DIGITAL PLAYGROU

The Hidden Politics of Children's Online Play Spaces, Virtual Worlds, and Connected Games

Digital Playgrounds explores the key developments, trends, debates, and controversies that have shaped children's commercial digital play spaces over the past two decades. It argues that children's online playgrounds, virtual worlds, and connected games are much more than mere sources of fun and diversion – they serve as the sites of complex negotiations of power between children, parents, developers, politicians, and other actors with a stake in determining what, how, and where children's play unfolds.

Through an innovative, transdisciplinary framework combining science and technology studies, critical communication studies, and children's cultural studies, *Digital Playgrounds* focuses on the contents and contexts of actual technological artefacts as a necessary entry point for understanding the meanings and politics of children's digital play. The discussion draws on several research studies on a wide range of digital playgrounds designed and marketed to children aged six to twelve years, revealing how various problematic tendencies prevent most digital play spaces from effectively supporting children's culture, rights, and – ironically – play.

Digital Playgrounds lays the groundwork for a critical reconsideration of how existing approaches might be used in the development of new regulation, as well as best practices for the industries involved in making children's digital play spaces. In so doing, it argues that children's online play spaces be reimagined as a crucial new form of public sphere in which children's rights and digital citizenship must be prioritized.

SARA M. GRIMES is an associate professor in the Faculty of Information and director of the Knowledge Media Design Institute at the University of Toronto.

Digital Playgrounds

*The Hidden Politics of Children's
Online Play Spaces, Virtual Worlds,
and Connected Games*

SARA M. GRIMES

UNIVERSITY OF TORONTO PRESS
Toronto Buffalo London

ISBN 978-1-4426-4744-2 (cloth)   ISBN 978-1-4426-6820-1 (EPUB)
ISBN 978-1-4426-1556-4 (paper)   ISBN 978-1-4426-6819-5 (PDF)

Library and Archives Canada Cataloguing in Publication

Title: Digital playgrounds : the hidden politics of children's online play spaces, virtual worlds, and connected games / Sara M. Grimes.
Names: Grimes, Sara M., author.
Description: Includes bibliographical references and index.
Identifiers: Canadiana (print) 20210165952 | Canadiana (ebook) 20210166142 | ISBN 9781442615564 (softcover) | ISBN 9781442647442 (hardcover) | ISBN 9781442668195 (PDF) | ISBN 9781442668201 (EPUB)
Subjects: LCSH: Internet games – Social aspects. | LCSH: Shared virtual environments – Social aspects. | LCSH: Computer games – Social aspects. | LCSH: Computers and children. | LCSH: Children's software. | LCSH: Play.
Classification: LCC GV1469.17.S63 G75 2021 | DDC 794.8083 – dc23

This book has been published with the help of a grant from the Federation for the Humanities and Social Sciences, through the Awards to Scholarly Publications Program, using funds provided by the Social Sciences and Humanities Research Council of Canada.

University of Toronto Press acknowledges the financial assistance to its publishing program of the Canada Council for the Arts and the Ontario Arts Council, an agency of the Government of Ontario.

Canada Council   Conseil des Arts
for the Arts   du Canada

ONTARIO ARTS COUNCIL
CONSEIL DES ARTS DE L'ONTARIO
an Ontario government agency
un organisme du gouvernement de l'Ontario

Funded by the   Financé par le
Government   gouvernement
of Canada   du Canada

Contents

Acknowledgments

Writing this book was a long and (ultimately) deeply rewarding process. It is the culmination of several years' and multiple projects' worth of research, exploration, and thinking. Getting the chance to revisit and reflect on this work was a precious gift. This book is also the product of innumerable conversations and debates with peers, colleagues, and acquaintances from academia, the children's media and game industries, the education and cultural institutions sectors, and (often most significantly) my personal life. Most of the research described in this book was supported by the Social Sciences and Humanities Research Council (SSHRC) of Canada, for which I am grateful.

Thank you to Leslie Regan Shade, Richard Gruneau, Alissa Antle, Sonia Livingstone, Jackie Marsh, Brian Cantwell Smith, Greg Lastowka, Rosemary J. Coombe, and Michael Levine for your mentorship and constructive feedback over the years, and for granting me the opportunity to develop my work in meaningful new directions under your guidance. A special thank you to Andrew Feenberg for always supporting my research, and for helping me "find my voice" as a theorist. Thank you to Danielle Deveau, Benjamin Woo, Tracy Ying Zhang, Jamie Rennie, Florence Chee, and the rest of my former lab mates in the Applied Communication and Technology (ACT) Lab at Simon Fraser University for your camaraderie as we trained to become academic researchers together. I am grateful for the ongoing support and encouragement of my colleagues at the University of Toronto, especially Cara Krmpotich and Patrick Keilty, and my collaborators in the Semaphore Lab, Matt Ratto, Rhonda McEwen, and Michelle Murphy.

My research and writing have been shaped in so many ways by my friendship and frequent collaborations with Deborah A. Fields. Thank you for your insight, your energy, your generosity, and for reading the first chapters of this book with such enthusiasm. I am so grateful for the contributions of the many student assistants who helped me conduct the research projects described in these pages, with special thanks to Tracy Munusami, Kristina Chin, Vinca Merriman, and Marco Piccolo. Thank you to Sarah Roger for your invaluable assistance in preparing the manuscript for submission.

Thank you to my wonderful family, especially Peggy Elliott, Tom Grimes, Colin Grimes, Melissa Grimes, Emilie Grimes, Annabelle Grimes, Leona Donahue, Celeste Irvine-Jones, Johanne Bouchard, Andreas Reichert, and Roger and Elizabeth Williams for cheering me on throughout this entire process, and for understanding every time (and there were many) that I missed an event or gathering so that I could "work on my book."

The village helping us raise our children is what made the actual *writing* of this book possible. I am profoundly grateful to the amazing nannies, housekeepers, caregivers, and teachers who have helped us care for our children over the years, with special thanks to Jenny Oriente and Elspeth Robertson. I acknowledge the privilege that enables me to benefit from such supports, and the crucial role that domestic/care labour plays within all academic work.

This book is dedicated to my husband and our children, the three loves of my life. Jonathan Williams, I am eternally grateful for your unconditional support and your tireless efforts to make sure our beautiful life together is filled with purpose and fun. You make everything possible. Brogan and Sorcha, being your mama is the very best thing that ever happened to me. I thank you both for your endless curiosity, your great big imaginations, your courage, and your thoughtfulness in everything you do. You are both my biggest inspirations.

DIGITAL PLAYGROUNDS

The Hidden Politics of Children's Online Play Spaces,
Virtual Worlds, and Connected Games

Introduction

For most of my childhood, I lived with my family in a cabin located about thirty minutes outside of a small town, nestled among the turquoise lakes and forested hills of the Upper Gatineau. This area of the world is cottage country, and although the region had once supported a thriving forestry industry, in my lifetime its greatest source of income came from tourism – vacationers and fishers in the summer, hunters in the fall, followed by snowmobilers and sugar bush aficionados in the winter and spring. My siblings and I spent most of our days romping through the forests, building snow forts or invading frog ponds (weather depending), and colonizing huge swathes of our neighbours' seasonally occupied properties. It was, in many important ways, the ideal environment for engaging in the type of pastoral, free-range play that is so often bemoaned as "lost," or at least "endangered," within contemporary discussions of children's play. Occasionally, our unstructured rambles through the Quebec countryside were interrupted by trips into town to visit the Lion's Club playground. An orderly mass of brightly painted metal bars, springs, and chain swings conveniently located just down the hill from my grandparents' house, this actual playground was unspeakably exciting. Highlights included brief interactions with strange and fascinating other children, as we manically ran from one piece of equipment to the next, making sure we got a turn on every one. Our trips to the playground invariably ended with at least one scraped knee, and it was always time to go before we were ready.

My own children are growing up across the street from a sizeable urban park, and although they are still very young, they already engage in many of the same play activities that I recall from my own childhood. The park itself is at once atypical (not all cities, and very few of the neighbourhoods within them, have parks this size) and stereotypical, in that it meets many – if not all – of our current expectations and definitions of the ideal city park. It contains wooded areas, sports fields, a community garden, bike trails, and dedicated dog parks. The park is relatively well kept, with plenty of "wild" (read: unmanicured) patches, although it is also, inevitably, interspersed with the discarded trash and broken glass that punctuates any cityscape. Notably, it also contains a fantastical playground designed and constructed by (and featured in an episode of) a reality television show (*Holmes Makes it Right*, 2012–2014) after the original burnt to the ground in 2012. Just like the park it is situated in, this playground reflects much of the current knowledge and contemporary standards about what built environments for children's play should look like. The structures are predominantly wood and are embellished to resemble a fairy-tale castle. They include nooks and undesignated spaces perfect for make-believe play. There's a climbing wall and sturdy plastic slides, and shock-absorbing wood chips cover most of the ground area. The playground is extremely popular and well attended by children of various ages, along with their parents, grandparents, and caregivers.

As a scholar who dedicates much of her time to understanding children's play, I am intrigued by the continuities and contrasts that I see emerging between my children's play lives and my own childhood – or more accurately, my *memories* of my own childhood. Both sets of childhood narratives are permeated by a deeply and unreliably emotional veneer: mine is soaked in nostalgia, while that of my children is viewed through a filter of parental hopes and fears. In fact, this type of perceptual filter is itself a crucial part of the story of children's play in contemporary society. It's part of what makes children's play such a contentious and emotionally charged personal matter, as well as a sociocultural issue. We are all nostalgic for some now-lost idea of childhood: the games we once played and the spaces we claimed for them.

At the same time, albeit sometimes conversely, many parents, caregivers, and educators are dedicated to ensuring that children have access to good play experiences. Our definitions of what good play looks like vary wildly and are associated with an array of very different preferred outcomes – from gaining specific development advantages to simply blowing off some steam before bedtime. Tied to this is a broader societal desire to protect children from the world's harms – both perceived and real. The amazing, built-for-TV playground across the street from my house is a perfect embodiment of dominant, contemporary concerns – from its designated "undesignated" imaginary play spaces to its shock-absorbent surface. The interplay of all of these ideas and emotions, along with the huge variations in how they are felt and articulated, fuel the tensions that surround children's play.

To complicate matters further, much of the academic research on children's play is changeable, contradictory, and highly ambiguous. Although most researchers agree that children's play is valuable, there is disagreement when it comes to explaining *why* it is important, and to identifying *which* types of play have the most or least value. As Sutton-Smith argues, much of this ambiguity can be traced back to the profound influence that hegemonic rhetorics have historically had on both scientific and popular ideas about play. Powerful "underlying ideological values" that "are both subsumed by the theorists and presented persuasively to the rest of us" are thus attributed to play, its science, and its theories.[1] These ideas shape how play is operationalized, how it is studied, and how this scholarship is ultimately interpreted.

Yet again, one only has to look as far as the local playground to see how these forces clash in ways that directly affect children's play experiences. As I write these words, many parts of the Western world are witnessing a trend in children's play theory and design that privileges so-called risky or wild play. This movement seeks to reincorporate some of the unpredictability, autonomy, and even quotidian hazards (e.g., rusty nails, sharp edges) that were common features of children's outdoor play not so long ago.[2] It also follows on the heels of a decades-long, sweeping reform of playground safety standards (e.g., the move away from concrete towards shock-absorbent surfaces), many of which are correlated with significant decreases in the number and severity of childhood injuries,[3] but also attract substantial criticism about the infantilization of children and the underestimation of their abilities.

Notably, both movements are not only bolstered by their own body of sound scientific research, but are also supported by intellectually convincing play theories. Where the wild play approach is said to allow children to explore the world on their own terms and build resiliency, the safer playgrounds movement claims to provide children with opportunities to test limits and make mistakes while remaining (relatively) unscathed. Although the two approaches are at odds, one can easily make a compelling argument for either one.

Children's play is political. It is the site of complex cultural conflicts that involve moralistic proclamations about parenting styles, and ideological assumptions about the nature of childhood. These in turn often reflect and reinforce enduring class and gender divides. While the ideological conflicts surrounding children's play are ongoing and unresolved, they nonetheless have tangible repercussions for children – and for the adults who care for them. This extends far beyond shifting playground design standards. The very space and time allocated to children's play has also changed dramatically in the past several years. For instance, recent studies show a decline in the amount of time and resources set aside for recess in elementary schools[4] and play activities in kindergartens.[5] Neighbourhood playgrounds, once the domain of children, are now overtly multigenerational spaces, where the absence of an on-site supervising adult can increasingly result in state intervention.[6] Meanwhile, stark divides persist when it comes to who has access to the play opportunities that are available. Children from lower-income neighbourhoods are less likely to live close to a playground.[7] Most sports and leisure programs fail to accommodate children with disabilities, even in areas with established accessibility mandates.[8]

Play is political for children as well. It serves as an arena for criticism of the social order, which, for children, is largely symbolized by adults. Indeed, throughout history, children's games have featured anti-authoritarian themes that transgress the boundaries of adult authority. For instance, in their foundational study of children's folklore, songs, and games, conducted in England from the 1950s through the 1980s, Opie and Opie found that children enjoyed subversive songs and rhymes for the undignified way they portrayed adults.[9] Many traditional schoolyard games, such as "Mother May I?" or "Simon Says," can be interpreted as a sort of burlesque of social etiquette and rules, as players confront and upend the dynamic between parental authority and disciplined children.[10] Schwartzman argues, "These games also often mock conventional power roles and frequently provide unconventional access to such roles (e.g., everyone gets a turn)."[11]

Despite all this, the political dimensions of children's play are rarely acknowledged as such. Just as childhood is largely viewed as a distinct stage of life, segregated from the adult world of accountability, responsibility, and consequences, children's play is treated as separate from everyday life. As much as we might passionately argue about where, what, how, and why children should play, the focus of these debates is almost always on perceived outcomes: on what the child will one day become *as a result* of this play activity, or the absence thereof. In so doing, however, we risk trivializing the activities themselves, downplaying their immediate implications, and disregarding the profound meaning that children make by engaging in them. If play is indeed "the work of the child," as Montessori claims, then what unfolds within and around it is every bit as important as what happens in and around adult workplaces, homes, schools, and public spheres. After all, with limited access to other forms of cultural participation, play becomes a key forum for children to congregate, negotiate, critique, and engage in political discourse.

Digitizing Playgrounds and Technologizing Play

A discussion of playgrounds and schoolyard games might seem like an odd way to start a book about digital games. After all, digital and traditional play are regularly positioned as antagonists within contemporary debates about what Plowman has termed the "technologization of childhood."[12] This is especially true of outdoor play, which is seen by many as an early casualty in the war that screens wage for children's attention. But I am starting this way in order to lay the groundwork for one of the main arguments that I will make in the chapters that follow, which is that playing in a virtual world or connected digital game has more in common with traditional playground play than is often assumed. I argue that these digital activities are best understood as belonging to the same genus of play activities, wherein play is performed, constructed, and experienced as a child's version of the public sphere.

While there are important differences between virtual and real-world play, the insistence that these differences represent some sort of oppositional divide prevents us from building a more nuanced, historically contextualized understanding of contemporary children's play and the politics that surround it. It draws our attention away from the fact that when spaces are designed and allocated for children's play, whether in the digital realm or in a corner of a public park, they become subject to rhetoric, emotional appeals, ambiguities, and debates. In short, they share many of the same underlying politics.

This book approaches digital games as recent entrants in the long and complex history of the politics of children's play. It explores the idea that certain genres of digital games have come to function as a new type of playground: places where children can assemble and socialize with one another, play and create a shared culture, as well as confront and challenge the social order. From multiplayer online games and virtual worlds to connected games played on console systems and handheld devices, an increasing number of children have access to a growing number of opportunities to engage in such activities. And just like traditional playgrounds, digital play spaces are subject to ongoing debates and ideological rifts about the role (if any) they should have in children's lives. This in turn has a tangible impact on the structures, shapes, and contents of the spaces themselves, which are generally designed and regulated by adults.

Of course, digital playgrounds also attract their share of controversies, hopes, and fears that don't apply to their real-world counterparts. Digital games and virtual worlds are firmly situated within the broader climate of uncertainty that surrounds the technologization of contemporary childhood. The rise and spread of information technologies, particularly digital and media technologies, within children's everyday lives is a source of both techno-utopianism and moral panic. This is especially the case with digital games, which not only serve as lightning rods of public controversy and academic debate, but are often at the centre of large-scale interventions into society's persistently ambivalent relationship with information technologies.[13]

On the one hand, playing with information technologies is associated with a range of beneficial, largely educational, outcomes. This association has been the catalyst for a number of recent big funding initiatives to advance the use of games in educational contexts, thereby increasing computer access, improving digital literacy, and bringing technical skill acquisition into classrooms – especially for those in disadvantaged and other target communities. On the other hand, digital games are routinely condemned as *the* (or at least *a*) root cause of a wide range of social ills, from mass shootings to childhood obesity. Concerns about the potentially detrimental effects of playing digital games have led to the introduction of bans, laws, and regulations aimed at limiting children's access to them.

Digital playgrounds are furthermore distinctive in their liminal location or "situatedness" within children's lives. They are at once public and private – online and communal spaces that are accessed through personal electronic devices. Indeed, a significant portion of children's online and connected play takes place at home. Accordingly, children's interactions with digital playgrounds – and the devices that enable their access – are mediated by parents and broader family dynamics. For instance, a study of the gaming habits of eight Swedish families conducted by Aarsand and Aronsson found that domestic gaming spaces are co-created by parents and children, through which children's gaming becomes embroiled in household politics and time management strategies. The parents in the study "frequently imposed various temporal restrictions on the children's gaming, limiting when gaming could take place, for how long, and interrupting gaming."[14]

Parents are by no means the only adults involved in the co-creation and regulation of children's digital play. From game designers and chat moderators to marketers and policymakers, a wide range of adults and adult interests contribute to the social shaping of connected games and the practices that unfold within them. While many of these contributions happen behind the scenes, they nonetheless have a profound impact on how digital playgrounds are structured, defined, and – ultimately – used by child players. Much like the designers of traditional playgrounds, these adult "actors" are themselves influenced by social factors, ideologies and biases, and professional standards and expectations, as well as technological innovations, market trends, and emerging research.[15]

As critical theories of technology demonstrate, artefacts such as online games embody and at times reproduce the cultural, economic, and political contexts within which they are created.[16] Arguably, this is especially true for artefacts made for children who, as we have seen, are already at the centre of recurring, emotionally charged, ideological and political debates. Designing for children almost always means juggling conflicting demands, including social and parental concerns, abstract cultural hopes and fears, shifting regulatory requirements, as well as the needs and preferences of children themselves. This juggling act in itself warrants further attention, as its results are often what end up determining an artefact's norms – the design standards that eventually become synonymous with how the artefact is used and perceived by the general public, as other options and iterations are closed off. The designers, marketers, and other actors involved in the production of technological artefacts thus play a crucial role in determining how children's technologies are ultimately defined.

When it comes to *digital playgrounds*, this role expands considerably. It now includes the ability to implement ongoing and iterative interventions into the artefact's design and cultural positioning through software patches and updates, for instance, or through advertising and branding. Notably, it also reaches directly into user practices, specifically those that unfold within the playgrounds themselves. Design parameters determine what users are technically able to say and do within these spaces. Meanwhile, always-on surveillance and data collection algorithms inform an ever-widening assortment of user management strategies, which can include anything from covertly cultivating a viral marketing campaign among eight-year-olds to policing a conversation between two preschoolers attempting to build an igloo for their virtual penguins.

The intense, quotidian involvement of corporate entities in the lives and actions of an artefact's users, let alone its child users, is unprecedented. It is simply not possible with traditional toys, playgrounds, and even non-connected videogames. The role that (adult) designers, marketers, corporate lawyers, and moderators currently occupy in children's culture is unlike anything we've seen before.

What This Book Is About

As digital technologies are increasingly incorporated into children's everyday lives, understanding the implications of this shift towards technologization becomes paramount. Through design decisions and legally enforced terms of use, developers are implementing their own resolutions to the ongoing debates about children's play and children's relationship to technology. Significantly, these resolutions are largely implicit and unacknowledged. They are also to some extent necessary, given the lack of consensus on the issues involved and the dearth of viable solutions provided by researchers and policymakers. But such resolutions are also deeply political, with profound implications for the children who encounter them. They strike a position on important matters, such as whether or not children have a right to freedom of speech online, and which genders will be explicitly invited to participate in a particular space or activity. Furthermore, they implement and subsequently enforce these positions on their users by banning those who do not conform or by designing the space in ways that afford desired behaviours. Moreover, as individual strategies and ad hoc resolutions spread and become the industry-wide standard, they combine to present a unified front – one that contains and promotes a particular ideology of childhood.[17]

Of course, even the most powerful ideological assumptions can be resisted, subverted, and outright rejected. As numerous studies show, many children engage in active reinterpretations, both offline and on. They participate in unanticipated activities, find workarounds to programmed restrictions, and come up with creative appropriations of even the strictest designs and most limiting discourses. Yet the research also suggests that the majority of children's interactions with digital technologies tend to stay within the intended parameters. For the most part, children acknowledge and respect the authority of a game's design. They mostly follow the rules, and they frequently internalize key elements of the corporately produced messages and discourses that they encounter.[18] It is therefore wrong to assume that the underlying technical code and design parameters of digital playgrounds aren't powerful and important, just because some children can resist them. Moreover, for those children who *do* engage in workarounds, reinterpretations, and creative appropriations, their actions should not be seen as apolitical, but rather as "tiny" yet meaningful acts of resistance.[19] Such activities reveal that digital playgrounds are the sites of complex negotiations of power between children, parents, developers, and other relevant social groups – wherein institutional forces have the obvious upper hand.

To fully appreciate the extent to which children do (and do not) exert agency and contribute to the social shaping of commercial play technologies, we need to gain a better understanding of what exactly they are up against. *Digital Playgrounds* aims to do just this, by taking a closer look at the actual contents and contexts of children's online play spaces, virtual worlds, and connected games. In the chapters that follow, I present an in-depth, critical exploration of the "stuff" these artefacts are made of – from the user interfaces and virtual objects that make up their designed infrastructures to the terms of service contracts and privacy policies that regulate their players; from the promotional materials and narrative features that expose the underlying motives of the games' corporate owners to the plethora of cultural content that children themselves create. I identify and deconstruct key trends that have emerged within the children's digital play landscape over the past twenty-five years, and discuss how these trends reflect and shape the broader cultural politics surrounding the technologization of children's play.

This book draws on research and experiences accumulated through several studies of online play spaces, virtual worlds, and connected games designed and marketed to children aged six to twelve that I have conducted and collaborated on since 2002.[20] Rather than simply review this research, however, *Digital Playgrounds* offers readers a comparative synthesis that reveals dominant patterns and provides theoretically grounded conclusions. Through this approach, I demonstrate how contemporary children's digital play reflects powerful industry trends and recurring public debates that first emerged in the late 1990s. A range of different games, game genres, cultural fads, and digital technologies are thus drawn into the discussion. In so doing, I present the necessary contexts – historical, social, cultural, and political – for better understanding the far-reaching roles that digital games have come to play in children's lives.

I also reveal how the developers of children's digital playgrounds have tackled complex ethical questions and regulatory grey areas during this period, establishing their own industry standards for children's privacy rights, the commercialization of children's play, the status of children's freedom of expression, and the space allotted to children's intellectual property ownership. I argue that the now-standard strategies for addressing these four issues reveal a heavily politicized and contentious, yet oftentimes hidden, set of cultural politics. I make the case that unpacking and challenging these hidden politics has become particularly urgent in recent years, as more children engage in deeper and ever-more intricate ways with corporately owned play spaces. How these issues are ultimately resolved will have profound implications for children's rights and experiences as digital citizens.

Digital Playgrounds dedicates a chapter to each of these four issues – privacy, commercialization, censorship, and ownership – and provides a concise history of their emergence and development within the children's online game environment. Concrete examples are used to illustrate the dominant ways each issue has been dealt with to date, and a review of the interplay between industry standards, government regulation, and public discourses is provided. In some cases, the result is a conservative approach, in which children's interactions are heavily restricted and play is narrowly defined. In others, however, game developers have come up with innovative responses in which children's rights, creativity, and cultural autonomy are met with recognition and support. Throughout this discussion, I lay the groundwork for a critical consideration of how existing approaches might be used in the development of new regulation and best practices for the industries involved in making children's digital play spaces.

A principal tenet of this book is that connected peer play is now a valuable and meaningful part of childhood. Furthermore, its value extends far beyond the potential contributions to learning and professional skill development that are so often emphasized in the press, in previous research, and in ongoing public discussions about the importance of children's digital play.[21] Therefore, the focus of this book is the play that occurs during children's free time – outside of schools and other institutional contexts. While the educational and developmental implications of digital play are compelling, there is clearly more to it than that.

Playing is not merely a conduit to other states of being or a means for achieving pedagogical goals. It also forms a core part of children's cultural experience and leisure time. It contributes significantly to their present happiness and overall well-being. And, notably, it includes a vast array of activities, behaviours, and experiences that run counter to the instrumental or purposive rhetorics underlying so many of the popular current theories about children's play. Children's play is sometimes dark, sometimes inane, and sometimes outright destructive. Although dominant ideologies of play don't always allow for its multifaceted messiness, this book assumes that children's play is both ambiguous and inherently worthwhile.

Why Looking Back Helps Us Move Forward

Today, we are witnessing an explosion of options for kids to play digital games with other people. An increasing number of web-enabled social gaming apps can be played on smartphones and other handheld devices. All of the current generation of videogame consoles support multiplayer gaming, along with additional social networking options. The emergence and spread of the Steam digital distribution system over the past several years has made connected, multiplayer computer gaming more prevalent and accessible than ever before. More recently, following the financial successes of industry-termed "toys-to-life" brands such as *Disney Infinity* (2013–16), Activision's *Skylanders* (2011–present), and *Lego Dimensions* (2015–17), the incorporation of embedded sensors and network connectivity into children's toys and other (tangible) artefacts – commonly described as "the internet of things" – is spreading.

Along with this increase in the number of connected gaming options available to young players, a growing proportion of children now engage in connected digital play. A decade ago, 63 per cent of boys and 40 per cent of girls aged eight to eighteen played videogames of some kind, including console, handheld, and computer games.[22] In 2005, a study commissioned by Sesame Workshop revealed that on a typical day, just under 40 per cent of three- to five-year-olds, and nearly 60 per cent of children aged six to nine, played videogames on either consoles or handheld devices. In 2008, a study conducted as part of the Pew Internet and American Life Project showed that digital gaming had reached near saturation among older children and teens, with 99 per cent of boys and 94 per cent of girls in the United States aged twelve to seventeen playing digital games of some type.[23] By 2015, a follow-up study revealed that 75 per cent of teen boys played digital games with others online.[24]

Notably, over the years, growing rates of participation have been recorded among increasingly younger children. For instance, a small but widely reported survey of families living in a low-income neighbourhood in Philadelphia found that, in 2015, 44 per cent of infants under the age of one and 77 per cent of two-year-olds used mobile devices daily to play games, watch videos, or use apps.[25] A more rigorous study conducted by the Joan Ganz Cooney Center in 2016 found that among four- to six-year-olds who played digital games, nearly half (48 per cent) played a few times a week, and nearly a third (29 per cent) played every day.[26] The spread of gaming among children of all ages is arguably not all that surprising, given that 80 per cent of households own at least one device used to play digital games.[27]

Then again, young users have long been at the vanguard of connected play. For one, they have been playing online games since the earliest years of the World Wide Web. One of the earliest connected opportunities for children, Circle 1 Network's *KidsCom.com* (1995–2019) featured a range of Java and JavaScript mini-games, as well as downloadable play activity sheets and puzzles. For many years, playing online games was the most popular form of digital gaming among elementary school–aged children, in both the United States and Canada. Studies conducted in 2003 and 2005 showed that approximately 90 per cent of North American youth played games online and that children spent more time playing online games than any other online activity.[28] Statistics from this era, including some of those cited above, don't always make this clear. For many years, videogames and online games – especially the free, browser-based, Flash games that children were most likely to play – were often studied separately, making participation rates appear smaller than they probably were. A widespread tendency to apply narrow definitions of what constituted digital gaming, along with an overemphasis on platform versus activity, meant that certain practices got lost or overlooked. As a result, historical accounts of this era frequently disregard the key role that children have played in the evolution of connected gaming since the 1990s.

Revisiting some of this research allows us to see that children have been at the forefront of multiplayer gaming as well. Some of the very first virtual worlds and massively multiplayer online games (MMOGs), including Numedeon's *Whyville* (1999–present) and Disney's *Toontown* (2003–13), were both targeted to and predominantly frequented by children and teens. Online communities popular among children in the early 2000s, such as *Neopets* (1999–present), were among the earliest providers of multiplayer gaming experiences. By the mid-2000s, children's virtual worlds *Club Penguin* (2005–17) and *Webkinz* (2005–present) drew unprecedented user populations estimated in the tens of millions – numbers that far exceeded those of the better-known, mainstream titles of the same era, such as *World of Warcraft* (2004–present) and *Second Life* (2003–present).[29]

Uncovering the hidden history of children's connected gaming is important for a number of reasons, not least of which is that it allows us to build a better understanding of how and why the children's digital landscape became what it is today. But also, it enables us to approach each new media hype and moral panic relating to kids and gaming with a much-needed critical perspective. While a shift of perspective alone may not provide us with firm answers to our enduring questions about children's relationship with digital technology (such as the perennial "Are videogames good/bad for kids?"), it does empower us to start asking a deeper set of questions about the nature, scope, and quality of this relationship. For instance, What does it mean that so many of the fads and alleged innovations that emerge in this area invariably involve the same handful of corporate entities? How does the ahistorical emphasis on the newness of children's digital play obscure the continuance, or even expansion, of business practices that only a decade ago raised alarm among ethics watchdogs, policymakers, and parents? Above all, surveying the landscape from a broader vantage point helps us to understand that many of the issues that arise today around children's digital play have contexts that date back to the earliest years of the internet. Others, meanwhile, stem from the complex function that children and childhood occupy within the dialectics of modernity.

The objective of this book is to provide such a vantage point through an in-depth critical exploration of the present and history of children's connected (online, networked, or otherwise web-enabled) games – what they look like, how they operate, who makes them, who regulates them, and what they are used for and why. My research and observations have shown me that digital play spaces have unique potential to serve as important sites of cultural participation, peer interaction, and leisure for children of increasingly younger ages. As such, these virtual playgrounds can be extremely valuable spaces for children to gather, collaborate, and play. In numerous examples, this is clearly the case, some of which will be discussed in the chapters that follow. But there are also many games, including some of the most popular, where this potential is greatly diminished by ulterior interests. These range from the use of online games to gain unprecedented access to kids' thoughts and ideas for market research to the interest groups and policymakers who use such spaces as battlegrounds for longstanding ideological conflicts and regulatory initiatives. Although the complex and interdependent relationships that unfold between ideology, political-economics, and design within children's digital playgrounds are largely omitted from public discussion and popular representations of these spaces, they clearly warrant our consideration.

Building a Children's Technology Studies Framework

As this book will demonstrate, online games are more than just spaces for entertainment and fun. They also serve as increasingly significant "public spaces" within which decisions are made about what constitutes appropriate play, speech, and behaviour for kids to engage in online, and in which complex new relationships are negotiated between children, parents, game developers, corporations, and governments. In order to construct this argument, I approach children's connected games from multiple angles: as crucial forums for children's play, culture, civic engagement, and well-being; as artefacts that contain a contentious set of cultural politics; as quasi-public spaces where important new relationships are forged between children, corporations, parents, and governments; and as a social phenomenon that raises urgent policy issues.

The research studies described in this book employ an innovative methodology, which incorporates elements of historical analysis, critical analysis, design analysis, discourse analysis, semiotic analysis, and an analytic adaptation of play testing. The theoretical framework draws on critical theories of technology,[30] semiotic approaches to user-technology relations proposed by science and technology studies (STS) theorists,[31] and political economy of communication traditions.[32] It also draws on concepts and ideas emerging from sources that include play studies, cultural politics, children's cultural studies,[33] and the new sociology of childhood.[34] This inventive, interdisciplinary framework enables an examination of the very issues that have been most often overlooked in the literature, including questions about how social norms, assumptions, and expectations about children – and play and technology – become embedded and reproduced within the design, contents, interface, packaging, and management of the artefacts that adults make for them.

The theoretical framework applied in this book also represents an important departure from the other academic work in this area. In conjunction with the spread of information and communications technologies (ICT) among young users, the literature on children and technology has increased significantly in recent years. Much of this work has concentrated on either identifying the potential effects of children's ICT usage or mapping children's situated use practices.[35] These works include studies of group dynamics among children playing with digital devices, children's use of media production tools, families' use of mobile technologies, and children's feelings about electronic toys. In situ research has been conducted in a range of locales, including schools and public places, homes and virtual spaces. Multiple methods have been used to explore the social implications of children's ICT use, including questions about regulation, digital divides, gender and identity politics, and the technologization of childhood.

This research provides a dynamic and nuanced body of knowledge on children's evolving roles as users and producers of digital technology. It also supports a core STS argument that, when it comes to understanding technology and how technologies are conceived and incorporated into everyday life, users matter just as much as designers, governments, and corporations do. Indeed, endless studies demonstrate that even young children "consume, modify, domesticate, design, reconfigure and resist technologies" in important ways.[36] Academic research also performs the crucial function of challenging some of the grand narratives that have surfaced within the press and other forms of popular culture, which tend to paint either a celebratory or a condemnatory picture of the effects that new technologies will ultimately have on kids, their development, and their well-being.

At the same time, however, the emphasis on use and uses – which have long preoccupied both academic and public debates about kids and technology – has produced a noticeable asymmetry, in that far less scholarly attention has focused on the structures and features of the actual devices and artefacts that kids engage with. Research that has examined these facets is dispersed across a range of disciplines and subject areas and does not necessarily form a coherent tradition of children's technology studies. Bringing these works together thus represents a key step towards developing a more comprehensive understanding of children's technologies and establishing a framework upon which future work might build.

For one, within the research on children's use of ICTs, several studies include some analysis of contents and functionality. Ito's research on the history of children's educational software includes an exploration of the sociocultural conditions within which these artefacts were designed, marketed, and adopted, and an overview of the contents of a number of examples.[37] The digital game studies literature, wherein analysis of design and user interaction (or "gameplay") is widespread, includes a number of works examining children's games.,[38] especially within the literature on girls and gaming.[39] Additionally, various works emerging out of education and design studies touch upon the role of affordances and usability.[40] For instance, Plowman's study of children's interactions with smart toys found that users became so frustrated with the toys' design limitations that most "preferred to play with it switched off."[41] While such studies tend to emphasize practical issues in technology or curriculum development, their findings contain important insight into children's technology production, industry norms, and ideas about users.

Scholarship on children's toys, drawn from media and cultural studies, can also be useful in this regard. For instance, many recent studies and foundational discussions of gendered toys address aspects of materiality and design as part of their analysis.[42] A particularly salient example is found in Forman-Brunell's discussion of the shift from rugged rag dolls to fragile porcelain dolls in the nineteenth century, which coincided with the emergence of new gender norms relating to girls' play.[43] Other scholars have examined the gendered discourses embedded within toys' designs and marketing materials,[44] providing compelling frameworks for examining comparable instances of design specialization and understanding how rhetorics of collectability, intertextuality, and "pedagogies of consumption" might surface within digital contexts.[45] The interplay between ideology, design, and consumer commercialization found in children's toys also features in numerous academic works applying a political economy of communication framework, some of which are discussed further in the chapters that follow.

Although several of the works described above incorporate themes and approaches similar to those found in STS, very few studies of child-specific technologies (digital or otherwise) make direct reference to STS scholarship. Even fewer include STS as a core part of their theoretical framework or analysis. Among the handful of notable exceptions are Aarsand and Aronsson's use of actor-network theory to examine children's gaming as an appropriation of space, Kearney's examination of gender scripts in media-making products marketed to girls, and Giddings's incorporation of actor-network theory in a study of preschoolers playing a computer game.[46] Conversely, crossover between STS and the more general field of digital game studies is not uncommon. For example, Bogost not only applies STS theories and literature in his analysis of digital game designs and users, but also draws directly on Badiou's notion of configuration in formulating his "unit operations" approach to digital game criticism.[47] Taylor's examination of how the end-user licence agreements (EULAs) found in teen- and adult-oriented, game-themed virtual worlds "formulate" their players as particular types of users draws on the STS notion of configuring the user.[48]

It is clear that STS theories have a key role to play in the establishment of a children's technology studies framework. A more concerted engagement with STS would not only contribute to a richer understanding of children's technologies and of children's relationships with technologies, but would also deepen our understanding of how childhood is understood and represented. As technologies are designed – or redesigned – in ways to specifically accommodate and configure child users, new conceptualizations of a technologized child emerge. As Druin, Stephen, and McPake argue, children "have their own likes, dislikes, and needs that are not the same as adults."[49] However, making games for children requires more than merely identifying child-appropriate themes and content that will interest them. It also demands a variety of special considerations and strategies for addressing issues of usability (e.g., clear and consistent feedback, intuitive user interfaces – also known as UI), literacy (e.g., instructions that take into account children's widely varying literacy, vocabulary, and reading rates), control layout and ergonomics (e.g., accommodation for smaller hands and shorter finger span), as well as the users' ability to "read" and navigate three-dimensional graphics.[50] Each of these considerations poses unique design challenges that models and industry standards are not necessarily able to meet. This is particularly relevant when considering the tendency to design using an "I-methodology."[51]

A different set of design decisions arise when children are considered as a "relevant social group."[52] Scholars of children's culture demonstrate that whenever artefacts are made for children by adults, an array of ideologically laden hopes and fears are necessarily also involved – in the form of adult desires to construct, control, and shape childhood in ways that reflect broader social ideals.[53] As users and co-shapers of such artefacts, children are both empowered (e.g., appropriating technologies in unanticipated ways) and at a unique disadvantage, as they are very rarely a core part of the design process. An STS-based framework for studying children's technologies would be particularly useful for uncovering how assumptions about children in turn become embedded in and negotiated at the level of technological design.[54] As STS scholars demonstrate, power relations, ideological narratives, and cultural assumptions can also play important roles in the social shaping of technologies.

A broader consideration of children's technologies would similarly benefit STS. Indeed, several STS scholars have begun exploring children's unique contributions, statuses, and experiences vis-à-vis the social shaping of technologies. This includes discussions of cases where health interventions (i.e., prevention and treatment programs) originally designed for adults were adapted for children;[55] studies of autistic youth's experience of structured routines and social order;[56] examinations of the medicalization of "childhood differences" by neuroscientists and psychiatric epidemiologists;[57] and studies of technological innovation among gifted children.[58] STS scholars are contributing to a growing body of literature examining the mobilization of "the child" as a key social and cultural construct within public discourses about technology,[59] and in technological diffusion initiatives such as the One Laptop per Child program.[60]

A key part of what makes STS such a compelling framework for investigating children's online games is that, much like technology, childhood is also a social construct. Although the term "childhood" is used to describe a specific series of developmental and biological stages, it also carries a wide range of cultural associations and social expectations. These are in turn flavoured by a changeable mix of nostalgia, romanticism, pragmatics, and politics, as described above. Our understanding of what childhood is, how long it lasts, what it should involve, and what it should exclude, has undergone dramatic transformations. Even today, there are important cross-cultural differences in how childhood is envisioned and in the roles children are expected to fill.

This argument recalls those made by feminist technology scholars in calling for scholarship aimed at uncovering the politics of gender within technological design and development. For instance, Berg and Lie argue that the compatibility between feminist studies and technology studies begins with the fact that both gender and technology are social constructs, and that both feminism and constructivism are concerned with the need to "blur the boundaries of categories normally kept apart."[61] They conclude that just as artefacts can be political, they can also be gendered. As such, hegemonic subjectivities (or subject positions) do not only become embedded in a technology's design, but also appear within discursive representations of its intended or ideal users. A critical awareness of power relations is fundamental to this approach, for, as Wajcman explains, technology is often "the result of conflicts and compromises, the outcomes of which depend primarily on the distribution of power and resources between different groups in society."[62]

Similar parallels can be drawn between technology and childhood, particularly as this latter category has been theorized within the "new sociology of childhood" literature.[63] While acknowledging that there is an obvious biological basis to childhood, scholars of the new sociology of childhood focus instead on the power relations, assumptions, and ideologies that contribute to the social shaping, regulation, and delimitation of childhood and children's agency. Within these processes, children are understood to be "agentic," which Ólafsdóttir et al. explain means that children are viewed as "competent and active participants in co-constructing their social worlds. They use their experiences, knowledge, and collective actions to produce and reproduce their peer cultures."[64] This constructivist approach directly challenges dominant notions of childhood, such as those found in traditional disciplines such as psychology, law, and medicine, "in which children were [historically] viewed as incompetent, dependent beings who were merely on the way to 'becoming' adults."[65] In addition to facilitating deconstruction and critique of the cultural politics of childhood, the new sociology of childhood posits that scholars must approach children "as subjects in their own right who develop their own and unique cultural milieus."[66] These arguments accord well with contemporary STS scholarship that challenges traditional notions about who constitutes a relevant social group within the construction or shaping of technologies, while broadening the focus of enquiry to better account for the roles of users and use within these processes.

In bringing together these traditionally distinct (yet epistemologically complementary) approaches, we find a more effective framework for studying children's virtual worlds from multiple perspectives – as digital media forms, as technological artefacts, and especially as sites of play. Unlike much of the previous work on children's digital play, this framework identifies the game or digital playground (the artefact) as the key site of enquiry, enabling a deeper understanding of what the spaces are made of, and how, and why. However, it is also a two-levelled exploration, emphasizing the importance of looking at both the artefact *and* its users. By drawing on user studies and feminist theories, the discussions that unfold in the chapters that follow account for the marginal status of children as an often-overlooked relevant social group – one with a unique and mutable set of needs, abilities, and challenges. As such, these discussions allow for a more comprehensive conceptualization of the power relations, ideological assumptions, communities of practice, and forms of resistance that come to shape children's technologies. The approach adopted in this book is moreover supported by the studies into children's play, toys, and media that emphasize the importance of addressing both text and context when conducting research on the complex, contentious, and changeable relationships that form between children's material cultures and children's cultural practices.

Chapter Overview

The first chapter serves as a preliminary introduction to both the world of children's online games and to the types of issues that will be examined throughout the book. It outlines the main arguments for taking a closer look at children's online games – why they are important (for children's play, cultural rights, and digital citizenship), how they're represented and discussed within popular policy and press discourses, and where they are situated vis-à-vis children's culture (including the children's media landscape, current social trends in children's play and leisure, etc.). In this chapter, I posit that online games exemplify many of the current debates about children and technology on the one hand, and children and play on the other.

I explain that over the past several decades, both topics have attracted controversy, powerful discourses of hope and fear, and policy initiatives – trends that are now carried over into children's digital playgrounds, as illustrated in recent news coverage and high-profile funding initiatives. I propose that, in some ways, online games intensify debates about children, technology, and play, as they are both more and less regulatable than traditional playgrounds. This chapter also introduces the idea that it is by paying closer attention to the overlooked, hidden, and taken for granted dimensions of children's online games – their commercial underpinnings, their design affordances, their regulatory frameworks, and their associated discourses – that we can begin to uncover the complex breadth of opportunities and challenges contained within these artefacts.

Chapter 2 provides readers with a brief history of children's online games. I start with the arrival of the first online games and play spaces for kids in the late 1990s, move on to the shift to game-themed virtual worlds and online communities in the early 2000s, then to the evolution of online games into multiplayer networks in the mid-2000s, and end with the more recent arrival of online games played on web-enabled console systems (e.g., Sony PlayStation and Microsoft Xbox consoles) and handheld devices (e.g., Apple iPad, Nintendo DSi). Similarities and differences between the types of children's online games that have emerged will be discussed, particularly in terms of how they are marketed and how they fit within the larger children's media landscape. The chapter considers how children's online games have evolved alongside the technologies, some of the recurring themes and genres that have surfaced over the years (e.g., storylines, game types), corporate ownership patterns and dominant business models (e.g., some online games make money through in-game advertising, others charge players a monthly subscription fee), as well as changing patterns in children's use and preferences.

Throughout this discussion, the reader is invited to consider how children's online games compare to those designed for general audiences and those made for teens and adults, in terms of their size, sophistication, accessibility, usability, and contents. This chapter also argues that many online games for children are marketed to parents as "walled gardens," a reference to a recurring theme (stemming from Romantic notions of childhood) found within public and academic debates about what constitutes appropriate play when children are involved.

In chapter 3, I argue that a closer examination of the structural dimensions of children's online games provides valuable insight into the processes through which ideas and assumptions about children (or technology or play) become embedded within the material and semiotic features of the artefacts themselves. This chapter reviews some of the structures found within children's online games – user interfaces, player management systems (e.g., moderators), codes of conduct, and rules of play – as well as the regulatory structures developers must conform to in designing games for children (e.g., federal and provincial policies, legislation, industry guidelines). It provides examples of the types of "scripts" or discourses that these structures contain, and it describes how certain design decisions can affect children's play.

The main theme explored in this chapter is commercialization and how promotional discourses can shape a game's design, contents, and even player behaviour. For instance, some branded games (games that tie in to other media or product lines) contain programmed features that effectively limit children's speech to phrases that promote the brand and its associated products. The discussion is grounded in a brief overview of some of the core concepts and theories that inform my research approach and theoretical framework, which resurface in later chapters.

In chapter 4, I describe the opportunities for free, open-ended, imaginary, and make-believe play found within many children's online games, particularly virtual worlds and "sandbox" games, as well as the forms of negotiation that take place between players, game designers, and game operators. Here, I address the limitations of the embedded scripts and structures examined in chapter 3, and highlight the many ways children are able to subvert rules, work around designed features, and make the games their own. I discuss recent industry trends towards "designed emergence" and towards providing opportunities for civic engagement (e.g., voting on content, community building).

The idea of the playground as the child's version of the public sphere is considered. The chapter also addresses how trends towards user appropriation and free play can come into conflict with the games' underlying structures, business priorities, social and ethical expectations, and/ or regulatory requirements. It discusses how these tensions between freedom and constraint reflect broader ideas about the role of children in public and civic life. It introduces questions about censorship and how children's right to freedom of expression is dealt with in online environments, as well as the implications for children's civic and cultural participation.

In chapter 5, I focus on the issue of children's privacy in online games – how it is represented and protected within the design and management of the games, and how it is at times infringed upon by common business practices. This chapter describes how children's privacy first became a major issue for online developers in the late 1990s, when child advocates and the US government discovered that many games were soliciting personal information from children for direct marketing purposes, which led to the establishment of new regulation and industry standards. Since then, developing for children has come with a variety of extra requirements, some of which overlap with the tensions and policy initiatives discussed in chapter 4.

This chapter introduces two additional practices that are now common in online games: data harvesting children's online interactions for market research and promoting (mandated) privacy protections as value-added safety precautions. I argue that both practices raise questions about the scope and effectiveness of privacy regulations, and about the ethical implications of collecting data without informed consent and misrepresenting the purpose of privacy policies to children and parents. Common data collection and market research practices are described as forms of corporate surveillance. The notion of "privacy as safety" is also addressed, for although safety is a high priority for both parents and children, it is often vaguely defined and used as a rhetorical device for advancing ulterior interests.

In chapter 6, I examine a growing trend within children's online games – the provision of tools, templates, contests, and forums where children can post original or "remixed" content. Examples of children's creative practices in connected games and other digital play spaces include fashioning virtual items and characters, designing game levels, submitting artwork, and writing fan fiction. This chapter describes some of the trends and benefits associated with these practices, which are furthermore discussed in terms of their implications for children's cultural rights, authorship, and engagement with fair use/fair dealing exceptions. Some of the issues raised in previous chapters, such as the tension between censorship and freedom of expression, are briefly revisited.

A key argument developed in this section is that both existing legislation and industry standards (as articulated in the games' terms of use contracts) are ill equipped to deal with the new questions such practices raise around who owns children's content, whether or not these ownership rights can be transferred, and what role parents should play. Concrete examples of how game developers are addressing such problems are examined. Another issue explored in this chapter is the relationship between creative and copyrighted content, as found in games that encourage children to use and remix materials (e.g., images of media characters). Similar questions arise around who owns remixed content and what consideration is given to fair use/fair dealing exceptions, which are discussed within the broader context of the prominent role that remixing has historically played in children's culture and learning.

The last chapter, chapter 7, provides a synthesis of key themes and arguments made throughout the book about how children's digital playgrounds are designed, regulated, perceived, and used. This sets the stage for a final critical analysis of the past and present of children's digital play, through which four enduring challenges are identified: the disconnect between children's privacy and children's need for autonomous spaces; the lack of support for children's freedom of expression online and its positioning in opposition to children's safety; the emerging question of who owns children's digital content and shared culture; and the tensions that arise when traditional models of corporate control and commercialization are applied to artefacts designed for and targeted to children. These four challenges represent problematic tendencies within the children's digital playscape, which have over the last two decades established a set of hidden yet hegemonic norms and standards of practice within an environment that is largely perceived as ever changing and user driven. In turn, the concretization of these tendencies into design features and other rules of play raises deeper questions about children's cultural rights online, and highlights the need for a better informed and more balanced discussion of the future and potential of children's digital playgrounds, and the broader technologization of childhood they exemplify. The book ends with a call to action and proposes an alternative way of thinking about children's digital playgrounds as a public sphere from which a diversity of spaces and practices can be carved, but which must foremost be actualized as places where children's rights are supported and children's digital citizenship is acknowledged.

1

The Importance of Digital Play

Digital playgrounds attract their share of controversies, concerns, optimism, and opportunism. On the one hand, they are approached as forums for children's play, and discussed as recent examples in a longstanding debate about the role and function of play in children's lives and society more generally. They are also defined by their incorporation of connected features and internet technologies, and are therefore embroiled in ongoing discussions about the perils and promise associated with life online. On the other hand, children's digital playgrounds also attract their own set of hopes and fears. This has been the case since digital games first hit the mainstream in the 1980s, when they were concurrently depicted as both a source of corruption (in the case of video arcades) and a key way for children to acquire computer programming skills. Contemporary examples abound. At the time of writing, *Minecraft* (2009–present) is being heralded by teachers and academics alike as the harbinger of a veritable evolution in effective, interactive, participatory educational curriculum delivery.[1] Concurrently, a book called *Glow Kids: How Screen Addiction Is Hijacking Our Kids – And How to Break the Trance* (2016), describes electronic media as "digital crack" that can lead to a range of clinical disorders and behavioural problems.[2] Elsewhere, the book's author claims that "your kid's brain on *Minecraft* looks like a brain on drugs."[3]

Taken together, and at face value, conflicting discourses such as these can make it seem as if the issue is at an impasse. To complicate matters, claims on both sides frequently rely on problematic research, questionable conclusions, or both. Studies professing to establish causal media effects are and should be critiqued, tested, and re-examined – what sample size was it based on, what methods were used, what questions were asked, how did the researchers reach their conclusions, and could any other factors be at play? It's important to take a closer look at what each side of the debate is basing itself on (e.g., research, theories, politics, ethics) in order to better understand where the underlying divisions stem from, what larger patterns they fit into, and what functions the debates themselves might be filling within popular and public discourse. Most importantly, it is crucial to revisit the basis of controversial claims and ongoing debates so that we can move past them: move beyond the outdated idea that issues involving children can only ever be positioned in polarizing terms that encourage all-or-nothing perspectives, which in turn prevent movement or decision making.

Just because something is controversial – and subject to contradictory claims – doesn't make it moot. Indeed, there is substantial, great research that does much to reduce the ambiguity by pointing the way towards more inclusive and effective strategies for helping children form and manage their relationships with digital technologies. Such studies emerge from a range of disciplines, including play studies, education, media studies, human-computer interaction, technology studies, and game studies. This research is often informed by cultural studies theories, as well as by methodological innovations emerging out of the new sociology of childhood approach. They engage and explain some of the scientific findings that otherwise lend themselves to decontextualization and over-generalization. These studies even avoid the extreme, deterministic positions or arguments that prevail within media and other popular discourses. Instead, they ground their discussions in practice and theory, adopting a child-centric perspective that demonstrates the profound value and meaning that digital playgrounds can have in children's lives, as well as the multiple ways digital play can benefit children's well-being.

This chapter highlights some of these studies, contextualizing them within relevant historical, ideological, and research traditions. It delves into some of the major current debates surrounding children's digital play, and it discusses how similar controversies tend to resurface every time a new technology or media form is introduced. Much of this discussion highlights contradictions found within the academic research, but it also addresses how this research both influences and is influenced by policy and media trends. I demonstrate that debates about digital playgrounds reproduce and reflect broader longstanding debates about children and play on the one hand, and about children and "mediatization" on the other. I highlight these relationships with the intention of moving beyond the standard polarizing polemic that has dominated, and in many ways stagnated, the academic discussion to date. This chapter lays a foundation for the rest of this book by shifting the focus away from binary debates and towards a more nuanced approach.

Conflicting Views of Children's Play

Although play is a universal phenomenon, children have long had a unique relationship to and special claim over it. Few things are as naturally aligned as childhood and play. In Canada and the United States, the mere mention of children's play is likely to evoke nostalgic memories of sun-streaked playgrounds, epic backyard adventures, cardboard castles, and endless sessions of dress-up and make-believe. Children's play is furthermore commonly associated with feelings of freedom and artistic inspiration, joy and self-exploration. Scholars trace this back to ideas that first emerged in the Romantic period that continue to have a profound influence on Western ideals and ideology. These include the works of Rousseau, a philosopher who popularized a sentimental linkage between children and the inherent beauty and goodness of nature, as well as that of poets Wordsworth and Blake, who wrote about childhood as a time of purity of spirit, incorruptible innocence, and unbridled creativity.

When it comes to children's play, there's a lot more at stake than mere nostalgia and romanticism. Children feature prominently within biological, developmental, and anthropological theories about the evolutionary function of play. They serve as evidence of the vast array of instrumental processes within which play is understood to fulfil a key role. This is especially the case within the multitude of studies and theories linking forms of play to healthy cognitive, emotional, and social development. Play is variably described as contributing to children's identity formation, socialization and acculturation, stress management, development of moral judgment, and refinement of fine and gross motor skills, among other things. Play is also central within contemporary theories of childhood education, with multiple approaches and programs emphasizing its role (or potential role) in children's learning. As Sutton-Smith, a foundational play scholar, argues, "There is no major play theorist of this century that does not make play out to be a positive force in child growth and child achievement."[4] The idea that children's play serves some greater purpose has concurrently taken hold within popular discourses. For instance, variations of the adage "Play is the work of children" appear everywhere from parenting manuals to town hall debates.[5]

Along with the belief that play is beneficial to children's development is an associated fear about what will happen if those benefits aren't achieved. For although play is often heralded for its positive outcomes, it has equally strong associations with frivolousness, disruption, and indolence. The public imagination is rife with horror stories about the allegedly dangerous consequences of letting children engage in the wrong types of play. In the 1980s, it was the demonization of the tabletop role-playing game *Dungeons & Dragons* (which originated in 1974), which was claimed to be a conduit into Satanic cultism. From the late 1990s well into the 2000s, videogames were frequently blamed for inciting real-world violence, particularly during the media panics that manifest in the wake of incomprehensible tragedies such as mass shootings.[6]

Scholars trace these associations back to an enduring, conservative cultural tendency, epitomized by the Puritan work ethic, in which idle hands are seen to be the devil's playground, and wherein play is placed in opposition to more productive and fruitful pursuits. In its most extreme forms, this tendency emerges as a general distrust and vilification of pleasure and all its trappings. More commonly, it manifests as a vague concern about the trouble that children will get themselves into if left to their own devices. The underlying assumption is that children have, and are naturally drawn to indulging in, destructive and inappropriate impulses. Central to this view is an accompanying belief that children's destructive tendencies can be avoided if their play is channelled by, contained within, and directed towards pro-social and other productive goals through educational games, organized sports, and other acceptable forms of rationalized leisure. This mode of thought gave birth to the organized leisure movements of the late nineteenth and early twentieth centuries, including the parks and playground movement that was based on the idea that "alternatives to the street and degrading commercial leisure must be provided by the government in safe, regulated fun."[7] The belief that unstructured, unsupervised play is detrimental to children, and that structured alternatives are in turn beneficial, continues to resurface in leisure-based programs and projects, especially those geared towards underprivileged communities.

Today, it is not uncommon to see child-targeted, organized leisure programs, educational toys, and other initiatives that present a particular form of developmentally (or otherwise) beneficial play as a solution or antidote to unstructured, and allegedly potentially detrimental, leisure. Indeed, there are entire industries fuelled by the widely held belief that children's leisure time is best spent on productive activities. Extracurricular lessons (e.g., violin, art, Mandarin), after-school clubs, and organized sports of all of kinds have become synonymous with the contemporary vision of a well-rounded childhood. While many children engage in such activities purely in the interests of fun and self-fulfilment (not to mention time management), the trend is also associated with what child psychologists and other experts describe as an "over-scheduled childhood" – a term used to describe the lives of children whose every waking hour is dedicated to some form of organized leisure or self-improvement activity. This phenomenon is not unrelated to the encroaching professionalization of childhood, as young people are expected to engage – at younger and younger ages – in leisure activities that will not only contribute to their personal development, but also provide a favourable extracurricular dimension to their eventual university and job applications.

At first glance, these perspectives may appear to be at odds. On the one hand, children must be given free rein to indulge in autonomous creative play, while on the other hand, they must be protected from corruption and interference – implying that they must be isolated to some extent from the sources of such corruption, whatever these may be. Children's play is understood to produce a wide array of developmental benefits and social advantages, and yet risks and detrimental impacts are thought to occur if their play doesn't unfold in a particular way. But there is actually an underlying congruence to these two positions, specifically in terms of their shared belief that there exists an ideal way for children to play, along with the subsequent insinuation that other forms of play are inadequate or detrimental. Furthermore, both perspectives advance the idea that it is the responsibility of adults to ensure that children have access to the good types of play and to protect them from the bad ones.

Play is thus a source of social anxiety, as parents, teachers, and caregivers try to decipher contrasting expert opinions in order to figure out which types of play will provide benefits, and how to avoid the types of play with negative outcomes. The institutions involved in providing services to children (e.g., schools, day-care centres, libraries) are also expected to mould and mediate play's potential impacts in ways that support broader organizational and societal goals. To complicate matters further, adult ideas about what constitutes good play often conflict with children's actual play practices. When left to their own devices, children tend to engage in practices that incorporate themes, technologies, and activities adults (may) disapprove of. At the very least, children's play often diverges from the idealized descriptions found in textbooks, curriculum plans, and policy papers.

Sutton-Smith argues that the contradictions within dominant conceptualizations of play reflect the underlying fact that the very essence of play is ambiguous and paradoxical. He argues that it is nearly impossible to describe play and games without falling under the paradigmatic horizon of at least one of the "seven rhetorics" that predominate in cultural understandings of play. These rhetorics include the notion of play as expression of self, play as progress, and play as frivolity, as briefly described above, along with notions of play as fate, play as power, play as identity, and play as the imaginary.[8] Here, the term "rhetoric" is used to refer to any "persuasive discourse, or an implicit narrative, wittingly or unwittingly adopted by members of a particular affiliation to persuade others of the veracity and worthwhileness of their beliefs."[9] When it comes to play, understanding the role of rhetoric is crucial. This is especially the case when considering the widely cited claim that play has a measurable, positive effect on child development. Sutton-Smith emphasizes that the notion that play is adaptive remains, for the most part, unproven. He cites Panksepp's comprehensive review of the literature, which concludes, "Of course, it remains very attractive to assume that the consequences of playful activities are adaptive in many ways, but there are no robust and credible demonstrations of that in either humans or animals."[10]

Despite non-definitive evidence, many play theorists remain committed to the idea that play serves an adaptive function. Such associations persist in much of our contemporary thinking and theories about children's play. As with other dominant discourses about childhood, this enduring cultural belief about play contains both a promise and a warning. Allowing children space and time to engage in self-directed play is viewed as crucial. Yet such spaces are consistently seen as under threat of corruption from adult interests and mechanisms.

Conflicting Views of Mediated Play

For well over a century, mass media have been identified as a key source of the alleged corruption of children's play (and childhood itself) that many believe to be taking place within modern Western societies. In the late nineteenth century, for instance, a brief but notable outcry emerged around the growing trend of including illustrations in books for children, as it was feared that the imagery would constrain young readers' imaginations. By the mid-twentieth century, attention had shifted to concerns that exposure to inappropriate themes and mature imagery, especially sexual and violent content, would affect children in other, potentially more serious, ways. Ongoing concerns about children's allegedly heightened susceptibility to harmful "media effects" have played a crucial role in the history of censorship and regulation of a wide range of media formats, from film and comic books in the early to mid-1900s to websites and videogames today.[11]

Conversely, mass media are also identified as potential conduits for a wide range of positive outcomes, particularly those relating to children's learning, development, and technical skill acquisition. The most universally recognizable example is the identification of children's literature – specifically, being read to – as a crucial pathway to literacy. Within specific contexts, electronic media share similar associations. For example, both the format and contents of *Sesame Street* are deeply informed by research supporting the idea that television can be effectively used to educate preschoolers, particularly those from disadvantaged backgrounds. Similarly, since the 1980s, a great number of child-targeted computer skills curricula and after-school programs have centred on the idea that videogames are (or can be) immersive and engaging stepping stones into coding.

Within both popular and academic discourses, children's media and play intersect and clash. For one, media and play are often positioned in conflict as mutually exclusive activities that are in competition for children's time and attention. Since the 1950s, there has been a well-documented, consistent increase in the average amount of daily screen time engaged in by children of ever younger ages. This increase has in turn been associated with a wide range of social ills, from the dramatic rise in childhood obesity rates to an alleged decrease in children's "creativity quotient" and ability to engage in self-directed, imaginative play. A series of moral panics have thus emerged around children's media use, which is positioned as harmful and something to be limited or avoided altogether, while traditional play activities are championed as the panacea. Most recently, public attention has shifted to the issue of addiction, a recurring concern when it comes to children and media technologies. The debate about "gaming addiction" came to a head in 2018, when the World Health Organization (WHO) formalized its status as a recognized disorder by adding it to the International Classification of Diseases-11 (ICD-11).[12] Time-use politics feature prominently in the WHO's classification and recommended assessment criteria. For instance, in an online Q & A on "Gaming Disorder," the WHO warns that "people who partake in gaming should be alert to the amount of time they spend on gaming activities, particularly when it is to the exclusion of other daily activities."[13] Here, as in previous media-related moral panics, much of the "evidence" relies on deterministic and reductionist conclusions about the negative "effects" of screen time. Critics of this approach highlight that the problems blamed on children's media consumption are more diverse and complex than these causal assessments make them out to be, and involve a matrix of deeper environmental, socio-economic, and behavioural factors.[14]

A second major point of intersection is "mediated play," a broad term that can include anything from playing with Harry Potter Lego sets to bouts of pretend featuring Rey and Finn from *Star Wars: The Force Awakens*. Here too, the discussion is driven by well-documented shifts within children's culture and play patterns. For instance, following the removal of regulatory restrictions in the United States in the early 1980s, the production and sale of toys based on children's media characters quickly mushroomed. By 1985, they represented 40–50 per cent of all toy sales.[15] By 2003, a study conducted by Rideout, Vandewater, and Wartella found that nearly all American children (97 per cent) under the age of six owned toys and other products "based on characters from TV shows or movies."[16] At the same time, studies conducted since the 1980s have shown an increased presence of media-based storylines and branded characters within children's own imaginative play scenarios.[17]

Once again, when it comes to making sense of this trend and what it means for children, the research and public opinion are both split. A number of scholars have tried to determine the potential consequences of these developments for the instrumental benefits commonly associated with children's play. Among the most compelling and controversial issues addressed are lingering questions about the extent to which licensing and cross-promotion influence the shape and contents of children's play practices,[18] and whether children can resist or even subvert commercial messages in their play.[19] These questions commonly emerge within popular discourse as issue-specific debates, such as the recent discussion about gendered toys and the "pink aisle," as well as the long-standing controversy about toy guns.[20]

Licensed Toys and Media Supersystems

The growing prominence of commercial messages, branding, and cross-promotional strategies within children's toy culture fuels its own set of academic and public debates. The contemporary academic conversation about the commercialization of children's games and online play spaces can be traced back to the 1980s, and the emergence of several studies examining the rise of "media supersystems"[21] and licensed toys. Scholarship in this area consistently shows an increased presence of licensed toys, media-based storylines, and branded characters – not only in children's toy boxes, but also in children's own imaginative play and storytelling.[22] Scholarship from both sides of the structure/agency debate support the idea that contemporary supersystem strategies foster a consumerist ethos that celebrates children's growing role as consumers and promotes a "pedagogy of consumption."[23] Each text (i.e., television show, film, digital game, book, graphic novel, etc.) promotes consumption of other related texts (or toys or artefacts) by promising that purchase of ancillary products will enable more intimate access to the narrative and its characters.

Scholars, critics, and educators argue that this development is detrimental to children's play and well-being.[24] For instance, they suggest that the commercialization of children's culture promotes a repetitive, simplistic, and stereotyped mode of play, which in turn decreases the benefits otherwise associated with play. Conversely, many others view such critiques as condescending towards children's own desires and preferences, and as dismissive of children's active participation in the broader, shared, and inarguably commercial, culture. Rather than bemoan the presence of media brands in children's lives, these scholars propose that attention should be given to the numerous ways children subvert, appropriate, and master commercial content through their play. Indeed, the very term "media supersystem" was coined by Kinder, who also argues that children assimilate, accommodate, and eventually master the intertextual relations and subject positions that are cultivated by commercial media cultures.[25]

Revisiting the children's commercial culture debate is useful for several reasons. For one, as Giddings argues, "The history of children's play with technology is inseparable from the emergence of a commercial children's culture."[26] Since the nineteenth century, a wide range of technologized toys and machines have been produced for and advertised specifically to children. From play construction kits and talking dolls to more recent entries such as digital games and electronic devices, the children's market for commercial consumer technologies has a long and established history. Second, unlike the violence in (digital) games literature, the scholarship on children's commercial culture is dominated by child-centred theories, as well as studies conducted with actual children – including numerous in-depth analyses of children's own practices, experiences, and perspectives. It provides a crucial historical and theoretical context for thinking about how traditional structure/agency dynamics are shifting as children's play increasingly unfolds within the corporately controlled, mediated, and moderated contexts of online games and other digital spaces. Moreover, many of the studies examining commercial dimensions of children's media and material culture include some form of textual or design analysis, upon which the current discussion seeks to expand.

On one side of the debate is a body of scholarship providing an in-depth critique of the commercialization of children's media and play culture. Much of this critique is supported by empirical, predominantly positivist, research suggesting that children are harmed by the presence of commercial messages and associations (such as the narrative associations between a licensed toy and the media text that it is based on). Here, children's play with licensed toys and media narratives is generally understood to be not only qualitatively different from traditional forms of children's play, but also less beneficial – if not outright detrimental – to children's development.[27] For instance, Greenfield and her associates argue that exposure to media and licensed toys inhibits children's "transcendent imagination" by reducing the number of imaginary items available to the child.[28] Playing with licensed toys and incorporating media characters into imaginative play is understood as something fundamentally different from traditional forms of make-believe, wherein children collaborate to create their own rules and themes, or even traditional gameplay, wherein rules can be negotiated or suspended at the whim of the players.

Another key critic, Kline, conducted several decades' worth of research on children's relationship with media and technology, including their play with media tie-in toys. In some of his earlier works, he uses the term "play scripts" to describe how themes, plotlines, and characters circulated within transmedia intertexts do not merely construct a narrative scaffolding around tie-in toys, but in fact determine key aspects of their use.[29] He argues that children are taught to internalize certain narrative themes and values as they watch toy ads and associated media programs, which they then incorporate into their own play. The media texts provide children with play scripts that they then attempt to reproduce in their interactions with the tie-in toys. Play scripts, he argues, assign toys a specialized set of rules and thematic conventions, confining the "possibilities for pretending" to those that conform with the child's understanding of the toy's encoded character and storyline. According to Kline, play scripts shape "sequential patterns of action and meaning which children replicate in their play."[30]

Yet the idea that licensed toys and their associated media supersystems limit children's play is also deeply contested. At issue is the deterministic relationship that the critiques of media supersystems construct – in this case, between mediatization and play. The causality implied in Greenfield and Kline's arguments has been challenged by researchers whose work instead demonstrates that play is shaped by multiple factors, not least among them the actions and interpretive agency of the children themselves. Many scholars in this opposing camp emphasize the creative ways children integrate, appropriate, subvert, and transform the narrative discourses provided by media texts and licensed toys, especially when playing with peers.[31] They highlight the individual's capacity for rich and subjective meaning-making, which they argue takes precedence over the simple storylines and hollow promotional messages touted by media and toy producers.

Paley and Sutton-Smith both demonstrate that children retain the ability to diverge from and subvert the play scripts found in toys and games, even when these scripts contain powerful narrative associations.[32] The children in their studies engaged in active appropriations, they negotiated meanings, and they reinterpreted the intended uses assigned to toys and other artefacts. Ethnographic work conducted over the past thirty years has revealed strong traditions of subversion, innovation, and appropriation across children's play culture.[33] Seiter explains that licensed toys can provide children with important opportunities for "creative ritualization, [and] victorious self-images," as well as "facilitate group, co-operative play" by providing children with a shared set of codes, references, and narratives to use in their make-believe.[34] As Willis points out, "Barbie can slide down avalanches just as He-Man can become the inhabitant of a two-story Victorian doll's house."[35]

More recently, many of these same arguments and findings have emerged out of studies of children's digital gameplay. For example, Giddings argues that children retain a high level of agency and creative freedom in their interactions with digital games, even when the game in question follows a seemingly prescriptive, linear design.[36] In his study of children playing with console games based on the Lego toy brand, he observed numerous instances of unscripted, subversive, and creative play. This included improvised games that emerged out of the children's discovery of programmed limitations in the game design, as well as the frequent reassignment of the game's formal rules and objectives. For instance, rather than abide by the formal game rule that equates death with defeat, the children in his study purposefully sought out new ways to make their avatars die. Children's digital play, Giddings argues, is "constituted by the complex interactions among the gameworld's physics; the affordances of software elements (notably those of the car/avatar); the transmedial suggestions and humour of this particular game (linking it to prior knowledge of the Lego franchise in its actual instantiations); and the characteristics of more traditional children's play with toys, notably the pleasures of exploration and creative destruction."[37]

These findings establish important continuities with previous arguments that children's play with licensed toys and media brands incorporates just as much creativity, subversion, and agency as their more traditional play activities do. They also highlight the limitations of assuming a game's design and intended uses predict actual player behaviours.

Moreover, research by scholars such as Jenkins, Ito, and Götz show that young people engage in informal learning and deep meaning-making through participatory fandom, in which media characters and narratives are reimagined, repositioned, and at times critiqued in the form of fan fiction, drawings, and role-play.[38] Marsh and her research team found similar patterns among elementary school–aged children in the United Kingdom, who frequently incorporated media themes and characters from television, film, and digital games into their make-believe play and playground games.[39] This work indicates that at least some children can assess and make their own decisions about whether to accept or reject the play scripts promoted by media brands and licensed toys. It also suggests that engaging in such activities is itself an important part of children's acculturation, socialization, and identity formation.

Changing trends in academic research and public opinion about the impact of licensed toys and other cross-promotional media on children are reflected in concurrent regulatory shifts that have unfolded in both Canada and in the United States. In the mid-1970s, concerns about children's vulnerability to manipulatory advertising tactics led to the implementation of restrictions in both countries on what and how commercial content could be incorporated into child-targeted media such as television, magazines, and films. In the United States many of these restrictions were loosened significantly in the 1980s and 1990s, in keeping with broader changes occurring in the regulatory climate of the time. In Canada, while the 1974 Children's Code remains in effect, government enforcement of established, industry-generated standards and restrictions on advertising to children is all but non-existent. As Jeffrey argues, "There is no evidence on record that the CRTC [Canadian Radio-television and Telecommunications Commission] has ever considered violations of the Children's Code to determine whether a licence should be renewed, revoked, or subjected to additional terms."[40]

The 1998 introduction of the US Children's Online Privacy Protection Act (COPPA) represents an important departure from the otherwise congruent trends towards government deregulation on the one hand, and a dominant academic emphasis on children's agency on the other. While the rule covers a range of issues relating to children's privacy rights online, it emerged in response to some troubling findings discovered by Montgomery and others demonstrating that advertisers and market researchers were soliciting personal information from children online. Montgomery argued that website owners and third-party advertisers were using various tools, including questionnaires and registration forms, to gain unprecedented levels of access to children through child-targeted games, forums, and other websites. The data were then used in direct marketing campaigns, as well as for research and development of new and existing products. With COPPA, a number of important restrictions were placed on the type of information that could be solicited from children online, along with requirements that websites targeted to (or simply known to be frequented by) children seek parental consent before collecting data from that child, and enable parents to have their child's personal data deleted upon request.

Since then, however, relatively little academic research has focused on understanding the commercial dimensions of children's digital games and other applications. This is noteworthy for various reasons, but especially because the children's digital landscape remains dominated by both indirect and direct forms of commercialization. Concurrently, although the COPPA Rule introduced important limits to how children's data could be collected and managed within online contexts, the buying, collating, and selling of personal data remains a key source of revenue for many child-oriented digital platforms. In addition, a disproportionate number of children's digital games and virtual worlds are connected to media supersystems and function predominantly as venues for cross-promotional initiatives. Many of the most popular children's games are either based on established media brands or quickly become the basis for tie-in toys, media, and other products. Meanwhile, the rapid spread of in-game/in-app purchases and other forms of content monetization across the digital landscape has extended into titles popular among children as well as those designed specifically for them. Nonetheless, children's digital playgrounds are rarely approached as a form of licensed toy or as a type of transmedia cross-promotion. As a result, their embedded commercial features are routinely overlooked.

Part of this oversight may stem from a consensus in current academic and popular discourses pertaining to digital games – that they are first and foremost sites of heightened levels of player agency. Most digital games scholars argue that connected games and virtual worlds (particularly MMOGs) are highly amenable to autonomous, creative, and unanticipated play.[41] Within such a climate, studies focused on structure are frequently dismissed as deterministic and authoritarian. Likewise, within the disciplines associated with children's studies, there is a growing body of research focused on uncovering and better understanding how children perform and experience agency in their interactions with digital games.[42] Much like digital game scholars, many children's scholars position themselves in opposition to early (and in many ways enduring) claims of negative, deterministic media effects, which equated digital gameplay with real-world violence, obesity, or anti-social behaviours, especially among children. As explored in the next section, the powerful spectre of the "dangerous games" rhetoric continues to haunt academic discourses about games and gaming. In children's digital games, the backdrop is even more politicized, as issues relating to children and childhood are subject to their own set of complex ideological rifts and clashing epistemologies.

Digital Game Controversies and Dichotomies

During the early history of digital games, children were not considered to be a major user group. Many of the earliest computer games were designed for hobbyist computer programmers, a demographic that by the late 1970s was already predominantly (although not solely) made up of young, white men from middle-class backgrounds.[43] Both the earliest personal computers (or microcomputers) and the first generation of home videogame consoles were marketed largely to this narrow, highly specialized group. Outside of the home, video arcades and arcade games became the targets of the first videogame-related moral panics. In the early 1980s, for instance, arcade games were frequently condemned by media watchdogs, religious groups, parents' organizations, and the press for their alleged addictive influence, violent content, and assumed "encouragement of aggressive behaviour."[44] Standalone arcades – which were depicted by these same groups as "sleazy" venues that attracted "bad kids" and fostered delinquency – were deemed unsuitable for children.[45]

A lot has changed over the past four decades. Today, not only do the majority of Canadian and US children play digital games, but they also represent approximately 21 per cent of the global digital games audience.[46] As described in chapter 2, market analysts also suggest that children represent a disproportionate number of "heavy" and "avid" gamers – terms used to describe those who engage in digital gaming most frequently and for longer-than-average periods. More than this, however, digital games have come to be strongly associated with children, a trend first established in the mid-1980s with introduction of the child-friendly (and child-targeted) Nintendo Entertainment System. During the 1980s, the idea that digital (specifically computer) games were an effective means of teaching children computer programming, and of attracting them to future careers as coders and other information workers, first took root. The alleged linkage between digital gaming and more serious forms of computer coding spread across school curricula and market discourses alike. In turn, as Bittanti argues, these dichotomous associations placed digital games at the centre of a recurring cycle of moral panics, public controversies, and court cases.

The pendulum dynamic that emerged around children and digital games – wherein playing games is viewed as beneficial on the one hand, and as detrimental on the other – is arguably the defining feature of the history of children and digital games. Today, it continues to play a vital role in the social configuration of children's digital games, influencing everything from how children's titles are designed and marketed to how they are regulated. It is therefore unsurprising that digital games are at the heart of so many of the current discussions about children's play, both popular and academic. Digital games consist of virtual, adult-constructed play spaces that seem to be at stark odds with the idealized pastoral visions of childhood play that still permeate our cultural consciousness. At the same time, the games also represent a perfect convergence of media, play, and technology, and thereby carry all the ideological baggage associated with each of these prominent and highly controversial areas of contemporary childhood. Accordingly, digital games serve as both lightning rods of controversy and as beacons of technological promise.

While key elements of this dual role can be linked to the traditions outlined above, children's digital games have also followed a unique trajectory, one characterized by rhetorical intensity. The cycle generally unfolds as follows: games are spuriously linked to some undesirable or worrisome social development through a media-fuelled moral panic, and a controversy is born. Some public discussion of regulatory change or disruption of the status quo occurs. Occasionally, initial steps are even taken to change laws or policies, or to enact new ones. This is followed by a widely shared, robust critique of the spurious causal linkages upon which the panic (and subsequent policy development) was originally based. Lastly, a neoliberal alternative is introduced and widely championed. This alternative is at times presented as a solution to the controversy, but more often it is used as a sort of sleight of hand – drawing attention away from the controversy and onto a more optimistic discourse. Predictably, the solution is almost always centred on increasing technological diffusion, expanding into new markets, and privileging self-regulation through the rhetoric of consumer sovereignty. In the 1970s and 1980s, the new market being targeted was children (and to a lesser extent, families). In the 1990s and early 2000s, it was girls. In both instances, children came to represent the untapped potential of digital gaming, which was concurrently positioned as a gateway into the development of hard computer skills, such as programming, and computational thinking. As is so often the case, the emphasis on purposive play found within these discourses functioned as a counterbalance to growing social concerns about the perceived dangers of unfamiliar new media, technologies, and play forms.

Dangerous Games and Risky Gamers

Social anxiety about the possible negative effects of digital games first emerged in the late 1970s and early 1980s, with the framing of standalone video arcades as unsavoury spaces that fostered delinquency, aggression, and addiction – especially among younger patrons. Since then, a series of high-profile controversies have focused on digital games in their various forms, leading scholars to term the medium a "lightning rod" for public scrutiny and debate.[47] Many of these controversies mobilize a rhetoric of "the child at risk" and reproduce many of the same dialectics that surround children's play and children's media, as explored above. Accordingly, regulatory responses to the controversies have focused largely on limiting children's exposure and access to certain types of games. Digital games scholar Williams notes, "The story of how games emerged, were quickly vilified and then earned some measure of redemption is part of a larger history of new media technologies. Previous media have encountered a consistent series of utopian and dystopian reactions to new technologies, often simultaneously. Over several cases, we have begun to see consistent patterns in these reactions.... Starting with film, each case led to a major series of social science–based media studies to determine what effect the newfangled technology was having on the unsuspecting populace, most frequently on children."[48]

Over the years, different interest groups have taken the lead in linking children's gaming to a wide variety of social ills and undesirable trends. A longstanding concern is that engaging in too much solitary gameplay results in underdeveloped social skills and even antisocial behaviour. More recently, concern has shifted to a perceived correlation between gaming – a sedentary, screen-based, indoor leisure activity – and rising childhood obesity rates. However, for well over two decades, the most widely held and well-known fear relating to children's gaming has been its purported association with real-world aggression and violence. Alarm about this alleged "media effect" not only makes up a significant share of the game-related controversies that have emerged since the 1990s, but is also credited with inciting numerous regulatory movements, court cases, and an entire sub-field of academic research.

In an in-depth examination of news media coverage of videogame controversies published between 1970 to 2000, Williams applies Gitlin's "media frames" theory to uncover a persisting conservative bias, in which videogames are first vilified and then partially redeemed. Williams argues that during the first three decades of their existence, videogames consistently served as "touchstones for larger struggles within the culture." Similar trends are uncovered in McKernan's analysis of the *New York Times* coverage of videogames and related issues between 1980 and 2009. McKernan concludes that overarching cultural codes relating to children profoundly shape how games are represented: "The New York Times' understanding of video games as a children's activity ultimately influences the manner in which the newspaper treats video games, resulting in coverage primarily focused on determining if video games are a threat or a functional benefit to children. In this sense, the New York Times' video game coverage is consistent with civil society's predominant understanding of children as a special population in need of protection and adult guidance."[49]

Children have played a central role within many of the regulatory and legal discussions relating to digital games that have unfolded over the past several decades. In a comparable review of digital game–related legal cases and public policies debated by US courts over the past three decades, Ferguson details a long series of failed attempts to regulate digital games, predominantly by placing limits on children's access and exposure to violent videogame content.[50] Of course, regulatory debates and media coverage commonly feed into other – high-profile media subjects often drive new policy development, while attempts to enact new laws and regulation are in turn newsworthy events. In this case, however, both realms were also responding to high-profile violent events, such as the Columbine High School massacre in 1999, in which violent videogames were alleged (by some) to be implicated. Although many of the bills introduced in the early 2000s aimed to do little more than institutionalize the digital game industry's own self-regulatory ratings system – a system managed, and already enforced quite effectively, by the industry-driven Entertainment Software Ratings Board (ESRB)[51] – they were frequently described by lawmakers as tools for preventing future mass shootings. The bills themselves stemmed largely from the common belief that playing violent videogames transformed players into violent offenders – an idea that had circulated quite heavily within policy hearings, news coverage, and associated media panics, since the 1980s.

Academic research also features prominently within both the news coverage and legal cases relating to violent videogames. This is especially true of studies and scholars that advanced deterministic, polarizing claims. Within the court cases reviewed in Ferguson's analysis, academics on one side of the debate were frequently called upon to present their research findings in support of increased regulation, while academics from the other side were asked to challenge the validity of these findings, along with the methods used to produce them. For its part, news coverage is generally oscillatory and ambivalent in its presentation of empirical research – even when the findings themselves don't create a dichotomy. Williams found that "media coverage over the past thirty years has drawn incorrectly on research results, often ignoring the null findings altogether. One column went so far as to suggest that research has proven that games are pathologically addicting children at epidemic rates."[52] This may simply be a function of the journalistic norm of a "two-sided balance in reporting."[53] Williams argues that, in some instances, dichotomies were also constructed after the fact – through the over-generalization of a study's actual findings, for instance, or by narrowly representing selections of a researcher's argument.

This practice of stoking ambivalence produces heightened uncertainty among audiences about "what is true" and confusion about how to "distinguish between more versus less valid claims."[54] Much has been written about the detrimental impact of this practice on the public's understanding of climate change science, for instance, which for many years has been depicted by the news media as an issue under debate, rather than the area of sweeping consensus that it truly is. Indeed, Harvey suggests that parental ambivalence vis-à-vis children's digital gameplay is quite common, even among tech-savvy parents: "No matter what the degree of fluency, competence, or interest, use [of digital game technologies] within the home was always shaped by the discourses of how parents and youth must negotiate the digital landscape, laden with benefits and opportunities but also rife with potential dangers."[55]

As for the videogame trials, the stakes involved were even higher, as each bill was challenged on the grounds that it infringed on freedom of speech rights. Justification for regulating children's access to digital games thus became contingent on the presence of *irrefutable evidence of harm* – a condition that the research falls far short of meeting. In ruling after ruling, the US courts – including the US Supreme Court – decided that the research did not support the widespread belief that videogame violence causes real-world violence. As Kline argues, the violent videogame trials essentially established causality as the new gold standard for media regulation.[56] In pure and applied science, causality is a principle in which a linear relationship between cause and effect is established. But in complex cultural and social phenomena, unfolding within the messy, mutable, and ambiguous contexts of everyday life, one-to-one causality is difficult to determine. Most social science research, including studies stemming from positivist traditions and disciplines, is instead designed to examine, establish, or measure correlations. Other studies employ descriptive research methods to track trends, patterns, and shared characteristics without establishing why they occur. Meanwhile, entire branches of the social sciences eschew positivist standards altogether and instead adhere to qualitative methodologies that emphasize building a holistic, contextualized understanding of individual perspectives, meaning-making practices, and experiences. All in all, claims of causality within social science research are quite rare. When they do occur, they are usually met with a heavy dose of scrutiny from the broader academic community.

When it comes to writing news stories and building legal arguments, however, claims of causality are highly sought after. Therefore, academics who are willing to make such claims often become overrepresented within public debates. This happened during the violent videogames debates of the early 2000s, which frequently featured testimony and soundbites by Craig A. Anderson, a psychologist and professor at Iowa State University. In addition to making regular appearances in the news media, Anderson was called upon in two high-profile cases to present the results of his research, which argued that exposure to digital game violence led to increases in players' real life aggression and attitudes.[57] While Anderson has continued to research in this area over the past decade, at the time his testimony was based largely on the results of a grossly unrepresentative survey, as well as a quasi-experiment, both involving his own undergraduate students. In response, an amici curiae (friends of the court) brief was submitted by a group of social science scholars challenging Anderson's methodological design and interpretation of findings. The brief outlined that most digital game research did not support Anderson's argument that playing violent videogames caused increased aggressive thoughts and actions among players. They critiqued Anderson's research for its small sample size, lack of direct causality, and overly broad definition of what counts as evidence of aggression. The fact that the respondents consisted of adult university students – not children – was also raised.

By focusing so heavily on the specific weaknesses in Anderson's research design and conclusions, however, the amici curiae brief implicitly validated the underlying idea emerging within the courts that videogame regulation could be justified only if proof of a direct and consistent causal relationship between gaming and repeated real-world violence was introduced into evidence. Omitted from this discussion was the large number of comparatively robust studies conducted over several decades examining correlation, potential harms, and risk factors. For instance, as Millwood Hargrave and Livingstone describe, the literature on television violence "suggests that, under certain circumstances, television can negatively influence attitudes in some areas, including those which may affect society (through the creation of prejudice) and those which may affect the individual (by making them unduly fearful, for example)."[58] Overall, the research indicates that for at least some children, heavy exposure to violent and disturbing media themes and imagery can be detrimental – negatively impacting children's world views, emotional states, and/or sense of well-being. However, within the violent videogame news coverage and court cases, little attention was paid to the more moderate findings and conditional conclusions of this larger body of research. Instead, emphasis remained on headline-stealing outliers, such as Anderson, who claimed that games and their players were outright dangerous.

The stakes and approach taken during these deliberations represented an important departure from the role academic research played in previous regulatory debates. Historically, evidence of potential harm or risk of harm was sufficient for justifying the introduction of numerous public policies and media regulations – particularly in instances where vulnerable groups were involved. For example, laws limiting children's exposure to pornography are based largely on cultural norms, ethics, and expert and judicial opinion, rather than on empirical evidence that it irrefutably harms children. Outside of the United States, a wide range of standards, arguments, and considerations still do come into play when new laws and government-enforced regulation are deliberated. By 2008, five Canadian provinces (Ontario, Manitoba, New Brunswick, Nova Scotia, and Saskatchewan) had passed legislation institutionalizing the US-based ESRB ratings system, making it illegal to sell or rent age-inappropriate games to minors. The same year, a sixth province (British Columbia) began regulating children's access to digital games through its pre-existing motion picture legislation.[59] By 2016, thirty-nine European countries required retailers to adhere to Pan European Game Information (PEGI) ratings, which, like the ESRB system, employ an age-based approach to classifying content.[60] In many parts of the world, governments are relatively protectionist when it comes to children and the media, placing limits on what the media and advertising industries can say and show to children, despite a lack of irrefutable proof of harm.

Failure to establish causality is therefore not the regulatory deal breaker elsewhere that it appears to be in the United States, where, by the early 2010s, nearly half of all states had tried and failed to pass comparable legislation. Invariably, bills to make the ESRB ratings mandatory and enforceable were subsequently dismissed by US courts, largely on the grounds that such a system would infringe on freedom of speech rights. Although Canada and the European countries that regulate digital games using the PEGI system also recognize freedom of speech as a human and legal right, their courts are much less likely to treat it as a pre-eminent right that supersedes all others. In Canada, for instance, laws against hate speech put tangible limits on freedom of expression. As Cohen-Almagor argues, such limits are based on the premise that "there is a need to strike a balance between the right to freedom of expression and the harms that might result from certain speech. It is argued that the right to exercise free expression does not include the right to do unjustifiable harm to others."[61] While striking a balance is an ongoing task and is itself a source of controversy and public debate, its prioritization within policymaking discussions has resulted in a climate that is much more open to (at least some forms of) media regulation.

Notably, in all three cases (United States, Canada, and Europe), the regulation in question is relatively moderate and non-interventionist. The age restrictions advanced in the US state bills, for instance, were based on categories defined and applied by a self-regulatory body of the digital game industry and arose only at the point of purchase. Parents could bypass the restrictions by purchasing the game for their child, just as movie theatre ratings could be bypassed with parental permission and/ or accompaniment. Moreover, and at the same time, many states still required theatres and movie rental stores to adhere to Motion Picture Association of America (MPAA) ratings in almost exactly the same way the videogame bills sought to enforce retailer compliance to ESRB ratings. However, the regulatory climate was clearly shifting away from such traditional approaches. During this period, several movie-related state bills were repealed. The last state to have such a law was Tennessee, which replaced it in 2013 with a vague restriction prohibiting movie theatres from admitting children to films found to be "harmful to minors."[62]

As scholars such as Williams and Ferguson maintain, in the United States, freedom of speech presents a formidable obstacle to digital game regulation. To date, the US courts have unanimously decided that there is insufficient empirical evidence to justify any form of videogame regulation that would infringe upon the freedom of speech rights of the digital game industry or those of players. It is important to remember, however, that there is something more at play within these discourses. The bills, their associated court cases, and much of the surrounding media coverage are all haunted by the spectre of the dangerous child. The emphasis placed on causality has a lot to do with the implication that when it comes to violent videogames, the child is first and foremost viewed as a subject at risk of *becoming* the risk – of embodying and perpetuating the violence contained within certain game genres and titles. Once again, public discourse is preoccupied with what exposure to certain forms of play will transform children into, rather than how these activities might inform children's experience or well-being in the present.

Games for "Good" Girls

The construct of the child gamer as risky or dangerous is inherently political. For one, it is frequently mobilized by politicians and anti-game pundits as justification for enacting government-enforced videogame regulation and other restrictions. It derives from ideological beliefs and fears rather than from empirical evidence – outside of a small body of contentious studies with spurious conclusions, as outlined above. Notably, it is also heavily gendered. As Walkerdine argues, "Boys but never girls are associated with violence and fighting and possible negative effects of computer games."[63] This is perhaps unsurprising, given that the perpetrators of the types of violent incidents that most often serve as the catalysts for renewed media and policy debates about digital game violence, such as mass shootings, are almost always male. Moreover, from the 1980s until recently, popular culture depictions of gamers, in film and television for instance, have been predominantly male.[64] As Shaw describes it, the dominant gamer image has long been that of a "White, heterosexual, male, teen."[65] This stereotype has gained additional support through its regular presence in advertisements, marketing strategies, and other "configurations of the user" perpetuated by the digital game industry itself.[66]

Although rates of digital game play are now roughly the same between boys and girls, during the violent videogame controversies that emerged in the 1990s and early 2000s, boys *were* the most likely demographic to play digital games. Notwithstanding the fact that the available statistics on who plays digital games have long been problematic – riddled with biased and narrow categorizations of what constitutes a digital game, for example – game scholars such as Schott and Horrell determined that at the turn of the twenty-first century girls and women made up only 14–25 per cent of the gaming market.[67] In addition, the digital game industry itself was then, as it remains today, predominantly male – with (young) men occupying most of the positions in development, programming, design, and even play testing.[68] From the ubiquitous presence of "booth babes" at videogame conventions to the prevalence of "crunch time" and other non-family-friendly industry working conditions, a male-dominated culture had already emerged around games and gaming. This "hegemony of play," as it was described by feminist game scholars Fron et al., "narrowed the conception of both play and player in the digital sphere."[69] This in turn produced a self-perpetuating cycle that worked to maintain the status quo while inadvertently lending support to the negative gamer stereotypes and the associations with deviance that circulated within the broader culture.

It is within this context that the "girl games" movement emerged. The movement itself was multilayered and multifunctional, but three facets stand out as particularly relevant to the current discussion. First, the girl games movement can be understood as an attempt by the digital games industry to expand into new markets, which coincided with the industry's own expansion through a surge in new, independent entrants, including a small number of girl-oriented and women-led start-ups. Second, interest in girl games was propelled by the efforts of several academics, educators, and advocacy groups seeking to address the gender gap that had arisen within game development and the mainstream gaming culture. Often, these efforts drew on the longstanding belief that digital games could serve as a gateway into computer programming and other technically sophisticated forms of information work. Finally, the combined results of these disparate interest groups served a third implicit function – that of providing an appealing and convenient other to dangerous games and risky gamers at the centre of the violent videogame controversies.

The origins of the girl games movement is often linked to the surprise success of Mattel's *Barbie Fashion Designer*, a computer game released in 1996 targeted specifically at girls. At the time, the game set a new sales record for PC games, selling half a million copies within its first two months. As Laurel writes, the game's success "stimulated a retail feeding frenzy."[70] Start-ups were launched, new titles were introduced, and the industry did all it could to replicate *Barbie*'s sales figures. During this period, a number of innovative games for girls were produced. For example, Her Interactive's *Nancy Drew* games won awards and for many years held the title of top-selling PC adventure game series – in all categories, not simply in the girl games genre. For the most part, however, the new girl games market was predominated by "pink games." Much like the "pink aisle" found in modern toy stores, the term "pink games" refers to the predominance of the colour used when designing and packaging toys targeted to girls. It also refers to a strategy that is often used when designing technologies ostensibly for women or girls, in which an artefact is appropriated and adapted through limited, superficial, and mostly aesthetic modifications. Many of the pink games that emerged during this era used pre-existing game engines and code, which were modified and "reskinned" to accommodate girl-coded aesthetics, as well as girls' presumed play preferences.[71]

The market research suggested that girls were turned off by the violence and male-coded themes that permeated the mainstream videogame market. This finding was corroborated by certain academic studies as well. For instance, Kafai's research on gender differences in children's own designs of the "ideal" videogame found that the girls in her study (unlike the boys) rarely incorporated violence in their designs, nor did they include stories centred on contests between good and evil. Greenfield and Subrahmanyam's review of the literature culminated in the argument that the "established" cultural preferences of women and girls – vis-à-vis literature, television, or play more generally – provide insight into the types of videogames that would most likely appeal to girl players.[72] Overall, these studies claimed that girl games should focus on traditionally feminine values, such as interpersonal relationships and co-operation, and feature traditionally feminine themes, like shopping, gossip, and beauty.[73] By the late 1990s, a new wave of girl games had flooded the market, many of which centred on stereotypically "girl-coded topics such as dating, fashion, hairstyles, and social protocols."[74]

Most commercial, girl-targeted games produced during this era failed to recapture *Barbie*'s audience size. Many of the pink games ultimately relied heavily on cross-media intertextuality but were otherwise poorly designed – filled with glitches – and offered limited gameplay. In at least some instances, the games were made up of recycled game code and engines originally designed for the mainstream (male) market, in which core features such as guns and shooting mechanics were removed to make the games non-violent and "girl-friendly," but were not replaced. This practice resulted in games with very few action opportunities and oftentimes incongruous objectives. They were also inconsistently marketed to their target audience. Overall, the industry showed a lot of impatience when it came to establishing a girls' game market. Companies pulled the plug on projects before they really had a chance to get off the ground, while others were underfunded. Little effort was put into advertising. In the end, the market for girl games never really took off the way everyone hoped it would.

Nonetheless, during the decades that followed, girls and women flocked to digital games. Across genres and platforms, they have found niches for themselves within a medium that otherwise remains heavily male-dominated. Girls and women make up a growing proportion of mainstream gamers – playing male-targeted titles and participating in (and at times at the margins of) the larger gamer culture. In addition, girls and women contribute significantly to the massive success of gender-inclusive titles such as Niantic's *Pokémon Go* (2016–present), Nintendo's *Mario Kart* series (1992–2017), and Blizzard Entertainment's *World of Warcraft*. Others sustain the remnants of the girl games market, buoying dark horse blockbusters such as Glorious Games's *Stardoll* (2004–present), and providing a market for girl-targeted science, technology, engineering, and math (STEM) initiatives such as GoldieBlox's *GoldieBlox: Adventures in Coding – The Rocket Cupcake Co.* (2016). Recent studies estimate that on any given day, approximately 40 per cent of girls aged eight to eighteen play digital games of some kind, and 78 per cent of girls between the ages of six and eleven play online games. As Shaw argues, "The dominant White, heterosexual, male, teen gamer image ... is consistently discredited, both popularly and academically."[75] Widely cited studies estimate that female-identified players' participation rates are now more or less equivalent to those of male-identified players, particularly when a broad range of game forms and formats are included in the count.

The girl games movement was always much more than a mere market strategy, however. It was also fuelled by a transdisciplinary surge in academic research on issues pertaining to gaming and gender, as well as the efforts of organizations and advocacy groups dedicated to promoting and supporting gender equality in different areas (e.g., media, technology, childhood). The marked disparity in who played, made, and appeared in digital games raised crucial questions about bias and representation, the marginalization of female-identified players, as well as early concerns about the emerging toxicity circulating within gaming culture. These elements were linked and mutually reinforcing, but until then had been largely overlooked in both popular and academic discussions about games and gaming. During the mid- to late 1990s, a growing body of academic, and especially feminist, scholarship on gender and games emerged. In 1998, MIT Press published *From Barbie® to Mortal Kombat*, a pivotal edited collection that featured a combination of academic research and a series of in-depth interviews with some of the girl games movement's most successful women developers and entrepreneurs. Since then, academic enquiry into gender issues and politics has become an established tradition within (digital) game studies.

During the 1990s and 2000s, the widespread interest in understanding and addressing the gender disparities associated with videogames was amplified by a growing awareness of comparable divides within computer programming, as well as in computing science and other technically sophisticated information professions. The "computing gender gap" seemed to begin in pre-adolescence, as girls and boys diverged in their use of digital technologies and skill with computers. As Vitores and Gil-Juárez describe it, "Most of the research indicates that middle school is a key moment of 'exclusion' and 'disaffection' formation because by high school, gender differences in computing interest (and thus, girls' lack of interest in computing or IT as a career option) are well established."[76] One explanation offered at the time was that boys' widespread attraction to videogames translated into deeper levels of comfort and familiarity with computers, along with the development of transferable technical skills. This idea had circulated since the early 1980s and drew on early scholarship by Papert, Greenfield, and others who linked playing computer games with increased computer literacy, as well as increased confidence and aptitude for learning and mastering new computer technologies and applications. The girl games movement included several studies and initiatives aimed at bridging the computing gender gap by increasing girls' familiarity, skill, and confidence with computing technologies through gameplay.

A connective thread weaves in and out of these seemingly disparate narratives – that of a third and largely implicit function of the girl games movement. Located in the liminal space between gaming's destructive and educational potentials, girl games and their subjects – girl gamers – at once legitimated the desire to transform play into a productive activity (as represented by the hope that gaming would lead to computer skill development and, eventually, future careers in computer science), while disavowing the violence associated with "dangerous" videogames. For one, girl games and pink games provided a convenient antithesis to the violent, competition-laden titles at the centre of the videogame controversies. Instead of guns and kill counts, most girl games revolved around themes of shopping, cuteness, and friendship. Similarly, the girl gamer provided a rhetorical resolution to the social ambivalence that had arisen around the dominant gamer stereotype during the 1990s and early 2000s. The studies and market research, which suggested that fewer girls played digital games because they disliked violence, played a key role in this regard. The idea enabled the focus to be shifted onto the beneficial dimensions of digital games, while suppressing the possibility of girls' aggressiveness.

A key weakness shared by many of the studies claiming marked gender differences within children's play preferences is that they focused predominantly on girls who did not play videogames. In many instances, these non-gamer girls were asked to speculate on what types of games they, or other children, *might* find appealing. Their responses were then interpreted as providing confirmation that gender norms and stereotypes are accurate representations of children's (innate) preferences. This line of reasoning is flawed, as it overlooks the fact that even young children are already embedded in specific sociocultural contexts. Emerging research indicates that even infants are aware of gender expectations and stereotypes. Toys, media, and play represent some of the first places children encounter gender norms, and they fast become masters in identifying what types of content, stories, or themes are meant for girls and what is intended for boys. Gender norms and stereotypes also provide children with a convenient set of shared cultural references – a vocabulary for connecting and sharing ideas. It is not surprising that children would mobilize gender norms in response to the types of questions and scenarios asked in the studies described above. It is much more difficult to ascertain the extent to which the studies truly reveal what girls do, or would prefer to encounter, in their play.

Another problematic feature of the girl games movement and its associated research was the underlying assumption that girls were autonomously choosing to not play videogames – that "not playing" was itself a preference. Yet girls have historically been given less time for play than boys, and recent research on children's time use shows that girls continue to enjoy less leisure time, and engage in more household chores, than boys. These trends extend to digital play as well. In a study of gender, gaming, and family dynamics conducted in the mid-2000s, Walkerdine discovered that parents were less likely to buy their daughters digital games and consoles, and were more likely to monitor girls' gaming.[77] In a three-year study of young people playing games in an after-school gaming club, Jenson and de Castell reported that "it became clear that nearly all of the young women we were observing had not spent much time playing console games; in fact, even when they did claim to have played ... many would say that they played by 'watching' their brothers, or uncles or fathers or male cousins play."[78] The girls in their study had limited access to console games in their everyday lives. Accordingly, they had limited knowledge of how to navigate the console interface, and no experience setting up or even turning on the gaming machine. In both studies, the researchers determined that lack of experience and access played a pivotal role in the girls' relationship with gaming, greatly limiting their ability to achieve mastery of specific game titles or of common gaming mechanics and control mechanisms. Tellingly, as the girls became more experienced videogame players, the "'gender differences' so consistently 'found' in gender and gameplay studies ... were far less evident and some of these were no longer present at all, once the girls had been afforded genuine access, support, a 'girls-gamer' model, and the right to choose what, when and with whom they would play."[79]

Since the nineteenth century, girls have not only enjoyed less leisure time than boys, they have also been more often encouraged to pursue functional leisure activities. From tea parties and doll play, to knitting and crafts, a significant proportion of the toys, play activities, and games aimed specifically at girls were intended to prepare them for their futures as wives and mothers.[80] Many of the underlying assumptions perpetuated by the girl games movement, therefore, have circulated in one form or another throughout the modern era. This includes the idea that girls prefer themes of nurturing and aesthetic arrangement, as well as the notion that girls should engage in leisure activities that will help them develop the "right" types of skills. At the turn of the nineteenth century, these skills revolved around housekeeping, child-rearing, and proper etiquette. In the case of the girl games movement, the preferred outcome has become the development of enhanced skills in programming and computational thinking. Research furthermore suggests that girls encounter additional purposive expectations, in that they are more often encouraged by parents to play educational games.[81] While the image of the "girl gamer" mobilized by the game industry, policymakers, and advocates served as a handy rhetorical counterweight to the "dangerous (male) gamer" stereotype imagined in the violent videogames controversies, it also shaped the social expectations and lived experiences that came to be associated with girls' everyday gaming practices.

The pursuit of girl games as a distinct market persisted throughout the 1990s. It not only operated as an effective antidote to the violence associated with boys' gaming, it also provided a way of effacing the (potential) violence of girl gamers, should they start playing in greater numbers. Lamb argues that this is typical of Western society, which largely denies aggression in girls while naturalizing it in boys.[82] Research into children's play, however, reveals that instances of aggression are common among children of both genders, as are antisocial behaviours generally deemed more acceptable for boys than girls – for example, engaging in subversive or macabre play. In interviews, young girls have expressed a range of thoughts and feelings about violent videogames: from dislike to outright enjoyment of competitive videogame violence to wondering if they themselves will become violent if they take too much pleasure in playing violent games. As Walkerdine argues, "There is little doubt that many girls like playing [digital] games. They joined the videogame clubs and were keen to play. They also can get [as] excited about killing and violence as the boys."[83] Despite findings that nearly a third of girl gamers play violent games regularly, girls who play and enjoy such games are routinely designated as exceptions to the rule. In any case, they are distanced as much as possible from the accepted, and acceptable, girl gamer construct.

Other scholars make similar arguments about the underlying gender dichotomy bolstering the girl games movement. According to Cassell and Jenkins, "For the most part, the girls' game movement has operated under the assumption that girls and boys want something fundamentally different from digital media, that it is possible to find out what they want from market research, and that the best way of responding to this situation is to create girls-only or girl-directed media that stand alongside more boy-centered media."[84]

Such assumptions not only "other" the girl gamer, but also simultaneously legitimize the male-centric tendencies of the existing game industry and the broader gamer culture. If girls and boys want fundamentally different things from their leisure and media experiences, the argument goes, then the preferred solution is to create girl-specific games. This approach extends gender segregation within the games market while ensuring that the "boy-centred" status quo remains unchallenged. Questions about gender inclusiveness in the contents, themes, characters, and even production of mainstream (i.e., male-targeted) games are, in turn, more easily deflected. After all, the game market's massive and ongoing success – in terms of sales figures and profits – serves as evidence that boys' and men's needs and preferences are being effectively addressed. The problem of gender disparity in games can thus be shifted onto girl gamers themselves – an elusive potential audience with mysterious and perhaps unknowable desires, and an emerging and undefined market segment that must be created and sold to separately.

Recent research investigating the cultural construction of the type of gendered play preferences introduced during the girl games era problematizes the methodology and findings of studies that claimed to have found "essential" differences. Other contemporary scholarship brings attention to the many girls and women who *do* play mainstream, male-targeted videogames, while critiquing girls' and women's exclusion from traditional discussions of games and gender.[85] Since the early 2000s, feminist game studies has evolved into an established academic tradition, and issues of gender, race, sexuality, disability, and intersectionality are now viewed as central to game studies.[86] Conversely, it is more difficult to assess the impact of the girl games movement outside of academia. As mentioned, girls and women now play digital games in sizeable numbers. Yet console gaming and hard core gamers are still predominantly male, as are the targeted users of significant numbers of Triple-A games. Moreover, contemporary commercials for videogames, while exhibiting "some diversity in the actors presented as players," nonetheless contain "certain patterns in how player diversity [is] presented, suggesting that the larger cultural perception is that videogame players are more likely to be white and male."[87]

Other developments emerging from the girl games movement had equally ambiguous results. While women and other visible minorities have clearly made headway in diversifying the game industry, the industry remains disproportionately male and white. A recent survey of professional game developers, the International Game Developers Association (IGDA), found that only 22 per cent of respondents identified as women, most of whom worked in management positions (37 per cent) and artistic roles (10 per cent game designer, 16 per cent visual art, 3 per cent UX/UI design). Only 11 per cent of women who work in the game industry self-reported as being employed as (game software) programmers – compared with 27 per cent of men.[88] Nonetheless, these numbers represent a significant increase. According to Graser, women made up a mere 3 per cent of the industry in 1989.[89] The IGDA statistics also constitute a noteworthy divergence from the trends found across computer science more broadly. For instance, at the university level, women's enrolment in computer science has markedly decreased since the 1980s, despite numerous interventions and campaigns to attract more girls and women to these programs. In 2006, Cohoon and Aspray pessimistically argued, "We have to face the fact that twenty-five years of interventions have not worked."[90] As Hayes concludes, "If this trend were to continue at the rate experienced from 1986 to 2006, there will be *no* women bachelor degree graduates in computer science by 2032."[91] The oft-cited goal of using gaming as a gateway into computer science remains unmet.

Meanwhile, the hostile extremism of the "Gamergate" movement, which peaked in 2014, brought to light a toxic facet of mainstream gamer culture. While a range of events and conflicts can be ascribed to the Gamergate crusade, a sizeable part of it consisted of a minority-led yet prominent backlash against the (potential) dissolution of gender inequalities within games and gaming. As Tomkinson and Harper note, "The increase in the visible contribution of female gamers to videogame communities has coincided with misogynistic reprisals against those who challenge the old hegemony of hypermasculine performativity within the culture."[92] At their worst, these reprisals manifested in the form of online and offline harassment, threats of violence (including sexual violence), death threats, doxing (posting private personal information, such as home address), and other instances of hate speech, which were aimed primarily at women, in coordinated and unrelenting bombardments. Several prominent women from a range of game-related fields, including journalists, cultural critics, players, and developers, were subjected to particularly vicious attacks. At one point, Gamergate's participants even directed their efforts towards the main professional association for digital game scholars (Digital Games Research Association), centring on studies and researchers that addressed gender issues, on the premise that the academic literature produced by feminist members of this organization was exerting undue influence on policymakers and game developers (if only!). The violent and deviant tone that characterized so many of Gamergate's activities is especially noteworthy in the context of the current discussion. It provides a perfect, albeit unfortunate, illustration of the dichotomy found within popular conceptualizations of digital games and gamers: dangerous boys retaliating against the increased presence of good girls on the digital playground.

Bad Game(r)s, Good Game(r)s

Today, most academic and popular discussions about violent videogames treat the issue as resolved: violent videogames were put on trial, and the (US) courts established that there is no link to violent behaviour. End of story. By all accounts, industry self-regulation is generally accepted to be (mostly) sufficient, whilst government-enforced regulation is increasingly framed as the antithesis of freedom of speech and free market economics. Popular discourse appears to have moved on to other, more novel alleged linkages – both negative and positive. Nonetheless, the idea that violent videogames cause players to be (or become) violent themselves continues to resurface, particularly in the news media in the United States and around the world. As recently as 2013, US politicians seeking to reignite the debate have used terms such as "violence simulators" to describe certain digital games – echoing the type of hyperbolic claims that were made by anti-game activists and lawmakers during the heyday of the 1990s violent videogame controversies.[93] Now, as then, such positions are quickly juxtaposed with opposing opinions, evidence, and critiques. Indeed, in the current climate, public opinion appears to be generally more sympathetic to the idea that digital gaming is not only harmless, but potentially beneficial.

Meanwhile, the objective of attracting girls and women to computing continues to inspire programs, summer camps, clubs, and other initiatives in which games and game design have a key role. For example, in 2013, the Girl Scouts of Greater Los Angeles launched a "game design" badge, in partnership with Women in Games International (WIGI). In media interviews, WIGI's vice-president and spokesperson explained, "By creating a STEM-aligned video game patch program for Girl Scouts, we're helping young women see what opportunities are open to them in these fields."[94] Notably, many of the girl-specific titles and programs associated with these more recent efforts to get girls into computing reproduce the very same stereotypical assumptions about girls' preferences that permeated the girl games movement in the 1990s. Granted, there is now an even greater number of initiatives that target both girls and boys, many featuring gender-inclusive characters and storylines, that are similarly centred on the idea that games, and especially game design, can serve as stepping stones into STEM or STEAM (science, technology, engineering, arts, math) learning. These initiatives, much like the ones that came before them, seek to integrate children's play into a sort of pedagogy of technologization, in which activities are valued for their contribution to children's future careers as information workers.

There are clear continuities between these trends and the broader Puritan traditions of prioritizing purposive leisure activities while vilifying non-purposive play. Notably, the two main camps involved in the social construction of this particular cultural dichotomy have assigned opposing labels to the same realm of activity – digital gaming. Although different game genres and different gamers were referenced within each of the discourses, the specifics often served as examples in support of the generalization that each camp sought to advance: that is, games are bad, or games are good. This trend reflects an oversight that permeates the broader literatures on children's play and on children's use of technologies – that very little attention is given to the technologies themselves. Instead, as Ito describes it, the technology is often framed in deterministic terms: "While the boosters and debunkers may seem to be operating under completely different frames of reference, what they share is the tendency to fetishize technology as a force with its own internal logic standing outside of history, society, and culture. The problem with both of these stances is that they fail to recognize that technologies are in fact embodiments, stabilizations, and concretizations of existing social structure and cultural meanings. The promises and the pitfalls of certain technological forms are realized only through active and ongoing struggle over their creation, uptake, and revision."[95]

As argued above, this dichotomous representation helps to fuel the ongoing debates. In so doing, it sustains a status quo approach to games, in which calls for change, be they regulations or other forms of intervention, can be perpetually dismissed on the grounds of reasonable doubt. The dichotomy itself is borne out of contradiction. For instance, many of the same methodological problems highlighted in the violent videogame trials arise just as often in the research linking gaming with computer programming (or future careers in STEM/STEAM). Yet the evidence for and claims of causality advanced in this later body of work are rarely, if ever, given the same level of serious attention and critique. As is typical of issues involving children's play, both camps are moreover focused on purported outcomes. One puts forth an outcome that is frightening and detrimental, while the other promises an outcome that is pro-social and instrumental, yet both are equally preoccupied with how games will transform children. Ultimately, what all of this points to is a continued, profound social and cultural ambivalence when it comes to children's digital gaming.

Moving Forward

While it is important to consider how digital games research is frequently dichotomized and mobilized for rhetorical and political ends, this does not mean that the literature itself is unworthy of consideration. Indeed, there is overwhelming evidence that digital gameplay can have enormous value and meaning for the children who engage in it, especially when playing with family or friends. Many digital playgrounds provide children with a unique forum for interacting with one another, for participating in cross-generational play, for creating and collaborating, as well as for discovering and exercising their cultural rights and responsibilities as digital citizens. Although academic opinion about the overall effects of digital gaming remains to some extent split, outside of positivist disciplines and research traditions much of the scholarship in this area has moved away from this line of questioning. Like the more recent literature on licensed toys, scholarship conducted within the fields of digital game studies and children's cultural studies tends to emphasize the importance of looking at specific contexts, people, and practices.

For example, works by Giddings, Seiter, Paley, Jenkins, and others demonstrate that ethnographic explorations of children's own inter-pretations and in-situ interactions provides a deeper and more nuanced insight into children's complex relationships with digital games. This approach is supported by a growing body of literature that examines everything from children's access to computers in public and at home to offline interactions among children playing with and around console games, from their creative appropriation of Web 2.0 tools and content to their use of locative mobile applications and devices. This body of research reflects a broader trend found in contemporary children's studies, which argues that more attention should be placed on chil-dren's subjective experiences and on their situated or embodied "use practices." Given how little children's perspectives are considered within mainstream academic research – and within the public sphere more generally – this emphasis is warranted. Accordingly, research in this area has produced a wealth of findings that both challenge and complicate previously accepted knowledge about how and why children play.

Notably, the findings of these ethnographic studies are not generalizable – but nor do they claim to be. Instead, they challenge the essentialist par-adigms that have traditionally dominated academic debate in this area, and that have historically shaped how so much of the previous research was conducted and interpreted. They provide evidence that alternatives to the digital game dichotomy described above are not only possible, but are indeed common within the messy spaces and practices of every-day life. They highlight the importance of looking at specific contexts of use. At the same time, however, although their findings often imply that textual and design features also fill important functions within these processes, the studies themselves do not always extend to such structural dimensions. Indeed, a lingering limitation found within many of these works is their failure to fully consider the role of structure and the ways design, regulations, and other "rule systems" shape, support, and some-times limit children's play and agency. The growing emphasis on use practices has produced its own emerging gap in the literature when it comes to understanding the material features and other structural forces that children must contend with – and at times negotiate – in their digi-tal play. Indeed, the academic literature in this area generally continues to neglect the technologies *themselves*.

Ito's analysis of the discourses and academic literature pertaining to children's computer software led her to conclude that a concerted, critical analysis of the technologies of children's play is required before the discussion can truly proceed. I wholeheartedly agree. Certainly, design affordances and promotional discourses are not the only actors involved in the social construction of child-specific technological artefacts. Children play a meaningful and prominent role in this process. Paying attention to the structural dimensions of digital playgrounds does not mean we should overlook the roles that children have in the social shaping of technologies' design, development, and regulation – including the ways technologies' unanticipated uses and children's subversive play can transform the technologies themselves. But that also does not mean there is no need for critical attention to and analysis of how children's technological artefacts are designed and managed. To construct a more nuanced framework for understanding the unique structure/agency dialectic shaping children's relationship with digital playgrounds and other technologies, both facets must be considered. Adopting this dual-level approach allows for a more nuanced understanding of how children's technologies are produced and consumed within specific social, historical, and cultural contexts.

This is particularly the case when dealing with commercially owned digital playgrounds, where an unprecedented iteration of the traditional dynamics between children, technologies, consumer culture, and media supersystems is unfolding. Whereas the relationship was once predominantly constructed and negotiated at the level of interpretation, structural features such as design, program algorithms, and corporately defined rule systems have now assumed a disproportionately prominent role. The continued possibility of unscripted or unanticipated play within children's digital playgrounds does not negate the fact that many of these spaces are stringently controlled by the corporations that own them. Many of them also provide users with a relatively limited selection of in-game affordances and action opportunities. Furthermore, the constructed, predetermined features of digital playgrounds are frequently embedded in commercial priorities and subtly intertwined with cross-promotions, third-party advertising, and branding initiatives. Although connected games and virtual worlds clearly share important similarities and continuities with traditional play spaces, including playgrounds, bedrooms, and family rooms, their status as programmed, proprietary artefacts also sets them apart.

Looking at "Stuff" and Structures

While much of the literature pertaining specifically to children's digital playgrounds tends to omit or downplay the importance of structural elements and features, a small but growing body of scholarship is working to disrupt such trends. These scholars are expanding the discussion to include critical, systematic analyses of design and semiotic features, considerations of commercial and legal/regulatory mechanisms, as well as studies of how users interact with the material and structural dimensions of digital games and virtual worlds. Together, these works are shifting the scholarly focus towards a broader consideration and understanding of the crucial role that structural features such as design, infrastructures, and texts can have in the shaping, containing, and configuration of children's digital play.[96]

When combined, this research helps advance the argument that a wide range of factors are involved in shaping the extent to which children can envision and express their agency vis-à-vis technological artefacts and systems. The factors that allow such agency can include the specific narrative elements of a media text, the features and affordances of an individual toy's design, the way an artefact is marketed and packaged, as well as how a game's privacy policy is presented to its users. Each of these factors adds to an ongoing filtering, interpreting, and challenging of the transitional meanings and functions that players bestow upon their toys, games, and other artefacts – both during play and after.

Instead of focusing solely on effects and outcomes, Hutchby and Moran-Ellis propose that the more important questions are, "What are the shapes and the outcomes of specific, situated encounters between children and technologies; how do children interact with, and in light of, the affordances that technologies have; how do those affordances constrain such interactions; and how is the complex of relations brought about here consequential for our understanding both of children themselves and of technological forms?"[97]

This approach expands the widely shared notion among children's scholars that the "contexts of play" are themselves a key factor in determining the roles and functions of both structure and agency within specific play cultures and experiences by extending the analysis to other *specifics* of technological interaction, including the design of the technological artefact used, the underlying systems or infrastructures, and associated texts (here understood as including textual, semiotic, narrative, and discursive elements). Some of the recent research on children's games and virtual worlds provides a superb starting point. While an exhaustive review of these works is beyond the purview of the current chapter, some notable examples include Fields and Kafai's examinations of tweens' appropriations and interpretations of specific design affordances in Numedeon's *Whyville*, Marsh's study of children's negotiation and performance of the action opportunities (e.g., avatar movements) available in Disney's *Club Penguin*, Black and Reich's qualitative analysis of the design and semiotic features of Ganz's *Webkinz World*, McAllister's political economy of communication-based analysis of branding strategies and rhetoric in MGA's *Be-Bratz* virtual world, as well as Carrington and Hodgetts's close reading of the gendered textual and discursive contents of Mattel's *BarbieGirls*.

Within the broader area of digital games studies, several studies now examine how design and discursive features can be aligned in ways that strongly promote a particular set of interpretations, specifically those that advance commercial priorities.[98] For instance, Hamari and Lehdonvirta's notion of "marketing as a form of game design" is useful in thinking about how promotional content and commercialization can materialize as integrated, and at times seemingly unavoidable, affordances.[99] Questions about the role of design also feature prominently within practitioner-oriented games research, which examines everything from interface design and game-engine coding structures to the relationship between narrative and game rules and questions about human-computer interaction.[100] In a similar vein, scholars have attempted to address the dialectical dimension of gameplay (or game/play), which is increasingly envisioned as a sort of continuous dialogue between a game's system (e.g., program code, rules, graphical user interface [GUI]) and its players. A key example can be found in Salen and Zimmerman's definition of "meaningful play," which they describe as emerging "from the relationship between play action and system outcome; it is the process by which a player takes action within the designed system of a game and the system responds to the action."[101]

Similarly, several feminist game scholars identify design as a key site in which gender norms and expectations are assigned to digital games, both as a leisure activity and as a techno-cultural form.[102] Indeed, some of the most compelling scholarship on the relationship between technology design and child users comes out of feminist technology studies and girl studies. Instead of talking about play scripts, these works focus on "gender scripts" both as a source of embedded ideology and as the structure against which children's agency is ultimately enacted. The term "gender script" describes how hegemonic gender norms, stereotypes, and expectations become encoded in many children's toys and games at the level of design, as found in hyper-masculine GI Joe action figures and hyper-feminine Barbie fashion dolls. As with play scripts, the concept of gender scripts seeks to describe the relationship between encoded discursive elements and the active meaning-making that girls and boys engage in during play.[103] A key difference is that scholarship on gender scripts does not generally argue that discursive and design features determine user behaviour. Instead, children are (largely) described as able, and often willing, to stray from the script. Even the most gender-stereotypical toys and games are understood as capable of embodying "multiple meanings" that reflect and reproduce the "gender contradictions" children experience in their daily lives.[104]

Each of these bodies of literature provides support, as well as a sort of road map, for extending our understanding and analysis of the structural dimensions of children's play technologies. Just as the ethnographic research of Jenkins, Giddings, and others problematizes the essentialist claims about play and users made by media effects researchers, a more nuanced and critical consideration of design/text *and* context challenges the sweeping assessments of digital games and other play technologies found within both academia and popular culture. This approach asks us to consider not only how technologies are consumed but also produced within specific social, historical, and cultural contexts. It reminds us that children's play does not exist solely in the realms of subjective experience or interpretation, but frequently involves and is enacted through material artefacts situated within particular networks of agents, systems, and infrastructures.

Resituating Children's Play

Any discussion about child-specific play technologies runs a risk of reproducing the same pattern discussed in the previous sections – that of idealizing and instrumentalizing children's play. So much of the literature on this topic rests its central argument on an impossible vision of children's play as largely and inextricably tied to an ideologically laden purpose or outcome. For instance, critics of licensed toys envision ideal play as children freely accessing their own natural, unbridled imaginations, uninfluenced by the crass, limiting discourses of commercial culture. For those emphasizing children's agency, however, ideal play is embodied in the subversive, resistant, participatory acts that children engage in when they use those same licensed toys in unexpected and unprescribed ways. The expectations and assumptions motivating each of these idealizations may be different, even in opposition, but they are equally out of touch with the complex, heterogeneous realities of how children actually engage in and think about play. Not all play is creative. Not all play is subversive.

Play – particularly children's play – is a non-rational realm of activity. This position is worth articulating as it runs counter to much of the literature and many of the dominant theories that have influenced the discussion and debates. Although traditional approaches to play conflict on many points, they share a belief in a purposive or functional understanding of play. Despite the "nondefinitive state of the evidence," Sutton-Smith argues, "many play theorists remain committed to the idea that play serves some adaptive function."[105] This idea results in a privileging of certain kinds of play – specifically, those activities that best "imitate the customs or beliefs of those who would control the society."[106] When other forms of play are considered, it is usually to better establish the ideal through contrast with its other. Undesirable play is thus labelled as exceptional and associated with deviance – as seen in the rhetoric of the risky gamer at the centre of the violent videogame controversies, as well as in the children in Kline's study who were unable to stray from the play scripts embedded in licensed toys. Much of the literature sets up an internal polarity of good play versus bad play, a dynamic that further serves a social function of constraining activities that fall outside normative notions of play. As a result, vast areas of play have been omitted, or even suppressed, from the discussion.

There are deep inconsistencies between these traditional, functional notions of play and children's actual play practices. For one, Sutton-Smith points out, "Different individuals participate in different kinds and levels of play, and some individuals avoid operating in playful ways most of the time."[107] Moreover, children's play – like the play of adults – typically includes a wide range of dark, destructive, subversive, offensive (especially to parents and teachers), and aggressive elements. In his foundational study of children's playground games, Sutton-Smith found that violent themes and "social testing" games made up a large proportion of playground play, where children engaged in play activities that adults disapproved of. Not only are such "undesirable" forms of play common rather than "exceptional," but the research indicates that they are oftentimes integral, meaningful, and pleasurable parts of children's play experience. Failing to acknowledge or allocate space for such activities within our definitions of what constitutes "acceptable" or "allowable" children's play is at best naive, at worst dismissive of a crucial facet of children's lived reality. Moving past such exclusionary tendencies requires accounting for the ambiguous aspects of children's play.

Such an approach would need to acknowledge the central role of the grotesque within children's culture, the at once terrifying and buffoonish games that children use to dispel their fears by laughing at them. Children's games such as Bloody Mary and the tradition of telling ghost stories often integrate elements of fear and laughter, while many popular toys, games, and other media feature monsters (such as *Sesame Street*'s Grover, or Sully from Disney's *Monsters Inc.*) who reconfigure the "aesthetics of the monstrous" in the form of silly and lovable friends.[108] Studies describe the grotesque dimensions of children's culture as involving combinations of adult repulsion and sensory pleasure, as exhibited by children's predilection for distastefully themed and strangely textured candies, obnoxiously loud cartoon programs, and sickly-sweet-smelling dolls.[109] Hendershot argues that while adults may find "children's tastes to be abject," children delight in finding practices and themes that illicitly transgress "adult standards of taste."[110]

In this book, I strive to apply a broad and inclusive understanding of children's play. Throughout the discussion that unfolds in the chapters that follow, I align myself with what I have come to see as a Bakhtinian tradition in children's play research, which can be found in the above-cited works advancing a middle ground or non-idealized approach to children's play. Bakhtin's theory of the carnivalesque provides a valuable starting point for acknowledging the transgressive, spontaneous, symbolic, and subversive aspects of play described in these studies; it enables us to approach play as a form of "symbolic action which is rarely mere play; it articulates cultural and political meanings."[111] The theory of the carnivalesque suggests that to understand play, it is important to first consider how its practice might function in relation to the ordinary rules, structures, and aesthetics of everyday life. For example, Bakhtin's concept of the grotesque describes how the carnivalesque seeks to distance itself from the quotidian, the beautiful, the sanctioned, and the sacred by representing all that is exceptional, repulsive, taboo, and profane within a particular cultural milieu. The same can be said of many children's play activities, which, as Schwartzman describes, are full of parody and critique of social worlds that are structured by adults.[112] Hendershot argues that children often transgress adult binaries in part *because* they are adult boundaries. This indicates that there is an underlying political dimension to children's play practices that has yet to be fully understood. Adopting a Bakhtinian framework enables us to approach children's transgressive, grotesque, and subversive play practices as symbolic action – in dialogue with larger cultural, political, and social discourses, and through which modes of (adult) authority are likely being negotiated and challenged much more than we might realize.

In addition to acknowledging the non-rational and non-idealized dimensions of children's play, the discussion in these pages seeks to shift the focus away from purposive and outcome-based valuations of play. While I recognize that play is most likely a contributing factor in "important forms of learning that occur in young children," the research also shows that it is "seldom the only determinant" – multiple other factors and influences are involved.[113] Similarly, play is multifaceted. Its role may be ambiguous, but its value and importance are undeniable. In this book, play is understood as fulfilling several key functions within

children's culture and everyday experience: contributing to their happiness, pleasure, and well-being; providing a forum for self-expression,
self-actualization, and identity performance; serving as a source of
agency, fun, and social interaction – along with a plethora of other roles
that have as much to do with who children are in the present as they
do with what children will (possibly) become in the future. Indeed, as
Sutton-Smith argues, children's own rhetorics about play tend to emphasize things such as having fun, being with friends, or not working.
In this way, their thoughts about the importance of play are strikingly
similar to those of adults when asked about their own play. We would be
wise to take children's own understandings and valuations of play more
seriously, and treat them with the same level of respect and deference
we accord to adults. Accordingly, in this book, play is seen as important
because it is fun and social, and provides respite from the work of school,
chores, and ordinary life.[114]

Conclusion

The scholarly debates reviewed above paint a picture of an ongoing
struggle between freedom and constraint, in which children's play constitutes a highly negotiated and ambivalent terrain of activity.[115] Like all
children's play, children's digital play simultaneously serves as a source of
moral panic and as a fount of unbridled optimism about what child players will ultimately become – violent delinquents or skilled information
workers, subversive cultural hackers or proscribed consumers. In both
cases, the emphasis is on outcomes – on becoming – and so children's
play continues to be framed in idealized, often politicized terms. This in
turn draws attention away from other dimensions of children's play, such
as situated practices, design features, storylines, and business models.
Despite the predominance of dichotomous tendencies within academic
and public discourses about children's digital games and playgrounds,
much of the literature in this area supports the idea that context, text,
and design all matter tremendously. It is by looking more closely at the
specific contexts of children's play that ethnographic researchers have
uncovered the diverse, spontaneous, and unanticipated ways that actual children engage with even the most seemingly prescriptive games
and toys. Similarly, it is by looking closely and critically at the stuff and
structures of digital play technologies that we will begin to form a more
complete understanding of the range and nature of the interactions,
negotiations, and power relationships involved.

The emerging consensus among children's media, play, and technology scholars about the importance of the contexts of play demonstrates

that differing approaches are not always oppositional. They can also intersect on a variety of points and issues. Moving beyond the old binaries, with their accompanying tendencies towards essentialism and idealization, requires a holistic approach, not only to research questions, but to the literature as well. A key component of this is the incorporation and synthesis of existing works, relevant findings, arguments, and insights, to build on what has come before as well as to consider how sometimes different perspectives may simply describe different facets or dimensions of the same phenomenon. For instance, a child player may well diverge in some ways from the intended use of a particular, branded videogame, and yet still be constrained in other ways by that game's design limitations and embedded commercial messages. As Ito describes it, "In contexts of play we see competing discourses and genres of participation jockeying for position in the micro-politics of kids' everyday lives."[116] While children bring a significant amount of agency, creativity, and situated knowledge to their interactions with (and within) digital playgrounds, so too do the designers, marketers, moderators, politicians, and other adults involved in making and managing these play spaces. These groups are rarely on an even playing field, especially where rules and structures are concerned. Embedded or inscribed within these "texts of play," we can also see competing discourses, agendas, and concerns vying for position and power. We just need to know where and how to look.

2

Small Worlds and Walled Gardens

Just as children's play occupies a distinct space within Western culture, children's digital games form a distinct sector within the broader digital games market. As described in the previous chapter, children's digital gaming attracts a particular – oftentimes highly politicized – set of discourses, concerns, and aspirations. Children's game development has subsequently followed its own trajectory, as designers have attempted to respond to (and capitalize on) the ebb and flow of hopes, fears, regulatory requirements, and controversies that surround children's gaming. Over the past four decades, the children's games market has diverged from the mainstream in other ways as well. For one, there's a strong tradition of making educational games for children, some of which are produced out of non-profits, universities, and other academic institutions. Furthermore, a significant proportion of the children's games market is generated by companies that do not specialize in digital game development, at least not solely. This is particularly the case with online games, among which the most popular are often those owned and operated by media and toy companies. Children's online games are associated with a range of unique historical trends and influences, many of which are not found within the broader gaming culture.

Ever since children first became regular users of the internet they have exhibited a preference for entertainment websites, especially those featuring games. By the early 2000s, a market analyst reported that 87 per cent of children aged seven to twelve listed "playing online games" as their favourite thing to do on the internet.[1] The same year, all of the top five online destinations most visited by children aged two to eleven featured online games of some sort.[2] For well over a decade now, playing networked or connected digital games has been a core part of how many children form and maintain friendships. A recent study indicates this is especially the case among teenage boys. In 2015, the Pew

Internet and American Life Project revealed, "91% of video-gaming boys play with others who they are connected with over a network; one-third [34%] of boys say they play this way every day or almost every day."[3]

These trends reflect the widespread popularity of digital gaming among children, who over the past twenty years have started to play digital games at increasingly younger ages. Here, digital gaming is a category that includes online games, but also offline computer games, console games, tablet and app games, and games played on cell phones and portable devices (connected or not). For instance, in 2003, nearly half of US children aged zero to six owned a videogame console, and in 2005, children aged eight to eleven were on average more likely to play digital games and to play for longer periods of time than older children and teens.[4] In 2007, children aged six to eight played 75 per cent more digital games than previously, adding nearly three hours a week to their digital playtime.[5] By 2016, the NPD Group reported that 34 per cent of "*avid omni gamers*, defined as those who game on an average of five different devices," were between the ages of two and twelve.[6] That same year, research by the Joan Ganz Cooney Center revealed that 53 per cent of boys aged four to thirteen years who played digital games did so every day, while 48 per cent of girls gamed played "a few days per week."[7] Today, in addition to playing digital games in greater numbers and playing more frequently than previous generations, children also play games on a range of platforms and devices. Among the children surveyed by the Joan Ganz Cooney Center, tablets were the most popular devices for playing games (73 per cent), followed by game consoles (69 per cent), computers (61 per cent), and cell phones (60 per cent). Notably, "Parents reported their children played on a variety of devices, as opposed to just one."[8] In short: children really like playing digital games.[9]

Of course, they don't always play games designed, let alone rated or otherwise classified, for them. Studies conducted by market researchers and academics show that kids play a wide variety of digital games. Many children play games designed for a general audience. For instance, in the early 2000s, a number of the most popular gaming destinations for children were all-ages gaming portals (which featured whole collections of Flash games) such as AddictingGames.com, Pogo and Yahoo! Games.[10] Moreover, the all-ages category has become an increasingly popular alternative to labelling titles as specifically (or solely) for children. A key example of this can be found in the evolution of Nintendo's *Super Mario Bros.* franchise (1983–present). Whereas early iterations of the game were heavily marketed to children, advertising for contemporary sequels and remakes tend to cast a much wider net. The move towards all-ages from child-specific target marketing is reflected to some extent in the prevalence of the ESRB's E for Everyone rating category. According to the ESA, "Of the 2,768 physical and downloadable console games assigned ratings by the ERSB in 2018" 42 per cent were rated E.[11] The E classification applies to any game containing content deemed thematically "suitable" for all ages, and includes a wide range of game genres – from cartoony adventure games to hyper-realistic sports titles. Similarly, there are numerous online games designed to appeal to a range of age groups, which may include children but are not exclusive to them.

In addition, many children also play games they aren't technically supposed to, defying ratings systems, design intentions, targeted marketing, and age restrictions. Studies have found that children frequently lie about their age in order to join age-restricted sites, and that many report a preference for games and sites "officially" designed for teens or adults.[12] This phenomenon extends to instances of children becoming active – although not always welcome – participants in T-rated multiplayer games and virtual worlds targeted to teens and adults.[13] For instance, as discussed in the previous chapter, Yee's six-year longitudinal study of highly popular massively multiplayer online role-playing games (MMORPGs) such as *Ultima Online, EverQuest, City of Heroes,* and *World of Warcraft* included players as young as eleven.[14] Recently, market research firm Dubit reported that 17 per cent of Canadian children and 25 per cent of US children aged five to fifteen years played *Fortnite Battle Royale,* a T-rated multiplayer online player-versus-player survival (or last-player-standing) game that has been played by 350 million players worldwide as of 2020.[15]

Even though children do not solely play games made specifically for them, there is a great deal of value in paying closer attention to how child-specific games are designed, marketed, managed, and played. For one, how child-specific games are designed – as well as how they are regulated, marketed, and talked about – tells us a lot about how children are envisioned as players by the games' designers, the broader games community, as well as policymakers and parents. What is and isn't included in a game when the intended end-user is a child reveals much about the underlying assumptions that have been made about children's abilities, capacities, and preferences. The resultant "vision" of the child user that is embedded within the design choices and marketing discourses surrounding these games in turn represents a particular ideal, which the games themselves work to both reflect and reproduce.

Examining children's games (those designed specifically for children) may not tell us everything we need to know about children's actual gaming practices, but it does provide insight into how children's gaming is imagined, supported, and constructed by adults. The purpose of this chapter is to provide an overview of the history and evolution of child-specific online games, starting with the arrival of the first online play spaces for kids in the late 1990s and ending with the emergence of online games played through web-enabled console systems and hand-held devices. The chapter considers how children's online games have developed in conjunction with technological advances, social expectations, and industry trends. Particular attention is given to the unique corporate ownership patterns and business models that have come to dominate this space. The chapter also examines some of the ways online games are marketed to children and parents alike as "walled gardens," thereby exhibiting important continuities with Romantic idealizations of childhood and children's play.

A Brief History of Children's Digital Playgrounds

While there are surely earlier examples, much of the literature places the emergence of online games designed and targeted to children in the mid- to late 1990s, coinciding with the dot-com boom.[16] Landmark texts such as Tapscott's *Growing Up Digital* (1997) and Jupiter Communications' annual "Digital Kids" conferences played a key role in documenting and propagating the establishment of the children's online game genre and its eventual association with market research and advergaming. In some ways, this association extended to many of the self-proclaimed "educational" titles that appeared during the same period. For instance, MaMaMedia.com (1995–2004), an award-winning web portal for children under twelve, at one point contained a Fruit Roll-Up advergame alongside its "educational" offerings, and engaged its users in various forms of market research. This emphasis on advertising and market research soon led to the establishment of some fairly distinctive trends within the realm of children's online gaming.

Early children's online games tended to fly under the academic research radar, especially when it came to comparative or multi-case analysis. As such, there is no way to accurately establish the types of trends or patterns that may have characterized the first years of the children's online gaming landscape. Among those games that were documented and analysed, scholars noted a tendency to reproduce some of the same formats that had been popular in the early arcade games – including games where players had to collect a certain number of coins or objects within a set amount of time, or destroy all the enemies encountered as they made their way to the end of a side-scrolling landscape. Within many of these examples, the games themselves consisted of "flash games" or "mini-games."[17] As such, they featured relatively underwhelming game designs and unsophisticated gaming experiences, especially when compared to the offerings targeted to older players during this same period. With some exceptions, children's online games were often short, meaning that an intermediate-level player could complete them within a few minutes.

By the late 1990s and early 2000s, children's online games often appeared alongside other cross-promotional offerings. Many of the most popular children's games were housed within larger, branded corporate websites. An illustrative example of this was the Cartoon Network website, CartoonNetwork.com (1998–present), a popular destination for children during this period. The site, or portal, contained numerous games featuring Cartoon Network television characters, as well as advergames promoting third-party products.[18] Another popular online destination for children's games in the early 2000s was Mattel's EverythingGirl.com, a branded "virtual community" that contained an assortment of fashion and beauty themed mini-games.[19] The popularity of children's online games produced by media and toy industries continued for well over a decade. Throughout the 2000s, games and gaming sites owned by television networks (such as Cartoon Network and Nickelodeon), media giants (such as Disney), and toy companies (such as Mattel and Ganz) consistently ranked among children's self-reported favourites and most frequently played.[20]

The early prominence of the traditional children's industries within the children's online game landscape is noteworthy for many reasons. For many of the companies involved, online games quickly became a forum for extending cross-media strategies, such as building brand identity and promoting tie-in products. For example, Nickelodeon used its website to showcase its media characters and product lines, but also to test out potential new properties with their target audience at low cost and little risk. In her study of the launch of the Jimmy Neutron media brand, Pecora argues that the company relied heavily on its website to generate online buzz in the months leading up to the character's official debut in the feature film *Jimmy Neutron: Boy Genius*. She describes how Nickelodeon viewers were introduced to the character through a combination of appearances on the Nick.com website and in short interstitials that aired between network program broadcasts. By the time the film was released in late 2001, the character had already achieved an "80 percent awareness score among its target audience."[21]

By significantly extending corporations' access to children's play lives, online games brought cross-media strategies to an intense new level. In addition to watching their favourite cartoon characters on television and playing with licensed action figures, children could now interact with them in an online environment that was shaped by and almost entirely under corporate control. Marketers could make note of which games children played and which brands they interacted with. Using games as promotional tools facilitated a fundamental expansion of the intertextuality that could be built around a media character or brand. Where television shows, movies, advertisements, and even toy packaging allowed advertisers to develop an ongoing storyline about a character, games enabled them to delve into the mechanics and physics of the worlds the characters lived in. More than that, games invited players to live in those worlds alongside the character – experience their excitement, share in their victories, and explore their topographies.

In addition to providing the children's industries with an immersive venue for cross-promotion, online games became a key forum for third-party advertising, market research, and other commercial activities. By 2001, the term "advergame" had emerged to describe games that were designed from the outset to promote a specific product or brand.[22] In addition to promoting media and toys, many of the advergames that appeared on children's websites or otherwise targeted children featured food brands, sugar cereals, and candy and were commissioned by food and beverage conglomerates such as Kraft and General Mills. These trends continued well into the late 2000s. For instance, one study found advergames on 81 per cent of the food websites advertised on Nickelodeon and Cartoon Network between August 2006 and March 2007.[23]

Online Games: Portals, Arcades, and Environments, 2003–2005

In the early to mid-2000s, games featured prominently on websites listed as the most highly rated and heavily frequented by children and youth.[24] A comparative analysis of the contents of seventeen of the "most popular" game-based online destinations revealed several dominant trends and common characteristics – not only in terms of how and where the games appeared within the sites, but also how the games themselves were structured, and the types of mechanics, themes, and promotional contents they contained. The seventeen cases included in the analysis could be grouped into four broad categories or genres: arcades, portals, themed game environments, and one MMOG.

The arcade sites provided a selection of discrete or self-contained mini-games, loosely grouped by category and/or by popularity. Users simply selected which games to play, with little to no interaction with other players and limited engagement with the site owners. In each case, players were required to register as members to access the site's full library of contents. Outside of the individual mini-games, arcades contained few if any interactive or customizable features. Most of the cases that fit into this genre were owned and operated by Yahoo, and many were sports themed. A fifth case was owned by Microsoft. All five of the cases in this category were identified by market analysts as suitable for players of all ages, and they did not contain text or other features that were discernibly addressed or targeted to children.

Like the arcades, the portals featured an assortment of discrete mini-games, grouped by theme or popularity. However, the portals provided players with customization tools allowing them to alter the appearance of the homepage, along with features that displayed users' personal information and gameplay statistics. They also included community support features, such as forums, chat rooms, and lists of the top scoring players. Players were also afforded opportunities to contribute to the site's contents by submitting game reviews, for instance, or responding to online polls and surveys. While all the portals analysed were heavily branded, the overarching sites tended to remain distinct from the narrative elements and themes contained in the mini-games. For instance, the EverythingGirl.com portal featured an animated guide named Pippa who introduced players to each game and activity, appeared in pop-up windows to direct players to different areas of the site, and granted players "Pippa Points" for playing featured games. However, Pippa did not appear as a character in any of those mini-games. Instead, the mini-games, most of which were advergames, featured established Mattel toy lines (e.g., Barbie, Polly Pocket) or promoted third-party products and media brands (e.g., Hilary Duff).

While the themed game environments also featured mini-games, they differed from the sites in the previous two categories in that their mini-games were integrated parts of a coherent, overarching metanarrative. The themed game environments also featured webpages containing news and information, plot developments, instructions, forums, and other features. Visual elements contained within the site were consistent and interconnected throughout. For example, in *Neopets*, users were positioned in the role of virtual pet owners, and their actions within the site were framed as contributing to the caring and maintenance of their pets. Games provided backstories and scenarios linked to the various species and realms of Neopia, and playing them produced NeoPoints, which could then be used to purchase pet food and other items. On these sites, users were positioned as players of a specific, coherent, and unified game throughout their interactions on the site. Within the themed game environments, opportunities for community participation were prominently featured. They included forums, surveys, and polls, as well as opportunities to submit user-created content such as artwork or news stories. The majority of these participatory activities revolved around themes, characters, and storylines found in the site's metanarrative.

The fourth genre, massively multiplayer online games, applied to only one of the cases in the sample (Disney's *Toontown*). Like other MMOGs, *Toontown* consisted of a three-dimensional virtual world that allowed multiple players to play together and communicate with one another simultaneously. *Toontown* featured a completely immersive game environment, in which players – each visually represented by a customized avatar – could explore, interact with, and play with aspects of the game in a perpetually evolving, animated online village populated by hundreds or thousands of other players. Notably, *Toontown* did not conform entirely to the norms and conventions previously established in teen- and adult-oriented MMOGs, instead espousing numerous child-safety protocols that limited inter-player communication and restricted player freedoms in important ways.

Several of the sites listed were in fact sub-properties of the same umbrella brand or corporation, with the seventeen games actually owned by only nine different companies. These included software and game companies such as Yahoo, Microsoft, and EA, as well as toy giant Mattel, which operated four of the most heavily frequented game sites of 2003, all of which were targeted to girls. Three of the sites were owned by Disney, while one of the sites, Neopets.com, was (initially) run by an independent market research company. The list included an online portal run by Kraft Foods, called Kraft Entertainment, which ranked number six among children and youth, and featured three sub-sites: Candystand, Nabiscoworld, and Postopia (1997–2016). It is therefore unsurprising that all seventeen of the sites contained some form of advertising or other promotional content. Many of them contained advergames. The brands and products promoted on the sites ranged from sugar cereals and movies to toys and clothing lines. In some cases, nearly all the games and interactive activities provided on the site related to products and tie-in merchandise.

Almost all the sites collected personal information of some sort from their young users. Two-thirds also featured polls and surveys, which often contained questions about products and favourite activities – information that would likely be of value for market research into the habits and preferences of a traditionally hard-to-reach demographic. Most of the sites also included social features, enabling players to interact with one another. Several contained forums or chat rooms, some included multi-player mini-games, while others provided players with an in-game email or e-card service. These findings raise questions about the sites' data collection and security practices, as well as their adherence to the then-new COPPA requirements. Since all seventeen of the sites in this study were US-based, their seemingly loose adherence to COPPA's

Table 2.1. The Seventeen Online Games for Children and Youth Analysed, 2004–2005

Genre	Game/website name	Site owner
Arcade	Yahoo! Games	Yahoo
	Yahoo! Fantasy Sports – Baseball	Yahoo
	Yahoo! Fantasy Sports	Yahoo
	Yahoo! Fantasy Sports – Football	Yahoo
	MSN Game Zone	Microsoft
Portal	EverythingGirl	Mattel
	Pogo	Electronic Arts
	EA Online	EA
	Disney Online	Disney
	gURL.com	Alloy/Hearst
Themed game environment	*Neopets.com*	Neopets
	DisneyChannel	Disney
	Diva Starz	Mattel
	Polly Pocket	Mattel
	Barbie	Mattel
	Kraft Entertainment (*Candystand, Nabiscoworld, Postopia*)	Kraft Foods
MMOG	Toontown Online	Disney

restrictions on the collection and display of children's personally identifiable information was problematic, as will be discussed in further detail in chapter 5.

Neopets

Out of all the children's online games that I researched during this period, *Neopets* was the most notable. It not only came up in more than one study I was involved in but, in retrospect, stands out as illustrative of several key trends found across the commercially owned, children's online games landscape, both then and now.[25] Initially, *Neopets* appeared as a bit of an outlier. At its launch in 1999 and during its first few years of operations, it was not (yet) owned by a media, toy, or food company, but rather by an independent company that eventually incorporated under the name Neopets Inc. Unlike most other children's game sites running at the time, which could be classified under the arcade or portal genres described in the previous section, *Neopets* unfolded as one big, fully integrated role-playing game.

By 2005, however, it had firmly joined the mainstream. The site was purchased by Viacom, a US-based media conglomerate with holdings in the traditional children's industries (primarily film and television). The shift in ownership was followed by a dramatic intensification of the transformation of *Neopets* into a full-fledged media brand. Moreover, the features that had once made it seem so unique had become widespread across the children's digital landscape. As it turns out, *Neopets* was not an outlier so much as it was a pioneer. From its heavy focus on market research and "immersive advertising" (a term Neopets Inc. actually trademarked), to its pseudo–"virtual world" design, core elements of the *Neopets* approach to children's digital gaming soon became the industry standard. As such, it foreshadowed many of the key trends and issues discussed in this book, including the appearance of powerful consumer discourses and player management strategies, the establishment of problematic privacy and safety protocols, and the use of designed emergence and participatory culture as methods of fostering player engagement and self-identification with the *Neopets* brand. It is therefore worth a closer look.

At the time of the above-mentioned studies, *Neopets* was a free online community containing dozens, if not hundreds, of interactive activities, mini-games, forums, and user-generated webpages, all of which centred on the adoption and caretaking of virtual pets, called "neopets." The concept was comparable to Bandai's Tamagotchi, an interactive handheld toy that was popular among Japanese and North American youth in the 1990s, which required users to feed, entertain, and otherwise tend to a virtual pet multiple times a day, every day. The virtual pets in *Neopets* (herein referred to as "neopets") also required ongoing maintenance through regular feedings and other forms of virtual nurturing (e.g., bathing, grooming, playing). In *Neopets*, the food, toys, and medicines needed to care for these pets all cost in-game currency, called NeoPoints. Players could earn these points by completing mini-games or "special quests" (which largely consisted of scavenger hunts), finding and selling items, or filling out polls and surveys. Beyond keeping a neopet alive, the game also encouraged players to "level up" their pets – developing their attributes by either engaging in specific activities (e.g., building strength by competing in the Battledome) or consuming specific items (e.g., buying and reading a "book" to them). At the time of writing, *Neopets* is still in operation and allegedly maintains a relatively high level of popularity worldwide.[26]

The neopets themselves look like a cross between Disney's signature anthropomorphized animals (e.g., Mickey Mouse) and Pokémon. While the site has long attracted players of diverse ages and backgrounds, early on it was designed and marketed primarily to younger users. For many years, it contained a multi-step – albeit poorly enforced – parental consent process, which children and their parents were "required" to complete upon registering to the site. The game also contained child-friendly features, from chat filters that forbade adult language and content to child-appropriate storylines and difficulty levels. For instance, while over-neglected Tamagotchi eventually "died," neopets did not. Although neglected neopets could reach "dying" status, players could always bring pets back to "healthy" status with food and other items, no matter how much time had passed.

By 2003, it was estimated that *Neopets* had over sixteen million regular users (NeoPets Press Kit, 2003), most of whom were children (39 per cent under the age of twelve) and teens (40 per cent between thirteen and seventeen). When Viacom purchased the site in 2005 for a reported US$160 million, the site had at least two unique selling points: it was enormously popular among young internet users, and it was unprecedentedly lucrative.[27] In its first year of operations, *Neopets* reportedly made US$6 million in revenues, a number that climbed steadily as the site's community grew exponentially.[28] Rather than charge subscriptions or other fees, the *Neopets* business model revolved around a trademarked strategy they called immersive advertising, an adapted version of product placement in which third-party advertisers could temporarily lease "spaces" and activities within the *Neopets* environment. For example, third-party advertisers could pay to have their products appear as in-game items that players could "purchase" using NeoPoints for their pets. Virtual versions of McDonald's hamburgers or Sunny Delight beverages were thus positioned in and amongst the regular, neopets items – distinguishable only through the inclusion of their real-world logos and brand names.

Soon after it was purchased by Viacom, *Neopets* expanded into a range of new markets, media, and product lines. This included a magazine (*Neopets: The Official Magazine*), a collectible card game, toy lines (including collectible plush toys), stationery and school supplies, action figures, and licensed clothing. In March 2005, the company signed a deal with Warner Bros. Pictures to produce a series of *Neopets* films (none of which were ultimately made). Later that same year, two console games were released: *Neopets: The Darkest Faerie* on the Sony PlayStation 2, and *Neopets: Petpet Adventures: The Wand of Wishing* for Sony PlayStation Portable. Concurrently, Neopets.com was expanded and made available in nine additional languages: Japanese, traditional Chinese, simplified Chinese, Spanish, German, French, Italian, Korean, and Portuguese.[29]

By 2005, *Neopets* had become a transmedia property. It promoted each new adaptation and tie-in product to its userbase through in-game ads and announcements on the *Neopets* website, which in turn promoted the site to its newfound audiences and consumers. For instance, many of its tie-in products came with activation codes that opened special items or activities on the site itself. In a sense, the entire site became an immersive advertising campaign for the *Neopets* brand. Significantly, at the time, this approach was becoming commonplace across the children's digital landscape. Over the next three years, branded, cross-promotional, multiplayer virtual worlds became a major trend within children's online gaming. Many of the most popular titles opted to forego third-party advertising entirely, focusing their online environment and its contents on generating transmedia intertextuality, on the one hand, and promoting the purchase of paid memberships, virtual items, and tie-in products, on the other. Unlike *Neopets*, these worlds often claimed to be ad-free because of their exclusion of overt third-party promotional content. All the same, they embodied an important next step in the evolution of the commercialization of the children's digital landscape.

The Virtual World Boom, 2005–2010

In 2005, the popular press began taking notice of two Canadian gaming websites that were enormously popular among children and pre-teens around the world. Both had skyrocketed to the top of most-frequented and favourite website lists in a short time, drawing in estimated player populations of around six million each.[30] The first, the then-independently owned *Club Penguin*, consisted of a cartoony virtual world designed and targeted to elementary school–aged children. The second, Ganz's *Webkinz World* (2005–present), was notable for initiating its own real-world toy-craze, through a virtual world that could be accessed only with the secret code that came with the purchase of a tie-in plush collectible. By the end of 2007, *Club Penguin* had been purchased by the Disney Company for US$350 million,[31] and *Webkinz* plush toys were among the top-selling toys of the year.[32]

Most significantly, at least from the perspective of the children's industries and their associated trade publications, the sites were turning child users into paying customers and translating their online play into significant real-world profits. Very few online properties for children had done that before. Furthermore, the sites applied innovative monetization strategies that were similar to those found within contemporaneous virtual worlds popular at the time in Asian markets but had yet to generate much interest or success among North American players. These included the premium memberships approach, wherein a "free to play" game concurrently provided a subscription option, which came with numerous advantages and perks, including access to exclusive areas of the game, rare items, and special costumes. Another example was the incorporation of "micro-transactions," wherein certain special items or exclusive access to specific areas and activities were available only through purchase, usually for relatively small sums of real-world money.

Indeed, *Club Penguin* and *Webkinz World* were both seemingly free to play, in that players didn't need to purchase (or install) any software or sign up for a monthly subscription to access them and start playing. This feature was widely reported in the surrounding media coverage of the sites and their players. However, their categorization as free to play was misleading. Many features in *Club Penguin* were accessible only to those players with a paid membership – a distinction that deepened as the site became increasingly popular. Similarly, *Webkinz World* was free only to those who had purchased a real-world plush toy containing an (unused) activation code. Even then, players' access to site would eventually expire, requiring them to keep purchasing new plush toys with new activation codes to continue playing. As young players progressed through these worlds, they soon encountered items and areas that were available only to those who paid for them. Given the sizeable profit margins reported by both companies, it is clear that a great many of them did just that.

It soon became apparent that *Club Penguin* and *Webkinz World* were the tip of the iceberg in the children's virtual worlds phenomenon. Market analysts estimated that 24 per cent of US child and teen internet users had visited virtual worlds at least once a month in 2007.[33] By April 2008, industry analyst Virtual Worlds Management had identified 105 virtual worlds and MMOGs for children and youth that were either live or in development.[34] Four months later, this number had reportedly grown to 150, and by early 2009, they published a follow-up report claiming that the market had grown to include over 200 youth-oriented titles.[35] These reports were widely covered by the popular press of the time and by all accounts demonstrated a veritable boom in children's virtual worlds development. Indeed, *Virtual Worlds News* reports continue to be widely cited by analysts and scholars and often serve as evidence of the breadth and vibrancy of the children's gaming landscape during this period.[36]

A content analysis of the titles included on these lists revealed significant discrepancies.[37] For one, forty-five of the worlds were still in development – some were in closed beta testing while others had merely been announced. Ultimately, several of these "in development" projects were never launched. An additional four worlds closed shortly after the lists were published. Only fifty-seven virtual worlds were actually available to the public, including both live and open beta titles. Virtual Worlds Management described the items on their list as "youth-oriented worlds." Given that in 2008 the majority of existing virtual worlds and MMOGs were targeted to teens and adults, the implication was that these titles were intended for younger players. Among the fifty-seven virtual worlds analysed, most (forty-two) were indeed targeted to children under the age of thirteen, while fifteen were aimed at adolescent or general audiences. However, forty-two is not close to the approximately two hundred being lauded by industry analysts. It soon became apparent that contrary to numerous claims that a children's virtual worlds boom had unfolded in 2008, a relatively small number of child-specific virtual worlds were actually up and running during this period.

Of the forty-two child-specific titles, all but nine were owned by companies based in either the United States or Canada, and most reproduced the same patterns already found across the children's digital landscape. For one, they were owned and operated predominantly by established media and toy conglomerates. As illustrated in table 2.2, eight of the worlds were owned by leading producers of children's television and other media, while an additional twelve were owned by top-selling toy manufacturers. Only four of the US and Canadian worlds were owned by companies whose stated focus of operations consisted of virtual worlds development. Notably, none of the child-specific virtual worlds listed were owned or operated by a company with established ties to the digital game industry (design, development, or publishing).

As in other children's online game genres, promotional content featured heavily in virtual worlds based in Canada and the United States. Several (thirteen) contained third-party advertisements, while the majority (twenty-six) of the worlds featured transmedia characters, themes, or brands, such as Mattel's Barbie and Nickelodeon's SpongeBob SquarePants. More than half (twenty-two) featured characters or other items that could also be purchased in "real-world" toy form. Nearly half (nineteen) of the child-oriented virtual worlds enrolled these toys in a micro-transaction system similar to the one found in *Webkinz*, turning real-world purchases into in-game privileges and assets. At least five of the titles reproduced the *Webkinz* model entirely and could be accessed only by registering on the site using a special code obtained by purchasing a real-world, collectible plush toy.

Overall, a significant majority of the child-specific worlds examined operated on some type of real money transactions (RMT) business model, including real-world toy purchases, micro-transactions, and purchasable downloadable content (DLC). This finding conflicted with industry estimates circulating at the time, such as Gibson's 2008 report that only 40 per cent of children's virtual worlds featured micro-transactions.[38] Conversely, most of the worlds were otherwise initially or partially free to play, and only five of them contained subscription models. These findings were consistent with research conducted during this period, which suggested children spent much more time on free gaming sites than on subscription or traditionally defined pay-to-play sites. For example, a survey of children's gaming habits conducted by NPD Group in 2007 found

Table 2.2. US and Canada–Based, Child-Oriented Virtual Worlds Analysed, 2007–2010

Virtual world	Country of origin	Site owner	Industry sectors	Company size
BarbieGirls	US	Mattel	Toys (media)	Conglomerate
Beanie Babies 2.0	US	Ty	Toys	International
Be-Bratz.com	US	MGA Entertainment	Toys (media)	Conglomerate
Bella Sara	US	Bella Sara	Toys (media)	International
Big Fat Awesome House Party	US	Cartoon Network	Media (toys)	Conglomerate
Build-A-Bearville	US	Build-A-Bear Workshop	Toys	International
Bunnytown	US	Disney	Media (toys, theme parks)	Conglomerate
Chaotic	US	4Kids Entertainment	Media	Conglomerate
Club Penguin	Canada	Disney	Media (toys, theme parks)	Conglomerate
Dizzywood	US	Rocket Paper Scissors	Virtual world development	Small
GalaXseeds	Canada	YTV/Corus	Media	Conglomerate
Handipoints	US	Handipoints	Virtual world development	Small
KidsCom.com	US	Circle 1	Market research	Small
Littlest Pet Shop	US	Hasbro	Toys	Conglomerate
Magi-Nation	Canada	Cookie Jar Entertainment	Media (toys)	Conglomerate
MinyanLand	US	Minyanville Media	Media	Small
MyePets.com	US	MGA Entertainment	Toys	Conglomerate
Neopets	US	Viacom	Media (toys)	Conglomerate
NFLRush.com	US	NFL	Media (merchandise)	Conglomerate
Nicktropolis	US	Nickelodeon	Media (toys)	Conglomerate
Pirates of the Caribbean Online	US	Disney	Media (toys, theme parks)	Conglomerate
Quest Atlantis	US	University-based initiative	Education (research)	N/A

(continued)

Table 2.2 (*continued*)

Virtual world	Country of origin	Site owner	Industry sectors	Company size
ShiningStars	US	Russ	Toys	International
Tamagotchi's Tama & Earth Expo	US	Bandai	Toys	Conglomerate
Toontown	US	Disney	Media (toys, theme parks)	Conglomerate
Ty Girlz	US	Ty	Toys	International
U.B. Funkeys	US	Mattel	Toys	Conglomerate
Vizwoz	US	Vizwoz	Media	Small
Webkinz	Canada	Ganz	Toys	International
WebWilds	US	Globio	Toys (educational)	Small
Whyville	US	Numedeon	Virtual world development	Small
Xivio	US	Xivio	Virtual world development	Small
Zibbie Zone	US	Cascade Toys	Toys	Small

that most (91 per cent) of the online gaming engaged in by children and teens aged two to seventeen was on free sites.[39]

A particularly surprising discovery that emerged from my own study was that very few of the child-oriented titles included on the Virtual Worlds Management report actually qualified as "virtual worlds." As part of the content analysis, the design features and contents of each title were noted and contrasted with a list of features commonly found in mainstream virtual worlds (i.e., those targeted to teens and adults). Namely, I was looking for the presence of features that allowed player activities to unfold within a persistent environment, multiple users to be present and visually represented within a shared space, and multiple users to interact with one another and the environment simultaneously.[40] Just over half (twenty-two out of forty-two) of the sites met all three criteria. Since many of the titles included in the report were furthermore described as MMOGs within contemporaneous press coverage, I also noted the presence or absence of features commonly associated with the genre.[41] While all twenty-two of my confirmed virtual worlds contained play activities, and most (eighteen) placed a heavy emphasis on imaginary or make-believe play, only four of the titles could accurately be described as MMOGs. Notably, one of these four titles was Disney's *Toontown*, the self-proclaimed "first MMORPG" for children, released back in 2003.

The content analysis has a number of important implications. First, in 2008, despite the headlines claiming a market boom was underway, children's virtual worlds development was still at a relatively nascent stage. Little more than half of the titles included in the original Virtual Worlds Management report had actually been launched, and many of the titles identified as "in development" were ultimately never released. While a majority of the live sites included on the list were indeed targeted to children under the age of thirteen, very few of them contained the design features or criteria required for classification as a virtual world. Moreover, several of the titles reviewed were not new or emerging, but had in fact launched years before the report was compiled. Overall, the increase in children's virtual worlds reported in 2008 should not be understood as a development boom, but rather the result of a much more gradual and modest market shift.

The Virtual Worlds Management report was not alone in its exaggeration of the virtual worlds phenomenon during this period. The same year, in a comparable review of a different trade publication's listing of mainstream (i.e., teen and adult-oriented) virtual worlds and MMOGs, Spence found that nearly half of those titles failed to meet the criteria for classification as virtual worlds, and only a few could be categorized as MMOGs.[42] There appears to be a trend of misrepresenting the scope of the virtual worlds market through the application of overly broad and ambiguous definitions of the genre. Since such reports tend to be widely cited within both popular and scholarly publications, this has important repercussions for public and academic knowledge of the virtual worlds phenomenon. In the context of the current discussion, it also raises important questions about our understanding of the history and evolution of children's digital playscape – an area in which very little comparative or survey work has been conducted, but which remains a topic of recurring and concerted public attention and debate.

Since 2007, the digital cultural landscape has changed dramatically. Immediately following the influx of children's virtual worlds and MMOGs that took place in 2007 and 2008, there was a pronounced dip in the market. While Virtual Worlds Management estimated that approximately US$1.4 billion was invested in virtual worlds during the 2007 fiscal year, investment in virtual worlds generally fell in 2008.[43] Indeed, several of the virtual worlds and MMOGs that had launched during my own study closed soon thereafter, including Mattel's *BarbieGirls* (2007–11) and the short-lived MMOG *Lego Universe* (2010–12). More recently,

Disney announced that it would be closing the *Club Penguin* online virtual world and shifting focus to "an entirely new Club Penguin experience for mobile" called *Club Penguin Island*.[44]

Conversely, although perhaps not as popular as they once were, virtual worlds are still an important part of many children's online experience. Some of the titles described above have maintained and even grown in popularity since 2008, spreading into global markets and new demographics, while also adapting to new cultural trends as they emerge. Meanwhile, several new virtual worlds have become global success stories, such as Mind Candy's *Moshi Monsters* (2008–present) and Renaissance 2.0 Media's *SecretBuilders* (2014–present). By 2011, 55 per cent of UK children owned a toy based on at least one virtual world.[45] By 2012, there were reportedly over four hundred virtual worlds designed and targeted specifically to children, many of which were corporately owned and commercial in nature.[46]

Another enduring legacy of the children's virtual worlds fad of the mid-2000s is the level of commercialization that it introduced into the children's digital playscape. In addition to making transmedia-oriented immersive advertising and other self-promotional strategies commonplace, the children's virtual worlds of this era also contributed to the extension and ongoing normalization of corporate surveillance within children's games. This includes continuous monitoring of players' in-game activities and contributions, which enables detailed analysis of how specific promotional efforts (and associated products) are received by players. While previous games, such as *Neopets*, rewarded children for filling out surveys and personality quizzes, the "always-on" nature of virtual worlds has instead enabled the passive but ongoing collection of rich, longitudinal, contextualized data on children's actions and interactions. This in turn has given market researchers unprecedented access to children's private thoughts and opinions, and insight into their peer play and social interactions.

Notably, the commercial dimensions of children's virtual worlds ultimately attracted very little public attention. Instead, popular press and policymakers were more likely to focus on the fact that virtual worlds were multiplayer spaces and could potentially be infiltrated by dangerous adults and cyberbullies. These concerns were reinforced following news media reports of a handful of high-profile instances in which young users had indeed been approached by child predators. These examples, along with others associated with social networking sites and chatrooms, fuelled a renewed moral panic about children's use of internet technologies, which then led to a series of attempts to pass new, protectionary regulations, ostensibly aimed at protecting

children from such risks by restricting children's access to online platforms. As will be discussed further in chapter 5, these policy initiatives
were largely unsuccessful. They were also broadly critiqued as reaction-
ary, overly restrictive attempts to ban children from the internet. The
fact remains that while stories of children being approached by predators online are deeply troubling, they are extremely rare, despite being
heavily covered by the media. Conversely, the problematic practices engaged in by corporations, data brokers, and market researchers within
children's online spaces are endemic but largely ignored. The lack of
attention being paid to the "actual stuff" of children's virtual worlds
inspired my own research into the phenomenon, in the form of a multi-
year, in-depth analysis of six commercial game-themed virtual worlds
for children, conducted between 2007 and 2010.[47]

Design Trends and Disparities

The continued expansion of the children's media and toy industries
into emerging forms of online gaming was far from unexpected. Not
only had these same industries dominated each previous genre and iteration of children's online games, but it seemed that virtual worlds lent
themselves particularly well to cross-promotional strategies and market
research activities. Yet, while the traditional children's industries' interest
in expanding into virtual worlds was not surprising, the game industry's
reluctance to engage with an increasingly profitable market segment arguably was. As Gibson described in 2008, the children's virtual worlds
market remained one of great, mostly untapped potential, as it was one
"in which most 'traditional' games companies appear largely disinter-
ested."[48] This was despite that fact that in 2007, children already represented approximately 25 per cent of the global audience for console and
other digital games, a market that at the time generated US$44.5 billion
in annual sales.[49]

In addition to the impact this likely had on the range of themes and
contents that ultimately appeared within children's online games, the
game industry's absence arguably had an adverse impact on design standards. The children's virtual worlds that emerged between 2005 and 2008
consistently contained older-generation programming and more limited
design features when compared to those found in virtual worlds aimed
at teens and adults. Although many of the children's worlds reviewed
allowed players to mingle and communicate with each other in a shared
visual space, the spaces themselves were static and two-dimensional
with few, if any, interactive environmental features. Overall, they were
markedly different from the massive gaming experiences increasingly

available to teens and adults – they had lower levels of design sophistication, were smaller in size and scope, and provided players with fewer and less complex affordances and action opportunities. This extended to significantly reduced opportunities for inter-player communication as well. While children may well have derived meaning and value from their participation in such spaces, a double standard was nonetheless emerging in design standards and user expectations for child-specific virtual worlds.

The disparity in design standards found in games made for children and those made for older players can be traced back to the early years of online gaming. Initially, the most popular online offerings across demographic groups consisted of single-player browser games with simple visuals and basic game mechanics. But numerous important shifts occurred in the late 1990s and early 2000s as online game design evolved in conjunction with rapid advances taking place in home computing and internet technologies, and with the steady spread of internet access, uses, and expectations. Within the mainstream market (i.e., teens and adults), rapid innovation soon gave rise to three-dimensional, graphic-rich, contiguous gaming environments, some of which supported multiple players and enabled interaction, collaboration, and competition within a shared game space. Key among these was the advent of game-themed virtual worlds or MMOGs, spearheaded by Sony Online Entertainment's *EverQuest* (1999–present), which brought three-dimensional, multiplayer gaming to an entirely new level. Conversely, the vast majority of children's titles available during this same period retained their first-generation aesthetics, technical specs, and design affordances. Well into the 2000s, most children's online games and virtual worlds were still two-dimensional and static, had basic designs and graphics, and shared a propensity for lagging and glitches. In terms of the underlying technologies involved, as well as the overall look and feel, children's online games in the late 2000s were very similar to those launched in the late 1990s, including *Neopets*. In some cases, the only real difference between them was the use of the term "virtual world."

The continued use of single-screen, browser-based environments meant that these games could not provide the same levels of "geographic contiguousness" found in other virtual worlds. Geographical contiguousness is a feature identified by Pearce as a principle characteristic of the virtual world genre, in that virtual worlds possess a "sense of spatial continuity or a reasonable premise for breaking that continuity."[50] This not only makes such spaces "mappable," but also "inherently explorable." For games that do not contain this feature, there is arguably a diminished sense of movement during gameplay. Whereas the mainstream MMOGs of early 2000s featured expansive, scrolling landscapes similar to those found in contemporaneous computer and console games, child-oriented titles almost all unfolded over a series of linked yet spatially distinct (or segmented), single-screen rooms. Moving from one room to the next required the player to momentarily exit the game and re-enter once the next room had been loaded. Only one room could be loaded onto the browser at a time, and each room had limited capacity in how many players could be in the same room together. Within many of the children's online games introduced in the 1990s and 2000s, this fragmentation and *in*-contiguousness was further aggravated by the common use of point-and-click control systems, in which movement within the virtual world space was achieved by placing a cursor over and clicking on the desired destination, and then waiting for the avatar to move itself across the space.

The repercussions of the design disparity that emerged between online games for children and those designed for teens and adults extend far beyond questions of production value. Over the past decade, much has been written about mainstream MMOGs and the enormous amount of cultural and social value that their players can gain from participating in them. As digital game scholars describe them, virtual worlds can be many things to many people – games, emergent cultures, social networks, spaces for experimenting with identity, for storytelling, and for collaboration. Virtual worlds are the sites of economic processes and legal battles, as well as philosophical discussions and debates about internet governance and digital personhood.[51] That these dynamics were unfolding within graphic-rich, highly expansive – and continuously expanding – shared environments with ever-evolving storylines and software updates was not irrelevant. The formal exclusion of children from these (mainstream) spaces was compounded by the above-noted absence of comparably rich, well-designed, child-specific offerings.

The lack of involvement of game companies in the establishment of the children's online games market arguably contributed to the heavy emphasis on commercial content found within this sector. For the toy and media companies who would eventually become the de facto leaders of the children's online playscape, games were initially positioned as supplementary, promotional vehicles for existing (or emerging) brands and products. That their games filled a void left by the absence, and the concurrent exclusionary practices, of the mainstream game industry is not insignificant. *Neopets, Club Penguin*, and their contemporaries offered children a version of multiplayer gaming that looked very different from the types of experiences being targeted to teen and adult audiences. Significantly, these games provided a unique forum for children, as they were rare, child-friendly islands in the sea of age restrictions that otherwise permeated the mainstream multiplayer online game market. They were extremely popular among young players. A handful of them generated massive profits by successfully translating children's digital play into real-world purchases and by mobilizing high levels of transmedia intertextuality. More importantly, research into player practices within these spaces, from *Neopets* and *Whyville* to *Club Penguin* and *Webkinz*, reveals that they served as important sites of meaning-making, peer play, informal learning, and creative appropriation for many children. However, the activities noted in these studies unfolded despite the games' rudimentary designs and limitations, and in negotiation with the games' commercial properties and priorities.

Beyond the Computer Screen

Since 2008, children's online gaming has not only expanded significantly in the range of the genres, designs, and content available to children, but also in the hardware involved. For one, as of 2005 (Microsoft Xbox 360) and 2006 (Nintendo Wii, Sony PlayStation 3), all three of the major videogame console systems now come with built-in, internet connection capabilities, allowing players to connect with each other directly through their consoles and television screens. Second, following release of the Apple iPhone in 2007/8 and the subsequent widespread adoption of smartphones and tablets worldwide, mobile devices have become integral technologies in the lives of a large percentage of children and teens. Although children use mobile devices for an array of different activities, playing games is among the most popular, and an increasing number of these games incorporate connectivity and multiplayer features. Third, the rise of the internet of things within quotidian consumer markets has enabled the introduction of a range of new web-enabled and otherwise connected (or "smart") artefacts into the realm of children's digital gaming. With it, a new game genre – centred on the incorporation of interactive, tangible toys, variably referred to as "toys-to-life" or "interactive gaming toys" by industry analysts – has emerged. The most popular examples consist of games designed and marketed to children, most of which are based on transmedia properties. While the online dimensions of such games are not always immediately apparent, especially to their users, they are nonetheless implicated in many of the same processes and relationships found in traditional online playgrounds.

Recently, a variety of new game makers, designers, and developers have entered the realm of children's online game production. They include established game companies, mobile game designers, as well as other app developers. Alongside the diversification of the market, however, the children's media and toy industries have proven themselves highly adept at keeping pace with their audience and their newfound competition. Many key players from within traditional children's industries, including some of those discussed in previous sections, have retained their relevance among young players by positioning themselves at the cutting edge of technological and cultural trends as they unfold. Over the past decade, these companies have continued to produce some of the most popular children's digital content across categories and platforms – from online games to mobile apps, collectible toys-to-life games, and even educational software. The enduring predominance of media and toy companies within children's online or connected gaming is significant, as is the profound impact they continue to have on the conventions, themes, and norms associated with this segment of the digital gamescape.

These developments, and the continuities and departures from early iterations of the children's digital landscape they represent, became a key focus of a series of studies I conducted between 2011 and 2019 on the rise of game-making and content-creation tools in commercial digital games, and specifically within game titles targeted to children.[52] A great number of the titles I analysed during this period were played on either connected consoles or mobile devices, and several featured "toys-to-life" game pieces. Out of this research, a more comprehensive analysis was subsequently conducted, establishing the scope and impact of these trends across the children's digital culture and its associated industries.

Web-Enabled Consoles

Just like smartphones and tablets, videogame consoles are essentially computers that have been packaged in a specialized form. Starting in 2005, all three of the major console system manufacturers (Sony, Microsoft, and Nintendo) began incorporating internet connectivity capabilities into their devices. Over the years, an increasing number of features embedded in these systems assume or even require consoles to be connected to an active internet connection to function optimally. This includes access to membership accounts, virtual shops, software updates, and web-enabled game titles. Current-generation console systems also include all the peripherals required for computer-mediated communication, including microphones and speakers that enable inter-player chat. In the case of Microsoft Xbox (360 and One), this extends to a built-in, voice-activated, multi-sensor video camera contained in the system's accompanying Kinect attachment, which can be used to record as well as engage in video chat (e.g., players can install the Skype app onto their Microsoft Xbox console). In addition to enabling multiplayer coordination and social interaction, these features also create an open and ongoing flow of data between players and the game industry. The systems are used by the game industry to monitor player behaviour and track player activities, while also collecting undisclosed amounts of data from and about them.

Since the introduction of the Nintendo Entertainment System in 1984, children have been counted among the most avid console gamers. In Canada, the majority (72 per cent) of households with children under the age of twelve own at least one gaming console, and nearly half of Canadian children between the ages of nine and twelve report playing console games daily.[53] Although there is very little research available on the frequency of children's online or connected play using game consoles, particularly within North America, a recent study conducted in the United Kingdom suggests that participation rates among children and teens are on the increase. This appears to be specifically the case with boys, who are much "more likely than girls to mostly use a games console (11% versus 1%)" to go online. Significantly, similar gender divides were uncovered in a recent Pew Research Center study of the online gaming practices of adolescents, which found that teen boys aged thirteen to seventeen were not only "substantially more likely than girls to report access to a game console (91%, compared with 70% of girls)," but also more likely to engage in connected gaming.[54]

From a political-economic perspective, the spread of online gaming to consoles is significant in its diversification of children's online game development. Indeed, while children's gaming on the World Wide Web has long been dominated by toy and media companies, the connected console landscape is still up for grabs, and a range of industry sectors appear interested in claiming it. For one, it has opened the way for the greater involvement of established game companies. Nintendo, which has led the children's console game market since the mid-1980s, now incorporates online play features into many of its child-friendly game titles. In addition to changing the look and feel of the children's connected play sphere, Nintendo's unique approach to inter-player communication and parental monitoring mechanisms represents a significant departure from the standards that emerged during the 2000s in relation to children's privacy, intellectual property, and surveillance within corporately owned online games.

For the most part, however, console systems and games are predominantly targeted to male teens and adults. As such, children are configured as a niche audience within this sector of the gaming landscape and are not as frequently targeted by game designs or advertisements. Although there are plenty of examples of child-specific titles to be found

in the game catalogues of all three major console systems, especially Nintendo, they remain disproportionately under-represented, considering
that children count for 27 per cent of the global games market.[55] Instead,
the trend is towards games, and some marketing, that are child-*inclusive*,
rather than child-specific. For example, the majority of videogames
released in 2015 were rated either E for Everyone (37 per cent) or E10+
for all players aged ten years and up (23 per cent).[56] This figure has been
typical for the last several years.

   However, an E rating does not mean that a game is necessarily designed
for or even with children in mind. The ESRB's rating system does not take
into consideration children's varying experience levels, literacy skills, and
situated knowledges. Rather, games are rated on the basis of whether and to
what extent they contain thematic and graphic content has been deemed
inappropriate for children. Therefore, a statistics-laden sports game such
as *FIFA 17* is E rated, while the extremely challenging platformer game
N++ is rated E10+. Meanwhile, the ESRB's EC for Early Childhood rating
appears so infrequently, it fails to register on recent distribution charts.
A search of the ESRB online database reveals that since 1994, only twenty-one games have ever received an EC rating, across all platforms. Notably, sixteen of these games were made for Nintendo (for the Nintendo DS,
DSi, or Wii). Moreover, none of the EC titles currently listed in the ESRB
database are for the current eighth-generation consoles.[57]

   Of course, the games that children elect to play, and/or that their parents select for them, are not necessarily those that have been designed
specifically for them – and many children and parents do not see this as
problematic. Nonetheless, this facet of the mainstream games market
warrants consideration, for it is obscured in the oft-cited statistics that
most games are rated E or E10+ and that most households with children
own at least one gaming console. It is too easy to overestimate the extent
to which children are in fact viewed as intended, as opposed to inciden-
tal, users of games and console systems by the majority of designers. If
such is the case for games in general, then it is especially so for connected console games, which introduce all the same special ethical, regulatory, and legal considerations that have historically deterred so many
online game designers from targeting (or even allowing) child players.
Alongside the larger trend of making games child-inclusive, albeit not
child-centred, there is a concurrent tendency to ban child players from
connected games and multiplayer features. For instance, Twitch, a highly
popular web-streaming service widely used by game players and fans, forbids users under the age of thirteen years from using or accessing its
services "at any time or in any manner."[58] Thus, although the advent of
web-enabled consoles did result in a greater number of traditional game

companies getting involved in the children's online game market, here too the default remains teen and adult oriented.

It is therefore not all that surprising to see that other patterns initially established on the World Wide Web have resurfaced within the console gamescape. One key example is the successful expansion and continued prominence of many of the same media and toy companies into children's console game development. For instance, among the twenty-one titles rated "EC" for "Early Childhood" listed on the ESRB database in 2017, eleven featured characters and storylines from transmedia properties owned by Disney, Sesame Workshop, and Nickelodeon. Another important carryover is the emphasis on transmedia cross-promotion. Although only a small proportion of videogames produced over the past thirty-odd years have ties into existing media brands, a significant number of the most popular and best-selling children's console games are based on toy or media brands.[59] From Lego's *Lego Star Wars* games (which sold over thirty million units between 2005 and 2012) to EA's numerous *Harry Potter* titles, children's console games are populated by familiar media brands and characters[60] Simultaneously, several highly successful children's media brands have emerged from original console titles, the most celebrated of which is Nintendo's *Pokémon*, which reportedly became the highest grossing media franchise in the world in 2018, generating an estimated $59.1 billion in revenues since its launch in 1996.[61]

Interestingly, connected consoles have not attracted anywhere near the same level of scrutiny and public attention as children's online spaces. In 2012, a number of newspaper stories appeared condemning the Microsoft Xbox 360 console system for enabling sexual predators to approach children, after one such incident had allegedly occurred in New York State.[62] The subsequent negative press and mounting concerns about the potential dangers of social interaction through gaming consoles led to the establishment of an industry-wide agreement to shut down the accounts of registered sex offenders (at least in that one particular state), thereby preventing them from interacting with others through a console system. For the most part, however, connectivity features have proliferated throughout console games and embedded services with little regulation or public debate. It is quite possible that the lack of attention is due at least partially to a lack of awareness on behalf of parents and policymakers. For instance, a study conducted by the Entertainment Software Association of Canada revealed that many parents were unaware that their children engaged in online gaming. Although 77 per cent of the children and teens (aged six to seventeen) surveyed reported playing games online, only 5 per cent of the parents surveyed believed their child accessed online games.[63]

Connected Games Go Mobile

Another important development in children's connected gaming links to the recent, widespread increase in children's access to smart mobile devices, from cell phones and handheld gaming consoles to tablets and e-readers. According to a report by Common Sense Media, in 2013, 40 per cent of US families with children between the ages of zero and eight owned an iPad or other tablet device, while 63 per cent owned a smartphone.[64] Research conducted in 2012 at Northwestern University found that 26 per cent of US children aged zero to eight regularly used a tablet, such as an Apple iPad. That same year, market analyst Nielsen reported that 66 per cent of households with kids aged six to twelve years owned a Nintendo DS or Sony PSP, as well as an Apple iOS device. More recently, in 2014, a national survey conducted by market analyst yconic found that 58 per cent of Canadian children aged nine to twelve used a tablet and 37 per cent used a smartphone daily.[65] Meanwhile, a small-scale study found "almost universal exposure" to mobile devices among children aged six months to four years of age living in a low-income neighbourhood of Philadelphia.[66]

Children use mobile devices to engage in a range of activities and different types of media consumption, but for most young people, playing games is among the most common. Furthermore, the NPD Group reports that on average, children are engaging in mobile gaming at increasingly younger ages (age eight in 2013 versus nine in 2011).[67] Notably, although social networking features are not incorporated to the same extent in children's mobile games as they are in online games or connected console games, data collection practices and one-click purchasing capabilities regularly are. However, there is also much to suggest that children's game designers have only just begun to explore the full potential of mobile devices. For instance, the next generation of videogame consoles, such as the Nintendo Switch, promises greater integration of multi-screen activities, in which portable gaming devices, phones, and other devices might be used to supplement gameplay.

Initially, the mobile game market was flooded by independent developers and diverse companies hoping to establish themselves in a widely hyped, still-emerging industry sector. As in other areas of the children's connected game market, however, established children's media and toy companies now predominate. Although spending on mobile games for children reportedly represented 7.8 per cent of the global mobile games revenue generated in 2015,[68] the market is frequently described as unsustainable by industry analysts and trade publications. As Traylor writes, "For companies that can afford to make such apps, these businesses may not be focused on generating revenue, but rather care more about generating brand visibility, brand engagement and cross-promotion of other non-app products."[69] Much like online games and console games before them, mobile games are increasingly used as vehicles for transmedia promotion and, potentially, market research.

The prevalence of self-proclaimed educational games represents another key trend in the children's mobile games arena. The patterns here are markedly like those that shaped the early decades of children's software development, where an emphasis on educational benefits and content served to justify the spread of computing technologies within children's lives while countering recurring social anxieties about possible harmful outcomes. Alongside reports and studies decrying the alleged negative side effects of children's mobile device use, there is a growing body of academic and industry research that instead claims linkages to learning and technical skill development. Accordingly, in addition to containing an increasing number of transmedia titles, the children's mobile game landscape is also dominated by "educational" titles and genres. This emphasis extends to how children's mobile games are marketed on platforms such as the Apple App Store, which regularly features education-focused categories including "Coding for Kids" and "Learning Made Fun" on the front page of its Kids section, and the Google Play Store, which includes genres such as "Learning Apps for Kids" and "Brain Games for Kids" in its Family section.

While such claims – that an app or a game has educational value and defined learning outcomes – are rarely questioned, the research suggests there is good reason to be critical of the industry's mobilization of educational terms and classifications. In her analysis of early children's educational software, Ito discovered that there was very little to support the categorization of these titles as specifically "educational."[70] Similarly, a study of self-described educational apps conducted by Vaala, Ly, and Levine found that little more than a third (36 per cent) of the top fifty paid apps mentioned involving a child development, education, or literacy expert in the development of the app, while fewer than a third (29 per cent) of all apps mentioned an underlying educational curriculum.[71] Very few contained the types of features that have been found to be the most effective for facilitating learning, such as content levelling (i.e., being able to set the difficulty level) and joint engagement features.

Along with the emphasis on learning, mobile games are frequently heralded for their perceived value in motivating children to become more physically active, particularly through the incorporation of geolocational and activity-tracking technologies. Two early examples of child-specific mobile games that promoted themselves as instigators of increased outdoor play and fitness were Bulpadok's *The Hidden Park* (2009) (for Apple iOS and Android) and Aspyr Media's *Treasure World* (2009) (for Nintendo DS). Both titles were among the first commercial game titles to tap into the geolocational capabilities of contemporary mobile devices, combining real-world maps, built-in camera phone capabilities, and digital content to engage players in fantastical, augmented reality scavenger hunts. Recently, the massive, global success of Niantic and Nintendo's *Pokémon Go*, a mobile, geolocation game based on the popular transmedia property released in July 2016, has rekindled interest in the genre and in its purported benefits. While initially free, premium items are available for purchase, through an embedded in-app system. According to market research firm App Annie, the game generated US$950 million worldwide in 2016 alone.[72] Notably, *Pokémon Go* incorporates multiplayer activities, although these require that players (or their phones) first be within a certain physical proximity. A mere seven months after its release, the game already served as a case study in the oscillating, polarized, academic discourses that surround children's digital gaming, with nearly two dozen articles in print from various disciplines and traditions discussing the game's risks and/or benefits.

Toys-to-Life and Cross-Platform Games

A final trend within the contemporary children's connected gaming landscape that warrants mention is the emergence of the "toys-to-life" genre – digital games that are played in part by manipulating real-world (i.e., tangible) USB or Wi-Fi connected figurines and other toys. The term toys-to-life is somewhat misleading, as the figurines themselves do not tend to have enhanced features or functionality beyond cuing specific events or unlocking associated characters (or other items) within the digital game environment, as well as downloading and storing game progress and other data through their embedded near field communication (NFC) chips. The genre is the recognizable descendent of *Webkinz* and the other tangible/virtual toy games popular in the mid-2000s, and (so far) shares their emphasis on collectability and endless cycles of consumption. Similarly, the toys-to-life market segment rose to prominence in conjunction with a seemingly sudden surge in popularity and financial success, which were directly linked to one or two highly popular titles. Between 2011 and 2016, the genre received regular, largely celebratory coverage within news media and industry trade publications, which focused heavily on its growing profit margins and seemingly infinite transmedia opportunities. By 2015, the toys-to-life segment was estimated to be worth US$4 billion,[73] much of it generated by four dominant properties: Activision's *Skylanders*, *Disney Infinity*, *Lego Dimensions*, and Nintendo's *Amiibo*.

The toys-to-life fad began in 2011 with the widespread critical and popular success of Activision's *Skylanders: Spyro's Adventure*, the first in what would eventually become a series of six *Skylanders* titles (in addition to a spin-off series exclusive to the Nintendo DS, as well as a multi-game or app series playable on all major mobile devices). The games are available on all three major gaming consoles but can only be played using the appropriate "Portal of Power" – a special, peripheral device that plugs directly into the player's console system. Using this portal, which looks like a stage, players can "transport" their collectible *Skylanders* toy figures into the game environment, where they appear as playable, digital avatars. Similar systems are found in both *Disney Infinity* and *Lego Dimensions*, wherein different in-game characters, areas, and actions are accessed (or unlocked) by placing the correct figurines or other objects onto the appropriate toy pad accessory, which is in turn plugged into the console system's USB port. Some variation from this format is found in Nintendo's *Amiibo* system, launched in 2014. While *Amiibo* also revolves around collectible figurines, the system is not limited to one specific game title or game series, but rather extends across a range of Nintendo console and handheld games, and it often incorporates (tangible) trading cards. The *Amiibo* system is likewise unique in that it does not require a plug-in accessory to enable and delimit interaction between its games and toys, but lets the devices communicate directly through NFC protocols. Conversely, the in-game rewards unlocked by the *Amiibo* toys are comparatively small and have minimal impact on gameplay, leading some market analysts to conclude that the figurines are largely purchased as collectibles by Nintendo fans.[74]

In the spring of 2016, Disney announced that it was discontinuing its *Disney Infinity* property and closing the in-house studio that had created it. The same year, despite strong initial sales of its figurines, it became apparent that Nintendo's *Amiibo* had failed to meet expectations of both market analysts and game critics. Soon after, trade publications began predicting the imminent death of the toys-to-life market, where growth had seemingly stagnated, and at least one major player was jumping ship. In many ways, however, the full potential of the technological and conceptual innovations underlying the toys-to-life genre has yet to be fully realized. While much has been written by academics and industry analysts about the promise of toys-to-life as a platform for not only acknowledging, but also supporting and extending children's affinity for transmedia play, to date the properties that have dominated this market segment have instead fixated on using it to promote endless cycles of consumption and little else. The very term "toys-to-life" is deeply associated with collectable toys and accessories, and the games' designs revolve heavily around this underlying business model. Levels, storylines, and gameplay mechanics are all designed to reinforce the idea that buying the next toy in the series is crucial for fun and successful gameplay. In fact, in most of the titles described above, players very quickly reach the limit of what they can do in the game without purchasing additional figurines or accessories. This in turn diminishes the games' longevity and playability for anyone but the most die-hard, not to mention affluent, player-fans.

It is likely that this narrow emphasis on collectability introduces other unintended limitations as well, both in the types of games that are considered suitable for the genre, and the sorts of games that developers view as able to be competitive in the toys-to-life market. For instance, if manufacturing an expansive toy line is seen as a requirement for making a toys-to-life game, the associated development costs would be prohibitive for most independent and small to mid-sized game design companies. Indeed, it is no coincidence that all of the toys-to-life properties discussed above are based on existing media characters. These games, and their toys, already have an audience and fan base. While such an approach is in no way a guarantee of market success, it certainly reduces the perceived and financial risks associated with launching an original property, populated by as-yet-unknown and therefore unproven characters and storylines. Moreover, this very logic is what increasingly drives production decisions across the children's industries.

Yet there is nothing inherent to toys-to-life technology that mandates the incorporation of multiple, collectible products. Such games could easily be designed to connect with a single toy. For instance, these games could also be designed around the presence and manipulation of a highly customizable toy, one that makes better use of the NFC chip to record and remember greater details about game progress and past actions, and uses these data to personalize the gameplay experience in deeper, more interactive ways. Rather than focus on an ever-increasing quantity of toys involved, these games could just as well be designed to emphasize and explore the quality of the relationship between games, toys, and players. Such an approach would tap into other important dimensions of children's transmedia play – dimensions that are largely ignored by existing toy-to-life properties. While (some) children do enjoy building collections of things, children also develop intimate, exclusive relationships with a favourite toy or character, as well as engage in meaningful identity play through the creation of unique personas or avatars.[75]

Indeed, from the child player's perspective, the most important consequence of the spread of online gaming across multiple platforms is arguably the introduction of new, technologically supported opportunities for hybrid modes of playing that more fully address or reflect how children themselves choose to play with their media, toys, and technological devices. As explored in chapter 6, this remains a notably understudied and underserved area of children's digital play. At the same time, however, emerging developments in research and children's game development suggest that at least some of these gaps may soon be filled. For example, several children's connected games, including *Minecraft*, now incorporate cross-platform features, enabling players to engage with the game through different devices, thereby expanding their gameplay into multiple contexts, locations, and modes of engagement. Meanwhile, Nintendo described its next-generation console, the Nintendo Switch, as a hybrid console that can function as both a home and mobile device, and it includes an NFC reader for *Amiibo* toys and other objects. Concurrently, as children's digital play increasingly unfolds within the public realms of digital game systems and social networking forums, the nuances and complexities of their cultures of practice are not only confirmed, but also work to highlight and contradict many of the limitations that have historically permeated the children's online gaming market.

Conclusion

In many ways, the children's connected games environment has changed significantly over the past two decades. Whereas child-oriented connected games once lagged behind their mainstream counterparts in technical sophistication, action opportunities, and diversity of contents, the category now includes several critically acclaimed titles, some of which have been groundbreaking for their design innovation and their approach to player participation. For example, Nintendo's *Mario Kart* was notable for its highly fluid incorporation of multiplayer competitions, through which, at the click of a button, users could play against other players of similar levels from all around the world. Similarly, Bulpadok's *The Hidden Park* was among the first commercial game titles to tap into the geolocational capabilities of contemporary smartphones to produce hybrid digital/alternate reality games – a clear precursor to the more recent *Pokémon Go* craze.

Conversely, the children's connected playground is still characterized by many of the trends that were first established in the very earliest years of the World Wide Web. The children's online game industry remains dominated by established media and toy companies – including many of the same companies that shaped the landscape when it first emerged in the late 1990s and early 2000s. Child-specific connected games contain remarkably high levels of commercial and especially cross-promotional (transmedia) content. With some important exceptions, the designs, aesthetics, and level of diversity found in this market segment are generally less advanced, less sophisticated, and less innovative than those found in the mainstream market. Although some of these differences are surely the result of informed, purposeful decisions to create games that are smaller, less expensive, and therefore more accessible to a greater number of child players, others – such as the high prevalence of bugs, lags, and design flaws – have no apparent justification. Commercial innovation and corporate priorities remain at the forefront, largely determining which and how children's online games are designed – as well as how they are managed, how policy is shaped, and how children are ultimately configured as players and digital citizens.

With the introduction of each new tool for engaging in online or connected gaming, previous controversies and concerns about risks, benefits, and effects are inevitably revisited. In at least some cases, public outcry results from a simple lack of awareness – oftentimes on behalf of the parents – that so many different devices can now be used to connect to the internet, to other people, and to corporations. In others, more immediate consequences, such as unexpected credit card charges stemming from real money transactions sneakily embedded in children's connected games, have led parents and advocacy groups into action. Yet, for the most part, we have yet to see a comprehensive debate or policy discussion that addresses the full range of implications – positive and negative – of the contemporary, connected gaming landscape for children's play experience, privacy, cultural rights, and overall well-being. Although children's digital play remains a frequent and popular topic of discussion, media (especially trade media) coverage often adopts an ahistorical approach that positions every new fad or technological innovation as unprecedented and subject to irresolvable academic disagreement.

A key example can be found in the 2010 controversy surrounding Capcom's *Smurfs' Village* mobile game. Rated as appropriate for players aged "4 and up" by the Apple App Store, *Smurfs' Village* was free to play but also featured an embedded micro-transactions system similar to the one found in Zynga's popular Facebook game *FarmVille*. Certain items could be acquired using in-game currency (i.e., play money), while others cost real money to purchase. In *Smurfs' Village*, RMT items ranged wildly in price, from ninety-nine cents to a reported ninety-nine dollars, and their purchase was integrated directly into regular gameplay.[76] To confirm a purchase, the player needed only to click "agree" (rather than input a password, for example). The process was streamlined by the fact that, like all iOS applications purchased through the Apple App Store, the game was directly linked to the device owners' accounts, and therefore to their credit card. Controversy arose when parents began to discover unexpected charges made to their credit cards after letting their kids play the game. In one well-documented case, an eight-year-old had spent US$1,400 while playing it. Soon after, the Federal Trade Commission (FTC) launched an investigation into the use of in-app RMT in applications targeted to children.[77]

The game was part of a larger class action suit launched by parents and consumer advocacy groups against Apple, which the company settled in 2013 for a reported US$100 million.[78] The following year, the company agreed to provide consumer refunds of at least US$32.5 million to settle the FTC complaint. In addition to the financial settlement, the FTC required that Apple change its billing practices to ensure express, informed consent before any in-app purchase is made. The controversy and its outcomes highlight the importance of public attention in mobilizing regulatory discourse on the commercialization of games, and of children's games especially. Conversely, the only issue that was properly addressed in this instance was the process through which the purchases were made, while underlying questions about the appropriateness of targeting a game built so centrally around RMT to children as young as four was barely mentioned. Similarly, the scope of this discussion was narrowly focused on games bought and sold in the Apple App Store. The fact that similar practices can be found within children's console games as well, for example, was not considered relevant. And yet, understanding the pervasiveness of embedded RMT and other forms of commercialization across children's gaming is crucial for unpacking its normalization within children's culture and its impacts on children's digital experience.

Important questions remain about whether commercially driven, transmedia-based games truly expand the gameplay experience into new spaces and play modes or merely work to extend commercial processes into an ever-greater portion of children's lives. After all, throughout their brief yet colourful history, children's online games have had a unique and persistent relationship with commodification, and questions about the impacts of embedded cross-promotion and immersive advertising have come up again and again. Concurrently, the full implications of the relationship between children, media supersystems, and the corporations who own and profit from those systems are obscured by the high-profile media hypes and panics that preoccupy the public's attention when it comes to children's digital gaming. It is also quite possible that the sheer ubiquity of commercialization in children's media, toys, and games has finally made it a tired subject for parents and child advocates.

Nonetheless commercialization remains one of the most powerful forces guiding children's online game design today. As the next chapter will explore, the primacy of commercial content and corporate priorities within the children's online landscape can be understood as reformulating children's relationships to the public sphere, to commercial entities, and with consumer practices in widespread, unprecedented ways. While such developments are not necessarily total or even proscriptive, they have significant impact on the shape and contents of digital childhood.

3

Commercializing Play(grounds)

In reviewing the history of children's connected digital playgrounds, it is apparent that many of the most popular titles to emerge over the past several years have been owned and operated by a handful of media and toy conglomerates – companies that dominate in multiple areas of children's consumer culture. Consequently, these games often contain many of the same characters, themes, and motifs found in other children's texts and artefacts – from toys and books to film and television. As such, the children's digital landscape is rife with cross-promotional content, branding initiatives, and transmedia intertextuality. Although children's online games fulfil a wide range of different functions and are interpreted in various ways by the children who play them, as cultural artefacts they are defined in no small part by their heavy emphasis on transmedia commercialization.

Children's connected games are notably distinct from other game genres and from other forms of children's media, where commercial content has a much more contentious track record and is often met with higher levels of public resistance. For example, overtly cross-promotional games targeted to teens and adults, such as games based on movies, have historically been less critically and financially successful than "original" titles. With a few exceptions for instances where product placement was viewed as enhancing the game's realism (as in the racing games discussed later in this chapter), the integration of in-game advertisements and product placement within T- and M-rated titles has been met with controversy and player outcry. Only recently has this tendency been challenged, notably through the introduction of a series of highly acclaimed interactive, episodic story games produced by Telltale Games, including *The Wolf among Us* (2013–14), based on the popular Fables comic book series, and a series of games associated with the Walking Dead transmedia franchise. Similarly, in previous years, far less commercial content was found in children's console games than in children's online games. As explored in the previous chapter, however, this too is now changing, as the children's industries expand their properties to include connected console gaming.

The uniquely high level of commercialization found within children's online games reflects broader political-economic trends found across the children's media, toy, and other cultural industries. Over the past three decades, a combination of corporate convergence, media deregulation, and shifting social norms has led to the widespread normalization of cross-promotional media and tie-in toys aimed at children.[1] Today, it is common for child-targeted media texts to arrive at the pitch stage with already built-in licensing deals and plans for future adaptations. Children's media properties are increasingly conceived from the outset to function as media brands, rather than as distinct texts (e.g., a book, a television series) or objects (e.g., an action figure, a doll). As discussed in chapter 1, this supersystem[2] approach is designed from the start to promote cross-consumption of ancillary media, as well as the purchase of tie-in products. Supersystems are fragmented, integrated, and cross-referenced in ways that make it seemingly impossible to access their full meaning unless their interlinked media and associated products are all consumed in turn. Although not always successful, the approach is prevalent within children's consumer culture.

Revisiting Supersystems and Structures

While it is impossible to deny that supersystems are prevalent within children's commercial culture, their significance and impact is much less clear-cut. While supersystems obviously introduce certain patterns and themes into children's lives, there is a longstanding debate among scholars about whether and to what extent they actually infringe upon children's agency and subjective experience. Although many academics studying children's commercial culture strive to avoid essentialism in their discussions and research, as in so many areas of children's studies, research on the commercialization of children's culture can provisionally be divided into two camps: works arguing that commercialization is detrimental to children, and works arguing that commercialization is easily contravened by children's natural tendencies towards subversion and creative appropriation.

As discussed previously, ongoing debates about the impact of commercialization on children's play often appear to reproduce the longstanding structure/agency dialectic that is found throughout the social sciences. The news media tend to depict the literature in this area and the issues involved as unreconcilable. Yet, in reviewing the academic research on the potential impacts of commercialization on childhood, it becomes clear that the work in this area is not actually at a standstill. Moreover, arguments from *both* sides have been used to support the establishment of new government regulation, industry guidelines, as well as cultural and social expectations. Much like the scholarship on violent digital games, scholarship investigating children's commercial culture has had far-reaching implications, not only for academic and public knowledge, but also for how children's relationship to consumerism, advertising, and materialism is conceived of and, at times, regulated. This body of work is also implicated in shifting social norms around the role of the market within contemporary childhood.

In order to navigate this precarious terrain, a more nuanced, flexible approach must be adopted – one that avoids the polarizing tendencies that have characterized so much of the previous literature on children's digital play. There are a range of sources to draw on in the works of scholars who have similarly sought to move beyond dichotomous frameworks and examine the roles of both structural forces and individual agency in the social construction of children's play. Children's media scholars such as Fleming and Kinder, for instance, highlight the importance of considering both *text* and *context* when attempting to understand children's relationship with licensed toys and media supersystems, and they acknowledge that some toys and texts are thus potentially more prescriptive than others. Similarly, research into toy and game design, conducted by Bergen, Plowman, and others suggests that certain structural features afford higher levels of creativity, appropriation, and interaction than others. These works advance the argument that the relationship between structure and agency that unfolds within children's play, especially technologized play, is complex and artefact/context-specific.

Texts and Contexts

A key insight emerging out of children's media studies is the idea that some toys, games, and media texts carry more "narrative baggage" than others, providing more or less structure or direction on how the story, characters, or toys should be played with. This suggests that the specific features of the texts themselves are also an important factor in shaping the contexts of play. Kinder, Fleming, and Zipes each highlight the enormous influence of narrative – including formal narrative elements and structures, as well as the specific attributes of the characters, aesthetic conventions, and thematic motifs – in determining the forms and functions of transmedia intertextuality within children's commercial culture.

Kinder's landmark study of transmedia intertextuality (in which she coined the term itself) found in children's media and toys identifies numerous examples that "encourage the kind of negotiated reading theorized by Stuart Hall ... where generational subgroups actively appropriate images from mass culture."[3] She points to innovative Saturday morning television programs from the 1980s, such as *Muppet Babies* (1984–91) and *Pee-wee's Playhouse* (1986–90), as examples of narratives that emphasize the reinterpretation of shared cultural texts and icons. By appropriating themes and imagery associated with (or directly taken from) other media, and by rearranging them in a fluid postmodern juxtaposition, these texts invite the audience to enter into an "intermediate space" of "interactive fantasy." Kinder argues that engaging with this particular form of transmedia intertextuality facilitates "transgressive identification across other borders of genre, generation, race, culture, and species."[4] Such texts reflexively generate a sort of concurrent pedagogy of intertextuality by providing a road map for mastering, accessing, and appropriating diverse cultural references, subjectivities, and meanings.

Similar arguments are made by Zipes, who highlights how the specific narrative structures, themes, and features that make up a particular media text (book, film, television show, game, etc.) have a profound impact on its meaning and reception. He describes, for example, how Disney's fairy tale films traditionally employ "techniques of infantilization, narrative strategies of closure, and the exaltation of homogeneity."[5] In contrast, other media texts, such as Jim Henson's *StoryTeller* (1987–9), apply bricolage, multimedia pastiche, satire, and parody, and subvert their own authority by transgressing norms and convention. Rather than simply promoting conformity to established scripts, structures, and consumer behaviours (although these features may nonetheless also be present), texts in the second category invite young viewers to "explore the tale's manifold meanings."[6] The narrative format of a media text can therefore reproduce and perpetuate the media industries' ideological repositioning of identity, imagination, and meaning-making as a commercially mediated process, as well as repositioning the underlying market relations (and consumption patterns) out of which transmedia intertextuality is constructed in the first place. Such texts promote conformity to established scripts, structures, and consumer behaviours. Conversely, transgressive texts "challenge the creative and critical capabilities of young viewers."[7]

Another useful concept is Fleming's notion of "mediatization," which describes the process through which toys become embedded in media-driven popular culture, "with meanings circulating through object and culture in mutually reinforcing ways."[8] Via the complex layering of meaning that media narratives generate around tie-in toys and ancillary products, a "thoroughly mediated relationship" is produced, through which even toys that do not have very elaborate or appealing qualities can become meaningful by their association with other media.[9] Akin to Zipes, Fleming argues that the structure of the narrative itself plays an important role in this process. He argues that effective transmedia intertexts such as *Star Wars* are characterized by "metonymic" narratives, which allow "for difference, for messier forms of identity, unraveled by fantasy, to take hold."[10] Unlike *metaphor*, the standard rhetorical strategy of clumping "meanings together into static, authoritative objects while laying claim to being the meaning in some idealised way," *metonymy* "disperses the meanings into fluid, more provisional and open-ended connections, with no single object claiming to encapsulate it all."[11] As the transgressive, ambiguous qualities of these texts are spread across the nodes of their associated transmedia supersystems, Fleming argues, the tie-in toys come to display a similar "semiotic complexity" and "cultural resonance."[12]

An additional analytic tool is found in Willis's notion of "packaging." In her use of the term, packaging refers, on the one hand, to the actual cardboard and plastic materials that envelope consumer products, and on the other hand, to the underlying processes involved – including standardization (of weights, etc.), sanitization, and as an important component of commodity fetishization. Willis draws on Haug's discussion of the "double reality" of commodities in her exploration of the many functions of packaging within consumer culture. Haug argues that many commodities have not only a use value, but also "more importantly, the appearance of use value," which is essentially detached from the commodity itself.[13] As Willis argues, "This is the aspect of the commodity form that advertising seizes upon and renders sensually perceptible in its words and images."[14] Within my own research on children's digital playgrounds, I have adapted this term to describe the virtual layer of webpages, advertisements, and registration procedures that players must first navigate (or "unwrap") in order to enter into the digital game or virtual world environment.

The idea that technologies contain narrative elements and iterations of "packaging" also appears in STS research, such as Akrich's "script theory" and van Oost's notion of "gender scripts." As van Oost describes it, notions of gender become transformed into "design specifications" that operate at the level of technological, aesthetic, or marketing design. Advertising in particular serves as an "important locus for linking an object to a specific consumer group."[15] The concept can easily be expanded to include other ways that artefacts become coded through narrativization, transmedia intertextuality, and media representation. Relatedly, Shaw proposes adapting Hall's encoding/decoding model for conducting a critical cultural studies–based analysis of design affordances, which focuses on better understanding their underlying meanings and power relations.[16] Hall's model, Shaw argues, "acknowledges that we are not simply free to interpret texts (or technologies) in just *any* way."[17] While individual users play a crucial role in negotiating and ascribing meanings to the technologies they use, these meanings are also always expressed through shared systems of representation and in relation to a (oftentimes hegemonic) system of meaning. Shaw's approach acknowledges "there are aspects of mediated experiences that are invisible to users," including affordances that "affect what users can and cannot do in online spaces, but operate out of view."[18]

Affordances and Design Limitations

The second level to consider is that of the artefact's technological design, and the role of specific design features in shaping, enabling, and delimiting children's play. For the most part, toy design makes only a cursory appearance in the scholarship examining the relationship between children's media, play, and commercialization. There are, however, a few notable exceptions, some of which are briefly reviewed here. Concurrently, there is now a small but growing body of work that addresses the literature's longstanding "design" gap in a more direct and systematic way, placing design at the centre of the analysis. Emerging out of both education and design studies, I have found these works immensely useful starting points for constructing a research methodology that considers key elements of technology design from a non-technical perspective. These works emphasize consideration of the user experience (rather than the more common focus on designer processes and intentions), and they enable critical analysis of the semiotic and discursive dimensions of technological artefacts, their packaging, and their targeting of specific, idealized users.

In their study of Mattel's Barbie doll toy line, Pearson and Mullins argue that highly specialized toy designs have dominated the market for the past thirty years as a way of perpetuating endless cycles of consumption.[19] Such toy lines are continuously being expanded to include new iterations, accessories, and tie-in products through new plot developments in the associated media narrative, such as the introduction of a new character or a new object-focused scenario. This part of their argument is similar to those found in the works of scholars such as Cook, Bianchi, Buckingham, and Sefton-Green, who suggest that games and toys built around accumulation (such as trading card games and collectible toys) advance a "pedagogy of consumption," through which players are introduced to the "habits and competencies required by our commercially based media culture."[20] Bianchi furthermore proposes that collection-based toys and games articulate a specific vision of consumer society, in which the selection and control of commodities is equated with fun, achievement, and play. In looking at the specific design features of one such toy, Barbie dolls, Pearson and Mullins build significantly upon this idea – demonstrating that toy, or even toy component, designs promote ongoing consumption in different ways, with varying degrees of effectiveness.

A key contribution made in the Barbie study is their discussion of the difference between "functionally distinct" and "materially distinct" accessories (or parts). Many of the "expansion" toys associated with collectible toy lines are merely "functionally distinct," meaning that they differ from existing products only in terms of their outward or superficial appearance, or their thematic motif. Many of the items in Barbie's seemingly infinite wardrobe are a perfect example. They serve the same material function but carry special and unique cultural or semiotic meaning. However, others are designed as materially distinct components of a larger system, a process Pearson and Mullins describe as the design equivalent of transmedia intertextuality. The purchase of one toy can *require* the purchase of many others at the practical level as well as the symbolic, with each additional toy, accessory, clothing item, and playset specifically designed to perform a unique function within the larger whole. Without them, those functions cannot be fulfilled.

Several children's media researchers have touched upon design elements in their analyses of "gendered" toys.[21] Although these works emphasize aesthetic elements and marketing rhetoric, facets of the toys' designs are also examined, to some extent. For instance, a recurring finding is that toys designed for girls are frequently less durable and less conducive to active play than toys designed for boys. Forman-Brunell traces this trend back across cultural and market shifts that unfolded in the late eighteenth and early nineteenth centuries, through which traditional, malleable, durable rag dolls were replaced by fragile, easily stained porcelain dolls. The shift in materials used to manufacture dolls coincided with the stricter, more widespread gendering of doll play as girls' play within product packaging and popular culture (e.g., in parenting magazines). It introduced tangible limitations on what could be done with the dolls without breaking them. Whereas rag dolls could be manipulated in a range of ways and contexts, including during outdoor play, porcelain dolls were promoted as display items and collectibles, or as props for tea parties and dress-up play.

The interplay between design and discourse is also the focus of Bergen's study of children playing with both talking and non-talking action figures based on a then-popular television program (*Rescue Heroes*, 1999–2013). Her work confirms the importance of considering specific design affordances in discussions of the limiting effects of licensed toys on children's play and imaginations. Overall, the play practices of the children who engaged with the talking toys and non-talking toys included many of the same actions and language, and none of the children were overly deferential to the *Rescue Heroes* narrative. However, the "children who played with the talking toys were more likely to have a rescue hero theme"[22] and tended to repeat the phrases and sounds made by the toys. Bergen concludes that talking toys have "highly salient affordances" that are specific to the individuals and contexts involved. Yet she also argues that the impact of these affordances can in turn be limited by physical, developmental, or other perceptual constraints. Here, Bergen introduces a crucial nuance to the discussion of affordances within technologies designed specifically for children, reminding us that children's perceptions fluctuate, change, and mature as they gain experience and move through the stages of cognitive development.

Research led by Plowman explores and challenges the idea that electronic toys afford constrained and repetitive interactions. In a study conducted with Luckin in 2004, children were asked to play with "smart toys" based on characters from a popular educational children's television program (*Arthur*, 1996–present).[23] The toys consisted of stuffed animals that featured motorized movements and embedded electronic chips designed to recognize certain inputs, and came with an accompanying, licensed CD-ROM game. In terms of scripts and affordances, Plowman and Luckin found that in some cases, children integrated the toys' technological features into their broader play, combining them with non-technological themes and playthings. For instance, the *Arthur* toys contained a time-telling feature. Some of the children were observed incorporating themes of bedtime and wake-up time when playing with the toys, a phenomenon the researchers thought was at least "partly attributable" to the toys' design.[24] Like Bergen, Plowman stresses the importance of acknowledging the perceptual differences between children of various ages. For instance, in the Arthur doll study, "Some children knew batteries powered the toy, although younger children tended to think it had feelings and could think and talk on its own."[25]

Plowman also emphasizes the importance of considering functionality and usability. The children in her study frequently became frustrated with the toys' design limitations, particularly when interacting with electronically enhanced features or the accompanying interactive CD-ROM game: "Many of the children in the study found that the talking became monotonous or irritating and preferred to switch it off."[26] These findings highlight the important role that child users play in determining the contexts of a technology's use – even when opportunities to directly influence design or shape affordances are out of reach. Plowman's study also reveals the limitations of marketing rhetoric and design intentions in determining how an artefact is ultimately used. Although the *Arthur* toys were promoted first and foremost as "interactive learning partners," children played with them in unpredictable ways – they sometimes became bored and refused to engage with them, and at other times integrated them into daily domestic schedules and traditional toy play. Plowman's research demonstrates the significance of context and the plural nature of "user experience."

Commercializing Gameplay

In order to better understand how the commercial priorities underpinning digital playgrounds can become concretized at a structural level, thereby affording certain types of play while restricting others, a critical consideration of the interplay between design and narrative and discourse is required. The embedding of commercial priorities manifests as design features and as part of the underlying program code, but also as reward systems, plot developments, and official game rules. When design and discourse are devised to operate in concert with branding and cross-promotional strategies, the prominence of the underlying consumerist ethos increases. Accordingly, when a particular commercial interest, such as raising consumer awareness about a new product, is supported at various levels of the game's design and implementation, its power to shape the parameters of gameplay increases substantially. In short, when the intended uses and interpretations become technologically embedded or otherwise afforded, their significance in setting the terms of play becomes more apparent.

While many of the commercial features found in children's online games are portrayed as optional, their close alignment with optimal or successful gameplay can also grant them preferred status. For instance, pay-to-play content is frequently depicted as enabling a better, more comprehensive, or more effective play experience. Even in games where engaging in pay-to-play is not a firm requirement, purchase of the additional levels, tie-in toys, or virtual currencies on offer is almost always linked with highly visible – and heavily promoted – benefits, rewards and special treatment. Commercial elements are frequently involved, and even central to the particular user configuration afforded by the games' designs and packaging. Here, the ideal player is depicted as the player who has purchased the premium, pay-to-play content. Similar dynamics are at work in games with other types of commercial content and priorities. In each case, the common theme is the equating of ideal play with engaging in a particular set of consumer behaviours – from viewing in-game advertisements and filling out surveys, to acting as a brand ambassador during interactions with other players.

Drawing on findings from my ongoing research on children's online games, virtual worlds, and connected console games, along with concepts and arguments found in the literature reviewed above, the remainder of this chapter outlines some of the methods used within digital playgrounds to shape, mobilize, and at times constrain children's play. In so doing, I argue that although the underlying play structures found in these spaces are not proscriptive or deterministic, they impose tangible limitations on in-game actions and provide players with a clear script (or at least a template) for how they *should* play. As such, embedded commercial structures come to function as informal, but not always contradictable rules of play, which impose a type of social order onto players and position them as consumers first and foremost. I have identified four main strategies commonly used by children's online and connected game makers to integrate commercial priorities into the very fabric of gameplay: velvet rope, cross-promotion, immersive advertising, and brand ambassadorship. Although very few of the games that I've analysed exhibit all four of these strategies, a great number of them contain one or more such features. Furthermore, the categories are not always mutually exclusive. As discussed in the final section of this chapter, they are in fact increasingly designed to intermingle as parts of a broader, synergistic system.

The Velvet Rope

A common promotional strategy found in digital games is what the marketing industry calls the "freemium" or "velvet rope" model. The terms apply to games, apps, and virtual worlds that initially appear to be free to play but contain numerous features and areas that are accessible only to those who purchase them (either through micro-transactions or through a paid subscription). While the paid-for content is not available to non-paying players, it is largely visible to them. The advantages and added value associated with the paid-for content are represented, or at least hinted at, within the free areas of the game – much as the VIP area of a nightclub or restaurant is set apart and sectioned-off (often with a velvet rope barrier, hence the name) but still visible to regular patrons. The idea is that eventually non-paying users will see or even just imagine sufficient benefit associated with paying for the "premium content" that

Table 3.1. Types of Promotional Content Found in Children's Connected Digital Games

Type of advertising	Description
Velvet rope	The inclusion, display, and promotion of pay-to-play areas, features, or other RMT that grant exclusive powers, benefits, or rewards to the players who buy them
Cross-promotion	Features that cross-promote the associated, overarching brand or property upon which the game is based, including its characters and/or tie-in products
Immersive third-party advertising	Features that expand upon traditional product placement through the integration of third-party brands or characters into the game environment
Brand ambassadorship	Features and activities that enlist players to serve as brand ambassadors by engaging them in forms of viral marketing, brand promotion, and social policing

they will start to engage in RMT. In the meantime, however, these games create a disparity between non-paying and paying players in access, affordances, and other advantages. Furthermore, in many instances, non-paying players are exposed to frequent promotional messages for premium content, and often encounter mounting pressure to upgrade their experience by paying for it.

Disney's *Club Penguin* (2005–17) provides an especially sophisticated illustration of the velvet rope approach. For much of its existence, the virtual world offered tiered membership options, which included the possibility of joining and playing some parts of the world for free. In order to access the site's full contents and features, however, a subscription membership was required. Here, the subscription membership was the premium experience showcased behind the velvet rope, and its promotion was integrated throughout the virtual world's narrative and gameplay mechanics. One way in which this was accomplished was through the central role fulfilled by in-game items. Although *Club Penguin* did not have game levels in the usual sense, progression and experience were instead represented through the accumulation and display of items such as avatar clothing, furniture, sports equipment, and other accessories. With a few notable exceptions, items could be obtained only by "purchasing" them using the official in-game currency, called "coins." All players earned coins by engaging in the activities and mini-games featured on the site. Earning coins was easy, and a large number could be amassed in a relatively short time. Until they were spent on items, however, the coins held no functional value of their own. Notably, a sizeable majority of in-game items could be purchased only by subscription members.

The items themselves fulfilled a range of functions. As every member, free or paid, started out with an unclothed, mostly identical Penguin avatar (the only customizable feature being feather colour), clothing and accessories enabled players to distinguish themselves from others. For instance, using wigs and clothing, players could assign a gender to their avatar and to themselves. Thematic costumes were useful for participating in both impromptu games of make-believe play and official, site-organized events. Items were also tied to action opportunities, in that a selection of special items "unlocked" their own exclusive avatar movement. For example, during the time of my study, wearing a construction hat allowed players to pull a jackhammer out of thin air and drill the ground beneath them. Items were also heavily promoted within the site's storyline, official announcements, and calendar of events. The world was continuously updated with new items, which were enthusiastically promoted in the in-game weekly newspaper (the *CP Times*) and on the website's front page (the landing page through which players would log in to the virtual world environment).

In addition to an avatar, *Club Penguin* players were each given their own "igloo" – a designated, personal "room" that they alone controlled access to, and that served as a sort of home base. This type of feature was common within children's virtual worlds of the era. It was configured within the site's narrative in part as a place to socialize with other players, by invitation only or by opening the space to the entire community of *Club Penguin* members. Above all, however, the igloo was configured as a space for players to display and arrange their items. It presented them with a unique opportunity to customize a small component of the game environment and provided them with a canvas for self-expression and community participation. It also enabled them to participate in the game's regular "Igloo Contests" – high-profile events in which players were invited to decorate their igloos (often in a specific theme, such as Halloween or sports) and submit them to a site-wide competition for the chance to win a prize (either coins or special items). During some of these competitions, all players were encouraged to visit participating igloos and vote for their favourites. Additionally, igloo customization could itself be a compelling part of gameplay, as a sort of iteration of virtual dollhouse play. As with avatar clothing and accessories, however, most igloo furniture and decorations were available for purchase only to players with a subscription.

In this way, access to an extensive and (predominantly) exclusive catalogue of items was a significant part of what made subscription membership appealing. Because the game was multiplayer, and social interaction was such a central activity, exclusive items were not merely encountered in the shops and promotional materials, but were in constant display on the bodies and in the igloos of other (subscription) players. The special actions and advantages these items bestowed were regularly performed for all to see, and they often filled a central role in whatever communal activity dominated at the time. Meanwhile, the ever-growing purse of coins inevitably amassed by non-paying members as they participated in the site and completed in-game activities served as a supplementary lure – a constant and highly visible reminder of the increasing number of items players *could* have access to, if only they switched to a subscription account. Additionally, access to purchased items was not permanent, but rather tied to the player's current membership status. Players whose subscription had expired saw their previously purchased items removed from their inventory and igloo, and placed in "Storage." Items in storage could still be viewed, but they could not be placed, worn, or used. Full access to these items could be regained only by renewing, and subsequently maintaining, the players' subscription membership.

The velvet rope model is designed as a promotional tool for stimulating desire and demand among non-paying players for the games' premium features and subscription membership options. In *Club Penguin* and other games like it, the velvet rope approach is also used as a form of bait and switch. While free gameplay is possible at first, it becomes increasingly difficult if not outright impossible to continue the game without the items and access that are granted to pay-to-play members. Today, this strategy most frequently appears in the form of micro-transactions, rather than monthly or annual subscriptions, wherein players are continuously invited to purchase the next level, better items, or enhanced skills. As in *Club Penguin*, although such pay-to-play features are publicly promoted as supplementary or premium, which implies that they are somehow superfluous to a standard or regular form of gameplay, they are often much more deeply embedded in the gameplay design than they initially appear. In fact, it is often only after a player has surpassed the initial levels or areas of the game world that the true significance of the so-called premium features is revealed. Rather than providing superfluous or added benefits, access to pay-to-play features is increasingly integral to successful and continued gameplay. Without it, the game serves primarily as an advertisement for itself – a sort of prolonged demo in which non-paying players can become invested in the game and its player community, but are prevented from engaging fully in either.

The velvet rope model defies traditional notions of fair play. Instead, it overtly places non-paying members at a distinct disadvantage, restricting their actions and access to the playing field. In so doing, it promotes the capitalistic belief that certain activities and affordances *should* be available only to those who pay for them. The resulting distinctions that arise between non-paying and subscription members establish a social hierarchy based almost entirely on willingness and ability to engage in (and afford) RMT. While social hierarchies are not uncommon within mainstream online games and MMOGs, research in the area suggests that they are normally based on player-driven criteria. Conversely, the hierarchy enforced by the velvet rope emerges out of, and works primarily to advance, corporate interest in driving and sustaining purchasing behaviours in order to increase profits. Even the limited access that non-paying members *are* given becomes problematic in this context, in that it always fills the concurrent function of providing a taste of the benefits of having a subscription. When used in this way, the velvet rope model inextricably links mastery and achievement – commonly understood[27] to be essential dimensions of the experience of playing a game – to monetary transactions.

Cross-Promotion and Branding

As described in chapter 2, many of the most popular connected children's games to emerge over the past fifteen to twenty years are either based on existing transmedia properties, or have themselves become the basis (or perhaps more accurately, the "flagship") for ancillary media and tie-in products. Indeed, there are several ways games can be and have been used as tools for cross-promotion, a term used here to describe the references, advertisements, tie-ins, and branding contained within a transmedia property that are aimed specifically at directing players towards the other media texts and licensed products in its own supersystem. Cross-promotion of this sort can manifest in games in various ways. For one, gameplay can be designed to afford, prioritize, and maximize players' exposure to cross-promotional content (or specific commodity) by directly linking its consumption to an in-game benefit. In other cases, players might be paid or granted an in-game reward for watching an advertisement for a tie-in toy. A new text, character, or product may be introduced to players through an in-game plot development. In yet other instances, cross-promotional content may itself be framed as a special feature or benefit – for instance, as occurs when a sneak preview of an upcoming tie-in film or episode is made available exclusively to a certain type of player (or fan). In this last example, special status is associated with the opportunity to see an advertisement before everyone else does.

While essentially any branded or transmedia-based game can be understood as employing this strategy, it is worth examining some specific examples to get better sense of how it manifests. Mattel's *BarbieGirls* provided an overt illustration of how virtual worlds can be used for cross-promotion. Although its narrative and aesthetics revolved around fashion and other themes associated with the Barbie doll toy line (and associated media tie-ins), in terms of both gameplay design and underlying commercial structures, *BarbieGirls* was very similar to *Club Penguin*. Much of the game centred on the accumulation and display of items as a way of customizing one's avatar and home base (or in this case, "bedroom"), as well as participating in collaborative events (such as multiplayer fashion shows or dressing up in costume for Halloween). As in *Club Penguin*, these items had to be "purchased" using an in-game currency ("B Bucks"), which could be earned by participating in various activities, such as completing mini-games. Moreover, although the game was initially free to play, most items were available for purchase only by players with a paid membership (which, for a short time, was linked to the purchase of a real-world commodity – a Barbie-shaped USB stick). Where *BarbieGirls* diverged from *Club Penguin* most significantly was in its incorporation of cross-promotional content into this economic relationship. The easiest and quickest way to earn B Bucks was to visit the cinema, where players could watch trailers for upcoming Barbie direct-to-DVD movies and other Barbie-related media products in exchange for significant sums of in-game currency.

In most of the games that I've looked at, however, cross-promotion seeps into gameplay in less direct ways. For instance, video ads for ancillary media could also be found in Nickelodeon's *Nicktropolis* (2007–10). *Nicktropolis* was one of the first commercial MMOGs introduced in follow-up to the early successes of *Club Penguin* and *Webkinz*, and it went through several transformations over the course of its three-year lifespan. Nonetheless, the game was consistently mobilized to cross-promote Nickelodeon media properties. Ads for Nickelodeon television shows appeared throughout the game in the form of clickable banner ads and video clips that ran while the game was loading onto the user's browser, as well as on embedded "TV screens" contained within the game's GUI, which aired trailers and even full webisodes. The layout of the world was akin to that of an urban shopping mall, with several common or central areas from which players could navigate into a range of thematically distinct "rooms," most of which centred on either a specific Nickelodeon transmedia property (e.g., the *SpongeBob SquarePants* "Bikini Bottom" room) or that of a third-party advertiser (e.g., in 2009, in conjunction with the release of the feature film, a *Harry Potter and the Half-Blood Prince* area was temporarily added). In the case of *Nicktropolis*, players were not "paid" to watch these ads, as they were in *BarbieGirls*. Nonetheless, frequent exposure to the embedded ads was strongly afforded through the emphasis the game-play design placed on "exploration." The game was set up as a sort of ongoing scavenger hunt, through which players earned currency and obtained unique items by finding them through a systematic exploration of the world's rooms and areas. Not coincidentally, treasures were most frequently found in rooms containing cross-promotional content.

The cross-promotional dimensions of transmedia properties are well established within the literature. Rather than focus on a single text or artefact, Kapur observes, cross-promotional strategies now emerge from the outset as portfolios of interconnected products, media formats, and activities. Increasingly, the transmedia texts themselves are created with these multiple formats and entry points in mind. Stories are written across texts, with the expectation that readers (or players) will grasp their full meaning only when the texts are positioned in concert. Perpetuating an endless, or at least ongoing, cycle of consumption is clearly a driving factor for the growing number of producers and other corporations currently engaged in the mobilization of transmedia intertextuality as a self-promotional or cross-promotional strategy. But consumerism permeates the meaning-making engaged in by players, readers, and audiences as well. Kinder argues that engaging with a transmedia supersystem provides "an entrance into a system of reading narrative – that is, a means of structuring characters, genres, voices, and visual conventions into paradigms, as well as models for interpreting and generating new combinations."[28] These models privilege and extend consumerism as the primary organizing system, and as such "help prepare young players for full participation in this new age of interactive multimedia – specifically, by linking interactivity with consumerism."[29]

Despite all of this, there has been a widespread reluctance, within the children's industries and public discourse, to acknowledge the highly commercial dimensions and intentions of most cross-promotional games. This is particularly odd, given the pushback that has emerged around child-specific advergames and branded games. Although transmedia games clearly also function as advertisements, oftentimes very effectively, they are rarely labelled as such. Indeed, in many cases, such titles have even been described as "ad free" by journalists and teachers alike, presumably because there are no third-party advertisements. Of course, their assessment overlooks the possibility that the corporations that own these games simply want to avoid promoting the competition or otherwise diluting their own promotional messaging. Concurrently, within academic and public debates about the commercialization of children's online play spaces, focus has similarly fixed on third-party advertising as a main point of concern.

A key example of the emphasis placed on third-party advertising can be found in the numerous studies and policy discussions centred on the prevalence of unhealthy food ads within children's websites and online games. The lack of attention given to content that seeks to promote a property's own media brand or tie-in products extends to games in which cross-promotion and velvet rope models overlap significantly – a strategy that is becoming increasingly popular with the normalization of micro-transactions throughout the gaming landscape. This is true even when the thing being promoted is a distinct commodity, rather than simply an invitation to expand the narrative experience or deepen one's sense of mastery over it. The fact that it belongs to the same story or character seems to efface its underlying promotional function. Or at least, it does for many of the adult stakeholders involved in the ongoing discussions about children's digital play. For the kids who actually play these games, I'm not convinced that this is in fact the case.

Immersive Third-Party Advertising

Within the children's digital playscape, third-party advertisements are rampant. From banner ads and videos that play while a game is loading, to embedded brand imagery and in-game product placement, this environment has traditionally featured a disproportionate amount of advertising and promotional messaging, particularly when compared to the mainstream games market. Indeed, as I've argued elsewhere, for many years, children's games served as a testbed for a wide range of new in-game advertising and marketing strategies. There are likely numerous reasons for this. For one, during the first decade or so of children's online gaming, most child-specific titles, and most of the games that children themselves flocked to, were free to play, and they generated revenues primarily through the incorporation of third-party ads. Additionally, children represent a lucrative, sought-after market segment, not only for the massive profits they generate for the children's industries, but also for the influence they yield over household purchases. Whereas advertising to children through traditional media is regulated and at times limited by government and industry, there are very few restrictions on advertising to children in digital games.

This situation is compounded by recent innovations in the types and depths of advertising strategies found within children's digital play spaces – especially online and connected titles – of which immersive advertising is a key example. Here, third-party advertisements, products, brands, or promotional messages are integrated directly into the gameplay design. The approach is intended to maximize players' engagement with the content being advertised, as well as enable tracking of players' ad exposure. In some cases, monitoring of players' interactions with the ads extends to the types of responses evoked, what the players say to one another about the ad or the product being advertised, as well as other forms of contextual data. As mentioned above, the immersive advertising approach was introduced and trademarked by Neopets Inc. in the early 2000s. More than merely including a static advertisement as part of the virtual world environment, immersive advertising consists of an interactive and deeply embedded form of product placement that allows players to engage with and even inhabit the advertising content. Since then, it has become commonplace. Accordingly, it has evolved significantly in the complexity and the diversity of its applications.

For instance, for a time in the early to mid-2000s, *Neopets* featured an immersive advertising campaign for McDonald's. It included an in-game restaurant where players could purchase McDonald's food items for their virtual pets, collect McDonald's-themed stamps, and acquire Happy Meal branded special items. Players could also compete in a McDonald's-themed "secret image" game, in which two players raced to be the first to identify the contents of a distorted image that gradually became clearer and easier to identify as time elapsed. Most, if not all, of the images featured in this game consisted of known McDonald's food items or mascots. Notably, the McDonald's campaign was just one of several observed during my study that promoted unhealthy foods, or foods high in salt, fat, and sugar. Other examples included Heinz EZ Squirt (multi-coloured, child-targeted variations of the best-selling ketchup brand) and Lucky Charms (a high-sugar cereal with a long history of advertising to children).

At the time, the immersive advertising approach of *Neopets* represented a significant departure from the type and volume of promotional content typically found in children's digital games and websites. Indeed, up until this point, product placement in digital games was relatively uncommon outside of a few important, yet infrequent, exceptions. For instance, at least since the 1980s, hundreds of racing games have featured actual car models, as well as in-game advertisements for car brands and car-related products. But apart from racing games and advergames, the incorporation of product placement and other forms of third-party advertising was a relatively underused strategy. As Bogost suggests, this is "possibly as a result of the small intersection between credible scenarios for real-world products and commercial videogame themes," which predominantly gravitate towards the fantastic.[30] *Neopets* was thus at the vanguard of a fundamental shift that unfolded in the early 2000s in how, and to what extent, promotional content was incorporated into digital games.

The *Neopets* approach was also unique in its seamless integration of product placement within the game's narrative and its "mechanics" (e.g., how the game is played, how in-game actions are made). Prior to this, product placement in games often involved displaying a static image of a product or a brand name somewhere in the game environment. Conversely, immersive advertising involved branding a space, object, or activity that players could engage with during gameplay. Immersive advertising afforded active and repeated user interactions with the product – interactions that unfolded repeatedly over an extended period of time and were embedded within the user's overall play experience. The approach relied heavily on transmedia intertextuality, and as such can be understood as analogous to the cross-promotional tactics described above. Immersive advertising similarly attempts to reproduce and extend the relationships that children traditionally cultivate with tie-in toys and fandoms. These interactions were further supported by audience measurement and tracking tools programmed into the very code of the game's software, which could be analysed, and potentially updated, in real time. Where immersive advertising diverges from cross-promotion is in comprehensiveness and exclusivity. Because these are advertising campaigns, paid for by third parties, they are typically contained in scope and length. Once one campaign ends, the space and players are made available to the next paying customer.

With the arrival of new gaming genres, applications of the immersive advertising approach have evolved accordingly. A prime example can be found in the *LittleBigPlanet* (*LBP*) game series (originally developed by Media Molecule), in which players are provided with tools for creating their own games and other content, including items, songs, and costumes that can be shared with other players through a built-in distribution system. The series includes three titles – *LittleBigPlanet* (2008), *LittleBigPlanet 2* (2011), and *LittleBigPlanet 3* (2014) – all exclusive to Sony PlayStation web-enabled console systems, a website (LPB.me), four spin-off games, and streamlined versions of the original that can be played on Sony PlayStation portable gaming devices (PSP and PS Vita). Since the series was launched in 2008, *LittleBigPlanet* players have produced and shared over ten million levels. These player-created games are largely made up of a combination of original creations, remixed items, and customized content, which the players discover as they navigate through different areas and levels of the game. However, players can also purchase DLC, such as costume packs to dress up their avatars, called "Sackboys," and level creation kits. The DLC can be purchased in-game via the *LBP* Store, using an integrated RMT system. When the game first launched, a limited number of DLC packs were available, and pertained largely to a selection of relatively generic themes, some seasonal and some genre-based. A small number of them were free.

It is within this unique context that *LittleBigPlanet*'s iteration of immersive advertising emerged. As the game progressed, a growing number of the DLC packs contained characters and themes drawn from third-party media properties. It soon became clear that these DLC packs were officially licensed by the property owners, and represented a new form of third-party, cross-promotional, transmedia advertising. Initially, most of the branded kits and costume packs available in the *LBP* Store featured characters and themes from classic Sony PlayStation games, such as *Metal Gear Solid* and *Heavenly Sword*, and longstanding transmedia properties, such as the Marvel superheroes and Disney's *Pirates of the Caribbean*. With the arrival of *LittleBigPlanet 2*, however, new patterns began to emerge in the subject matter and timing of new DLC releases. Specifically, DLC packs, especially those featured on the store's front page and on LBP.me, began including an increasing number of third-party transmedia properties, several of which aligned with real-world marketing campaigns, release dates, and branding initiatives.

By the time the game's sequels were released, the store featured several licensed creation kits containing characters and themes linked to recently released films or videogames.[31] For example, *The Muppets* costume packs were introduced a couple of weeks after the Disney feature film hit theatres, while the *Infamous 2* mini pack became available about a month after the game was released on the Sony PlayStation 3. In some ways, the DLC packs were configured as a type of digital merchandise, through which fans of the transmedia property could express their fandom and extend their engagement with a beloved text. The emergence of these packs during the early stages of the release cycle, however, suggests that the DLC packs also served a concurrent, promotional function. And yet players still had to purchase them to access and create game levels with them. The DLC packs represented a new hybrid of RMT and immersive third-party advertising, wherein players paid not only to be advertised to, but also for the privilege of becoming part of the promotional machine. As players produced their own levels and avatars using the licensed content packs and published them to the broader LBP community, the DLC and its associated transmedia properties were promoted anew to other players.

Immersive third-party advertising can intersect in other important ways with cross-promotion and branding. In some games, the inclusion of third-party ads serves as a way of downplaying the self-promotional quality of the broader content. Cross-promotion of a transmedia property's other texts or tie-in toys can become effaced or subsumed by the presence of overtly promotional third-party advertisements, which stand in contrast and are sometimes labelled as such. For instance, during my analysis of *Neopets*, most of the third-party advertising I came across carried the disclaimer "This is a paid advertisement" written in small print either above or below the ad. However, when it came to areas that linked with or otherwise promoted the Neopets Trading Card Game, for example, no such disclaimer was provided. As discussed above, the cross-promotional function of transmedia children's games is largely overlooked as a form of marketing or advertising. The oversight is intensified when cross-promotional content is configured as the "other" of third-party ads.

Traditionally, the children's media industries and advertisers are restricted from engaging in this type of ambiguous blurring of ads and content. As discussed in chapter 1, television producers, broadcasters, and advertisers in Canada and the United States must follow regulations and industry codes that establish clear boundaries between promotional material and programming. Immersive advertising, however, seems designed to efface these very boundaries. Through a convergence of regulatory loopholes, jurisdictional ambiguities, and "after the fact" monitoring of individual companies' adherence to industry guidelines, a significant amount of the advertising that unfolds within this realm is kept in check only by the limits of what the players themselves will put up with.

Certainly, children do exert a significant amount of agency within these spaces. They can choose not to play games that contain too many ads or feature ads deemed to be overly disruptive or unsuitable, and they can simply ignore the ads altogether. They can also subvert and resist the "strategic limitations" of promotional content by bypassing it or finding workarounds, engaging in creative reappropriations, or forming their own negotiated and resistant readings. It is also worthwhile to consider that adult player pushback against in-game advertising effectively stalled its progress for multiple decades. Writing about product placement's long yet surprisingly peripheral history within the context of mainstream digital games, Bogost points to the "anti-advergames" movement, comprising groups who "have tried to take matters into their own hands and rally against the profusion of commercialization in games in particular."[32]

However, children's games have already followed a very different trajectory, where virtual pets have long been eating McDonald's fries, and unknown numbers of players have paid for the opportunity to dress their Sackboy in a trademarked Disney Princess gown. The norms are already established, and therefore much harder to resist and overturn. At this point, a sudden, concerted pushback of the kind described by Bogost is highly unlikely. Moreover, it's important to remember that not all children have equal access to the skills and knowledge required to establish agency.

Indeed, the research tells us that many young children struggle to discern hidden marketing messages, while others are not always able to fully comprehend the function, and especially intentions, of advertisements – particularly those crafted specifically for them, filled with familiar characters and messages of fun, happiness, and excitement. The prevalence and increasing *embeddedness* of immersive, hybrid, hidden, and unfair third-party advertisements within children's digital play spaces is problematic, no matter how clever and savvy children can be in response.

Brand Ambassadors

The last significant commercial strategy found in children's online and connected games is the mobilization of players as unofficial "brand ambassadors." Traditionally, the term "brand ambassador" describes a person who is paid by a company to endorse their brand or product. In recent years, more integrated and subtle iterations of the approach have emerged, particularly within social media forums. This includes paying or otherwise rewarding celebrities and opinion leaders to share pictures of themselves using specific products or brands, to discuss the brand in a positive light with followers, or to integrate it in some way as a part of a desirable lifestyle. It also includes a range of more diffuse tactics, in which average users become associated with a product or brand within contexts relevant to them and their personal networks. A common example is the Facebook practice of narrowly advertising to a specific user's Friends network that the user "Likes" a product or brand. The ads appear only on the Friends' news feeds, and oftentimes users are unaware that their Likes are being utilized for this purpose. Diffused brand ambassador strategies are fuelled by the unpaid, affective labour of average users (or players), and they unfold within quotidian contexts and everyday use as users engage with one another and with the broader culture.

Within children's online and connected games, the diffused version of the brand ambassador strategy crops up. In games that employ a velvet rope model, the special status or benefits accorded by the game design to players who have a paid subscription or who have purchased exclusive RMT items is often communicated to other players in some way. For instance, players' status as a VIP may be represented in some feature of their avatar's appearance (e.g., an embedded special icon), or through the presence and/or variety of their clothing and other items in their possession. In others, wearing or displaying exclusive items purchased through RMT can serve the same function. In *LittleBigPlanet*, player-made game levels featuring cross-promotional, branded stickers, backgrounds, and soundtracks work to promote the RMT pack itself, as well as its associated transmedia brand. On one level, these marks of distinction generate the added value of the games' pay-to-play features, providing paying customers with additional benefits and services that would justify the ongoing financial investment required to maintain a monthly paid subscription or engage in micro-transactions. However, they also remind both paying and non-paying players alike about the existence of these exclusive features and accentuate their desirability. By embodying and showcasing the special status associated with a game's velvet rope features, paying players serve as living, breathing promotional vehicles for them.

Another strategy found in children's virtual worlds and MMOGs was to embed promotional messages in the games' chat system designs. Each of the games examined in my study contained a safe chat mechanism aimed at providing younger players with a more controlled and heavily moderated forum for interacting with others. This appeared primarily in the form of programmed limitations on what players could say to one another through the in-game chat systems, as well as the absence of tools that would enable direct and private inter-player communication (such as direct chat or mail – both features commonly found in mainstream virtual worlds and connected games). Within the six games I analysed, the primary safe chat mechanisms used were dictionary chat, which limited in-game text input to words that appeared in a pre-existing list or inventory, and predetermined chat, through which engaging in inter-player communication meant making selections from a drop-down menu of available phrases. Notably, three of the games included overt references to products and brand names within a non-negligible portion of their predetermined chat phrase options. The incorporation of branded phrases into children's chat represents a particularly alarming demonstration of how game design can be used to advance commercial priorities – in this case, conscripting players as brand ambassadors by literally putting words in their mouths.

The branded chat phrases contained in these games were not always in the form of overt advertising slogans, and were not always explicitly promotional, in their contents and the language used. Most often, they instead consisted of conversational statements about a cross-promotional feature or product, or related to a third-party immersive advertisement found within the broader game environment. That said, the branded phrases I uncovered were invariably positive or even celebratory. Predetermined chat systems rarely enabled players to say anything critical or negative about the brands, pay-to-play features, or third-party advertisers. In fact, only one of the branded phrases recorded in my study allowed players to communicate dislike about a branded feature: *GalaXseeds*

Table 3.2. Cross-Promotional and Third-Party Mentions in Predetermined Chat Systems

Game	Total phrases available	Cross-promotional phrases	Phrases referencing third-party ads
BarbieGirls	323	45	30
Club Penguin	322	0	0
GalaXseeds	8,200	0	17
Nicktropolis	634	237	0
Toontown	228	0	0

(2007–2010) players had the option of saying "I don't like Hive'n'Seek," in reference to an in-world, multiplayer game (based on the traditional hide-and eek) sponsored by Post Honeycomb cereal brand.

In all three of the virtual worlds that featured branded chat phrases (*BarbieGirls, GalaXseeds,* and *Nicktropolis*), there was a clear connection between the way in which the way the chat system was used as a promotional device and the game's underlying commercial structures. Games featuring third-party ads also featured branded phrases containing references to those same ads or to their subject matter. Games driven by cross-promotional strategies featured branded phrases relating to tie-in media and transmedia intertextuality. As discussed elsewhere, this suggests that branded chat was used largely as a way of extending or supplementing promotional initiatives. The overall proportion of phrases dedicated to brands and product references found in these three games is also noteworthy. This is especially true given the generally limited range of chat phrases, themes, and ideas that are made available to players through the predetermined chat system. For instance, the *BarbieGirls* virtual world safe chat system contained only 323 predetermined phrases, touching on a highly limited range of topics and sentiments. Nearly a quarter (23 per cent) of them contained promotional references – to the Barbie transmedia brand, toy tie-ins, or third-party product lines.

As mentioned, the clear majority (all but one) of the branded chat phrases recorded in my study were highly positive in tone and sentiment. This trend was particularly explicit in *Nicktropolis,* a virtual world used by Nickelodeon to cross-promote its television shows, films, and other web properties. The game featured a safe chat system in which over a third of the available chat options (37 per cent) were cross-promotional. It included phrases such as "Wahoo! There's a new '*Zoey*' in TurboNick!" in reference to the television series *Zoey 101,* and "'*Unfabulous*' is my favorite show!" in reference to the television series *Unfabulous.* It also contained catch phrases associated with its television shows, such as "It's time to Jo-ordinate!" – a phrase used by the main character of the popular Nickelodeon sitcom *Just Jordan*, as well as phrases about specific characters and plotlines relating to its transmedia properties. For example, players could state, "My bending skills are unparalleled!" in reference to the magical abilities of characters of Nickelodeon's widely popular *Avatar: The Last Airbender* media brand. Branded chat and velvet rope strategies also overlapped in some of the games examined, turning players into brand ambassadors for paid subscription membership areas, status, and other perks. Among the three games that featured a subscription membership option (*BarbieGirls*, *Club Penguin*, and *Toontown*), a significant portion of the branded chat phrases referred directly to features and areas that were available only to subscription holders.

The inclusion of branded chat phrases represents an attempt to substitute spontaneous peer interaction with corporately contrived promotional speech, thereby transforming players into brand ambassadors. When used by players during their interactions with others, they work to promote third-party ads, subscription memberships, and micro-transactions, as well as extend transmedia intertextuality. In the cases outlined above, it is important to note that this attempt further involves the appropriation of a self-described safety mechanism as a vehicle for commercial interests. Players, and their parents, likely have very different reasons for using the safe chat system. For some, it may present a desirable alternative to more open systems, through which the child may encounter inappropriate themes or troubling interactions. For others, it provides a practical way to transcend personal limitations vis-à-vis the technical skills or literacy required to engage in (timely) text typing. No matter the users' motivations, however, accessing the safe chat system often meant receiving an arsenal of tools built for spreading promotional messages. This is particularly troubling, given how few alternative options were provided to these players in the form of non-promotional phrases, let alone those that touch upon equally compelling topics.

When Stories, Designs, and Commercial Priorities Align

Over the years, many different types and genres of children's digital playgrounds have been designed to serve, at least in part, as forums for promotional and other commercial interests. As commodities, children's games are embedded in marketing texts, ads, and imagery that serve to position them within a specific niche market, in which children are the primary consumers. However, the commercial processes and strategies contained within many of the most popular connected and online game titles extend much farther than the initial "point of sale." Indeed, many of the titles described thus far contain mechanisms, content, and other features aimed at sustaining cycles of consumption, fostering fandom and transmedia intertextuality, and establishing open lines of communication between the children's industries and child players. While much of the scholarship in this area emphasizes the open-ended, player-driven, collaborative, and social dimensions of digital play, these qualities are not always readily afforded by the types of action opportunities, storylines, and commercial structures that characterize much of the children's connected gaming landscape.

Instead of challenging lingering concerns about the limiting potential of commercial narratives and packaging for children's play, a closer look at the design features found within several cross-promotional digital games shows that this potential is actually much greater and is more deeply embedded than presumed. These games do not merely contain discursive and aesthetic elements that advance transmedia intertextuality or promote third party advertisers. Rather, they afford and limit players' in-game behaviours, interactions, and even speech at the structural level of the GUI programming or software code. In short, the games contain multiple, oftentimes overlapping, design affordances aimed explicitly at aligning users' in-game activities and experiences with the game owners' underlying business interests. Here, design affordance does not simply refer to what is available within a technological device or artefact, but rather to what presents itself as the most appropriate or most natural action to take. In digital games, however, design affordances take on heightened importance, as intended uses are more easily imposed on users through their translation into software code, and their integration into the technical system upon which the game world operates.

In games, desired player moves can be automatically rewarded by the system (in points, currency, or special access), while undesired actions can be omitted through exclusion. If the game code does not let you command your avatar to jump or to say the phrase "Go away," then short of hacking the system, you will not be able to perform these actions. At least, not within the context of the game world. The roles of narrative and packaging within this dynamic are ambiguous, as established within previous work in the area, but nonetheless warrant further consideration. Within many of the games I have analysed, commercial priorities are not only embedded at all three levels – i.e., in the design, as part of the storyline, and in how the game is described and managed by its corporate owner – but coordinated to operate in mutually supportive ways. Affordances that are consistently presented within a game's design, narrative, and packaging have a much greater potential to shape gameplay and guide player behaviour. They strongly suggest what the game "is" and how it is "intended" to be played, reward compliance, and minimize opportunities for divergence.

There is much more going on in children's play spaces than a mere expansion of transmedia intertextuality or conveyance of a "pedagogy of consumption." In so many children's titles containing cross-promotion, RMT, or third-party advertising, consumerism is configured as an integral part of successful gameplay. Rather than merely emphasize the acquisition of collectibles or accessories (although this is certainly part of it), these games equate consumer ideology and its associated practices with play itself. Of course, branding initiatives are often described as attempts to build and mobilize emotional bonds with consumers. Children in particular frequently develop emotional bonds with toys and media characters, and this tradition is widely encouraged and enabled by adults. Children's complex and intimate relationships with material goods and transmedia properties represent a core characteristic of contemporary childhood, and as such form the basis of innumerable branding initiatives and transmedia strategies. Previous research demonstrates that children can similarly form emotional relationships with brands and corporations, developing brand loyalty or "Lovemarks" that stretch from one product or experience to the next.[33] That these relationships might extend to a key area of children's everyday lives – play – is therefore unsurprising. But it certainly challenges dominant notions of children's play as an extra-economic space for creative autonomy and self-actualization.

From *Neopets* to *Club Penguin* to *LittleBigPlanet*, many children's games contain features that foster and mobilize children's emotional investment, whether vis-à-vis an avatar or virtual pet, regarding social relationships and interactions with the broader player community, or centred on a sense of pride and ownership over in-game digital creations. Once invested in this way, child players generate a crucial form of affective labour, as they come to not only learn, but also perform and reproduce the game's underlying consumerist ideology. Because so many popular children's titles are linked with transmedia properties, a concurrent goal driving this process is the extension of children's investment and labour contributions to the world beyond the game – joining fandoms, developing brand loyalty, and purchasing ancillary products and media texts.

Questions and concerns about the commercialization of digital play are not limited to children's scholars. While the children's gamescape contains uniquely visible and highly concentrated cross-promotion and advertising, mainstream games are not impervious to commercialization. As discussed previously, this is in fact increasingly the case. Accordingly, numerous mainstream game scholars have discussed the political-economic implications of the commercialization of games, questioned the repercussions for internet governance and user rights, and raised concerns that deepening links between games and real-world economics are detrimental to the play experience. For example, Castronova warns that the more real-world meaning permeates online play spaces, the more likely it is that "their status as play spaces will erode, and norms of contemporary Earth society will increasingly dominate the atmosphere."[34] Allowing economic imperatives to encroach upon digital play spaces, he warns, could compromise players' rights to enjoyment, leisure, and escape from the widespread commercialization of the real world. The more real-world economics and laws are applied to game spaces, the more players' own actions and decisions will start to carry real-world consequences – and the less play-like the whole thing will become. Of course, Castronova's argument relies on a definition of play in which games are fundamentally separated from the real world – an approach that overlooks the quotidian experiences of actual players and the myriad functions play fulfils within their lives.

A more compelling argument is found in political-economic analyses of what happens to players' agency and freedom in spaces where they are configured primarily as "key selling points" or recruited to serve as brand ambassadors. Connected games often rely on player participation, to function as intended (e.g., many contain quests or other activities requiring more than one player to complete) and to attract and retain new players. In games that revolve around peer play and social interaction, the gameplay experience depends on the quality and diversity of the social relationships available. In games where user-generated content (UGC) is central, the gameplay experience relies on a steady supply of new player-made content (e.g., game levels), as well as a constant flow of players to engage with it and potentially give feedback. Lastly, for games featuring third-party advertising or other marketing activities, the more players who view or engage with the ad, the higher their value as an "audience commodity."[35] The presence or absence of an adequately sized and sufficiently active player base can therefore be a key determinant of an online game's ultimate fiscal and cultural success. However, when players become such an integral part of a game's commercial system, they also become subject to much higher levels of management and corporate control.

When users are positioned within a game system not merely as players and consumers of a finished product (or service), but also as a key selling point, as brand ambassadors, and as producers of content, their behaviours and compliance with corporate priorities become of increasing import. Because players are unpredictable, the more emphasis is placed in a game's underlying business model on adequate and appropriate player involvement, the more impetus there will be to incorporate design features or rules of play that will help increase the likelihood of desirable player behaviour. Conversely, rules and design features may also be put in place in order to prevent players from devaluing the brand through misbehaviour or from failing to fulfil their commercialized "duties" as members of the player population. The aims and brand image of each game, the business and revenue models that it uses, along with the perceived needs and vulnerabilities associated with the targeted demographic or consumer market, are all factors likely to influence how and to what extent this relationship will ultimately manifest as part of a game's design.

When compared to games that are truly ad-free – in that they are not only devoid of third-party advertising but also do not contain a heavy emphasis on cross-promotion, tie-in products, or RMT – commercially infused children's titles tend to provide players with a narrow scope of action opportunities and a limited toolset for creating content and communicating with others. For example, the restrictive designs and limited interactivity of the early child-specific virtual worlds that I studied in the late 2000s distinguished them considerably from the sprawling, three-dimensional, rich graphic environments that were fast becoming the standard among mainstream virtual worlds and MMOGs. In each case, player behaviours were furthermore constrained by the game's implicit linkage of player agency with commercial priorities – wherein players had to pay to gain access to a fuller range of action opportunities, areas, or creative freedoms. In each case the result was similar, in that the promise of a massively multiplayer gameplay experience was not adequately sustained by the shape (e.g., affordances, action opportunities, rules of play) or the contents (e.g., narrative structures, cross-promotion, commercial emphasis) of the games' designs. As described above, I have found evidence of the same correlation in other genres of children's online games, connected console games, and mobile games as well.

By creating opportunities for children to play with digital versions of their favourite toys and media brands, all within the confines of a corporately controlled and branded environment, the children's industries have gained unprecedented access to children's time, attention, and cultural practices. Corporate entities are making detailed, largely behind-the-scenes decisions about what children can and can't do within these spaces, what they can and can't say to each other, and what they can and can't contribute to the gaming landscape. These same entities are making powerful choices about what children are told about key facets of life online – from what constitutes "legal" and appropriate cultural participation to what their rights and responsibilities are as digital citizens. They are even presenting one-sided revisions of ethical doctrines such as fair use/fair dealing and fair play. In assuming such prominent roles in the social shaping of children's digital play, the children's industries extend their reach into play more generally, into the private or domestic spheres where much of children's interactions with connected technologies unfold, as well as into the secret spaces of childhood that previously were accessible only to children themselves. In many of the commercial strategies described above, promotion and play become nearly indistinguishable. In the case of young children, many of whom already have difficulty distinguishing between content and advertising, the increasing prominence of these strategies represents a highly deceptive and problematic new challenge – one that is seldom fully understood by parents or teachers and that has yet to be adequately addressed by policymakers.[36]

The mobilization of transmedia intertextuality as a self-promotional tactic deepens and solidifies the already complex relationship between commercialization and children's culture. When applied (or extended) to digital games, the approach advances the ongoing synonymizing of consumption and play, traditionally promulgated by tie-in toys, collectible card games, and the like. Within the traditional supersystem scenario, resisting this particular ethos often meant simply not purchasing ancillary products. And while the spread of transmedia intertextuality has resulted in the inclusion of an increasing number of cross-references, Easter eggs, and other narrative linkages between associated media texts and products, for the most part games and media are still made in ways that concurrently enable them to stand alone to some extent – to serve as an entry point for new audiences to build relationships with the transmedia property. In this model, while there can be immaterial costs associated with refusing to buy a tie-in toy or to watch the TV show spinoff of your favourite movie, these costs do not extend to that initial movie-watching experience – at least not unduly or to the point of disrupting your ability to access it in the first place. Within many of the children's games I've looked at, however, the idea that a text should also be able to stand alone as a distinct and gratifying experience no longer seems to apply. Instead, the games are embedded in storylines that are (presumably) told elsewhere, contain game areas and features that are accessible only via some sort of RMT, and segregate players and play spaces to manufacture social hierarchies that support and promote commercial interests.

Conclusion

As with any text or artefact designed for children, online and connected games are shaped by powerful and oftentimes conflicting ideas, desires, and assumptions about who children are, what their roles should be within digital culture, and what "good" play includes and looks like. These assumptions span the formal and informal rule systems contained within children's playthings, and they ultimately become embedded within the artefacts themselves as design features, narratives, and packaging. Just as critical scholars of technology argue that power relations are reflected and reproduced within features of the technological design, children's media theorists such as Kinder and Fleming describe that power relations, specifically market relations, are reflected and reproduced within features of the specific narrative structures used to generate transmedia intertextuality.[37] For instance, Kinder notes that flexible narratives and liminal characters are more likely to evoke feelings of empowerment and active engagement among players, even as they enter cycles of consumption driven chiefly by corporate interests and profit motives.

Uncovering how the design and arrangement of a technological artefact can establish and maintain a particular set of ideological assumptions and power relations is key to understanding their underlying meaning and hidden politics. As I have argued throughout the current chapter, doing so is crucial where the assumptions and priorities embedded at these three structural levels are designed to collude and coincide. When the synergistic associations that are required to produce cross-promotional tie-ins or generate transmedia intertextuality are implemented within the fully mediated context of a digital game, opportunities for divergence can be tightly controlled by what is included and excluded from the program code. The point is that a toy or game's narrative often *does* matter (at least to some extent) to the children who play with them. But it matters even more when that narrative is effectively supported by a design that pushes players in the same direction while concurrently limiting opportunities for divergence. It is not a coincidence that the tendency towards more limited designs, more constrained spaces, and more restricted affordances has characterized the children's online games landscape since it emerged in the late 1990s. Then, as now, children's media and toy companies have dominated the market.

It is of course important to remember that children's connected digital playgrounds are also and above all hybrid spaces – simultaneously operating as games, technologies, and media platforms, as well as sites of social interaction, creative expression, and cultural practice. The ambiguity of these spaces, and their concurrent function as sites of negotiation, meaning-making, and even, occasionally, political activism for the children who engage with them, is the focus of chapter 4. Nonetheless, as I have attempted to demonstrate here, throughout their brief history, these artefacts have functioned predominantly as promotional venues. Their popularity among young users has consistently been mobilized by the children's industries to extend the reach and presence of transmedia brands within children's lives. This is not accomplished merely through the incorporation of in-game advertisements, or by featuring a beloved media character, but rather through the increasingly sophisticated integration of commercial priorities within the narrative and design of the games themselves. Throughout this process, successful gameplay and "good" players become intertwined with brand values and, ultimately, with real-world market exchange.

4

From Rules of Play to Censorship

There are clear continuities between how children engage in traditional and digital play activities. Given the number of misconceptions and moral panics that continue to circulate around children's technology use, it is important to reiterate this fact, while situating digital play within a broader cultural-historical context and positioning its practice as one among many that contemporary children enjoy engaging in. But digital playgrounds are also distinct from their traditional counterparts. With a few important exceptions,[1] everything that appears *within* a digital game, virtual world, or mobile app is designed, predetermined, or vetoed by the adults who make and manage them. A digital game's makers not only decide what objects will appear in the game, and what the game will look and sound like, but they also choose what words can be uttered and what actions can (and can't) be undertaken by the players. When players engage in forbidden or unanticipated actions, the game's moderators or managers determine an appropriate response – from banning specific players, to omitting certain words from the chat system, to updating the program code to exclude those actions from the game.

This is not to say that traditional toys and play spaces aren't similarly influenced by ideas and rules introduced by adult designers, playground monitors, teachers, and parents. Most playground structures are designed in such a way that excludes children with physical disabilities. Many schools and day care centres have strict rules against rough-and-tumble play during recess. Similarly, parents place individual restrictions and expectations on children's play at home. But the rules imposed in such contexts are localized, mutable, and – to at least some extent – open to negotiation. Although traditional rules of play are not always self-evident, they are generally much easier to uncover and identify than the commercial mechanisms, design affordances, and programmed limitations found in online and connected children's games.

Conversely, the level and depth of top-down control available to the makers of digital playgrounds are unparalleled, only minimally regulated, and largely unchallenged.

Of course, this does not mean that children do not play a role in determining the parameters and contents of their online digital play. Quite the opposite. Children retain the ability to exert power by simply electing not to play, for instance; they can usually quit the game at any time. Some children refuse to use the games as intended – finding ways to work around design limitations and sharing alternative interpretations of the game's meanings with other players. Like any users of technological artefacts, children hold high levels of agency and situated knowledge, and their engagements with digital games and other play technologies necessarily include unanticipated uses and appropriations. These in turn produce outcomes that have not been pre-emptively addressed by the games' designs and rule systems.

Indeed, children's situated knowledge can and often does conflict with the assumptions made about children by designers, parents and teachers, and the broader gaming culture. At the same time, not all game developers seek to control player activities to the same extent, nor would they all benefit equally from a technically afforded alignment of user behaviour and corporate priorities. In fact, a growing number of child-specific and child-inclusive games are now designed and marketed as spaces that foster greater rights and freedoms, and that provide opportunities for emergent play and participatory cultural engagement, even among younger players. For example, a key selling point of the wildly popular *Minecraft* is its open-ended design and hands-off approach to game rules. In its original incarnations, the game did not contain any real instructions or tutorials on how to play the game, and many of its most beloved contents and activities were presented as emergent design features.

Under certain conditions, it is possible for emergent play and unanticipated uses to result in meaningful change, democratic rationalization, and transformation of a technology's design or implementation. For instance, children's unanticipated use of a particular design affordance can be reappropriated by the game's makers and inspire the expansion or modification of the original feature. Instances of subversive and emergent play can lead to player-driven reconfigurations of a game and its meanings. These reconfigurations can then become incorporated into official storylines or integrated into advertising and marketing materials. Although it is clear that design features, narratives, packaging, and formal and informal rule systems can at times function as technologically embedded play structures, children can and will nonetheless find ways to express and negotiate their own needs, interests, and ideas within and against such structures.

And yet.

Even though children do contribute to the social shaping of digital games technologies, it is important to remember that most connected games are not only designed by adults with their own goals and interests, but are also managed and monitored by them. Undesirable uses – and users – can be tracked, limited, and shut down. Sometimes these player management activities are enacted by algorithms (i.e., automated systems) that fail to consider context or intention. Unlike a traditional toy or playground, connected games are under the constant surveillance and partial control of their corporate owners. As mentioned above, if – or, more accurately, when – something unexpected happens, the game's owners are the ones who decide whether to allow it to continue, or incorporate it into sanctioned gameplay, or ban the activities or players in question altogether. How much a game's owner will try to control and manipulate player behaviour in accordance with corporate priorities can depend on a wide range of factors. For instance, the specific functions assigned to the game will likely play an important role, as will the amount of influence wielded by the player community, or by their parents and teachers, in accordance with the particular dynamic that has emerged between the game's owners and its users. Although at times child players (and their parents) do directly inform decision-making and design choices – as do regulatory bodies and social expectations – most of the maintenance work performed by children's game owners occurs behind the scenes. In many cases, decisions are black-boxed behind the UI: embedded in an inaccessible, proprietary, underlying program code, and enacted by complex, seemingly "neutral" algorithms. Others are protected as trade secrets and touched upon only vaguely in jargon-laden terms of service agreements, or they are presented as "improvements" that will benefit players and enhance the gameplay experience.

Technologies are often sites of struggle, as users, designers, policymakers, and other stakeholders vie to shape what the technology is, how it is used, and how it is perceived. In children's digital playgrounds, child players are arguably at the forefront of such a struggle. Despite their continued exclusion from most design processes and policy debates, children must be seen as active agents or relevant social groups with respect to the artefacts and spaces that are designed for and used by them. But it is a struggle in which children also have a clear disadvantage, where the playing field is explicitly and implicitly uneven. This chapter explores how these uneven power relations play out within children's digital playgrounds. It examines several forms of negotiation that take place between

players, game designs, and corporate owners. It furthermore considers
the delicate interplay of freedom and constraint that emerges out of this
dynamic. The aim of this discussion is to explore how the play structures
identified in the previous two chapters challenge and *are challenged by*
player agency, while also highlighting some of the many ways children
subvert rules, work around design features, and make games their own.

The Primacy of Rules in Digital Games

Foundational play theorists emphasize the crucial function of rules in
separating ordered games from free-form play. Huizinga argues that
the value of play comes from the fact that play brings a limited, tempo-
rary perfection into the imperfect confusion of everyday life through
the player's voluntary submission to a set of made-up rules. The rules of
play "[demand] order absolute and supreme. The least deviation from
it 'spoils the game,' robs it of its character and makes it worthless."[2] For
Caillois, games with rules are evidence of advanced civilization. As societies progress "from turbulence to rules" within their play, play itself is
transformed "into an instrument of fecund and decisive culture."[3] Both
theorists emphasize the importance of rules within their definitions of
play, along with the temporal, spatial, experiential, and ethical isolation
of games from everyday life. Similarly, Suits highlights the crucial dual
function of rules, which not only delineate the parameters and goals of
each specific game, but also evoke the very attitude required for a player
to engage meaningfully (and voluntarily) in gameplay. He concludes,
"To play a game is to engage in activity directed towards bringing about
a specific state of affairs, using only means permitted by rules, where the
rules prohibit more efficient in favour of less efficient means, and where
such rules are accepted just because they make possible such activity."[4]

The primacy of rules within modern play theories and definitions of
games is directly related to the notion of "play as progress" discussed in
chapter 1, and the ways this ideology highlights the rational qualities of
organized games and leisure. The privileging of formal rules supports
purposive understandings of play as a realm of activity with measurable,
instrumental outcomes. Playing by the rules is often linked with perceived
benefits, such as learning (and "learning to learn"), sportsmanship and
other prosocial attributes, along with the development of physical and
cognitive skills. Such associations reveal the underlying gender bias
found within many traditional definitions of games, which are drawn
primarily from a relatively narrow consideration of games and sports that
were historically associated with male leisure, from chess to basketball.
Yet even within works aimed explicitly at shifting the emphasis away from

the purposive and rational qualities of games, or towards play forms and players historically excluded from the discussion, rules remain a central theme. For some, such as sports scholar Gruneau, it is within the dialectical relationship between game rules and gameplay, "between socially structured possibilities and human agency," that play becomes a form of social practice.[5] For others, such as children's play theorist Schwartzman, it is in the transgression of game rules, and the subversion of the underlying social order that rules represent, that the transformative potential of play is realized.[6] In each case, rules fill an enormously important role within theories of games and play.

Within digital games, rules gain additional significance. Since rules can now be standardized and embedded at the level of the program or software code, these spaces can be designed to virtually exclude certain forms of deviation and rule-breaking. The dialectical dimension of the interplay that unfolds between rules, designs, and play within digital games is a key topic of interest within game studies. It is often approached as a sort of continuous dialogue unfolding between a game's players and its underlying system – its program code, rules, and features of its UI. Salen and Zimmerman argue that the rules generate "the formal identity" of a game.[7] More recent work in this area highlights the points of disjuncture that always exist between rules and design, and the space this provides for players to engage in unintended uses and unanticipated actions. These include cheating, exploiting glitches and workarounds, creative appropriations, and other expressions of player creativity and innovation. That these acts of agency remain possible within the fully constructed context of a technologically mediated, digitally encoded, and corporately controlled game environment is a fascinating and important phenomenon.

The rules contained within digital games more or less delineate how the game *should* be played. In some cases, they are mere suggestions. In others, however, they are material impositions. Whether they are ultimately obeyed, negotiated, ignored, bent, or broken, rules provide players with a shared toolset for measuring success and for distinguishing between "strategic and nonstrategic action" – the moves that will contribute to their advancement and result in rewards, and the moves that ultimately prove to be futile or even detrimental.[8] In their traditional form, a game's rules and other rational qualities, such as point systems, standardized equipment, or governing bodies, may shape gameplay, but they never fully determine its contents. Conversely, in digital games, player moves become standardized as action opportunities, while the rules of play are concretized within and enforced by the game's design. Within digital games, the primacy of the rule system is intensified by its technical mediation. The articulation of the game's rules, along with many aspects of their enforcement, is delegated largely to the technology itself. They are enshrouded in a black-boxed design that most users perceive as inaccessible and non-negotiable. The technologization of game rules thus alters the conditions within which divergence from the rules is even possible, let alone practical.

The situation is complicated to some extent by the presence and popularity of games designed to foster greater feelings of agency among players, while enabling the creation of player-driven, rather than system-driven, rules and objectives. Recent trends in this direction include the establishment of non-linear game genres, such as open-world or sandbox games, as well as the spread of tools and platforms for players to create and share their own UGC. Such shifts not only represent an important expansion in the types of play afforded by digital games, but also contribute to a deeper sublimation of the rules, parameters, and design limitations that are necessarily contained in the underlying game code. This in turn can also increase opportunities for emergent play – or *emergence* – a term used to describe the space that is "opened up" for player agency and unanticipated uses within any designed system. The term seeks to describe how "complex possibilities are the result of a simple set of rules" and can be applied to a broad array of gameplay and design phenomena.[9] Instances of emergence are evidence that the behaviour of an overall system cannot be "obtained" or predicted by "summing the behaviors of its constituent parts."[10] According to Salen and Zimmerman, emergent play can serve a variety of functions. In some cases, players might engage in forms of emergent play that overtly defy the programmed game rules. Such instances reveal both the "special disconnect between the rules of the system and the ways those rules play out" and the "friction that can occur between games and their cultural contexts."[11] Not only are game designs becoming more open-ended and unstructured, but as game systems become more complex they are also less predictable and more amenable to emergence in its many forms.

The relationship between a digital game's players, its rules, and the rules of its underlying system (herein referred to as "design rules") is *also* complex and at times unpredictable. It is important to acknowledge that emergence is always possible, and that players are never entirely rule-bound. That said, a digital game's underlying structure and social order carries disproportionate authority within this relationship. The official rules of a game, the way it is designed, what it contains, and how it is played are not trivial aspects of the gameplay experience. Nor are they always malleable or open to the whims and wills of its players. In many instances, design features, gameplay mechanics, and menu items set, or at least suggest, the rules of play by establishing the parameters and underlying "reality" of the game world. At times, they are akin to the rules of physics – representing the mostly unquestioned and largely unalterable properties inherent to a game environment. Other times, they emerge as any other game rule might – advancing an idealized vision of appropriate play, reflecting assumptions and biases, promoting corporate agendas and priorities – and as such present as rules that players might choose to follow, but might also choose to challenge or reject. Similarly, although the official rules of play can sometimes be ignored, bent, or even broken, in other instances they are not so easily negotiated. For example, some official rules can be embedded and imposed at the level of the game's design. Others are enforced by adults who are hired by a game's operators, such as professional moderators who monitor player interactions. Yet others are a combination of the two, as in companies that specialize in finding IP infringement in games and other online forums through the use of copyright bots and legal firms. Although players retain significant agency in their interactions with (and within) digital games, clearly the rules themselves also assume important new levels of primacy and authority within these spaces.

Design(ed) Rules

As argued above, the way a game is designed – the types of objects and spaces it contains, the moves a player can (and cannot) make, its internal physics, and so on – functions as its own sort of rule system. Play is guided and constrained by two key elements of a game's design: its affordances and, relatedly, its action opportunities. The term "affordances" describes the characteristics and action opportunities that are not only made available but privileged and prioritized to some extent. A design affordance does not simply refer to what is possible within a game (or other program), but rather what presents itself as the appropriate or most natural action to take when interacting with a particular technology. As Mateas and Stern observe, "There should be a naturalness to the afforded action that makes it the obvious thing to do."[12] The obvious thing to do when playing a game that has established rules and objectives is to try to win, to accumulate points, and to achieve the game goals. In digital games, these aspects of gameplay are translated into code and become part of the underlying system upon which the game world operates. Because the game rules are part of the program, certain player moves and activities are automatically rewarded (in points or currency) by the system. Although other action opportunities or emergent features may still be available or possible, they aren't recognized by the system as part of the ludic logic of the game. Traditionally, there is a clear link within digital games between affordance and ludic structure. The affordances that are present within a game's design therefore significantly shape the gameplay – by suggesting (both discursively and structurally) what the game "is" and how it is "intended" to be played.

For example, Disney's *Toontown* contained design affordances encouraging players to participate in the game's overarching narrative and underlying ludic system by completing multiplayer missions battling the Corporate Cogs. Completing "Cog Missions" was not only the most efficient way to level up one's avatar, but numerous facets of the designed environment reminded players of the importance of these quests. Several non-player characters (NPC) based on familiar Disney characters, such as Mickey Mouse and Donald Duck, were interspersed throughout the game world to "chat" with and provide information to players. These NPCs often invited players to participate in Cog Missions as part of their predetermined dialogue. Players who accepted a Cog Mission but were delaying commencing it would receive a timed message via pop-up window reminding them that their mission was waiting. Upon completion of one of the world's many standalone mini-games, players were automatically and immediately transported to the "Gag Store," where the items ("Gags") required to effectively complete Cog Missions were available for purchase using Jellybeans, the in-game currency. Since players earned those Jellybeans by completing mini-games, the direct link back to the Gag Store implied that players should now spend their Jellybeans on Gags – items primarily, if not solely, used in Cog Missions.

At the same time, there are also child-specific connected games geared towards unstructured play and social interaction. In games such as *Minecraft*, ludic objectives such as winning, competing, or achieving a set goal are available but secondary to the game's chief emphases on exploration, creation, and peer play. My research in this area has found numerous children's games that promote themselves as *social* playgrounds. These games often provide open spaces for engaging in make-believe play and role-play. Notably, however, the inclusion of such features does not necessarily translate into the provision of a greater number of action opportunities or moves through which players can freely express themselves or fully determine the contents of their make-believe play. Rather, games such as *Club Penguin* afford a type of peer play centred on the players' use of "performatives" – utterances and other speech (or in this case, text) acts that are themselves actions, or that serve as a key component of action.[13] Most children have extensive experience using performatives in their play, as they feature prominently in traditional forms of make-believe and imaginary play, both solitary and peer-based. Moreover, children commonly use performatives to establish, negotiate, and challenge a game's rules and parameters, as well as to assert (and reassert) their own roles, identities, and experiences within it.

Recall, however, that most of the child-specific digital playgrounds I have examined over the years impose heavy restrictions on players' in-game communication. As discussed in chapter 3, the safe chat systems found in many child-specific virtual worlds limited players to a very narrow range of speech options and topics. The alternative or regular chat options that were available either contained programmed restrictions on specific words (e.g., swear words, email addresses) or, more commonly, limited chat to words appearing on an approved list, a strategy I call "dictionary chat." These mechanisms automate part of the moderation, but they also extend it by preventing certain words from ever being uttered in the first place. In games with dictionary chat systems, this meant that most words ended up being excluded, along with the vast majority of misspellings and typos. An example from *BarbieGirls World* provides an apt illustration of the arbitrary nature of the type and range of words excluded through such systems, where during several months of my data collection, players were unable to say the word "lion." Given that the players of these games consisted of young children with varying and developing levels of literacy, such systems almost certainly encumber inter-player communication. The resultant censorship of players' speech seemed at odds with the concurrent emphasis the games' designs and narratives otherwise placed on performatives and make-believe peer play. At the very least, it introduces an unexpectedly strict set of rules about what themes, subject positions, and even topics players are allowed (or able) to make-believe *about.*

Another way that rules of play are embedded and expressed through design features is in the presence of multiple affordances involving virtual items. Many children's games position virtual items as props, status symbols, creations, or merely shared references for players to use in their make-believe play. But the meanings and functionalities associated with virtual items varies greatly from one game to the next. In *Minecraft,* for instance, players have access to hundreds of pre-made items (ready-to-use tools and other objects that come with the game itself), as well as to "blocks" of materials that can be combined in a multitude of ways to make their own (albeit predetermined by the program) items. Many of these items have multiple possible functions, and some contain emergent properties for players to discover through experimentation (or by visiting a cheat site). Conversely, in *Club Penguin,* most virtual items consisted of props or accessories that could be displayed but that had no inherent actions or "moves" of their own. There were several exceptions, including numerous hats that enabled players to enact a special "move" with their avatar whenever it was worn, but even the exceptions were often limited either to specific areas of the game world or to specific events.

Games also frequently afford forms of player interaction that are mediated through virtual items – through their display, manipulation, and sometimes exchange. As in *Minecraft* and *Club Penguin*, virtual items are also often afforded at different levels of a game (e.g., in its storyline, packaging, design), each of which supports the idea that items are important, valuable, and associated with successful gameplay. Players are frequently rewarded with virtual items, or with an in-game currency they can use to purchase items. As a result, items are tied to player progress and can at times function as an alternative (or supplementary) points system. Moreover, many games encourage players to customize their avatars using virtual items, and they make progress dependent on the level and properties of the items worn. Similarly, specific items can be required to complete certain missions, levels, or activities. In both cases, virtual items function either as a necessary step in a player's trajectory, or as a barrier to entry into the higher levels of a game for those who fail to obtain them. In most games, items have degrees of perceived and inherent (or pre-set) value: some items are rare, some are expensive, some have desirable properties or functions, and others do not. Virtual items are commonly the basis of in-game economies, are regularly linked in some way to players' progress, and frequently carry additional affective value among the players themselves. Notably, virtual items are also the basis of many of the real-world business models upon which contemporary games operate. Increasingly, virtual items can be obtained – sometimes exclusively – using real-world money, through in-game purchases, or through tie-in products containing redeemable codes. Within many games, virtual items form the basis of an important, yet implicit, set of rules about how to progress through a game, as well as how to assess the progression of other players.

Design limitations can also act like rules by determining what cannot be done within a game. For instance, the MMOGs in my study contained far fewer programmed moves than what was typically available to players of teen and adult-oriented MMOGs. They also contained extensive chat restrictions and provided few tools for other forms of in-game communication. These limitations advanced a fairly narrow vision of how the game was supposed to be played. For example, while Corus Entertainment's *GalaXseeds* players could walk, dance, and wave, they couldn't jump, kick, or throw. Such limitations concurrently reinforce the importance and emphasis placed on the game's affordances. *GalaXseeds* encouraged players to explore its many worlds in search of seeds and other treasures, but little could be done with the items and areas once they had been discovered (and/or collected). After a seed was acquired and planted, there was nothing to do but continue exploring. Once the seeds sprouted, their plants could be tended, but only intermittently (real time had to elapse between interactions). The player's "pod" (i.e., home base) could be decorated and rearranged. But the actions involved in these activities were all quite simple and quickly executed. The lack of follow-up or alternative action opportunities available within the game design pushed players back to what was available and afforded.

A game's design can also introduce implied rules and parameters that conflict with or even contradict its other rule systems. For instance, despite the rhetorical emphasis on make-believe play and creativity found in the games' official texts, descriptions, and promotional materials, none of the titles included in my analysis of children's virtual worlds provided players with tools for *creating* content. In fact, *GalaXseeds* was one of only two MMOGs available during this period that contained an in-game system for players to *exchange* virtual items. Notably, this feature was incorporated only after members of the player community had started engaging in the practice as a black market, using workarounds, and in contravention of the official rules of play (itself an interesting example of a disconnect between design rules and written rules of play). Relatedly, despite a shared emphasis on virtual items, none of the games I examined enabled players to design or make their own. The customization tools provided in all six games were highly limited, including those provided for avatar creation. For the most part, engaging in creative self-expression was encouraged, but afforded only through the purchase, display, and arrangement of a limited selection of prefabricated virtual items. Because those items were invariably commercialized, and oftentimes monetized, this furthermore meant that self-expression was positioned in these games as a privilege that one had to earn or purchase. The confounding of customization and consumerism with creativity presented a problematic, but not at all uncommon, vision of children's cultural production and agency. This in turn added to the ambiguity that surrounded the games' objectives and rules. These worlds were "open" but very contained, and they celebrated creativity that conformed to strict parameters.

Until the introduction of UGC games such as *LittleBigPlanet, Roblox* (2005–present), and *Minecraft,* digital playgrounds generally provided very few opportunities for players to directly affect items and environments.[14] UGC games, by contrast, contain a range of tools, templates, and spaces that players are encouraged to use to create their own levels, games, or other content (such as virtual items). These titles are more firmly centred on creative play, often lack in top-down structure, and contain (near) limitless possibilities. Such games are referred to as "sandbox games" which, as Weise suggests, "refers to open-ended game design, but there are many types of open-endedness. In the loosest sense almost any game that does not funnel player navigation into some obvious path could be considered sandbox."[15] All the same, many still see these games as "possibility spaces," in which players can explore, make choices, create, and remix items in unique, or at least highly individualized, ways.[16] In addition to several titles focused on original user-made content, many of the most popular UGC games provide tools and sanctioned forums for players to remix, appropriate, and otherwise engage with specific transmedia properties. Games such as *Lego Dimensions* and *Disney Infinity* offer players more or less undirected free play with familiar media brands and characters, where they can diverge from the official storyline, roam through its fictional world, and manipulate objects, spaces, and contexts.

At the same time, the terms "open-ended," "sandbox," and even "user-created" also function as marketing rhetoric, and as such are frequently mobilized as "key selling points" within game packaging and promotional materials. The terms are at times used to describe games that do not actually contain non-linear designs or afford limitless creative freedom. As Bak uncovered in her analysis of *Disney Infinity* (editions 1.0 through 3.0), while the game's marketing materials revolved around notions of child creativity, its design and gameplay mechanics imposed numerous limitations on players' agency and access. Many of these limitations reproduced Disney's broader, longstanding emphasis on extending whilst also maintaining full control over its intellectual properties. Although the game allowed players to engage with popular Disney characters, storylines, and settings – and even let players combine these elements in new ways – it did not allow them to stray very far from the official Disney script. As a result, "unlike the tools available to video game modders, which function at the level of code to permit both structural and aesthetic changes, *Infinity* users are restricted to highly structured customization without the possibility of reappropriating elements."[17] Although the game's promotional materials evoked a heavily romanticized vision of the child creator as "playfully excessive, unruly, unrestrained," its design, action opportunities, and programmed limitations left "little room for transgression or reappropriation of any sort." Here too, the design features worked to operationalize creativity as a relatively narrow set of activities and interpretations.

Through its affordances, limitations, mechanics, and even imagery, a game's design can introduce all sorts of abstract concepts into the gameplay experience. In *Disney Infinity*, the promise of *more* – of a blank canvas and the creative freedom to use it – was not limited to the game's marketing materials. It loomed throughout the early stages of gameplay as well.[18] The title sequence and tutorial stages repeated the idea that this was a game in which players used their imaginations. However, upon commencing gameplay, it became immediately clear that in order to exercise their imaginations, players first needed to purchase the proper real-world items. *Disney Infinity* was a toys-to-life title, wherein tie-in figurines, power discs, and other accessories not only facilitated players' progression and enhanced the gameplay experience, but were integral components of the game's mechanics and structure. Purchasing real-world (or tangible) toys did more than merely unlock new avatars and areas – it also opened up the creative capabilities of the game. Without these ancillary products, gameplay was extremely limited, especially regarding the creative features touted so heavily in *Disney Infinity*'s narrative and promotional materials. The design of the game thus enforced the broader, discursive emphasis found within *Disney Infinity*'s marketing materials on extending the digital gameplay experience into the real world, primarily by building a collection of figures and accessories. What was obscured within this rhetoric was the paucity of gameplay features provided when the game was played *without* accessories (in which case it was essentially unplayable) or with only a limited number of them. The game's design and UI, meanwhile, communicated the crucial nature of accessories in multiple, immediate ways – from depictions of locked doors and character outlines (to be unlocked with the purchase of the right toys) to prizes that could be won but not used until the right game disc was placed on the "Infinity Base." At various junctures, the design rules suggested that the tie-in accessories were not merely supplementary, but necessary for a complete and successful gameplay experience.

Like commercials, storylines, and community norms, design features all play important roles in determining what is possible – as well as what is emphasized – within a digital game. Yet most of the decisions that are made about a game's designs and contents unfold beyond the purview of the user and of the public at large. They are often obscured by the "illusion of technical necessity" that emerges once a technology begins to achieve closure, at which point its features and materials begin to appear inevitable or seem like the best or only options.[19] However, there are ways in which technologies "mirror back" or communicate their underlying social order – the assumptions, ideals, objectives, and ideological positioning informing decisions about the game's design and strategies for managing its players. As explored in chapter 3, one way is through the images, stories, references, and discourses that are embedded or "inscripted" in a game's marketing and packaging.[20] It is also expressed in the institutional frameworks within which specific games are implemented, and through which their use is promoted, monitored, and regulated.[21] The underlying social order of technologies is communicated through design affordances, which guide users and encourage specific ways of using and interpreting a technology, as well as in the types of uses – and types of users – that are excluded by the design.[22] The synergizing of design features and market priorities represents just one of the many ways that children's digital playgrounds are shaped and informed by rule systems. Design rules can also reflect, extend, and even at times contravene the official rules of the game, along with its associated legal policies and technical codes.

Written Rules, Rulebooks, and Codes of Conduct

Digital games often include some form of preliminary introduction to the rules of play. These can take a range of forms, including tutorials and integrated tutorial levels, orientation activities, beginner areas, written rulebooks, or narrative ploys instructing new players on how to play the game, how to win, or what to avoid. Within connected games, rules of play often also include guidelines about how to behave and interact, as well as prohibitions on certain forms of (in-game) behaviour. Within games where players interact and chat with other players, codes of conduct that explain at least some of the game owner's expectations of how players will act, interact, and communicate are not uncommon. These types of texts are distinct from TOS contracts or privacy policies, but they often repeat some of the same information – particularly items that pertain directly to players' in-game actions and utterances. Generally, rulebooks describe and supplement the embedded rules of play encountered in a game's design by setting (or at least suggesting) limits on actions and behaviours that are *possible* but nonetheless discouraged or forbidden. For instance, the design of a children's MMOG might afford make-believe play through the inclusion of open spaces, costumes, action opportunities, and inter-player chat systems through which players can share and perform imaginary scenarios. There may be some programmed limits on what players are able to say to each other, but it will almost always remain possible to engage in some form of disruptive or abusive behaviour. Written rules against bullying or harassing other players might therefore be included in a game's rulebook, and enforced through reporting systems, live moderators, or algorithms.

The children's MMOGs that I analysed all contained a formal, written rulebook or code of conduct of some sort. While these rulebooks often introduced players to some of the basic conventions of multiplayer gaming, they were predominantly used to caution players about the kinds of behaviours that would be deemed inappropriate or unacceptable by the game's owners and moderators. Just as the MMOGs themselves encompassed numerous features and action opportunities that extended beyond the game itself, the rulebooks covered much more than mere rules of play. In *Club Penguin*, where certain forms of exploratory and emergent play were encouraged, the rulebook included a prohibition against the exploitation of design glitches. In *BarbieGirls*, where inter-player chat was the central action opportunity, players were warned that they must never "say anything naughty or mean" and "always be super nice" when chatting with others. If they broke these rules, they "could be banned from the site!" In fact, very few of the rules I examined related to play at all. Out of the thirty-four different rule categories recorded across the six games, only seven applied to gameplay. The majority (twenty-seven) addressed inter-player relationships and interactions. Many pertained to disruptive behaviours such as harassment, bullying, soliciting personal information, or introducing inappropriate topics of discussion. All six of the MMOGs had explicit rules against bullying or "being mean," along with rules prohibiting foul language and inappropriate talk.

Another trend was the predominance of rules aimed at defining and delimiting the complex legal, economic, and social relationships that exist between the game's players and its corporate owners. Most of the rulebooks included rules that repeated elements of the game's privacy policy. For instance, all six rulebooks forbade players from giving out their passwords – a restriction that also appeared in the privacy policies. Moreover, three of the rulebooks (found in *Magi-Nation*, *GalaXseeds*, and *Toontown*) reiterated terms already outlined in the games' TOS contracts. These included assertions of the game owners' intellectual property claims over in-game items, prohibitions on copyright infringement, and restrictions against players using the game environment for personal business purposes. Overall, these three rulebooks contained nine rule categories that dealt specifically with issues of governance, corporate liability, and accountability – all of which are standard components of most website (and other software) TOS contracts. Compliance with the TOS contracts becomes integral to the rules of play.

Of course, it is difficult to determine the extent to which players comply with either rule system in their everyday use of connected games. Game owners are rarely forthcoming about their player management activities, let alone their effectiveness. For example, many connected games rely to some degree on large-scale moderation to find and weed out inappropriate content (either before or after it is posted), and/or to verify content flagged as inappropriate by other users. Moderation can include live moderators, or automated moderation systems (i.e., algorithms), or some combination of the two. However, although moderation systems and practices have been a core part of online culture for decades, there is very little academic literature examining their inner workings or outcomes. It is often outsourced, increasingly to underpaid workers located in the Global South, and conducted largely in secret under non-disclosure agreements.[23] Details about how inappropriate content is defined, identified, evaluated, and addressed are notoriously hard to find. Little is known about the effectiveness of online moderation or its impact on either user communities or forum contents.[24]

The obscurity under which moderation systems operate has important implications for children's digital play. Within the context of the current discussion of rulebooks and the social order they reflect and seek to reproduce, the hidden parameters and people involved in making sure the rules of a game are followed give them a form of panoptic power. Game owners claim full discretionary rights to banish or suspend players for breaking the rules, but they provide very few details about how such events unfold, let alone if there is any recourse for players to protest or make amends. Meanwhile, the rules themselves are quite vague. To return to the *BarbieGirls* example above, what does it mean to "always be super nice"? How exactly is that defined and assessed? And by whom?

Notably, most of the games analysed delegated responsibility for ensuring that the rules were followed to the players themselves. For instance, most of the rulebooks included a requirement that players report rule-breakers. Previous studies show that child players do often take it upon themselves to police and enforce social norms, particularly when playing in traditional contexts such as schools and playgrounds. However, the norms that children themselves enforce frequently include a mix of both official (i.e., developer-driven) and unofficial (i.e., player-driven) rules of play. They are also open to negotiation and reinterpretation. The threat of "I'm going to report you" is itself a powerful tool among children, and it is often sufficient for moving past the rule-breaking behaviour and getting back to playing. The formalization of reporting (or "telling") by making it a rule or requirement of the game usurps the authority of the child player, while also threatening to make the child complicit. Players who do not report rule-breakers become rule-breakers themselves. In other games, this is taken a step further, as rules requiring that players report rule-breakers are included in the rulebook and advanced through design features that reward players for monitoring the game space and reporting unruly other players. This was the case in *Club Penguin*, where players could apply to become "secret agents" and "help be our eyes and ears throughout the Club Penguin world," in exchange for a monthly salary of 250 Coins. Players are not only asked to assume (some) responsibility for ensuring that the game world remains pleasant, fair, and rule-abiding, but are also asked to serve as surveillance mechanisms – watching and reporting on their peers' ability and willingness to play by the rules.

The official rules of a game are not always mandatory, but nor are they always open for negotiation. As argued above, this is particularly the case when the same rule is enforced at multiple levels of the game's structure, and especially when it is inscribed in the game design. Although players can engage in emergent play, technological appropriations, and other unanticipated uses when interacting in a digital playground, the playground's designed rules always carry disproportionate power. Through the "illusion of necessity" that tends to enshroud design choices once a technology becomes part of everyday life, for instance, design features begin to appear inevitable. When rules of play are purposefully embedded as (or in) a game's design, and authority becomes delegated onto technical features, they can begin to seem incontrovertible or impervious to challenge.

Who Follows the Rules Anyway?

As anyone who spends time around young people already knows, children don't always play by the rules. Learning and negotiating the rules are themselves central parts of children's play, and these processes can often take up a significant portion of children's playtime. Research from a range of disciplines and traditions involved in the study of childhood demonstrates that elementary school–aged children have a particularly ambiguous and fluctuating relationship with game rules – as a concept and as a set of practices. The idea traces as far back as the early works of Piaget. In one study, Piaget analysed children playing the game of marbles, using their murky relationship with game rules as an entry point for understanding children's moral development (how they come to distinguish between right and wrong).[25] Specifically, he examined how children of different ages applied rules when playing marbles, and their ideas about the role and nature of game rules.[26] While the resulting framework or stages model of development itself has limited applicability because it relies on essentialist classifications of children (by age and by gender), Piaget's findings are nonetheless useful for thinking about the unique, emergent, and polymorphous relationship that children have with game rules, and how this relationship evolves as they play, interact, learn, and grow.

For instance, Piaget found that by age seven or eight, most of the children in his study had a sufficient understanding of game rules and structures that they would try to win when playing a game. They also worked to ensure that all the players involved were following the same rules of play by negotiating and policing each other's moves or actions as the game unfolded. Game rules were largely "regarded as sacred and untouchable, emanating from adults and lasting forever," and alterations were interpreted as transgressions.[27] Concurrently, at this age most of the children in his study had notably vague ideas about game rules in general (e.g., what they were for, how they were determined, and why). Moreover, Piaget found that "when questioned separately, [they gave] entirely different accounts" of what the rules were. The apparent contradictions that underlie children's ideas about game rules illustrate the liminal or fluid nature of the role that rules occupy within children's play practices. Yet children also appear to grow out of this fluidity, at least to some extent. In Piaget's study, most of the respondents aged eleven or twelve and older described the game's rules with striking consistency. They also understood that game rules were "law due to mutual consent," and that one followed the rules to "play along and be loyal to the group." Accordingly, the older children tended to think that rules could be changed if the players all agreed to it.

Of course, knowing the codified rules of a game is not the same as following them. Regardless of how accurately they can describe a game's rules to an adult researcher, children of all ages can also choose to break those rules – and do so for a wide range of reasons. Deviating from the rules, reinterpreting them, cheating, and changing the rules outright are all common occurrences in children's play. These activities in turn generate a significant amount of discussion, disagreement, and negotiation among the players, as unforeseen or illegal moves are challenged, defended, considered, and sometimes reconciled. Observations of children engaged in debates about what is or is not allowed within a particular game or play scenario – that is, the rules – are found throughout the literature in this area, even among young children whose grasp of the rules is the most tenuous.[28] This research suggests that children "are constantly probing and exploring what counts as acceptable or not in game participation in the production of social and moral orders. Even though rules, in one aspect, can be seen as governing play and game activities, they are foremost open to negotiation and are used for different practical purposes in the players' interactions."[29]

In children's play, rules have a function that extends beyond the game and the individual players. This notion draws on sociocultural play theory found in recent studies on children's gameplay, which posits that "children's developing understandings of the rules and roles of society are reflected in children's play."[30] In their study of girls playing board games in a Swedish preschool setting, for instance, Karlsson et al. found that game rules served as a locus for players to engage in complex negotiations, challenges, and compromises that reflected and fed into their real-world friendships. Formal and informal rules provide a context within which social interactions unfold, vis-à-vis which social relationships and hierarchies are worked out. Karlsson et al. found that during peer play, the children in their study used "rules to renegotiate activities as a way to control others and to bend the rules in their favour and, in so doing, advance their positions."[31] Similarly, Martin and Evaldsson argue that rules "provide an interpretative framework for coordinating activities and a resource for negotiations, enforcement, and discussions as well as a resource for children to make sense of ongoing actions."[32]

As Cobb-Moore, Danby, and Farrell point out, such findings reflect broader patterns found in children's everyday interactions, which "typically involve children invoking and monitoring rules to manage each other's actions."[33] Indeed, children's play practices often seep in and out of the other areas of their lives. This is, Alcock argues, a key part of how children collaboratively produce their own meanings and cultures within and in relation to external (i.e., sociocultural) roles, artefacts, and routine activities. Young children bring "playful flexibility" to non-play routines as a way of connecting with each other and with the world around them, while also making the routines themselves more meaningful and enjoyable. She explains, "Roles acquire personal meanings as children use their imaginations to improvise and play with rules, thus working the dialectic between reality and pretense, between rules and roles."[34] In so doing, children transform the otherwise potentially mundane parts of their day into "playful collaborative shared activities."

Accordingly, the research shows that children apply playful tactics in their interactions with adults and adult-initiated rules – within the context of playing games and throughout their everyday lives. However, there also appear to be some important differences in how children experience and interact with peer-initiated and adult-initiated rules of play. For one, the literature shows that children often do follow the rules put forth and enforced by parents, educators, and other adults. A recent study by Ólafsdóttir et al. found that it was often obvious that "the children knew the rules and did what was expected of them." But they also challenged, adapted, and resisted adult-initiated rules, "displaying that they are able to make decisions about their everyday lives."[35] Resistance to adult rules occurs both individually and collectively, and it does not always mean refusing to follow the rules. Instead, it often involves finding ways of bending, appropriating, and working around them. The literature indicates that even young children employ sophisticated strategies to cope with and manipulate adult-initiated rules without *breaking* them. In Ólafsdóttir et al.'s study, for instance, preschoolers were observed making up their own alternative rules of play in times and places when they were "not obviously visible and audible" to their teachers. Through the employment of such strategies, children are able to maintain their relationships with adults and standing within adult-controlled contexts, whilst engaging in their own peer-oriented cultural experiences and social orders.

Children also mobilize adult-formulated rules for their own ends in their peer interactions and peer play. For instance, Cobb-Moore et al. argue, "Children often draw on 'higher order rules' that is, the social order and rules of the teacher and the classroom" to "increase their own power and position within their peer cultures."[36] A key example is how children mobilize notions of "cheating" in their peer play–based negotiations of what constitutes "appropriate" game action. Numerous scholars have observed children using "argumentative moves of cheating," both as a means of managing or controlling other players and as a way of gaining personal advantages. Although many children do purposefully – sometimes gleefully – cheat at games, there nonetheless appears to be a consensus among most children that cheating constitutes a moral transgression, though one that can clearly be justified and forgiven under the right circumstances. In the aforementioned study of young girls playing board games in a school setting, instances and accusations of cheating became the focus of extended debates and disputes among the respondents, as well as a basis for the co-construction of "a shared moral order in the peer group."[37]

As explored above, children interact similarly with the design rules embedded in the artefacts, structures, and environments that are on hand during play. The designed features and affordances, physical properties, and user configurations that are found within game pieces, playground structures, and other technologies of play can also figure prominently within children's rule making and gameplay. Here too, adult-initiated rules become resources for children to mobilize in their social interactions and in the development of peer cultures. As with other rule systems, design features can be evoked, manipulated, and subverted during play. For instance, in Bateman's study of how children used "playground huts" (small, permanent structures similar in design to a treehouse, but placed on the ground) during morning outdoor recreation time at a Welsh preschool, four-year-old respondents frequently used the huts' affordance of serving as "enclosures" to enact games of exclusion and inclusion, which were in turn used to (re)negotiate friendships and social standing among peer groups. Here, the physical properties of the huts provided an external locus of social order upon which the children could construct and maintain their own social hierarchies – by endowing the huts with their own "laws," claims of ownership, and other meanings. Rules thus do much more than simply constrain and prescribe play. They often also provide a structure against which children can exercise their agency and freedom, as well as a sort of shared vocabulary through which children can voice their creativity, autonomy, and power.

Why Breaking Rules Is Important

In reviewing the literature on children's mutable and ambiguous relationship with game rules, it becomes clear that idealized notions of children's play are largely inconsistent with children's actual play practices.[38] Contemporary childhood studies demonstrate that children's play is multifaceted, nebulous, and filled with themes and behaviours that adults neither anticipate nor approve of. There is a clear need for a more nuanced social understanding of children's play, one that moves away from limited binaries and ideological projections of adult hopes and fears for the future. A deeper consideration of the tensions between ideals and situated practices is also warranted, particularly as they unfold within specific games and play contexts. Indeed, the tensions themselves are important and occupy a crucial role within children's lives and cultures. Ólafsdóttir et al. propose that children challenge and resist game rules to "gain more control of their lives" and to display that "they are able to make decisions about their everyday lives."[39] For children, breaking the rules of play can be understood as a form of "interpretive reproduction," a notion advanced by Corsaro to describe how "children create and participate in their own unique peer cultures by creatively taking or appropriating information from the adult world to address their own peer concerns."[40]

Resistance to adult rules occurs individually and collectively. However, collective acts of resistance are especially significant in that they contribute to children's sense of belonging and to group cohesion. Corsaro maintains that this in turn helps shape children's peer cultures. These findings are reminiscent of arguments advanced in works by Sutton-Smith and by Götz, who similarly emphasize that peers often play an important role when children engage in resistance vis-à-vis adult-produced mass media texts and licensed toys. From subversively reinterpreting the plotlines of feature films to playing with licensed toys in ways that deviate from the provided "script," children's interest in challenging narrative authority and appropriating mediatized design features appears to be enhanced by the presence of peers. In her study of children playing with electronic toys, for instance, Bergen found that the presence of peers significantly increased the quality and creativity of children's play, and seemed to facilitate divergence from design affordances and user configurations. Opportunities to exercise agency are not only important for the development of peer relationships and cultures, but the reverse is also the case: the presence of peers contributes to children's sense of agency and provides unique opportunities for children to resist adult rules and other forms of social order.

Practices such as breaking, bending, and reinterpreting the rules provide children with entry points into the adult-controlled social order – openings through which they can access, confront, negotiate, and even reject adult authority to fix meanings and set standards. Children's play is rife with such practices. For instance, many children's games challenge adult definitions of taste and propriety. Hendershot argues children often delight in finding practices and themes that illicitly transgress "adult standards of taste."[41] They seek out distasteful smells, jarring sounds, and gross actions in defiance of adult standards of taste, and they take pleasure in their power to evoke adult repulsion. Other games feature dark, disturbing, or age-inappropriate elements, a practice that Schwartzman argues provides children with an important forum for managing fears and other anxieties. Sutton-Smith makes similar arguments in his discussion of the prevalence of violent themes and "social testing" games within children's playground play. Such games frequently emerge in response to rules, prohibitions, and parameters that adults have put on children's play.

Children's transgressive play practices may moreover function as a form of symbolic action, in dialogue with larger cultural, political, and social discourses, and through which modes of adult authority are continuously negotiated and challenged. By providing a forum for engaging with the exceptional, the repulsive, the taboo, and the dark, transgressive play can provide children with a break from the quotidian, the beautiful, the sanctioned, and the sacred. Within this dynamic, play can provide a valuable space for processing and rejecting social roles and expectations. For instance, dolls are often viewed as artefacts that embody and afford traditional gender ideals and sex-role stereotypes. Nonetheless, doll *play* has long been associated with gender role subversion and the rejection of adult expectations. Throughout history, dolls have served a dual and contradictory function – as pedagogical tools promoting feminine ideals, as well as weapons for thwarting social norms and undermining parental restrictions. While historically many girls (and boys) played with dolls in prescribed ways, Forman-Brunell notes, "Evidence reveals that doll players [also] pushed at the margins of acceptable feminine and genteel behaviour."[42] Common practices – such as doll torture, doll body modification, doll bashing, and doll funerals – demonstrate that even in the nineteenth and early twentieth centuries, dolls were often used to "maneuver between gendered expectations and more daring identities."[43] In practice, girls and boys interact with dolls in diverse and unanticipated ways.

Children's playful transgressions of socially accepted distinctions between putrid and pleasurable, appropriate and inappropriate, good and bad challenge adult-defined binaries. These practices provide children with a way to reassert control over their own bodies and a forum for exploring thoughts, desires, and feelings that might otherwise be excluded or even forbidden. Moreover, transgressive play provides children with a context for distancing themselves, temporarily and safely, from the adult world and its many expectations. Through these practices, children create a space that belongs to them within the physical places of everyday life – places that are designed and controlled by adults. It is a space within and between, a liminal or third place that is accessible only to the children involved. James sees this phenomenon as crucial to the emergence of a "social world of children," which, while dependent on and embedded in the world of adults, is also separate. As James observes, many children engage in practices aimed at delineating, protecting, and disguising such spaces, which are used to hide the "true nature of the culture of childhood" from adults.[44] She concludes that children benefit significantly from having their own spaces and peer cultures. Within the secret spaces of childhood, children exercise their agency and authority, experiment with ideas and social norms. Here children are temporarily liberated from the myriad constraints, rules, and structures that predominate in their everyday lives.

Negotiating Encoded Rules

Digital playgrounds contain codified, adult-initiated rule systems. In addition to the "written" rules of play examined above, many commercial games also seek to shape player actions and interactions in ways that will align them more closely with corporate interests, real-world laws, and social expectations (as found in safety protocols, privacy policies, and TOS contracts). Some of these rules are implicit, others are overt. In each case, they are codified or "official" – rules set by the adults who make and manage the game space and its contents. In addition, design features, affordances, and limitations provide their own set of rules, which inform and constrain how play unfolds within the digital game environment. Digital games are indelibly programmed. For something to "happen" in a digital game, it must first be made possible or "anticipated" by the game's underlying program code (although not necessarily anticipated by the programmers, as demonstrated by the phenomenon of emergent design). For better or worse, digital games are fundamentally more prescriptive and programmable than tangible toys or games could ever be. They also consist of artefacts made for children by adults, who bring to this task a range of interests, biases, and ideologies, which are in turn embedded in the artefacts' codes and algorithms, in their texts and policies, as well as in their narrative, discursive, and semiotic features. Where a game's rule systems become synchronized and are implemented in ways that mutually reinforce their authority over the game space and the players, they are surprisingly effective and difficult to contravene.

Nonetheless, research in this area indicates that children's tendencies towards rule-bending, transgressive play and subversion of adult authority can often carry over to the digital realm. Studies of children's digital play reveal that pockets of innovation and creativity can be found in even the most tightly structured and rule-bound games. Works by Giddings, Fields and Kafai, Marsh and Burke, and others demonstrate that children bring a significant amount of agency and situated knowledge to their digital gameplay.[45] Their action choices, discoveries of emergent play opportunities, transgressive behaviours, and technological appropriations all contribute meaningfully to the social shaping of children's digital playground technologies. Other studies examine children cheating, bending, and breaking the rules of play within digital games, identifying behaviours comparable to those found in traditional play. While little is known about the frequency with which children engage in such practices, this literature provides important insight into how and why some young players resist, challenge, or outright defy the programmed formal and informal rule systems contained within digital games. A key takeaway from these works is the sense that digital games provide an important forum for children to address and make sense of a relatively new source of social order that permeates much of Western contemporary culture. This social order emerges out of the intertwining of technological and commercial systems, and it underlies most contemporary digital applications, including digital games and playgrounds, along with their associated technological devices.

Noteworthy examples from the previous literature involve children experiencing tension or limitations vis-à-vis a game's programming, and children incorporating commonly encountered design features into their imaginary play scenarios. For instance, in Giddings's study of children playing *Lego Racers 2*, one of the children was observed gleefully and repeatedly driving his avatar into the sea to purposefully make it "die."[46] Giddings described this as a "game within the game," the goal of which "was the identification of, and the edging around, the precise point at which the game switched between life and death." However, he also linked the behaviour to the fact that the child in question lacked the hand-eye coordination to effectively compete in the game's preferred mode of playing, which pitted players and their avatars against non-player vehicles controlled by the computer in an increasingly challenging series of car races. The child's initial attempts to race the computer resulted in repeated and immediate defeat. It is meaningful that death itself became the focus of this child's subsequent transgressive play. In digital games, death is routinely used to communicate defeat, even as players are given multiple and sometimes even unlimited lives with which to attempt victory. In this context, playing at death and defeat can be understood as a form of symbolic action through which dominant definitions of achievement and mastery are challenged, and personal limitations are reconfigured.

In Giddings's example, a child is observed engaging in innovative technological appropriation and meaning making. Much of it takes place at the subjective or interpretive level as part of the child's experience and understanding of the child's own gameplay practice. It also unfolds within the physical location of the child's family living room, where the researcher and his respondents (the child and his younger brother) are engaged in a reflexive, sense-making discourse. Indeed, many of the examples of transgressive play discussed in the literature involve practices and processes that unfold, at least in part, outside of the games themselves. For instance, Kafai and Fields's large-scale study of the tween-targeted virtual world *Whyville* uncovered hundreds of websites dedicated to sharing cheats, walkthroughs, hints, shortcuts, solutions, and other information about the game's various areas and activities. These cheat sites were created by individual players (or small groups of players) outside of *Whyville*, but were broadly known about across the player community. The researchers report that the cheat sites and their contents fuelled debate among young players about the ethics of cheating and were the topic of over a hundred player-written articles in the virtual world's official newspaper (*Whyville Times*) during the study period. As Kafai and Fields explain, "Just as in the commercial gaming world, cheating was a hotly debated topic in Whyville and the newspaper articles criticize the practice of using cheat sites to increase salaries illegitimately: 'when just one person uses cheats it could affect our whole town.' By far the predominant view of cheating in the articles was that cheating is bad, lazy, dishonest, and unfair. Many of the arguments were based on the idea that such practices are wrong in real life and therefore are also wrong in virtual life."[47]

The fact that this discussion unfolded within an official, in-game forum is itself significant. It reveals a quotidian blurring of the boundaries widely assumed to exist between in-game and non-game, real and virtual, legal and illegal, within children's connected games. This finding suggests that children's gameplay often occurs within *and* outside the formal game space and involves multiple locations, practices, artefacts, and meanings. Many of the works cited above support this conclusion and describe comparable instances of children playing in, out, and across gaming contexts. In children's play, adult distinctions and boundaries are not only subject to transgression and challenge, but are often encountered as fluid, hybrid, ambiguous, and negotiable. This is, after all, part of what makes transmedia intertextuality such a prevalent practice, not to mention industry strategy, within children's culture. Children routinely extend their engagement with media texts, toys, themes, and characters across the milieus and activities of their everyday lives.

At the same time, it is equally noteworthy that the cheat sites – and the transgressive elements they reflect – are situated outside the game world. The players can discuss the ethics of cheating in the *Whyville* newspaper, but the game's operators and community do not appear to allow the world-wide sharing of cheats among players in-game. Through writing about cheating (broadly defined) in newspaper articles, players are afforded a contained way of enacting their resistance to the rules and interpretive freedom within the official game space. However, this falls short of a full integration of the cheating and rule-breaking those players are presumably engaged in. Moreover, many of the cheating practices described by Kafai and Fields are not necessarily discernible to the broader community of players. After all, knowing the answer to a riddle because you looked it up on a cheat site often *looks* identical to speedy problem solving. Game mechanics standardize user input, and in many instances this effaces the visible difference between fair and unfair player moves. The players themselves may know that they (or others) are cheating, but the play that is ultimately represented in-game and performed to the rest of the population can often come across as rule-abiding. This obfuscation raises important questions about what then happens to the benefits that play theorists associate with rule-breaking and other acts of resistance, and the importance of peers within this dynamic. Are the children able to build the same sense of belonging and generate peer cultures when (some of) their acts of resistance are made invisible? Does this alienation of children's transgressive play have any impact on their ability to create their own secret spaces of childhood within these game worlds? Or are sufficient resources on hand that children remain able to coordinate and engage in collective acts of transgression within digital game environments?

Of course, child players also engage in acts of resistance that are not obscured by mechanics and UIs, but rather are on full display to other players. This can include engaging with affordances in unanticipated ways, exploiting glitches in the programming, and discovering emergent design features. Some children furthermore participate in more radical acts, such as blatantly engaging in forbidden speech or behaviours, or even employing technological interventions such as modding (a player-made modification of a game's features or appearance) and hacking. However, more radical forms of resistance are also more likely to be formally prohibited by the games' designs and written rules, and are therefore much more likely to be policed, by the games' operators and by other players. In heavily monitored games, penalties for engaging in radical rule-breaking range from getting barred from the game to potentially facing criminal charges. In other games, rules are bent and broken frequently, with few to no repercussions.

Many of these questions tie back to how stringently a game's rules are administered, and the extent to which its overlapping rule systems are synchronized to work together. As argued above, in titles where gameplay mechanics are designed to afford or even require players' adherence to codes of conduct (or to corporate agendas), straying from the rules is more difficult. The same can be said of games featuring continuous moderation (live and/or algorithmic), accompanied by detailed rules about what players are and are not allowed to say in-game. Notably, the synchronization of rule systems is particularly common within child-specific connected games, such as children's virtual worlds and MMOGs, as well as child-targeted, multiplayer console games and apps. Although the genre is frequently identified by game scholars and children's gaming advocates as highly conducive to collaborative, creative, player-driven culture-building activities, the reality is that a great number of the most popular connected games designed and targeted to children are among the most restrictive with respect to player freedoms and agency.

Children Bending, but Not Breaking, the Rules

In my own research on child-specific connected games, I found that most of the actions and interactions that unfold *within* these spaces do follow the rules – or at least they appear to.[48] In my study of the public interactions of the player populations of Disney's *Club Penguin* and Mattel's *BarbieGirls*, I found relatively little evidence of conflict or divergence from the games' rules. My findings contradicted much of the scholarship in this area, which argues that virtual worlds are in their essence forums for challenging and negotiating systems of social order. Instead, *these* players largely appeared to conform to the games' official rules, parameters, and thematic motifs. They *mostly* used features in expected or afforded ways. They interacted with other players through public group chat, and they made use of the full range of available action opportunities. The majority of the players who congregated in public areas participated openly and overtly in game-wide events and activities – dressing their avatars in Halloween costumes near the end of October, for instance, or competing in hidden object scavenger hunts. In both worlds, it was quite common to see large groups of players simultaneously engaged in the same activity while sharing inside jokes and references through group chat. The limited action opportunities and chat restrictions contained within these worlds had a clear impact on the depth and diversity of the play activities and social interactions that players *could* engage in within the virtual environments. Even minor acts of transgression were relatively rare and by no means representative of the majority of the play that unfolded within these games during this period.

Nonetheless, subtle signs of tension were uncovered. As is typical of children's peer play in more traditional spaces, it was apparent that the players of these games spent a significant amount of time negotiating the parameters of play and otherwise coordinating the contents, strategies, times, and places of their interactions with one another. Through these negotiations, the games' own rule systems and storylines were at times subsumed in communicative chaos, as players resisted "playing along," demanded different roles from those assigned, or otherwise subverted the prescribed play scenarios afforded by the game worlds. Instances of players bending, and sometimes breaking, the rules were uncommon when compared to the much more prevalent pattern of playing *by* the rules. Nonetheless, these examples provide unique insight into children's *in-game* and publicly performed negotiations of the games' adult-initiated rules of play. They highlight the "margin of manoeuvre" found in the limited action opportunities and menu options for players within both *BarbieGirls World* and *Club Penguin*. Specifically, in both games, limited avatar customization options became the focus of forms of appropriation and creative play, as well as a key means through which players expressed their agency and interpretative freedom. The following case studies illustrate the types of transgressive play recorded during this stage of the study.

ICE GOTHS AND BARBIEBOYS

In *BarbieGirls*, players were represented in-game by a Barbie-esque avatar. Players could customize their avatars by dressing them up in different combinations of clothing and accessories, as well as selecting skin tone and hair and eye colour from a limited palette. Indeed, not only was the range of customization options limited, but many core attributes (such as body size, shape of nose, etc.) could not be altered. These fixed attributes tended to conform to the same stereotypical, hyper-feminine, European beauty ideals that have long characterized Barbie dolls and tie-in media characters. As a result, all of the avatars in *BarbieGirls* looked very similar. This look was furthermore congruent with the aesthetics associated with the Barbie media brand, upon which the game was based. Much like Barbie toy advertisements and packaging, the game heavily configured its users as girls. The idea that the game was intended for girls was reinforced in the language used to promote the game in advertisements, as well as in the text displayed on the virtual world landing page, both of which addressed users as "girls." Most notably, the avatar customization tools did not include an option for gender. Along with the avatar's numerous, gender-encoded fixed attributes, the implication of this design limitation was that all avatars were girls. The game itself contained videos, mini-games, and written texts (including descriptions and instructions) that centred on themes and storylines traditionally and stereotypically targeted to girls in Western culture – such as shopping, beauty and fashion, caring for small animals, and being kind and friendly. On multiple levels, *BarbieGirls* was configured as a hyper-feminized, girls-only space.

As with Barbie dolls and toys, many of the game's action opportunities, narratives, and underling mechanics centred on fashion and dress-up play. A hub of activity during the study period was the "Club Beauty" area, a "shop" (i.e., contained room) decorated in the style of a hair or beauty salon. What made Club Beauty unique was that it contained a feature that allowed players to give each other "makeovers." Players could either request a makeover or act as stylists, though both parties had to consent (e.g., click "Agree") before a makeover could commence. Through the makeover interface, the player acting as the stylist could make changes to the other player's hairstyle, hair colour, skin tone, and make-up. The player acting as customer watched the changes as they were being made. Once the stylist was done, the customer could either reject the changes and revert to the previous look, or accept them and pay (in B Bucks) for the changes to be applied to the in-game avatar. Notably, Club Beauty afforded one of the only forms of multiplayer interaction available in *BarbieGirls* outside of chat. It was also the only mini-game that had outcomes that carried over into the broader game world. Playing the game also gave players exclusive access to several hairstyle and make-up options that were not otherwise available to them. Given how heavily frequented the area was during the study period, it was clear that it offered players a unique and valuable experience.

One year, just before Halloween, a compelling trend emerged as increasing numbers of *BarbieGirls* avatars began sporting a look reminiscent of the "negative gothic" or "ice goth" style found in goth (or gothic) sub-culture.[49] In contrast to the more familiar all-black aesthetic, ice goths utilize white and pastels to play with, or even subvert, visual conventions associated with traditional goth fashion. In *BarbieGirls*, this translated into avatars customized using only the lightest colours on the palette, and making jarringly juxtaposed clothing, hairstyle, and make-up selections. One avatar featured the palest white skin tone available, paired with dark magenta/red irises, long white/platinum blond hair with light purple streaks, and a pastiche of frilly, white, or pastel clothing items. It is worth noting that in *BarbieGirls*, reproducing a traditional, all-black goth aesthetic was challenging. For instance, the avatar customization options did not allow for the type of dark make-up commonly viewed as a staple of the goth style (e.g., black eyeliner, dark blue or red lipstick). Instead, the avatar customization palette contained an assortment of light colours and pastels – the same colours found throughout Barbie products, media, and toy packaging. The emergence of an ice goth fashion trend drew on resources already readily available and afforded by the game design and its associated aesthetic motifs. At the same time, however, the ice goths diverged markedly from Barbie's brand identity.

The unconventional combinations that marked the ice goths as a distinctive subgroup, such as pairing white skin with red eyes, clashed visually, but also semiotically, with the clean-cut, bubble-gum imagery of the surrounding game world. This tension is reminiscent of dynamics described by members of real-world goth subcultures. For instance, in her study of the gothic communities in Los Angeles and Austin, Schilt found that "goth girls" often adopted fashion and make-up choices that exaggerated and thereby transgressed dominant cultural norms and beauty ideals: "The total effect of such gothic makeup serve[s] to challenge and almost to parody what a 'beautiful' woman looks like."[50] The disjuncture that arose between the ice goth avatars and their surroundings shone a similar light on the cultural norms embedded in the *BarbieGirls* game and, by association, in the Barbie brand as a whole. As mentioned, *BarbieGirls* reproduced many of the same themes found throughout other Barbie toys and media texts, which for the past several decades have consistently promoted a heavily hegemonic, heteronormative, and hyper-feminine vision of girls' play and girlhood.[51] Although Barbie is a fashion doll whose looks and outfits are always changing, in Barbie-based media and advertisements, Barbie and her friends are depicted sporting stylish but highly mainstream preppy or clean-cut clothing, hair, and make-up. The sudden infusion of a non-mainstream style associated in real life with an anti-establishment subculture under-scores the lack of diversity contained within such representations – at least in relation to fashion and style, although the potential for a deeper or more expansive critique is certainly present.

By contrast, Pearson and Mullins argue that Barbie not only promotes the reproduction of "femininity," but also its negotiation as a social construct, specifically as it relates to shifting social assumptions about labour and leisure, private and public space.[52] Barbie play troubles traditional understandings of consumption, domesticity, and beauty by repositioning these once private practices within public contexts. Barbie has a Dream House, but she is also a girl about town. Many of her toy lines and media texts work to extend, normalize, and publicize the traditionally domestic, historically hidden, "backstage" labour of grooming and caretaking associated with femininity. Similarly, *BarbieGirls* invited players to engage in backstage practices as part of a communal performance unfolding within a public, commercialized space (i.e., the virtual world). Within this space, feminine ideals and expectations were certainly afforded by the game's design and often reproduced by its players, but they were also negotiated as players interacted with the design features and with each other. The ice goth trend was not against the rules. Moreover, it was realized using action opportunities already present within the game's design. Nonetheless, the ice goths introduced an element of emergent or transgressive play to the game world by disrupting its visual and semiotic homogeneity. Their presence broadcast an alternative reading of the game, opening a "possibility space" within which players might diverge from anticipated uses, ideological assumptions, and user configurations.

The potential for transgressive play contained within the game's limited customization options was even more evident in a second trend observed during the study period, in which players used avatar clothing colours and styles to identify themselves or others as male. Initially, avatars were designated as "boys" or "guys" if they dressed all in black, wore long-sleeved tops, and long pants. Later, the code extended to include the shortest hairstyle available in the avatar customization menu. Players who were not familiar with the trend and unknowingly dressed their avatar in all-black clothing would find themselves bombarded with gender inquiries (e.g., "Are you a guy?") and requests for dates. Indeed, that is how I myself first discovered that dressing all in black connoted male to a sizeable subsection of the player community. Unlike the ice goth trend, this "game within a game" appeared to be somewhat reliant on chat-based performatives or utterances, through which players could broadcast their identities and intentions. For instance, some players dressed all in black would immediately identify themselves as a guy or boy upon entering a room. Others would ask if there were any girls in the room, thereby asserting their own not-girl status. Still others would enter the room asking if there were any boys. The trend drew on many of the same rules and parameters found in traditional forms of make-believe play, where conversation regularly fulfils a crucial function in the establishment of the shared play scenario and the players' roles within it. It is also a primary means through which players negotiate and challenge parameters, shifting storylines, and subject positions as the game unfolds.

The BarbieBoys trend stood in direct defiance of the "girls only" configuration of the game world, and its narrow gendering of the entire player population through the limited avatar customization options made available. It exposed and problematized the design decision to include only girl avatar options, its implied assumption that boys would not want to play the game, and its reinforcement of gender binarism. The presence of BarbieBoys also made visible an underlying tension or disconnect between the game's homosocial design and the heteronormativity otherwise promoted across and throughout the Barbie brand. Indeed, even within *BarbieGirls*, heteronormative dating and romance were by far the most popular narrative themes. During my data collection, for instance, four of the seven "movies" playing at the "B Cinema" featured animated videos of Barbie and her friends (who, like Barbie, were all young women) preparing for and then going on a group date with "the guys" (Ken and his friends, who were all young men). Two of the other "movies" centred on the story of a friend meeting a new (heterosexual) romantic interest.[53] While the inclusion of such narrative elements seemed, on the one hand, to provide players with a sort of play script for Barbie play, the game design did not afford a direct make-believe or role-play of the script's main themes, on the other. With its girl-encoded population, the game design only afforded dates and romance between Barbie girls – thereby queering its own heteronormative rhetoric. Through the use of creative workarounds, however, the community devised their own makeshift, or rather "make do," way for boys and gender-fluid players to be represented within the game world. While this strategy was subversive on many levels, it concurrently worked to restore the heteronormative social order within the game space, enabling players to role-play the same types of heterosexual dating scenarios found in Barbie texts and across the children's media landscape. Notably, while it is likely that at least some of the self-proclaimed boy avatars were played by children who identified as boys or as gender-fluid in real life, others were almost certainly played by girls. For one, the "I'm a boy" game most often transpired in negotiated, fluid, and temporally fixed ways. Moreover, Mattel reported that during the study period 85 per cent of its players self-identified as "girls between the ages of 8 and 15 years."[54]

The potential for transgression within *BarbieGirls* highlights the inherently performative and parodic dimensions of dress-up play. It also
evokes the concept of the "'masquerade' of femininity," which suggests
that there is potential for gendered subjectivities to function as "roles
that can be assumed, played with and then discarded" within even in
the most programmed and feminized of spaces.[55] This is perhaps especially true of children's play, wherein gender norms and sex roles surface as prominent and recurring themes. As Schwartzman observes,
socio-dramatic role-play is both a shaper and indicator of gender difference and identification. She argues that children's play often serves as
a caricature or satire through which adult behaviours and norms, especially those exhibited by mothers and fathers, are exaggerated and par-
odied.[56] Through these practices, children engage in what Sutton-Smith
calls "games of order and disorder."[57] Rather than mere mimicry, many
of these games seek to model the dominant social system in order to
then symbolically destroy it. Schwartzman points to the numerous examples of children's games containing antiauthoritarian themes, including
"Mother May I?," which may appear to reinforce maternal or parental
authority, but can also be reinterpreted as a sort of burlesque of social
etiquette. While the "mother" looks away, the "children" inch forward
trying to subvert her authority and trick her.

However, the masquerade of femininity is not in itself subversive. It is
often complicit with traditional gender norms, and with the social practices through which these norms are circulated, made sense of, and rein-
scribed. While the potential for subversion and change is often present,
or at least hinted at, within transgressive play practices, they most often
culminate in a restoration of the status quo. Bakhtin makes a similar argument in his exploration of the "carnivalesque." The medieval carnival
provided a spatially and temporally contained forum for social disruption, critique, and mockery of the dominant ideology. But it rarely served
as a catalyst for revolution or other forms of permanent social change.
Although Schwartzman herself argues that not enough attention is given
to how children's sex role and gender play might *challenge* the status quo,
she also describes that most of the scholarship in this area focuses on the
pedagogical or socializing function of such games. The main argument
advanced in the literature is that children engage in such play as a way
of experimenting with and making sense of but ultimately learning and
internalizing social expectations and ideals. The implications for queer
and trans children, who might already feel unsafe and marginalized
within digital playgrounds, are especially concerning. Concurrently, it is
important to remember that these particular masquerades – of femininity *and* masculinity – are inextricably intertwined with the overarching

cycles of cross-promotion and consumption that permeate the game world and its mechanics. In *BarbieGirls*, the acquisition and display of virtual clothing and accessories is not only a core component of gameplay but also a key driver of its in-game economy. Any activities centred on avatar customization are commercialized by design.

The players of *Club Penguin* also engaged in transgressive play through unanticipated uses of pre-made virtual items and limited avatar customization options. In this game, all players were represented by a penguin avatar. Their physical characteristics, such as body type and facial features, could not be altered, and so all the avatars looked strikingly similar. Avatar customization options were limited to changing the colour of the penguin's feathers and dressing it up in different outfits and costumes. The game contained a relatively large catalogue of clothing, wigs, shoes, and accessories, although a significant proportion of these items were available for (in-game) purchase for only a limited amount of time. Exclusive avatar customization items were also frequently rewarded to players for attending special events or completing missions. A certain amount of rarity was thus built into the world's virtual items system, and a heavy emphasis on items was found throughout the game's texts (storylines, announcements, etc.). Concurrently, items featured prominently within the game world and the activities and player interactions that unfolded within it.

A phenomenon frequently observed during the study period was for large groups of players to colour-coordinate their avatar feathers. It usually began with one player "calling out" a colour (through text-based chat), such as, "Everyone red." Sometimes, this game emerged in response to the coincidental presence of several penguins already sporting the same colour. Other times, colour-coordinating was proposed as a way of marking a special event, or to make a particular statement (e.g., "Turn green for the environment"). In any case, the purposeful homogenization of large groups of avatars allowed the players to reappropriate the lack of diversity and customization options made available to them by the game's design. The colour-coordinating game functioned as a sort of group performance – a virtual flash mob. In some cases, colour-coordinating was paired with engaging en masse in the same movement – such as waving or dancing. These fleeting but widespread moments of collaboration provided a fun and easy way to connect with the broader player community. Participating in these activities clearly generated meaning for the players. At the same time, however, the resultant visual spectacle of sameness and conformity made visible one of the game's design limitations. After all, the reason the flash mobs were so easy to initiate was because of the limited customization options and action opportunities available.

The participatory dimension of the *Club Penguin* flash mobs warrants further consideration. For one, although social interaction is such an integral part of play within connected games aimed at teens and adults, many child-specific titles enforce heavy restrictions on players' speech and other interactions. Consequently, children do not always have access to the same tools, or the same freedom, to form and sustain in-game communities. In order to do so, they must work within and around a wide range of restrictions, design limitations, and other rules of play aimed explicitly at controlling and containing the players' relationships to each other. Framed and performed within this context, the flash mobs serve to both express and promote social cohesion. In this way, the colour-coordinating game can be understood as a form of symbolic action. Concurrently, the lack of variation available in the game's design becomes itself a tool for a new type of creativity that comes out of synchronously engaging in a mass spectacle. In a sense, players were performing their own version of political pageantry, of what Kracauer terms "mass ornament."[58] Their flash mobs not only manifest a sense of communal belonging, they also make visible key components of the game's underlying social order. For children, digital playgrounds can thus function, or at least have the potential to function, as a sort of public forum. Within these spaces, children practise at exercising their right to assemble. They subvert rules and protest structures. They assume conflicting subject positions – as actors, as consumers, as products, but also as citizens. Through these processes, they experience the political possibilities of democratic action.

Notably, some of the players observed in this study also used the game's limited customization options for more deviant forms of play: a digital reinvention of the "copycat game." Here, the term "copycat game" refers to an informal playground game in which one person repeats back everything the other person says and sometimes mimics everything the other person does. The goal of the game is usually to mock and annoy the person being copied. In connected games, the copycat game sometimes emerges in players' chat interactions, with one player retyping everything another player types. In both *Club Penguin* and *BarbieGirls*, however, a different adaptation of the copycat game was observed, in which players exploited the games' limited customization tools to quickly make their own avatar identical to someone else's. Whereas this aesthetic homogeneity served as a mode of group expression and cohesion in certain contexts, in other contexts it functioned as a tool for disruption and "griefing." Exchanges such as these are compelling for several reasons. First, they illustrate that even limited action opportunities can have uses beyond those intended or afforded. They also reveal how so-called disruptive behaviours can occur almost anywhere and can manifest in ways that cannot be viably prevented by design features or filtering algorithms. For instance, although many of the safety mechanisms contained within *BarbieGirls* aimed to prevent bullying and "meanness," players nonetheless found ways to antagonize and annoy one another. Of course, deviant and dark forms of play are common not only in digital playgrounds but also throughout children's play culture. Children often manipulate, antagonize, or attempt to control one another during, and through, play. The copycat game is merely one incarnation of this tendency. The presence of the copycat game within these digital playgrounds is compelling because it reveals the inevitable ineffectiveness of automated systems designed to prevent subversive and disruptive behaviours. Perhaps most importantly, it reveals the inadequate way in which such behaviours are defined as problematic to begin with.

Playing in the Margin of Manoeuvre

In even the most tightly rule-bound of spaces, children can find innovative ways to engage in transgressive play. In the examples above, players exploited what Feenberg calls the "margin of manoeuvre" – the space or potential for unanticipated uses and outcomes contained within the underdetermined aspects of a technological system or device.[59] Within this margin, players find the resources that enable them to stray from the script. They do this by appropriating design features and action opportunities in unexpected ways, employing workarounds, and inscribing their own (subversive) reinterpretations onto the game space. They also uncover emergent properties and phenomena within the game design, engaging in what Salen and Zimmerman call "emergent play." Here, moves and outcomes that appear to stray from a game's programming in fact reveal the "special disconnect between the rules of the system and the ways those rules play out."[60] Within both *BarbieGirls* and *Club Penguin*, players made full use of the narrow range of action opportunities available to them to generate new, playful, and at times transgressive forms of social play. Players used the limited avatar clothing and colour options to identify with others, to antagonize them, to diverge from the official storyline, and to build a virtual community. Their regular divergence from the preferred modes of play, so heavily promoted in the games' storylines, rulebooks, and design affordances, contradicts the idea that children's play is prescribed by their toys, media, or technologies. It also serves as a reminder of the complex and heterogeneous nature of children's play.

Concurrently, however, it is important to consider how rules can inform and shape play, even as they are being negotiated and challenged. Many of the examples of user initiative explored above were markedly "reflexive." In this context, reflexivity refers to in-game activities that are self-referential and exclude themes and activities from outside of the constructed reality of the game world. While these activities deviated in some way from the norm, they nevertheless operated in direct dialogue with the game's underlying rule systems. They engaged, highlighted, and at times critiqued formal aspects of the game, such as its rules, design limitations, aesthetic conventions, or narrative themes. But these elements originated from the game's design and designers – not the players. In practice, the players may (and did!) exhibit elements of the type of spontaneity associated with free and unstructured imaginative play. But their actions and interactions were defined predominantly in reference to the game rules. Resistance was possible but could be enacted only in terms of what was allowed by the tightly managed parameters set by the games' designs and rules. Consequently, many of the examples of transgressive play observed in *BarbieGirls* and *Club Penguin* mobilized design features and directly referenced themes found in the games' narratives and packaging. The ice goths diverged from the typical Barbie doll aesthetic, but they were still perfectly in line with the game's overall emphasis on fashion as a mode of self-expression. The BarbieBoys defied the game's configuration as a girls-only space, but their presence also worked to restore heteronormative gender expectations. Although the *Club Penguin* flash mobs were player-driven, the idea of sporting a specific colour en masse also appeared in the game's store catalogues and in the *CP Times*, where it was promoted as a way for players to communally celebrate special events.

That the game's rules and parameters were so frequently the subject of the players' expressions of resistance and subversion provides further evidence of their prominence within the gameplay experience. This focus on rules is reminiscent of Schwartzman's argument that many children's playground games contain subversive critiques of the social order by mocking the authority of adults. Within digital playgrounds, where authority is relegated largely to the game's programming and other technological features, design restrictions become subject to comparable forms of subversion. Yet this type of reflexivity is also typical of the user–technology relationship. It is present within the dual-level process through which users at once strive to understand (and adhere to) a technology's rules, affordances, and intended outcomes, while simultaneously exhibiting "initiative" in the ways they do *not* conform to those rules and expectations, instead innovating new modes of engagement and uncovering unanticipated outcomes.[61] It is through this process that users come to strategically position themselves in relationship to the object. It is also how they come to find and access the margin of manoeuvre, along with the opportunities for user appropriation, emergence, and unanticipated uses that it contains.

However, when the margin of manoeuvre is too narrow – when too few aspects of a technological artefact are underdetermined – the potential for user initiative is diminished. In many of the child-specific connected games that I and others have examined over the past two decades, opportunities for players to engage directly with the games' technological designs, contents, and even other players have been sparse and tightly controlled. Of course, many forms of user initiative are invisible. Research in this area shows that a significant proportion of children's transgressive play practices have more to do with make-believe, interpretation, and what happens beyond the screen than it does with in-game actions and utterances.[62] Children's digital play is much more than a series of interactions and inputs. It is first and foremost an experience created by and within the players themselves – through their shared and negotiated interpretations of that space, their unique applications of the action opportunities and customization features available to them, their meaning-making and imaginative play. Nonetheless, within connected digital playgrounds, all of this unfolds within parameters laid out, and at times enforced, by the game's design and other rule systems. Perhaps most importantly, in many connected games there are very few ways for players to share, perform, or communicate this dimension of their play with other players – at least, not within the context of the game space. This design limitation is profoundly significant, given the crucial role that peers occupy within children's cultural experience and how their presence contributes to children's sense of agency. As argued above, peer play provides unique opportunities for children to resist adult rules and other forms of social order. However, it is unlikely that these same types of opportunities are available, let alone afforded, within digital playgrounds designed to limit and contain expressions of resistance.

Conclusion

It is common for child-specific digital playgrounds to restrict player expression and inter-player communication. These restrictions are often framed as necessary precautions for protecting children from predators, from other children, and from themselves. In reality, they emerge out of a much more complex, ideologically laden, and ambiguous set of concerns and priorities. In many countries, for instance, privacy laws require that children's personal information be given special protection and treatment. In other instances, restrictions on players' speech and in-game actions are imposed as a way of ensuring that the game's operators are not held responsible for things that unruly players might say or do. By preventing bad words, disruptive behaviours, and inappropriate imagery from ever entering the game in the first place, their potentially negative consequences can (allegedly) be avoided altogether. Children's games are often designed in ways that aim to minimize risks – not only the perceived and real risks that children might encounter when they go online, but also the legal and reputational risks to the game's operators, who might be held liable if something untoward were to happen on their game servers. What gets lost in the shuffle of brand management strategies, user needs, risks assessments, and regulatory responses is any in-depth consideration of how such restrictions can harm children's rights and freedoms. In other contexts, sweeping limitations on player speech would immediately be viewed as censorship. In mainstream games, diminished action opportunities and customization options would be cause for critique. Discourses about child safety have taken a disproportionate precedence within public discussions about children's connected play. The prioritization of this facet of children's online experience takes attention away from other concerns and interests. Meanwhile, several of the preferred industry strategies that have emerged over the past few decades adopt what might be described as an extreme approach to children's speech (and other modes of expression) online and in connected spaces. It is not unusual for child-specific titles to omit opportunities for inter-player interaction altogether, for instance.

In digital playgrounds, responsibility and authority for things such as player safety are partially delegated to the technological artefacts themselves. These delegations manifest as design features and limitations, algorithmic filters, and user management systems, as well as what has been excluded or omitted from the game world. Aspects of the design perform the function of automatically and imperviously enforcing a particular rule of play, a vision of safety, or an idea about what constitutes appropriate play. Through this process, power is seemingly relocated onto the technological system, where it is also diffused, mediated, and sublimated. It is clear from the examples discussed in the previous section that in some cases this technologically embedded social order becomes the focus of reflexive, transgressive play, as well as the site of negotiation and challenge. Throughout this exchange, however, the true sources of power and social order remain obscured. As design decisions become normalized and concretized, it becomes easy to forget that they are made by actual people, who bring to these decisions a messy and subjective assortment of assumptions, biases, cultural politics, and socio-economic contexts. The slippage between safety and censorship found in many children's digital playgrounds is the result of the complex balancing act through which their creators and operators must weigh individual decisions with corporate strategies, best practices with available resources, user needs with social expectations. In a sociocultural climate where children's cultural rights are so rarely on the political or public agenda, it is not surprising that children's freedom of speech rights are not always considered as part of this equation.

However, the fact that something is unsurprising does not make it immune to critique. The lack of consideration given to children's rights within so many areas of the digital realm is unsustainable. Children retain their rights across contexts – including those that are virtual and those that are dedicated to play. The systematic constraint and even effacement of children's ability to freely express themselves within online spaces constitutes an infringement of these rights. The playful nature of digital playgrounds does not diminish the negative affect that the curtailment of children's rights has on children's sense of agency, quality of experience, and overall well-being. The inclusion of a right to leisure and play opportunities within the United Nations' Convention on the Rights of the Child is telling in this regard, as it demonstrates the importance and value that is given to children's recreation and participation in cultural life in countries all around the world. It also shows that play is already understood as integral to broader discourses and definitions of children's fundamental rights and freedoms. In addition, as explored in an earlier section of this chapter, it is important to remember that engaging in the negotiation, challenge, and rewriting of game rules is a central part of children's play. In many ways, rule brokering, bending, and breaking represent key forms of cultural participation for children – as do the incorporation of dark, scary, and taboo themes in children's games and make-believe play. These practices provide children with access to and into the adult-controlled social order. They also serve as building blocks for the formation of peer cultures and relationships. When a space fails to provide children with opportunities to engage with and trouble the rules, it is not only precluding children from the full play experience but also from engaging in children's unique version of cultural life.

For some, the trade-off may seem reasonable. Many parents and children would gladly sacrifice some of their rights to ensure a safe online play experience. Such trade-offs are made every day in the name of protecting children from dangerous others, from disturbing content, as well as from mistakes they themselves might make if left to navigate such complex terrains unconstrained and unassisted. But corporate rhetoric about risk and safety is rarely straightforward and often involves a much more complex and ambiguous set of practices than it lets on. The term "safety" is used in varying ways, for divergent purposes, and with intended outcomes that are difficult to define and almost impossible to measure. As the next chapter will demonstrate, parents' fears about their children's safety are often exploited within popular and commercial safety discourses. The social conceptualization or configuration of the "child at risk" is heavily circulated and highly ideological, but also quite far removed from the actual practices and experiences of (most) children online. These discourses are frequently used to obscure underlying business practices, drawing attention away from the fact that many of the mechanisms and policies found in children's digital playgrounds are required by laws aimed at protecting children's privacy and regulating how their personal information is used by corporate entities. In some games, restrictions on players' speech and expression are concurrently used to promote and foster brand identity. In others, censorship of players functions in accordance with broader strategies to protect corporate copyright and intellectual property, as well as encouraging players to engage in RMT and other pay-to-play features. The trade-off involved is far from straightforward, and very few everyday users are made aware of the full matrix of factors and interests involved. Meanwhile, the restrictions placed on player speech, access, and agency are stringent and excessive, yet largely represented as in the children's best interest.

5

Safety First, Privacy Later

Children's online privacy emerged as an issue of public concern in the earliest days of the World Wide Web, as companies began using websites, quizzes, games, and other online tools to solicit personal information from children for direct marketing and advertising. By the late 1990s, these practices had become widespread, leading to the establishment of child-specific privacy legislation, most notably the US Children's Online Privacy Protection Act (COPPA). The new children's privacy laws aimed to regulate what and how personal information could be gathered from children by requiring service providers to follow a special set of criteria and other guidelines in their interactions with children under the age of thirteen. Since then, numerous studies and reports have tracked the continued expansion of corporate surveillance and data collection throughout children's connected sites, technologies, and spaces.[1] Research in this area pays special attention to how the children's industries have adapted their strategies to comply with the requirements outlined in the act, and in the Personal Information Protection and Electronic Documents Act (PIPEDA) in Canada.[2] It is worth noting that since a large proportion of popular children's websites and users are US-based, as well as because PIPEDA does not provide detailed guidelines for data collection involving minors, online applications targeted to North American children are likely to feature privacy policies that conform to COPPA requirements no matter their point of origin. As a result, for the past two decades COPPA has heavily influenced corporate responses to children's privacy.

The research also suggests that, among developers and service providers, COPPA compliance tends towards the bare minimum. Meanwhile, studies of users have found that a large proportion do not really understand privacy laws, nor do they take the time to read privacy policies. Nonetheless, COPPA and other privacy legislation have had a significant impact on the scope and contents of the children's digital landscape – introducing important limitations, ideals, and assumptions about children's relationships to privacy and anonymity, secrets and selfhood. As with so many facets of children's digital experience, these relationships are ambiguous and often contentious. The ambivalence that surrounds children's privacy reflects a broader, and currently mounting, social unease about how our digital data are collected, used, and manipulated by large corporations and government agencies. The recent discovery in the United States of a monumental case of election meddling, which used personal data and online behavioural trends to misinform voters and ultimately sway public opinion, has brought renewed attention to the problematic dimensions and potential risks associated with unfettered information flows.

It is worth considering that until recently, researchers such as Raynes-Goldie argued that a cultural shift was unfolding in young people's expectations and definitions of privacy. Whereas in the pre-Facebook era, people tended to think of privacy in terms of "institutional privacy," or "how institutions such as governments, banks and other businesses, use or misuse ... personal information," Raynes-Goldie concluded that contemporary uses of the term tended instead to involve social relationships and modes of expression – how personal information was used in daily activities, how it was mobilized for peer pressure or ridicule, or the extent to which users felt they could freely express themselves online and in public.[3] Such a shift would certainly help explain why so many users of connected technologies share so much of their personal information online – despite the role these data play in an increasing number of economic, political, and other institutional transactions. Its purported emergence moreover coincided with the rise and spread of neo-liberal ideals – ideals that celebrate (among other things) data transparency and the "death of privacy."

If such a shift was indeed underway when Raynes-Goldie conducted her research in 2010, more recent studies show that today institutional privacy concerns are increasingly prominent and prevalent. A 2018 survey conducted by Common Sense Media found that the majority (69 per cent) of teens aged thirteen to seventeen thought it was "extremely important" for sites to ask permission before selling or sharing their personal information. The current cultural climate appears to be moving towards a return to more traditional notions of privacy, with key concerns centred on the ways large entities such as corporations and governments use, share, analyse, and profit from our data. This idea finds further support in the mounting calls for the review and expansion of privacy regulations in the United States and Canada. Policymakers and advocacy groups pushing for stronger privacy rights for North American users point to the recent, sweeping changes in privacy regulations and requirements that have unfolded in the EU with the 2018 implementation of the General Data Protection Regulation (GDRP), the repercussions of which have been felt around the globe.[4] The new regulations include a comprehensive framework for protecting children's privacy and other rights, while providing support for their participation in life online. Concurrently, the European Commission launched its European Strategy for a Better Internet for Children (or "BIK Strategy"), which has been heralded by some as a key source of best practices and potential guidebook for future policy development in this area.

This section provides a brief introduction to children's privacy issues as they relate to Canadian and US contexts. It starts with an overview of *Neopets* and other early playgrounds, which exemplified the problems that had emerged in commercial data collection practices and the lack of protection for children's online privacy in the late 1990s and early 2000s. Some of these problems led directly to the introduction of privacy regulations (including COPPA in the United States), yet many others resurface in contemporary digital playgrounds and other connected spaces for (or used by) children. The discussion then shifts to a more focused consideration of the COPPA Rule as the primary site of governmental regulation and discourse pertaining to children's privacy rights, and how the rule has evolved to accommodate new technological forms and user practices. I then revisit my children's virtual worlds study, focusing on trends found in the games' privacy policies and safety-oriented design features, which I argue illustrate how regulation and commercial rhetoric can become translated into restrictive design features, paternalistic management strategies, and narrow user configurations. This is followed by a deeper engagement with the implications of commercial trends that confound privacy and safety, arguing that they allow corporations to obfuscate their own role as (potential) privacy infringers, while placing undue constraints on children's freedom of expression. In the final section, I turn the discussion to the importance of "secret spaces" in children's culture and consider some of the methods children use to bypass, subvert, or simply escape overly restrictive or oppressive interpretations of "safe" play.

Children's Data and Privacy

In the mid- to late 1990s, online commercial sites, games, and portals directed specifically to children began to proliferate, and they quickly attracted the attention of academics, child advocacy groups, and policymakers. In addition to questioning the high levels of commercialization found in so many popular children's sites, a key issue was the growing use of online games and other entertaining websites as venues for soliciting personal information and other valuable data from children for marketing purposes. For example, the Center for Media Education (CME) began investigating the use of children's websites for market research as early as 1995. The group, led by children's media scholar Kathryn Montgomery, drew attention to sites such as *KidsCom.com*, a self-proclaimed online "playground" that generated its revenues by packaging data collected from child users and selling the data to high-profile clients such as PepsiCo and Blockbuster Video.[5] The mounting criticisms against using children's websites for invasive market research played a key role in the establishment of COPPA. In 2000, after several years of public consultations, reviews, and congressional debates, the COPPA Rule first came into effect. In the twenty years since then, the FTC has monitored and enforced compliance to COPPA among operators based in the United States, and failure to follow its rules can result in law enforcement actions and substantial fines. COPPA has had limited but important repercussions for children's digital content developers across North America and beyond, as it requires that operators of websites or any other online (or connected) services directed to or knowingly used by US children under the age of thirteen meet a set of requirements aimed at protecting children's privacy. Notably, COPPA not only restricts how websites collect and use the data they obtain from child users, but it also forbids them outright from displaying children's personally identifiable information. This includes data and content that children might post themselves as they participate in forums or via in-game chat systems.

From the outset, the COPPA Rule largely equated children's privacy with parents' ability to control access to their child's "personally identifiable information," such as real name, home address, email, and so on. Many of COPPA's original requirements were therefore focused on how children's personal information was collected, displayed, stored, and transferred. COPPA stipulated, for example, that a child's personal information must not be knowingly collected, shared, or made publicly available without prior parental consent. Operators had to secure *verifiable* parental consent and provide a reasonable means through which parents could review what information had been collected from their child, as well as revoke consent for the continued storage and use of those data. Operators had to keep any personal information that *was* collected from child users secure, and they had to provide details to parents about the type of information collected, upon request. They were also required to refrain from making the disclosure of excessive amounts of personal information a condition for participation. While the rule's definition of "personal information" was expanded in 2013 to include geolocation information, photographs, and video, as well as persistent identifiers, the requirement that parental consent must be secured before the collection or display of children's personal information remains, with some updated and streamlined conditions for how and when this consent is obtained.

In these early years, for many operators, the additional costs and efforts involved with ensuring COPPA compliance provided justification for excluding child users altogether. As a result, "bans" and other restrictions of users under the age of thirteen years (and in many cases, eighteen years) became commonplace across the internet. In many instances, the age ban was more of a formality, an attempt to bypass COPPA, than an enforced age restriction. For instance, in 2002 four different Yahoo! Games titles appeared on the Nielsen/NetRatings and Hitwise lists of most popular sites among children and teens, despite the fact that the games officially banned users under the age of eighteen. The games contained themes, characters, and contents drawn from other children's media or culture, and the age restrictions themselves were essentially buried in the sites' accompanying terms of service contracts. During this period, COPPA compliance rates were quite low, and age restrictions, while common, went largely unenforced within large swathes of the digital landscape. By the turn of the millennium, however, a significant segment of operators and market researchers started moving away from direct forms of data collection, such as online surveys and requests for home addresses. For many, young users were no longer seen as susceptible to these more blatant commercial tactics, but rather as savvy and even cynical when it came to online ads and interactions with corporate entities. Accordingly, strategies for advertising to children began to include more diverse and nuanced approaches. It was during this same period that industries involved in data collection, mining, and brokering began to shift their attention towards aggregated but also longitudinal and rich data sets that tracked patterns in children's behaviour and interactions over time and across a range of sites and platforms.

Almost all of the children's online game sites that I analysed during this period collected some form of personal information from their young players. Email addresses, date of birth, and gender were the most common types of data that players were asked, and oftentimes required, to supply during the mandatory registration. Some also asked for the user's name and at least some components of the home address, such as state/province, country, or zip code/postal code. Two-thirds featured surveys, polls, or customizable features directly relating to – and soliciting players' opinions about – specific products or brands. Privacy scholar Steeves has written extensively about the practice of using online personality quizzes for market research. While often presented as a form of entertainment, quizzes are in fact frequently used as tools for getting children to reveal valuable details about their likes and dislikes, personal interests, and daily activities.[6] While user responses to these quizzes does not necessarily qualify as "personally identifiable information," almost any data provided online can be tied back to the computer they originated from, and therefore back to the user (and/or parent). In addition, aggregate data gathered from thousands, or even millions, of children – an otherwise difficult to reach demographic – are themselves a highly valuable resource, providing important insight into demographic trends and cultural fads, which in turn can be used for new product development, and for designing targeted advertising.[7] Despite COPPA's original purpose of curbing the activities of online marketers, compliance to its requirements has not much impeded the industry's ability to collect data from child users.

The COPPA Rule Revised

Throughout the 2000s, scholars and critics argued that COPPA's definition of what falls under the protected category of "personal" information was much too narrow. Defined at a time when the web was still quite nascent, COPPA did not initially include data derived from more recent technological innovations on its list of protected information, including common things such as geolocation data and persistent identifiers. It did not appear to extend to multimedia such as photos and videos either. Critics furthermore contended that the requirements for parental consent were problematic at best, and at worst ineffectual. When it came to securing parents' verifiable consent, allowing them to view their child's data and request its deletion, studies showed low compliance rates among operators, a general lack of awareness among parents, as well as inadequate enforcement by the FTC. Privacy watchdogs voiced their concern that the information collected from children on COPPA-compliant sites could subsequently be shared, or more likely sold, with non-compliant third parties – a loophole through which a growing number of child-targeted sites, games, and apps had begun to generate a significant portion of their profits. Finally, children's privacy advocates demonstrated that industry standards for the retention and the eventual destruction of user data were opaque and, in many cases, inadequate.

From 2010 to 2012, at the urging of some of these same critics, advocacy groups, and privacy watchdogs, the FTC conducted an extensive review of the COPPA Rule, which involved consultations with stakeholder groups, including industry representatives. In 2013, it released a revised set of guidelines to update the rule, with emphasis on how its terms applied to (then-)emerging technologies such as mobile apps and practices such as UGC. As mentioned above, this included an expansion of its previous definition of personal information to include geolocational data, photos, and video, with acknowledgment that new technologies such as facial recognition software made such data personally identifiable (or at least potentially so). The 2013 update was aimed at addressing technological developments and shifting trends in children's online and digital behaviour. For instance, during its consultations with experts, the FTC debated issues such as the impact of the rule on children's ability to make and share UGC online, and the obscure ways in which persistent identifiers often flow between companies. While the revised COPPA Rule responds to many of the shortcomings identified in its first iteration, scholars such as Turow argue that its overall effectiveness in protecting children's privacy remains moderate at best. Above all, the rule is limited by its narrow approach to children's needs and vulnerabilities within the digital realm, which are multifaceted, complex, and often context-dependent.

Within COPPA's text and surrounding discourses, children are constructed as inherently vulnerable users of adult-made technologies and content. Their potential rights and autonomy as digital citizens, creators, and authors are largely overlooked by a regulatory framework that prioritizes protectionism while bestowing very little agency to the child users it seeks to protect. Parents are concurrently framed as the ultimate authority on children's online transactions – they are the ones who must give or revoke verifiable consent, and they are the ones held responsible for knowing and keeping abreast of the details of the economic and legal relationships their children enter into by participating in a website, playing a connected game, or otherwise engaging in networked activities.

The expansion of the rule's purview to include pictures and check-ins filled an important gap in the privacy regulation – one that was becoming all the more noticeable, given the continued popularity of smartphones and apps that gather geolocation data and other persistent identifiers. Along with these technological innovations, posting pictures and videos to social networking forums such as Instagram, Facebook, and Snapchat have become common practice. While the sites themselves may still forbid, limit, or otherwise place conditions on children's participation, the scholarly research and popular coverage of these sites suggest that they are nonetheless used by many older children, and possibly by younger children as well. Concurrently, children's personal information is often included within the broader data flows that are generated by parents' own uses of digital technology – both overtly, through "sharenting"[8] practices, as well as inadvertently, through automated tags and other associations made behind the scenes by big data algorithms. Although there is little research on how prevalent participation in social networking forums is among Canadian and US children (under the age of thirteen), studies conducted in the EU indicate that the rates are quite high. Back in 2011, Livingstone, Ólafsson, and Staksrud found that "one in five 9–12 year olds have a Facebook profile, rising to over 4 in 10 in some countries."[9] A study of Canadian children and teens conducted in 2014 found that one-third of children in Grade 5 and almost half of children in Grade 6 had their own Facebook account – in defiance of the site's well-established age ban.[10] Recent research suggests that participation in online social networking among underage children has only increased since the early 2010s. A study of Norwegian children aged six to eleven years conducted in 2019 revealed that 23 per cent reported using Snapchat, which was the most popular platform among this age group, followed by TikTok (18 per cent).[11]

At the time of writing, the FTC is in the midst of a new review of the COPPA Rule, considering updates "in light of evolving business practices in the online children's marketplace, including the increased use of Internet of Things devices, social media, educational technology, and general audience platforms hosting third-party child-directed content."[12] The review commenced shortly after a group of US consumer advocacy groups (led by the Campaign for a Commercial Free Childhood and the Center for Digital Democracy) and policymakers filed complaints with the FTC, calling for an investigation into YouTube's handling of children's data. A key component of the complaints was the disconnect between YouTube's claim that the site is not intended for children under the age of thirteen years, and the fact that it is "filled with videos designed for viewing by kids."[13] It is not yet clear how, or even whether, an updated COPPA Rule would respond to these emerging issues, or to the contradictory business practices that they stem from.

Of particular interest is what role the GDPR might play in the FTC's review, and any subsequent changes it makes to COPPA's definitions of "personal information" or "age of consent." For instance, the GDPR's definition of "personal data" extends far beyond the direct, and explicitly personal, identifiers outlined in COPPA, and includes "any information relating to an identified or identifiable natural person ('data subject'); an identifiable natural person is one who can be identified, directly or indirectly, in particular by reference to an identifier such as a name, an identification number, location data, an online identifier or to one or more factors specific to the physical, physiological, genetic, mental, economic, cultural or social identity of that natural person."[14]

The GDPR's attempt to address identity rather than mere identifiers can be seen as representing a more holistic way of thinking about privacy – one that is less instrumental and less focused on meeting legal criteria or on limiting itself to only the most invasive of direct marketing practices. While the regulation is too new to assess how its approach to personal data might shift broader public or legal discourses about people's privacy *rights* online, and away from an exclusive emphasis on protections, it has already had the widespread impact of forcing operators around the globe to review and update their privacy policies. Notably, however, while inviting comments on all aspects of the COPPA Rule as part of its most recent review, the FTC did not include specific questions about its definition of personal information in its request for public comment, held in the second half of 2019.

Meanwhile, COPPA maintains an ambivalent relationship with YouTube and other popular social networking forums that, in their current form, are unable to officially allow children to participate without breaking several stipulations of the COPPA Rule. To become COPPA-compliant, the sites would first need to make significant changes to their designs and operating policies, including the incorporation of site-wide systems for securing parental consent. Such changes risk undermining the culture of sharing and personal connectedness that has established itself among users. Until now, by formally excluding children under the age of thirteen from joining, and banishing unauthorized children when they are discovered, popular social networking platforms have remained ostensibly exempt from the COPPA Rule. Meanwhile, increasing numbers of children join these sites "illegally" (i.e., lying about their age), and the sites themselves are filled with content that caters to this "underage" audience. Ironically, many children do use these platforms with their parents' knowledge and permission.[15] The current COPPA review is timely and vital, not only because of the massive technological innovations that have unfolded over the past decade, but also in light of the increasingly urgent need for social networking platforms to directly address – and hopefully reconcile – the growing disconnect between the traditional industry response and contemporary user practices. Until then, many of the sites and services through which children *and* their parents share enormous volumes of personal information are operating outside of COPPA regulation.

This last point warrants further consideration, as the research indeed indicates that parents are some of the biggest culprits when it comes to sharing children's personal information online.[16] Adults regularly post personal data, photos, videos, and other information about their own and others' children on social networking sites and other forms of connected media, oftentimes without the child's knowledge or consent. A recent study conducted out of the University of Michigan found that nearly three-quarters of parents who used social media knew of another parent who (in their opinion) shared too much information about their child online. This included "embarrassing information" about the child (56 per cent), information that could lead to the identification of the child's physical location (51 per cent), as well as "inappropriate" photos of them (27 per cent).[17] Ostensibly, many of these activities are not covered by the COPPA Rule. However, as Steinberg argues, little legal scholarship has focused on the "intersection of a parent's right to share online with a child's right to privacy on the internet," or addressed the issue of "a child's right to privacy from the parent."[18] These gaps are likely linked to the tendency among US courts to show reluctance in acknowledging children's privacy rights within family contexts. Deference is instead given to the parents' rights to exercise control over their child and to determine the specifics of their child's upbringing. According to Steinberg, "Many laws aimed at protecting children's privacy are written from the paternalistic viewpoint that the parent has exclusive control over the disclosure of a child's personal information. Privacy laws provide little guidance, prohibitions, or remedial measures for children needing privacy protection from their parents' online disclosure. This reality is partly based on the idea that society generally accepts the notion that parents will always do what is best for their children."[19]

Of course, most parents *do* want what's best for their children and strive to protect them from harm and negative consequences. But the deferral of responsibility onto parents to *always* act in their child's best interests rests on an underlying assumption that parents will have the knowledge and resources required to accurately assess the interests at play. The literature suggests this is not always the case. Many parents struggle to understand the complex relationships and ever-changing technologies that they and their children engage with. Moreover, children's privacy scholars emphasize that the processes through which "parental consent" is obtained remain largely undefined and poorly enforced.[20] Steeves also points out that the definition of parental consent is not equivalent to informed consent, despite the COPPA Rule's purported emphasis on ensuring that parents retain control over their children's data and, to some extent, children's relationships with corporate entities online. Meanwhile, users of all ages are unaware of the underlying political, economic, and technical processes that drive popular internet applications and connected devices.[21] At the same time, there are myriad tangible positive outcomes associated with using connected technologies – from community building and fostering personal connections to self-expression and participating directly in the creation of our shared culture. As Steinberg notes, "Sharing common parenting experiences brings communities together and helps connect similarly situated individuals around the globe."[22] Children are a "central" part of every parent's life story, she argues, and parents have an interest and a right to freely express their stories and experiences online. The situation is complicated and ambiguous. Parents do not always fully understand what might happen to the child's information once it is posted online. Meanwhile, their own interests sometimes conflict with those of their children – even though the conflicts are not always immediately apparent.

A key place to look for evidence of such conflicts is in children's own assessments of the roles and impacts of connected technologies on their everyday lives. In a study of families' experiences with digital technologies in the home, which included a survey of 249 parent-child pairs, Hiniker, Schoenebeck, and Kientz found, "Children were twice as likely [as parents] to report that adults should not 'overshare' by posting information about children online without permission."[23] The researchers concluded that the discrepancy between the children's responses and those of their parents was among the study's most notable findings. They argue, "Children's frustrations with parents' oversharing stands apart as a challenge that transcends existing power dynamics. Child participants reported that they find this content embarrassing and feel frustrated that parents publicly contribute to their online presence without permission."[24] The results led the researchers to conclude, "Children's need to control their online image is undermined by the common parent practice of sharing information about children online."[25] Steinberg makes a similar argument in her review of the legal implications of sharenting and the potential tensions that arise between children's right to privacy and parents' right to express themselves. She suggests that parents can avoid many such conflicts by adopting a best practices approach to sharing children's information online, including familiarizing themselves with privacy policies (and related issues) of the sites on which they share content and giving their child "veto power" over disclosures, images, and other content relating to them. As in other contexts where children's rights are considered, Steinberg explains, "The weight given to the child's choice should vary with respect to the age of the child and the information being disclosed."[26]

The issues and tensions associated with sharenting are relevant to the current discussion because of the substantial emphasis that the COPPA Rule places on parental consent and authority. Both in its approach to how children's privacy is defined, as well as how it is regulated, parents are positioned as *the* consenting party. In fact, the rule barely addresses whether and how consent might be sought from the actual children from whom data are collected. In its official *Complying with COPPA: Frequently Asked Questions*, the FTC provides the following general description:

"The primary goal of COPPA is to place parents in control over what information is collected from their young children online." Ensuring that parents have control over their children's information is envisioned as one of the main responsibilities that corporations are required to shoulder in protecting children's privacy online. While the rule comes with a handful of additional responsibilities, including making sure children's personal information is shared only with "service providers and third parties capable of maintaining it securely," most of its requirements revolve around the parents' rights, rather than those of the child.

It is therefore unsurprising that the rule overlooks and at times conflicts with important dimensions of children's online experiences. As mentioned, for instance, COPPA ties parental consent requirements to the public display of children's personal information, including information that children themselves may try to share with others online. This makes the inclusion of chat systems or other forms of UGC a much more challenging prospect if children are present. User communications must either be heavily monitored, unfold through systems designed to prevent or exclude the sharing of personal information, or both. Opting to simply ban users under the age of thirteen can seem easier and more cost effective than ensuring COPPA compliance. As a result, entire swathes of the internet have been closed off to younger children – at least officially. As mentioned above, social networking sites are key examples of this trend. Most have a minimum age requirement for participation, and they forbid users under the age of thirteen from creating an account. The formal exclusion of children from such spaces restricts children from entering whole categories of quasi-public space – some of which are now central to participation in (certain forms of) public life. While many young users ignore or bypass these restrictions, sometimes with the permission of their parents, their formal exclusion from such spaces arguably limits their legitimacy and authority as participants. As will be explored later in this chapter, another common strategy for ensuring COPPA compliance found across the children's digital landscape is the restriction or outright exclusion of tools and other design features that would enable children to share content and communicate online. Both strategies have a similar result of placing significant limits on and hurdles to children's access and freedom to participate fully in online culture.

Reframing Privacy Protections as Safety Mechanisms

The COPPA Rule was originally introduced to protect children from predators and regulate how marketers and other corporate entities solicited and used personal information collected from children online. Over the past twenty years, it has evolved into an even more complex piece of legislation. For one, the rule itself has been updated in response to new developments, both technological and social, and now applies not only to websites and digital games but also to mobile apps and smart toys.[27] Through this process of updating and clarifying the COPPA Rule, its reach has expanded in some ways and contracted in others. For instance, its definition of personal information has grown, while its ban on the public display of children's personal information was removed (or as the FTC claims, it merely "clarified" that the display or "disclosure" of children's personal information is contingent on parental consent). It is moreover the source of numerous social assumptions, beliefs, and misconceptions, which in turn have shaped users' behaviours and industry practices. In many ways, the ethical problems identified in the late 1990s have only intensified in the years since COPPA was introduced. While it may no longer be common to display children's personal details online or send "direct mail marketing" to their home address, as was the case two decades ago, the depth and extent of information collected from and about child users today is staggering. With the spread of always-on smart devices, such as the Amazon Echo and Mattel's Hello Barbie, there is a renewed interest among policymakers, parents, and advocacy groups concerned with children's privacy rights and information security. As with other major issues relating to children and technology, however, privacy is the subject of an ebb and flow of public debate, concern, and panic. Interest rises with the introduction of a new technology or following some noteworthy event (such as a large-scale security breach) and then wanes again once the news cycle has run its course.

Meanwhile, industry standards have emerged to create a relatively homogenous, widespread framework for dealing with children's personal information online. This framework is indeed COPPA compliant, but it concurrently allows operators to reconfigure children's privacy in corporate-friendly terms focused on "user safety" and "optimal user experience." Glimpses into this industry-standard approach can be found embedded within features of child-specific artefacts and spaces. The remainder of this section will focus on two of the most prominent and influential among these: privacy policies and design features promoted as safety mechanisms.

Privacy Policies

The COPPA Rule requires that websites and other digital media targeted at or otherwise known to be used by US children under the age of thirteen contain and prominently display a written privacy policy. As a result, a sizeable proportion of apps, games, and other connected play spaces that are aimed at (or knowingly used by) children under thirteen residing in the United States contain a privacy policy of some kind. Although the research indicates that users (of all ages) rarely read privacy policies, the documents themselves nonetheless provide unique insight into the hidden politics of children's digital play. While the policies serve primarily as mechanisms for ensuring regulatory compliance, they also often function as "position statements" on regulatory issues and debates. For one, they describe – often in great detail – a company's understanding of its own rights and responsibilities vis-à-vis children's privacy, as well as the rights of its users and their parents. Moreover, over the years, privacy policies have come to serve a multitude of additional functions. For instance, it is often within the privacy policy that a game's owners will attempt to define appropriate player behaviour and configure players (and their parents) in particular subject positions. Privacy policies can reveal some of the ways the social order is not only reflected in the designs of children's digital playgrounds, but in their management and governance strategies as well. They contain important insights into the technical code or broader socio-political climate out of which the associated children's game, site, app, or other digital playground emerged.

Although privacy policies are meant to inform parents and children about a site or game's data collection practices, what privacy protections are provided, as well as what rights and responsibilities users are accorded within the virtual space, the documents themselves are not always accessibly written or even easy to find. Moreover, the tone and contents of most privacy policies are far from user-centric. Instead, they tend to focus on setting terms that will enable site operators to meet COPPA Rule and other regulatory requirements, claim a range of corporate rights, and delimit corporate liability. For instance, many of the virtual worlds I analysed contained privacy policies that read a lot like rulebooks in which users and/or their parents were told what they could and could not do within the virtual world. In fact, many of the exact same terms and clauses included in the games' privacy policies also appeared in the official rules of play. All but one of the rulebooks I analysed included a ban on divulging personal information – a clear carryover from the privacy policies that prohibited users from publicly sharing personal information as a way of addressing the COPPA Rule's initial requirement that operators must not display the personal information of children under the age of thirteen. In some cases, the players themselves were additionally tasked with reporting any other player seen divulging or attempting to divulge personal information within the game environment. This conflation of privacy rights with rules of play is important, as it shifts the discourse away from how and when corporations are legally responsible for safeguarding young users' data, and instead places emphasis on the users as a source of potentially deviant, rule-breaking, privacy-infringing behaviour. This is just one of many ways the original purpose of government-mandated privacy policies has been obscured and reimagined within the commercial children's digital playscape

As explored in chapter 3, many children's digital playgrounds contain interactive advertising, branding, and cross-promotional content. They are also frequently used for market research and data harvesting. From *Neopets* to *Club Penguin*, the unique levels of access enabled by connected technologies are mobilized to gather unimaginable amounts of personal information, thoughts, and opinions from child users.[28] Common methods include surveys and polls disguised as personality quizzes, data mining chat logs and other communications between players, algorithms that track and monitor players' in-game actions, and data analysis of children's fanart and creative writing.[29] Information such as behavioural patterns, usage habits, and conversations among users can all be analysed and utilized for marketing and product development. Aggregated user data are data-mined and packaged as demographic trend reports, while full data sets can be shared or sold to other companies. A wide range of linkages and associations are made between the data collected in digital playgrounds and the users' broader digital footprints – along with those of their parents and other members of their households. Data harvested from children's games, apps, and websites can be highly valuable to the children's industries, from those involved in the production and promotion of children's consumer goods to those involved in the design and creation of children's media and other content.

All six of the children's virtual worlds selected for in-depth analysis contained a privacy policy that described an extensive array of data collection practices, extending from the personally identifiable information requested during sign-up, to behavioural data gathered using online tracking technologies, to data collected from users' submissions, UGC, and chat exchanges. The scope of user data listed within these policies was staggering. All the case studies specified that most of the information they collected from users was "non-personally identifiable," and that personal information was collected only where necessary for effective operation of the game and services. While many made a point of suggesting that the data were collected primarily in order to improve the game for its users, all six allowed that the data could also be used for marketing and product development. The *Club Penguin* privacy policy, for example, read, "We also may use information in the aggregate to analyse site usage, as well as to offer products, programs, or services." The policies

Table 5.1. Six Virtual Worlds Selected for In-depth Analysis

Name	Launch date	Population size	Owner	Market sector
BarbieGirls	Apr. 2007	1 million	Mattel	Toys, media
Club Penguin	Oct. 2005	4 million	Disney	Toys, media
GalaXseeds	Feb. 2007	Over 60,000	Corus Entertainment	Media/TV
Magi-Nation	Feb. 2008	Unknown	Cookie Jar Group	Toys, TV, collectible card game
Nicktropolis	Jan. 2007	4 million	Nickelodeon	Media/TV, toys
Toontown	Jun. 2003	1.2 million	Disney	Theme park, media/TV, toys

Source: Adapted from Grimes (2010).

all specified that some of this information might be shared with third parties. For instance, the *GalaXseeds* privacy policy stated, "Sometimes we may share aggregate, non-personal information with our partners or advertisers (i.e., 20% of our members are girls from Chicago), however specific members are never identified." Among the six case studies, *Club Penguin* was the only virtual world that stated in its privacy policy that it did not share any data with third parties. Given that this world was owned by Disney, however, the lack of third-party data sharing was not all that surprising. As one of the most prominent and expansive media conglomerates in the world, Disney tends not to share data about its users, but rather keeps and uses it internally.

A deeper exploration of the type of information protected by the COPPA Rule may help clarify the widespread practices of gathering, sharing, and selling non-personal information. The primary emphasis of COPPA is the protection of children's "personal information," originally defined as data (or "identifiers") that permit identification or physical contacting of a specific individual, and "personally identifiable information," which includes any information gathered from the child when combined with a "personal information" identifier.[30] This significantly limits the scope of COPPA, in that children's *non*-personally identifiable content does not receive any special protection unless it is directly linked to personal identifiers. As a result, a lot of the information deemed valuable by entities that harvest and mine data, such as personal opinions, aspirations, beliefs, habits, preferences, and social relationships, is not covered by COPPA or by most commercial privacy policies.[31] The addition in the 2013 revision of an expanded definition for "persistent identifiers"[32]

removed the previous requirement of a direct link with personally identifiable information in order to warrant protection. Thus, there are now
restrictions on collecting information such as IP addresses for purposes
such as targeted marketing, unless parental consent is secured. This move
can be seen as an attempt to address some of the practices found in many
commercial digital playgrounds. Indeed, given the massive amounts of
user data that are exchanged among companies, an IP address is often
enough to make all the connections necessary for detailed and specific
identification of individual users and their associated households.[33] On
the other hand, an individual child's personal information and persistent identifiers are not always required for their data to be useful to data
brokers, analytics algorithms, and market researchers, where the focus is
on aggregate data and demographic trends anyway.

Within many of the children's digital playgrounds that I have examined over the past two decades, details about the operator's approach to
children's data and privacy have been obfuscated by a heavy rhetorical
emphasis on safety. Most of the privacy polices reviewed in the virtual
worlds study, for instance, contained terms such as "safe" and "safety"
to describe the site's activities, data collection procedures, and design
intentions. As in other areas of the commercial digital landscape, these
terms were amorphously defined and applied. They appeared in other
official texts and advertisements aimed at parents as well, including
game descriptions, parent guides, and parent pages. This trend was consistent with previous research in this area, which has found that notions
of safety are frequently used as rhetorical devices for convincing parents, teachers, and other caregivers that a site or game is appropriate or
even beneficial to children. While the application of these terms within
promotional discourses is variable and often arbitrary, they are also
systematically used to tap into parental anxieties about children online.
In addition to their potential promotional function, a rhetorical emphasis on safety also reframes children's privacy in ways that de-prioritize
children's privacy rights, while also advancing the idea that corporate
entities and commercial processes protect children from ambiguous
harms. The subtle repositioning of children's privacy as a safety issue
helps obscure the fact that the COPPA Rule was initially designed to
protect children from commercial exploitation arising out of online
marketing and data harvesting. Instead of openly identifying operators
as COPPA-compliant collectors of children's digital information, as the
rule requires, privacy policies are used to reconfigure COPPA compliance as a key selling point – or even as a type of public service.

While the confluence of privacy rights and protection from online
predators produces very real advantages and has benefits for children's

safety – and for their enjoyment of digital spaces and artefacts – it none-theless distracts users from the commercial relationships and market research that privacy policies are meant to address. For example, my study uncovered a tendency among virtual world operators for describ-ing rules aimed at restricting players from sharing their real names, ages, hometowns, or phone numbers as there to protect children from other players. Little, if any, mention was made of the fact that this particular safety feature was actually required by the COPPA Rule as a way to end a once-common practice among operators and marketers of using con-nected play spaces to solicit children's names and contact information for direct marketing. The identification of stranger danger as the biggest risk associated with sharing personal information takes attention away from the more prevalent industry practices of collecting, using, manip-ulating, and selling children's data. These practices clearly play a much greater and more direct role in the infringement of children's privacy rights online. The emphasis placed on safety also polarizes the other-wise ambiguous distinctions within COPPA and other privacy legislation between personal information, personally identifiable information, and other types of user data. The significance of the widespread use of digital playgrounds to gather extensive amounts of information about children becomes sidelined when privacy is equated with safety. The mundane and largely obscure relationship between children's digital play and the global data economy cannot compete with the immediate gravity evoked by hot-button issues such as cyber-bullying and online predators.

Privacy policies are often re-appropriated to serve myriad additional functions, including relaying corporate mission statements, setting ground rules and rules of play, acting as promotional tools, and con-tributing to a subtle repositioning of the industries' relationship with children's privacy and other rights online. Their increased utility has coincided with a marked increase in the prominence and visibility of pri-vacy policies across the children's digital landscape. Since the mid 2000s, most connected playgrounds aimed at (US) children do contain a pri-vacy policy. Many sites and games include it in the registration process, and a great number make efforts to ensure that their policy is clearly written and accessible to users and their parents. This was the case in the children's virtual worlds study, where five out of the six worlds selected for in-depth analysis included a review of the privacy policy as part their new account creation process. All five of these policies included a section written in child-friendly language. More recent studies confirm the wide-spread presence of privacy policies in the children's digital realm. For example, my analysis of child-specific digital media-making platforms, published in 2015, found that 90 per cent of the 140 sites reviewed contained a privacy policy.[34] The trend of making privacy policies more visible to users is noteworthy, as it diverges from the conclusions of research conducted in the early 2000s, which found that most sites failed to provide privacy policies at all, and those that did most often buried the policies in small print at the bottom of the page.[35]

However, this increased visibility has not translated into increased transparency, particularly of behind-the-scenes processes addressed by the policies themselves.[36] Data collection practices are often described in vague and potentially misleading terms, which frequently include portrayals of commercial data flows as beneficial to users and their online experience. An example of this tendency was found in *Habbo Hotel*'s "Privacy Pledge" which, prior to the passing of the GDPR, included the following statement: "We promise that you will only hear from Habbo Hotel on behalf of carefully selected companies about cool offers that we think you might be interested in. Rest assured that we will not divulge your information to anyone without your prior consent. You can relax and enjoy the hotel in complete safety!"[37] The use of reassuring language and the emphasis on safety work to obscure the lack of details that are actually provided about the extent and nature of the data exchange involved. How are the offers "carefully selected," and what type of information is given (or rather sold) to these third-party companies? While the data flows underlying the information society are certainly complex, other examples show that it is indeed possible to describe data practices in ways that are both honest and easy to comprehend. Recall, for instance, the *GalaXseeds* privacy policy (from the same time period), which stated, "We use non-personal information – like gender, birth date, country and state/province – to customize our site for our users. Sometimes we may share aggregate, non-personal information with our partners or advertisers (i.e. 20% of our members are girls from Chicago), however specific members are never identified."[38]

The mobilization of safety rhetorics, commonly found in children's privacy policies, itself draws attention away from the privacy rights, implications, and relationships that are constructed within many digital play spaces. While privacy policies are more prominent and widespread across the children's digital landscape than they were two decades ago, they still represent a very limited and problematic tool for protecting children's privacy rights online. Not only do very few users read them, but a significant proportion of young users misunderstand what a privacy policy is even for. As Steeves discovered in her study of Canadian children in Grades 4 through 11, "68% incorrectly think that the presence of a privacy policy on a website means that the site will not share their personal information with others."[39] But the problems with privacy policies extend far beyond individual awareness and comprehension. Common industry practices, the rise of big data economies, and the limited scope of privacy regulation in North America present greater obstacles to children's privacy online. It is important to remember, for instance, that although operators rarely divulge the true extent and nature of their data collection to children and their parents (e.g., in privacy policies), the activities themselves are predominantly in accordance with current federal and provincial/state privacy legislation. In this way, the limited impact of privacy policies is simply emblematic of a much larger oversight within our regulatory approach and cultural conceptualization of what children's privacy entails, what it looks like, and whom it pertains to.

"Safety" by Design

Industry responses to regulations and broader social concerns about children's privacy online also surface in the form of design choices. In many games, apps, websites, and platforms, mechanisms for ensuring COPPA Rule compliance extend to design features intended to limit players' ability to publicly share personal information or to engage in other types of "undesirable" or "inappropriate" communication. In at least some cases, the presence of such features indicates a child-centred approach to user experience (UX) design, wherein the unique needs and vulnerabilities of children as an intended user group are placed front and centre as decisions are made about how the playground will function, what it will look like, what it will include or exclude, and so on. By incorporating COPPA Rule requirements into the very fabric of the playground's design – its interface, structure, and action opportunities – this type of approach enables children's participation in an online social experience that is consistent (and compliant) with legislation enacted to protect their interests. Yet a great number of these mechanisms accomplish this by essentially censoring player speech at the level of utterance, and by otherwise systematically restricting players' ability to express themselves. For instance, many children's digital playgrounds contain heavy restrictions on inter-player chat and communication, through which words, themes, and entire subject areas are banned from the space altogether. Many other playgrounds opt instead to simply exclude tools or features that would enable players to communicate with one another or to share content publicly.

In many of the sites I have looked at over the years, privacy policies and privacy-focused design features are very closely linked. Accordingly, many playgrounds refer to their embedded privacy design features as "safety mechanisms." The recurring emphasis on safety within children's games, apps, and other playgrounds is significant. For one, it is consistent with broader trends found across the digital landscape. As Shade argues, "Adult fears surrounding security and safety of children online have been a feature of popular media discourse since the popularization of the Internet in the mid-1990s. A veritable industry of online child safety experts and the creation of technological remedies, such as filtering software, have developed to assuage parental and adult fears."[40] Such fears are further compounded when the online technology in question consists of digital games, which come with their own history rife with controversy, panic, and ambivalence. While the safety features found within children's connected playgrounds serve a range of functions – including ensuring compliance with US privacy regulations – they also often represent a subtle manipulation of parental concerns. These encompass everyday concerns for children's interests and well-being, as well as media-fuelled fears about the risks (perceived and real) associated with children's use of online technologies. They include apprehensions about children's privacy and personal information, worries that children might become the targets of cyber-bullying or predators, as well as anxieties about children's potential exposure to inappropriate and mature content. As many digital play spaces are connected on multiple levels, from the multiplayer features contained within individual games and apps to device-specific networks, some of which are embedded and some of which are peripheral, the opportunities for risk can seem endless and incomprehensible.

The situation is almost certainly aggravated by the pervasive lack of parental awareness about children's use and proficiency with these technologies, as found in the previous research in this area.[41] Through the inclusion and promotion of safety features and discourses, parents are given (some) reassurance that their concerns are being addressed. It is therefore common for child-specific connected playgrounds to contain safety protocols of some form. In some instances, a separate "safety policy" may be provided, which users, or more specifically their parents, are encouraged to read during the initial registration process. In others, live moderators are on hand to monitor for and remove any unauthorized information or content, as well as to penalize the rule-breakers through warnings or account suspensions. In addition to written rules and moderators, features of the design itself can function as embedded safety mechanisms. These range from overt features such as tightly restricted or algorithmically filtered chat systems to subtler, implicit design decisions such as including only a handful of avatar move options. The resulting constraints that these limitations place on individual children's freedom of speech, expression, and creativity are frequently justified as ensuring the increased safety of the child player population. The underlying assumption is not only that children are at heightened risk, but also that they *pose* a higher risk to one another if they have too broad a range of moves or words available to them. Yet it is important to remember that design features, including chat restrictions and other safety mechanisms, introduce both limitations and affordances into the user's experience. Safety features contain but also guide children's communication away from undesirable or risky topics and *towards* themes deemed appropriate to the game space and its young population.

In this way, design features introduce additional "rules of play" – ones that are particularly difficult for the average child user to bypass or negotiate. As with so many dimensions of children's digital play, the definitions and interpretations of "safe" that are inscribed within these design features are laden with ambiguity, ideological assumptions, and idealized visions of childhood. They also exhibit a conspicuous lack of consideration for how this emphasis on safety might have an impact on children's rights to freedom of expression, access, and autonomy, or on the quality of their experience. Moreover, the widespread appearance of safety mechanisms and discourses across the children's digital landscape contributes to the broader social configuration of the child user as at risk. Here children are positioned as vulnerable and in need of protection, from other users and from themselves. Such rhetoric in turn serves as justification for the incorporation of strictly imposed and technologically enforced rules designed to weed out any unsafe speech, behaviours, and – ultimately – users. There is a sort of vicious circle at work, in which the appearance of safety mechanisms contributes to the perception that connected spaces are otherwise unsafe for children, and vice versa.

Many of the most common parental concerns involve children's interactions with others – what words, ideas, or details might be exchanged in conversation, what images or videos might be sent through private message or email systems. Accordingly, safety-oriented design features often focus on limiting what children can do and say within a shared game space. In multiplayer virtual worlds and connected games, this commonly involves restrictions on children's access to in-game chat (text or voice) and to tools for creating and distributing UGC. In some cases, these restrictions are contained in a separate, child-specific account option, which exists alongside an all-users (or older users) account option. This "kiddie table" approach is quite common in children's virtual worlds, MMOGs, and other connected games where inter-player communication is limited to text-based chat and instant messaging. In other cases, however, operators have opted to outright exclude children from chat and UGC sharing by not providing the tools needed to engage in such activities within the context of the site or game. Within digital games, banning children from participating in online components has historically been a common and convenient response to the problems associated with supporting child safety. In some games, this has meant that players with a child account or child designation are not only unable to access peripheral tools or extras, they are also given a limited or reduced version of the game itself. The recent, broad integration of voice chat across many multiplayer games and console systems has resulted in an expansion of this approach.

The trends described above are well illustrated in the example of the Sony PlayStation 4 console system's Parental Controls tool. The system allows parents to customize the level of access to content and networking features associated with any and every child user registered on a particular console or otherwise associated with the parent's account (in the form of a "sub-account"). For instance, version 5.05, released in January 2018, enables users with a Family Manager or Parent/Guardian account to determine whether "communicating with other players" and "viewing content created by other players" is allowed or not allowed for "Child Family Members." These configurations apply not only to the console's own player networking forum (Sony PlayStation Network, or PSN), but to any game playable on the Sony PlayStation system as well. The console's Parental Control system can also be used to technologically enforce age ratings (i.e., a game or movie will not play if it carries an age rating outside of the "level" selected for that child user account), block certain types of websites, disable internet browser access, and set monthly spending limits on how much real-world money each user can spend on games and in-game purchases. The system addresses possible scenarios and responds to at least some of the specific needs and (potential) vulnerabilities of individual children.

The system also relies on two assumptions that may not apply to all families. First, that the adult in charge of setting up and managing the child accounts is aware of and able to navigate the settings and decisions involved. Second, that the children sign into their assigned account every time they use the console. Nonetheless, the PSN parental controls system is noteworthy, because it reflects and responds to a wide range of the most prevalent safety issues associated with children using and interacting with connected technologies. In each case, the system establishes rules of play that can be tailored to some extent, but are ultimately reduced to binary options (allowed or not allowed, off or on), and enforced through technological delegation. As such, opportunities for negotiation, exceptions, or alternative interpretations are omitted from the system. Instead, divergent "contexts" of play are resituated within the realm of family dynamics, where they require parental involvement, understanding, and authorization to unfold.

The PSN parental controls system has undergone updates since it was introduced in the mid-2000s. During this time, it has also – and at times relatedly – come into conflict with child players and their parents. These instances of conflict between design and use demonstrate how programmed safety controls can sometimes impose overly stringent restrictions on children's play. When it was released in 2011, for example, child players of Media Molecule/Sony's *LittleBigPlanet 2* with accounts set to not allow communication with others discovered that they were unable to access any of the user-made games either. Since player-made levels make up the vast majority of the playable content associated with the *LittleBigPlanet* games, a systematic lack of access to them constitutes a significantly diminished gameplay experience. Furthermore, the same rules did not apply to the first title in the series, *LittleBigPlanet*, where players identified as not allowed to engage in chat could (reportedly) nonetheless access user-made levels. For parents and guardians with young children who wanted to play *LittleBigPlanet 2* in 2011, the choice thus became to either allow full access to others on the child's sub-account ("all"), or else limit their gameplay to the "story mode" levels included as part of the game software ("nothing"). Both options had obvious and serious drawbacks. Notably, neither one exhibited any real consideration of the value and importance of peer interaction for children's play – even though the game itself was built around this very notion.

While ostensibly designed to improve children's online experience, safety protocols can be sweeping and therefore overly restrictive. Some promote essentialist and reductionist classifications of user speech and behaviour that spill over into other aspects of children's play and social interactions. This in turn can have unforeseen and sometimes unintended consequences for children's ability to make autonomous decisions, communicate with peers, and exercise their creativity and freedom of expression. Such is particularly the case when safety protocols are enforced through technological delegation – that is, when they are inscribed in the program code, and forbidden user inputs are automatically and systematically censored. By outright excluding certain words, behaviours, and ideas no matter the context or intent, these systems vilify entire swathes of children's play and social experience. In so doing, they reproduce many of the same idealized and impossible visions of childhood found throughout popular culture.

At the same time, however, safety protocols are not always reliable. While many games and playgrounds targeted to children claim to be safe for young users, in practice the safety protocols found in these spaces vary wildly, not only in specific formats, tools, and methods applied, but also in their effectiveness in preventing unsafe things from happening. From *Neopets* and *Habbo Hotel* to *Xbox Live* and *Roblox*, a great number of the most popular children's games have at least one incident in their history wherein a young user was bullied in-game, or was approached by a (potential) predator, or worse. As in other areas of the internet, the filtering algorithms, moderation systems, and user/self-reporting features contained in many children's digital playgrounds are far from foolproof. Where safety protocols are most effective is in their function as a rhetorical device – one that many users will incorporate into their own understanding of what a given space is, how it functions, as well as what is allowed or forbidden within its confines.

Safety as a Key Selling Point

The trends described above are likely linked to the fact that commercial children's playgrounds, from *Neopets* to *Club Penguin*, often function at least in part as expanded advergames. A great number of the most popular games, sites, and apps that are designed and targeted to children serve as both promotional tools (e.g., for advertising to children, for fostering brand loyalty, for building transmedia intertextuality, etc.) and as reservoirs of personal information and other data. There is a clear impetus for operators to configure these spaces in ways that are appealing to child users and their parents, while minimizing the potentially negative implications of the commercial processes at work behind the scenes. However, they are rarely discussed as such. Very few of the commercial strategies used in contemporary children's digital culture have attracted the same attention or criticisms as third-party ads and advergames did in the late 1990s. This is surprising, given the similarities between current forms of self-promotion (e.g., cross-promotion, branding, and transmedia intertextuality) and older practices such as "host selling" and "program-length commercials," which have long been subject to regulation as a result of their potential to exert undue sales pressure on young audience members through the manipulation of children's often strong feelings and attachments to beloved media characters and narratives.[42]

For instance, since the 1970s, governments in Canada and the United States have prohibited manipulative promotional strategies within television programming aimed at children. Yet the use of comparable strategies online is, for the most part, either unregulated or left to the industries to self-regulate. As is the case with so many areas of children's online experience, government response in both countries has tended to be delayed and partial at best. For instance, it took several years for the Federal Communications Commission (FCC) to recognize the widespread use of promotional websites by the children's television industry. It wasn't until 2004 that the FCC finally regulated the display of website addresses within children's programs originating in the United States.[43] Meanwhile in Canada, children's digital games, apps, websites, and their associated advertising content are tempered by an uncoordinated assortment of federal and provincial government policies, some of which predate the digital era, as well as a handful of largely voluntary self-regulatory industry guidelines. With some important exceptions, the regulatory climate in both countries reveals that there is hesitancy to limit what and how marketers and other corporations interact with children online. The bulk of the responsibility for moderating those relationships falls to the parents, through the emphasis on parental authority and parental consent within legislation and privacy policies, as well as to the children themselves, through the inflated social expectations that have emerged around the efficacy of media literacy campaigns and the extent of children's own digital skills and savvy.

The commercialization of children's play spaces carries its own set of implications, several of which were explored in chapter 3. But the concept of commercialization pertains to the current discussion of children's privacy as well, in that it adds an additional layer of complexity to what is happening with children's personal information within digital playgrounds. There is relatively little public awareness about the highly sophisticated, deeply integrated promotional strategies that appear throughout the children's digital landscape. There is a similar lack of public scrutiny of the economic value and extent of the industry practices that have emerged around the harvesting, selling, and analysis of children's (and other users') data. In both instances, there is a clear interest, and an economic advantage, in maintaining the status quo. By changing the subject of the conversation – away from children needing privacy from corporations, and towards children needing protection from dangerous others – the focus is shifted to risk and safety. This shift enables operators to reposition themselves as the potential solution, rather than the source, of the problems associated with children online.

After all, commercial playgrounds provide parents with a familiar alternative to the otherwise unrestricted, and not always child-friendly, world of connected games and virtual environments. As in the past, mainstream connected games are often predominated by teens and adults, and many contain themes and imagery that parents (and children) deem inappropriate. Conversely, games such as WildWorks's *Animal Jam* (2010–present), a cross-platform virtual world with 4.5 million monthly users, promote themselves as walled gardens – friendly and safe places for kids to "meet and chat with new friends."[44] By presenting themselves as fun *and* safe places – where kids can be kids, while also protected from dangerous others – commercial digital playgrounds reshape themselves as market-based solutions to the fears that many parents still have about children interacting with others online. As with *Neopets*'s COPPA compliance claims back in the early 2000s, these assurances of safety and age-appropriate content make exposure to a bit of cross-promotional content seem like a necessary trade-off.

Tellingly, since the early 2000s, governments in both Canada and the United States have had consistent trouble formulating and passing new regulation to reduce the types of risks that parents and children are most concerned about. This is especially true in the United States, where policies aimed at safeguarding children have been systematically challenged on the basis that the protocols involved would also infringe upon freedom of speech. The problems associated with these policy initiatives often run much deeper, however. From overly sweeping mandates that would likely result in the banishment of children from the internet, to ill-considered definitions of what constitutes risk, legislative attempts to ensure children's safety online have been riddled with problems, oversights, and unfounded assumptions. Accordingly, the policies proposed thus far have garnered a healthy dose of criticism from lobbyists, experts, child advocates, and other stakeholders and have subsequently failed to pass into law. Of interest to the current discussion is the tendency of these policy proposals to disregard children's rights, and their failure to adequately account for the benefits and opportunities associated with using connected technologies. Neither country has managed to introduce a nuanced, informed, and balanced alternative to these clearly problematic policy proposals. The status quo is therefore maintained. Meanwhile, the UK government recently published its new Internet Safety Strategy in the form of *The Online Harms White Paper*, which was produced after consulting with academics and other experts in children's online risks and safety. Yet as Livingstone, one of the lead researchers consulted, argues, the initiative "tends to pit technological and market innovation against safety, but does not propose a strategy for enhancing the benefits of the internet for the British public, including children. This is a weakness, and a missed opportunity – it should not be left to the private sector to fill this crucial gap."[45]

Recent research indicates that parental anxiety about children's internet use is growing. In 2017, for instance, a study of UK parents and children commissioned by the UK Office of Communications (Ofcom) discovered, "Although parents whose child goes online continue to be more likely to agree than to disagree that the benefits of the internet outweigh the risks, agreement has decreased since 2016 among parents of 3–4s (47% versus 55%) and 5–15s (58% versus 66%)."[46] A survey conducted by the US-based *PC Magazine* found that "76% of parents have some level of concern for children's online safety, and 51% are harboring significant or major anxiety about it."[47] While these concerns include many of the same risks that have long dominated the public discourse about children online – including predators, cyberbullies, hackers, malware, and computer viruses – a growing proportion of parents cite privacy as a key source of concern. In the UK study, "the concern most likely to be nominated by parents of 5–15s, of the nine potential concerns about their child's internet use we asked about, was 'companies collecting information about what they are doing online,' cited by 46%." Meanwhile, a 2018 survey conducted by US-based non-profit Common Sense Media, found that "the majority, 69% of teens and 77% of parents, responded that it is 'extremely important' for sites to ask permission before selling or sharing their personal information. The vast majority, 97% of parents and 93% of teens, also agree that it is at the very least, 'moderately important.'"[48]

Reconfiguring privacy as a "safety" issue obscures the other, more mundane ways that children's personal information is collected, used, and manipulated within digital playgrounds, as well as the other ways that children's privacy is infringed upon within these spaces. It also fails to address the full breadth of concerns that parents and children carry with them as they venture online. Although the connection is rarely made explicit to child users or their parents, a great number of the standard safety features found in children's digital playgrounds are primarily the industry's response to requirements mandated by federal laws meant to protect children's personal information from being misused, specifically by marketers. Some embedded safety mechanisms may also address the "risks" posed by bullies or hackers, but it is often unclear if, how, and to what extent such risks are actually being eliminated. There is a systematic lack of transparency among operators on tangible details about their moderation practices, efficacy rates, and outcomes. The fact remains that although privacy and safety can overlap in important ways, they are not equivalent.

Like most privacy legislation, the COPPA Rule is focused predominantly on daily transactions and commercial activities involving children's personal information, and it is limited largely to ensuring that parental consent and authority are maintained throughout these exchanges. The rule does not necessarily seek to protect children from the physical and emotional harms that have come to be associated with the idea of being "unsafe" online. Despite its frequent rhetorical positioning as a (partial) solution to hot-button issues such as cyberbullying and online predators, COPPA is aimed at preventing commercial entities from *mis*using children's personal data, and at regulating the new and ever-deepening commercial relationships between children and online operators. Meanwhile, the obfuscation of these very commercial relationships creates a missed opportunity for operators to build better, more transparent, more informed, and more ethical relationships with young users and their guardians. If the current trends continue, and if awareness of and concern about children's privacy online continue to grow, the long-held industry strategy of presenting privacy protections as safety mechanisms may soon start to backfire. Either way, however, positioning children's safety or privacy as a mere selling point misses the much more important fact that children's rights and well-being must be acknowledged and supported, no matter the context.

Freedom of Expression as a Collateral Cost of Safety

Privacy is not the only right that can be sidelined by an over-emphasis on safety. In their quest to make connected, multi-user spaces safer for children and more appealing for parents, many games, apps, and websites place substantial limitations on users' speech, actions, and UGC (or at least, on what is visible to other players). Of course, by forbidding the display of children's personal information in any form, including information shared as part of children's own communications and user-made content, without verifiable parental consent the COPPA Rule already restricts children's freedom of expression (or freedom of speech) in important ways. The consent requirement, Simmons argues, introduces barriers that extend "past speech related to personal information and potentially restricts a child's access to a free speech forum online."[49] The limits introduced by COPPA and other privacy legislation are indeed noteworthy, but they are also minor in comparison to the levels of censorship enacted by some of the industry practices and design norms that have emerged over the last two decades. While largely presented as protections to eliminate children's exposure to dangerous people and content, a great many of the safety mechanisms that appear within children's connected playgrounds exclude meaningful areas of activity and subject matter by omitting them from the game space. Across my studies of children's digital games and virtual worlds, this pattern has proven to be consistent over time, as well as across genre and platform. Within these "safe spaces," entire realms of children's everyday life experiences, cultures, and knowledges are invariably excluded from the context of the game world. This is particularly the case in titles where the task of ensuring children's safety is delegated to the technological artefact itself – embedded as design features and action opportunities, for instance, or otherwise enacted through automated processes and algorithms contained within the game's underlying programming.

A compelling example of this trend is found in the commonly used strategy of restricting chat within games, sites, virtual communities, and other social networking forums made for children. The children's MMOGs included in my study, for example, all featured in-game, text-based chat systems that were designed to prevent users from sharing inappropriate words and topics (an approach I term "dictionary chat"). These systems differed from those found in mainstream sites in important ways. For one, in-game chat systems usually start as open access systems, upon which filters to exclude certain words may be subsequently added. Live moderators may also filter words out as they are input (sometimes with a slight time lag or approval period that enables them to remove the words before they become visible to other users). Finally, users are often given tools or instructions for flagging unsanctioned or offensive content themselves. Conversely, most of the case studies contained chat systems based on the reverse approach, applying variations of a closed system through which only words or phrases that were already included on an approved list (or dictionary) would be recognized by the system as legitimate and subsequently be displayed to others.[50]

In many cases, the list of available words was not revealed to the players. Instead, they had to be discovered through trial and error. Whenever a player attempted to input words that were not on the list, they appeared to other players as either gibberish or as blank spaces. For example, imagine a player wanted to communicate a preference for zebras. If the word "zebras" was not included in the chat system dictionary, the player's sentence would appear to others as "I like ######" or "I like____." Notably, the exact same redaction would appear if the player tried to utter an expletive. Forbidden words were thus quite effectively excluded from the game world, but so were a wide range of other words – including all unanticipated words, no matter how benign, as well as slang terms, typos, misspellings, and so on. Players were not only tasked with discovering the *right* words to use to communicate with others, they also had to make their ideas and interactions fit within the limited selection of topics deemed appropriate by whoever had compiled the chat system dictionary. These lists of approved words derived from choices made by one or more adults, situated within specific sociocultural contexts, and conducted in response to a politically charged set of demands and constraints. Restricted chat systems therefore represent a tangible manifestation of how design features can be used to determine what children can and cannot say online.

All but one of the case studies also offered an additional, even more restrictive chat option, which I refer to as "predetermined chat." In these systems, players must scroll through a series of drop-down menus and choose from a limited selection of phrases in order to communicate with others. These menu items were grouped by theme, although the types of themes included varied significantly from one game to the next. Interestingly, in all but one of the cases (*BarbieGirls*), predetermined chat was set as the default chat system and presented as a safety mechanism. To switch to the less restrictive dictionary chat, parental consent had to be given through email. An inventory of the chat phrases available within each of these predetermined chat systems confirmed that they dramatically restricted player interaction and expression. The scope and range of the sentences made available to children was highly limited and consisted largely of "closed phrases" that could not be modified or customized. One exception was found in *GalaXseeds*, which included several customizable sentences in its predetermined chat, enabling players to mix and match phrase portions to create several different combinations. This expanded players' different chat phrase options to approximately 8,200 – far more than any of the other predetermined chat systems reviewed. As discussed in chapter 3, all five of the predetermined chat systems I examined featured phrase options containing promotional messages. This trend raises questions about how notions of safety may concurrently be used to expand commercialization strategies.

Systems such as dictionary chat and predetermined chat are described by operators as features designed to ensure, or at least increase, children's safety. Yet they do so by omitting an excessive number of words and ideas from children's in-game conversations. These exclusions include expletives and other content that parents, and many children, would agree are best kept out of a child's playground. But the majority are arbitrary – they simply consist of things that were not included on a relatively short list of things that a person, or perhaps design team, assumed children would or could talk about. The systems enact an obvious and very direct form of censorship on the children who utilize them, effacing words at the moment of their utterance within the virtual space, in the case of the automated systems such as algorithmic filters, or soon thereafter, in systems using live moderators. In addition to curtailing children's speech, such systems introduce other challenges into the play space. For instance, navigating such systems often demands a significant amount of time and effort in order to find the right words or chat options to communicate with others, not to mention the huge variations in children's spelling as they move through the stages of writing development.

Table 5.2. Total Predetermined Chat Phrases Available by Game

Game	Total chat phrases	Closed phrases	Customizable phrases
BarbieGirls	323	323	0
Club Penguin	322	322	0
GalaXseeds	8,200	177	25 (x options)
Toontown	228	228	0
Nicktropolis	634	633	1

The additional labour involved in engaging in social interaction within these spaces likely has a limiting effect all of its own.

Considering the diverse literacies and typing abilities found among child users, the application of innovative, child-centred design strategies in the construction and management of in-game communication is clearly warranted. In theory, the inclusion of a predetermined chat system could very well function as an important mechanism for increasing the games' overall accessibility to younger children – those who are still learning to read, or those who are able to read but cannot yet type quickly enough to sustain a real-time text-based conversation. Yet none of the examples I looked at described their simplified chat systems in terms of their potential for making the spaces more accessible or more responsive to children's developing and varying literacies. Rather than focus on the supplementary uses and benefits that young players might derive from a simplified chat system, the systems were configured almost entirely as safety mechanisms. The linkage between the systems' restrictive designs and government-enforced children's privacy protections was often downplayed, buried within long, complex privacy policies. The safety rhetoric found across all six of the games included in my study also obscured the fact that the chat systems were concurrently used for building transmedia and promoting third-party advertisers, as well as enlisting children as brand ambassadors and viral marketers.

While it is possible, even likely, that players can and do work around some of the built-in restrictions described in this chapter, the subversive potential of these actions is limited. At least the subversive potential is limited within the context of the digital playgrounds themselves, which provide too few opportunities for users to communicate their design appropriations with one another, or to engage in the type of collaborative reinterpretation and meaning-making often associated with subversive action. Outside of the official play space, however, opportunities abound. A key example within the connected landscape is cheat sites, which have long served as largely unsanctioned yet very popular ancillary outlets for players to subvert the (game) system. Beyond the screen, children often discuss and recreate the digital games they play at home with "real-world" friends and classmates. Tips and hints about games are exchanged on the non-digital playground, as are myths and rumours. But not all children will have access to such resources and alternative venues. For instance, younger users may not know about cheat sites or how to find them, or they may be discouraged from doing so by well-meaning parents and teachers (cheating is largely disapproved of, after all). Other children may not have a network of fellow players to talk to about their preferred online game or available opportunities to show and share information about it. Finally, the fact that *some* children *may* find ways of working around or subverting design limitations does little to justify the technologically enforced censorship and other undue restrictions found in so many children's digital games and play spaces.

The presence of automated, programmed safety mechanisms can transform a children's digital playground in deep and tangible ways. They change the contents and parameters of the interactions and play forms that are accessible to players within the context of the digital space. They function as an additional, and in some instances incontrovertible, set of rules, guiding and limiting what constitutes appropriate player behaviour and allowed player action. While unanticipated and subversive interpretations of these design restrictions are of course possible, the restrictions themselves nonetheless have a concrete, limiting effect on the play space and its players. There is always a loss of nuance and context when responsibility is delegated to a technological artefact or system. Even the most sophisticated algorithms are largely unable to account for the more complex, contextual dimensions of human interaction, such as intention, humour, and meaning. Recent studies showing that the popular Amazon Echo smart device struggles to understand and respond appropriately to child users illustrates the limitations of such systems.[51] Meanwhile, the restrictions and algorithms themselves are guided by design decisions that contain their own sets of limitations, assumptions, and biases. In this way, the systems reproduce many of the same trends found throughout popular discourses about children and technology. They reveal and promote an ideological, and often quite narrow, vision of what children *should* experience, talk about, and care about when they play together online.

Secret Spaces and "Unsafe" Places

In the world of adults, discussions of privacy commonly centre on concerns about government surveillance, about the use and misuse of personally identifiable information by corporations, and about individuals' ability to control how their information is shared across personal and professional relationships. Privacy scholars identify a wide range of types of privacy that adults of different generations and diverse backgrounds generally care about. When instances of widespread or unexpected forms of privacy infringement are uncovered by the press or by lawmakers, public attention, outcry, and debate soon follows. As discussed above, much of the research suggests that children and teens also care deeply about their privacy and the privacy of others, but many young people have idealistic misconceptions about the extent to which their information and content is protected within connected spaces and interactions. However, it is important to remember that children don't generally have a lot of privacy in their everyday lives. This is especially true of younger children, a significant proportion of whom are under almost constant adult supervision, authority, and surveillance. The lack of privacy in children's lives is not reserved to the online world. To the contrary, it is something that most children experience across spaces and contexts, at school and at the public playground, but also at home and even in their own bedrooms.

While childhood is always embedded in a world of adults, children negotiate this dynamic by delineating, protecting, and distinguishing certain spaces as *children's* spaces. As James argues, "Hence, the true nature of the culture of childhood frequently remains hidden from adults, for the semantic cues which permit social recognition have been manipulated and disguised by children in terms of their alternative society."[52] The secret rites and places of childhood provide crucial forums for children to exercise agency and authority, as well as experiment with ideas and social norms. Children are highly skilled in the art of creating their own social worlds within the world of adults, and they benefit significantly from having their own dedicated spaces and cultural experiences. Across age groups and cultures, people use personal space, both physical and mental, to mediate and manage interpersonal boundaries – between parent and child, between friends, between self and other. Altman argues that these boundaries are crucial to our "understandings of selfhood."[53] Conversely, a widespread lack of privacy, secrets, or personal space can "threaten our ability to manage our boundaries, with potentially drastic consequences for the processes by which we articulate our identities, define our beliefs, and formulate our politics."[54]

Relatedly, the secret spaces of childhood provide a key forum for children to engage in play activities that adults don't understand or approve of, including social testing games and make-believe scenarios featuring dark or mature themes. As discussed in chapter 1, play scholars such as Sutton-Smith and Schwartzman view these activities as crucial parts of children's cultural and personal experience. These activities are how children make sense of their interpersonal relationships, come to terms with cultural expectations, and negotiate their roles within the broader social structure. The dissolution of available, unmonitored, and unprogrammed spaces and times within which children can make these territorial claims, engage in taboo play, share or keep secrets, and experience personal space is therefore deeply problematic. Always-on surveillance systems and programmed limitations on speech and behaviour do more than direct and contain children's peer play. By encroaching on children's privacy and failing to provide them with opportunities to delineate their own shared "secret spaces," these practices strip connected playgrounds of some of their most valuable potential functions.

Meanwhile, overly strict chat systems, panoptic parental controls, and design limitations push at least some children to seek out more flexible alternatives. One example is the use of workarounds, which Salen and Zimmerman describe as "ways of 'legally' working around game structures" that allow players to subvert design limitations and programmed restrictions.[55] Indeed, restrictive designs can often afford workarounds, as users are pushed to discover and innovate in order to perform even the most basic of actions. A fascinating outcome of the dictionary chat safety mechanism found in many of my case studies, for instance, was that it often appeared to drive players to develop skills that allowed them to not only work with the chat systems, but to work around the systems as well. In their communications with others, players engaged in frequent trial-and-error sessions to find the "right" (i.e., pre-programmed and correctly spelled) words to express themselves. None of the case study MMOGs provided players with guidance about what or how many words were contained in these systems. Instead, players were left to figure it out for themselves during gameplay. This delegation of responsibility onto the players to find the words themselves thus afforded experimentation with the chat systems. Through these experiments, the players discovered much more than just which words were allowed – they also uncovered loopholes, workarounds, and gaps in the systems themselves. For at least some children, however, the more enticing alternative is found in games and virtual worlds that don't contain safety features or child-specific designs, specifically playgrounds designed for and targeted to teens and adults.

Unsafe and Risky Play

Although most children play digital games online in one form or another, most connected game titles are still targeted – at least officially – to teens and adults. Popular multiplayer games such as *Fortnite* and *World of Warcraft*, for instance, carry a T (for teen) rating from the ESRB. Moreover, many online games forbid younger users from playing, through the inclusion of a minimum age requirement (of either thirteen or eighteen) in their EULAs and privacy policies. While age restrictions in games are linked at times to a game's inclusion of more mature imagery or thematic content, the mere presence of social networking features – such as in-game Voice over Internet Protocol (VoIP), text-based chat, UGC, or other forms of player-to-player interaction – can serve as adequate justification for banning children aged twelve and under. In so doing, game operators can avoid the extra costs and moderation requirements associated with COPPA compliance, along with the restrictions on player speech that often come with managing a multiplayer system where children are present. An official age restriction might also protect the game operators from certain forms of liability, providing a handy way to stop young players from engaging in disruptive or dangerous behaviour within the context of the game space (i.e., immediate account suspension). Although age restrictions alone do little to prevent children from joining a game, they do provide quick recourse for removing "problematic" children before they can get themselves, or the game, into hot water.

Of course, as with most other restricted cultural materials – from R-rated movies to adult magazines – children find ways around these formal age restrictions. In fact, many children report that they prefer to visit sites that are designed for adults.[56] These practices are consistent with children's consumption habits across media formats and cultural experiences.[57] Indeed, some scholars argue that the presence of age restrictions can *itself* become part of the appeal, a process described in the "forbidden fruit theory."[58] Here, children are understood to engage in acts of "psychological reactance," which Nikken and Janz describe as occurring when "restricting a person's freedom of choice motivates him or her to evaluate the eliminated alternatives more positively, and to try to restore the freedom."[59] For other children, Buckingham argues, an element of "aspiration" is likely involved, since "children frequently aspire to consume things that appear to be targeted at a somewhat older audience" (particularly to teens), who are "seen to embody a degree of freedom from adult constraints."[60] The literature indicates that the most common strategy for bypassing age restriction is simply to lie about one's age. Indeed, most connected games contain minimal (if any) mechanisms for verifying a user's actual age and rely heavily on accurate self-reporting. Concurrently, there are children whose parents allow or even enable them to contravene official age restrictions, as household rules and parents' own assessments of the appropriateness of a game or site, or even an entire form of online activity, take precedence over ESRB ratings and EULA contracts.[61]

Nonetheless, children's participation in teen and adult-oriented connected games is often a contentious issue. And it is easy to see why some game operators and older players might want to avoid having to deal with unauthorized children in their game space. For one, it implies that a certain amount of censorship, self-imposed or imposed by the system, will (or should) be placed on players' speech and behaviours. Not all adults want or expect to have to accommodate children in their personal leisure time. It bears mentioning that mainstream gaming culture is also notoriously toxic and routinely features themes and behaviours that are far from child-friendly. There has been a noted resistance among certain players towards any attempts to change or even moderate these tendencies, through claims that any limit to speech constitutes an infringement of players' rights. In at least some cases, resistance to the presence of child players can translate into aggressive forms of ostracism. In 2007, industry blog WomenGamers.Com posted a story about an after-school gaming club for children aged eight to sixteen whose young members were frequently subjected to verbal harassment by adult players when they participated in competitions on *Xbox Live*. In a written exchange with one of the club's adult organizers, a harasser explained that they disapproved of children playing M-rated games (including *Tom Clancy's Rainbow Six: Vegas* and *Gears of War*), and were enforcing the "adult only" nature of the game space. In this case, formal age restrictions were mobilized as justification for informal, problematic forms of social disciplining and exclusion.[62]

Children, however, can also act as aggressors and disruptors. As discussed previously, children's play contains its own elements of transgression and aggression, which can surface in ways that either fortuitously or purposively antagonize other players.[63] Some children actively (at times delightedly) participate in "flame wars" and "trolling," engage in online bullying, pose as adults, partake in "griefing" or "stealing," and enact other forms of disruption.[64] Such practices can in turn work to support a perceived need for age restrictions among adult players and game operators. As Taylor argues, although many adult players of *World of Warcraft* condone and even encourage the presence of children, "there is also a strong undercurrent you hear in conversations ... that lays blame for the ills of the game at the feet of '12 year old boys' or 'the kids.'"[65] She identified several guilds that set their own minimum age requirements and conducted thorough background checks to ensure that players weren't lying about their age before granting them membership. At least some

adults are under the impression that flaming and other disruptive practices are characteristic of child players, even though these activities are
also commonly engaged in (perhaps even more so) by teens and adults.[66]

The reasons children engage in disruptive gameplay are multiple and
complex, but it is important to remember that they are also – for the most
part – an expected part of children's play. Donovan and Katz argue that
"disruptive" and "deviant" activities can also serve as sites "of invention
and discovery as well as resistance to various technological fetters," and
can help children "understand and control their environments (technological or otherwise)" through demystification and appropriation.[67]
Similar arguments are found in the literature on children's play, wherein
the incorporation of transgressive acts and dark themes is often viewed
as a means of not only making sense of the social order, but also negotiating and at times challenging it. Setting considerations of the (potential)
underlying function and meaning of transgressive play aside, however,
the fact remains that it is an enduring part of childhood. Moreover,
as Tanenbaum points out, much of the game studies and game design
scholarship posits that play is inherently subversive.[68] Yet so few digital
games designed and targeted to children allow for non-idealized, let
alone transgressive or subversive, forms of play. Indeed, essentially none
of the connected multiplayer games that I have examined grant children
much flexibility or agency in core aspects of the gameplay and available
modes of social interaction. From the range of words that can be uttered,
to the types of moves that can be enacted, to the forms of UGC that can
be shared, the users of child-specific connected playgrounds find themselves narrowly defined and tightly controlled. It is therefore unsurprising that so many children seek out other, less limiting places to play. That
such places contain a certain element of risk is likely seen by some as a
small price to pay. For others, it's part of the fun.

Livingstone and Smith point out, "The more children use the internet, and the more digital skills and confidence they gain, the more
deeply and broadly they use it, thus encountering more risks as well as
opportunities."[69] Indeed, risk and opportunity are often intertwined. For
instance, uploading content to a connected platform usually requires
divulging personal information to the platform's owners/operators, just
as making a new friend commonly starts as an interaction with a stranger.
In attempting to minimize the risks to children online, opportunities
are reduced, or even eliminated, in the process. Within the context of
commercial digital playgrounds, it is a particularly costly trade-off. Here,
players are contained and restricted, while data harvesting and corporate surveillance continue unabated, enabled by games designed to perpetuate an idealized image of safe, good, appropriate play. Then again,

leaving the playground altogether comes with its own repercussions, as children are left to fend for themselves in game worlds that are not meant for them and at times do not welcome their presence. As unauthorized players, they are mostly left with few rights or legal standing on which to draw if something goes wrong.

The research suggests a similar disconnect between public policy and the types of risks that children *themselves* are most bothered by. For instance, when Livingstone and her research team asked internet-using children and teens aged nine to sixteen "What things on the internet would bother people about your age?," the most popular responses by far involved content risks (58 per cent). The number one risk identified by both girls and boys was exposure to pornographic content. In close second among boys and younger children was the risk of exposure to violent content. Violent content was also the most cited risk associated with playing digital games (39 per cent). Notably, only 14 per cent of the risks mentioned by the children in this study involved contact with others (usually adults). Just as corporate rhetoric often confuses children's privacy with safety, public discourses are disproportionately focused on stranger danger for children online. Meanwhile, it is worth considering how the overly restrictive designs and safety strategies that dominate the children's digital landscape might be pushing young users to seek out more flexible play experiences in game titles that are *also* more likely to contain the very violent themes and imagery they are most bothered by.

Conclusion

In 1981, following several high-profile lawsuits, academic studies, and government reports highlighting the prevalence of childhood injuries stemming from playground accidents, the first *Handbook for Public Playground Safety* was published by the US Consumer Product Safety Commission. Over the next two decades, playgrounds across the United States, as well as in Canada and the United Kingdom, replaced and updated their equipment, configurations, and materials in response to evolving safety standards. As Rosin reports, these standards were set largely by engineers and lawyers, with "little meaningful input" from those with expertise in children's play.[70] Despite a widespread compliance with safety standards, the overall rate of childhood injuries sustained on playgrounds has reportedly remained consistent. In 2002, a group of influential agencies in the United Kingdom released a position statement arguing that a fear of litigation and an associated emphasis on safety was leading play providers to focus on "actions having the appearance of minimizing the risk of injury ... at the expense of other fundamental objectives such as the right to play, the need for interesting and challenging play environments, and the opportunity for children to learn about risk in a reasonably safe environment."[71] A growing body of research now supports the idea that risky play is important – to children's development (cognitive and physical), learning, peer relationships, and identity formation. Some scholars posit that early risk-taking experiences might even help children to avoid accidents and injuries in the future.[72] Sandseter argues, "The feeling of strong exhilaration is sought during the [risky play] activity and manifested in the feeling of mastery the children experience when managing the play they did not think they would dare to do."[73] Allowing children to engage in risky play empowers them in meaningful ways.

In many countries, including Canada, new spaces and opportunities are emerging for children to engage in unsupervised (or, more accurately, minimally supervised) forms of risky play. Several of these initiatives are nature-based and targeted to younger children (i.e., preschoolers), two trends that also surface within the academic literature in this area. The "free-range childhood movement" and other approaches aimed at fostering children's independence and resilience are increasingly discussed within parenting forums and the popular media, where they are offered up as antidotes to the "helicopter parenting" style that became popular at the turn of the millennium. Yet these developments remain somewhat isolated from the broader discourses and cultures of childhood. They have yet to spill over into other areas of children's everyday lives, and a public conversation about the role of risky play within different arenas of contemporary childhood – online and off – has yet to unfold. Meanwhile, ambiguous notions of risk, danger, and safety continue to circulate, shaping policy and design decisions, informing individual parenting strategies, and delimiting children's access to spaces, experiences, and technologies. Within connected playgrounds and other online forums, discourses about risk and safety have had a tangible impact on where, how, and when children are invited to participate in digital culture. They draw attention away from deeper questions about the forms, quality, and diversity of the actual opportunities (e.g., the games, platforms, apps, sites) that are available to children for engaging, creating, and participating online. Instead of debating how we might best support children's newfound roles as digital citizens and empower them to tackle the risks and challenges associated with life online, the focus remains on protecting children from others and from themselves. Within this climate, the secret spaces of childhood take an obvious backseat to the "safe spaces" produced by the children's cultural industries. And while secret spaces may very well emerge within and between those child-safe digital playgrounds, the potential for this is limited by design.

Secret spaces of childhood are first and foremost "free from adult supervision."[74] Singer and Singer describe them as existing in a "make-believe dimension, a controlled, reduced-to-size realm that is the child's domain of personal power (agency)."[75] Access to places and spaces where children can exert control, grant or deny access, and engage in activities and fantasies that adults may disapprove of is not only important for children's play, but is also a core part of children's identity formation, socialization, and everyday life experience. Our understanding of the function and value of children's privacy rights is greatly enriched by a deeper consideration of secret spaces and their importance within children's lives. The integration of these two concepts helps us to better understand that sacrificing children's freedom of expression in order to provide them with increased privacy is inherently contradictory, as children often use private and secret spaces to experiment with subversive ideas and exercise their agency, free from the authority and judgment of adults. These practices depend on creative freedom, and they often revolve around unanticipated and inappropriate themes. Yet these are some of the very things that are commonly excluded from commercial digital playgrounds targeted to children. Limited action opportunities, restrictions on player interactions, and other embedded safety features work to minimize opportunities for transgression and innovation, while encouraging players to stick to the approved, highly idealized, adult-determined script.

Within the commercial rhetoric, as well as most policy discourses, the relationships between children's privacy, secret spaces, selfhood, and expression are rarely addressed. Instead, privacy is defined largely as keeping personally identifiable information safe from unwelcome strangers and other external threats. Digital playgrounds can be fully COPPA compliant while concurrently collecting massive amounts of data from and about their young users. They can analyse, package, and sell these data with little interference and minimal government oversight. Within these spaces, children are subject to constant surveillance as algorithms track, tag, and sort their activities, as moderators review their communications, and as market researchers and designers watch to see how their play unfolds. In some cases, parents or teachers may also be provided with tools that enable them to monitor their child's in-game activities and contributions, from regular reports of how much time the child spent playing the game to detailed transcripts of their interactions with other players. Public awareness of the surveillance activities that unfold in these spaces is partial at best. As discussed above, the industry's (potential) role as infringers of children's privacy is often subsumed by corporate rhetoric, where obfuscations and even misrepresentations about how and why children's data are collected are common. As a result, surveillance can appear to be a necessary part of ensuring children's safety, and/or it can be seen as required to make sure that the playground itself is responding to players' needs. Meanwhile, it is highly unlikely that children or their parents are granting truly informed consent to have their data appropriated to this extent.

While children and parents today are more likely to identify institutional privacy as a key concern, current trends in children's technology design include the incorporation of "smart" features, which expand the reach of corporate surveillance datafication within the home and beyond. The rapid diffusion of always-on domestic assistants such as Amazon Echo and Google Home, for instance, are granting corporations unprecedented access into the lives of children and families, who may not be fully aware of how the devices work or what happens to the reams of data they gather. Many of the same processes emerge around artefacts associated with the "internet of toys," which Smith and Shade describe as "an array of play related websites, games, toys, and apps [that] are scaffolded upon the internet to engage children and their caregivers to disclose data or personal information for analysis and use by corporations, or other actors."[76] While these developments are occasionally the subjects of controversy and debate, much of the public and media attention has centred on high-profile data breaches and the potential threat of hackers – rather than on the comparatively mundane, everyday processes of corporate surveillance and datafication. The internet of toys builds on well-honed, longstanding traditions of using children's digital play spaces for conducting market research, as well as for big data collection and analysis. These practices were established during the earliest days of the World Wide Web, and they formed the economic basis of many of the most popular online destinations made for and targeted to children over the past twenty-five years. From *Neopets* to Hello Barbie, the children's industries have steadily used games and toys to solicit and gather information from children. The full implications of the convergence of always-on surveillance, and the widespread reframing of children's privacy as a safety issue rather than a matter of data and personal autonomy, are not yet known. What is clear, however, is that fundamental, historically private experiences of childhood are being resituated and transformed in the process, from the construction of secret spaces to the formation of the self.

6

Playing as Making and Creating

Since their emergence in the mid-1990s, digital playgrounds have been associated with myriad benefits, positive experiences, and meaningful contributions to children's culture. Many of them have concurrently provided corporations and other agents with unique opportunities for accessing, recording, and manipulating the inner play worlds of children. From using games to conduct covert market research (by tracking users and collecting personal information from them), to embedding product placement and corporate messages into the very fabric of the game world, to restricting players' speech and actions in ways that promote branding and viral marketing, digital playgrounds have been used for a wide range of business purposes that contravene children's needs and interests. Other children's digital playgrounds do not engage in such activities, including titles produced by universities and non-profit organizations, as well as those made by corporate and independent developers who follow their own ethical design standards. Overall, children's digital playgrounds are ambiguous – containing opportunities for and challenges to children's agency and access to meaningful play experiences. One playground may provide children with a range of tools for creative expression while concurrently prohibiting fair use of copyrighted materials. Another may afford seemingly endless experimentation but invade children's privacy rights. As in most areas of children's lives, the digital playscape is rife with contradiction and dissonance.

Children nonetheless retain a high degree of agency and creativity within digital playgrounds, despite the realm's variable and capricious terrain. No matter how narrowly a digital playground is designed or managed, it can always also become a site of struggle and negotiation, as children construct their own interpretations of the structural elements they encounter, share alternate readings of promotional features, and construct their own "social worlds of children" within adult-controlled spaces. Despite the expansion of stringent copyright regimes and definitions across their cultural milieu, children continue to appropriate media brands (i.e., characters, storylines, and settings drawn from mass media texts) to explore, remix, and deconstruct popular and commercial discourses. When opportunities to engage in such activities are not made available, some children seek them out elsewhere. For instance, most of the children's virtual worlds analysed in my previous studies were the focus of fan sites made by players and hosted on private servers or third-party platforms – far beyond the confines of the official game worlds.[1] These unauthorized, ancillary spaces were often filled with player creations, from DIY world maps and screenshots to fan fiction, machinima, and fine art. This phenomenon is well documented within the academic games literature, where Consalvo and others refer to it as a form of "meta-participation."[2] In addition to extending gameplay for their creators, the materials produced via meta-participation can eventually come to function as "paratexts," helping to "shape the reader's experience of a text" and "give meaning to the act of reading."[3] As they are posted online, paratexts can shape how players interpret the games themselves – informing their folklore, serving as reference points, and transforming their shared cultural experience.

Children also use digital play spaces to engage in more overtly transgressive undertakings, including activities that challenge, defy, or circumvent rules and design limitations. A common example is the "cheat site," an online forum where players exchange tips, information, and tools for winning game levels, earning extra points or currency, and realizing achievements without following the intended trajectories. For instance, Fields and Kafai identified over two hundred cheat sites for the tween-targeted virtual world *Whyville*, at least some of which were used by young players to find the correct answers to in-game science problems or to uncover design exploits that allowed them to collect in-game currency more quickly. Players visited (and sometimes contributed to) large, collaboratively made cheat sites, but some also made personal sites or pages, which they used to "display their knowledge about *Whyville*."[4] Discussions about cheat sites and their associated practices frequently appeared within player-written articles published in the *Whyville Times*, where "the predominant view of cheating ... [was] that cheating is bad, lazy, dishonest, and unfair."[5] Yet cheating is rampant across digital gaming cultures and practised by players of all ages and skill levels. While players may have differing opinions about its ethical standing, cheating is by its very nature an expression of agency. It subverts the top-down shaping of the rules and contexts of play otherwise afforded by a game's design and management structures.[6] In creating cheat sites – forums for sharing alternative and transgressive ways of interpreting and manoeuvring a game's designed features – players contribute to a communal reappropriation of the game as artefact, as practice, as system. In this way, the sharing of cheats, mods, homages, and other reimaginings is a meaningful and consequential form of cultural engagement. It transforms a private or individual act of defiance into an opportunity for collective action.

Over the past decade, corporately owned UGC games have become a compelling locus for children's participatory culture and for the complex economic relationships that now exist between children and the industries that cater to them. Building on the broader emphasis on making and the influx of STEM and "learn to code" movements in contemporary children's culture, UGC games offer an entry point into specific forms of content creation. The cultures that have emerged around these games are, at times, empowering and innovative. Many of the most popular UGC game titles and platforms, however, are fuelled by circuitous business models that draw on a complex amalgam of immaterial labour, transmedia intertextuality, corporate copyright regimes, and real money transactions.

On the one hand, UGC games such as *Minecraft*, *Roblox*, and *LittleBig-Planet* provide easy-to-use tools for children to create their own game levels, contents, and assets – all without programming or other advanced technical skills. Many also provide infrastructures that enable children to share their creations, either publicly or with select others. The genre represents a meaningful and potentially transformative shift within children's digital game culture, away from its traditional, top-down, adult-centric production norms, towards something that is much more inclusive, diverse, and child-centric. More than merely informing game decisions made by adults, children are now intervening at the level of design – assuming the tools of production and expressing their own ideas, imaginings, and voices. On the other hand, and as in so many other areas of the children's digital playscape, many of the most popular UGC games also contain safety, promotional, and other structural features that delimit children's freedom of expression, advance commercial agendas, appropriate players' creative works, and exploit their labour.

This chapter explores children's shifting roles as *makers* of digital games and other connected play spaces. It examines the relationships, responsibilities, and rights that UGC games and other Web 2.0 media creation platforms have introduced into children' lives, and it considers how these developments diverge from and yet also reproduce longstanding patterns found in children's digital culture. The chapter starts with a discussion of children's UGC games, their history, and their implications for children's creativity and autonomy. The focus then shifts to an exploration of some of the legal implications of children's participation in UGC game design – including children's potential roles as authors and as holders of intellectual property rights – and it asks questions about children's access to fair use/fair dealing exceptions. I examine how these implications have been addressed by the children's industries, looking primarily at the standard form contracts that are used across the digital landscape to set the terms of both service providers' and users' rights and responsibilities within connected spaces (commonly referred to as "terms of use" or "terms of service" agreements). I present findings from multiple studies demonstrating a widespread tendency for these agreements to focus narrowly on expanding corporate producer rights (such as copyright) and securing unfettered industry access to user data while diminishing or omitting children's cultural rights as producers. I argue that existing industry norms and regulatory regimes are insufficient and largely ill-equipped to deal with the current rise in children's online cultural production.

There is a gap between how children are perceived (e.g., the roles they are assumed to occupy or not occupy, the activities they are assumed to engage in), and how children are engaged in digital culture. This gap is particularly evident when considering the prominence of remixes and fandom within children's digital creations. UGC games are a phenomenon that overlaps and conflicts with industry trends. On the one hand, many UGC games are designed to enable and encourage players to engage with transmedia intertextuality – to play with branded characters and storylines, deepening brand loyalty, and promoting cycles of consumption. From titles linked to established media supersystems such as *Super Mario Maker* and *Lego Dimensions*, to emergent properties such as *LittleBigPlanet* and *Minecraft*, instead of providing players with blank canvases and encouraging bottom-up creation, a great number of UGC games revolve around, and strongly afford, remixing and customization.

Indeed, this is a key part of what makes UGC games a distinct genre: the presence of easy-to-use tools that enable sophisticated levels of customization, rather than direct engagements with the game code or entirely original creations. While original works are occasionally possible, the emphasis in UGC games is on appropriating and remixing existing content into innovative configurations and new interpretations. This is part of what distinguishes the UGC game genre from media creation platforms such as Adobe Illustrator (a commonly used graphics editor) or Unity (a popular game engine). On the other hand, the widespread adoption of highly conservative, strictly interpreted approaches to copyright often places game owners in conflict with their own design affordances – problematizing the very transmedia engagements that UGC games would otherwise seem to invite. As a result, several popular UGC games have ended up placing important restrictions on what, how, and when players can create. These restrictions tend to extend far beyond the usual concerns of player safety and privacy, and instead reflect a prioritization of corporate copyright and brand integrity. The ambiguous relationship between children and corporate copyright that often surfaces within UGC games provides a compelling entry point for thinking about the ethics of making, playing, and branding in the digital playground.

Playing and Making Digital Games

Most of the digital games that children play are made and managed by corporations and other adult-run organizations. They are made *for* children *by* adults, and as such they embody and reproduce the complex web of relationships, hopes, fears, and expectations that characterize the adult/child dichotomy. Increasingly, however, children also make their own digital games. This phenomenon defies many of the trends already explored in this book. It also challenges traditional modes of production. (Here I am not referring to the interpretive creativity that all players engage in – to at least some extent – while playing a digital game, or to the "improvised games" that Giddings observed among children playing with and around the official game-as-artefact. Rather, I am describing more formal game-making activities, such as coding, utilizing game engines, and engaging in other types of creative but also technical intervention.) Although little is known about the prevalence of digital game *making* among young children, evidence abounds that it is increasingly common, within and outside of school settings.

There are now several popular, child-specific game design programs and platforms, including Scratch (2002–present), a browser-based platform for creating games and animations that claims an active worldwide userbase in the millions, as well as Gamestar Mechanic (2010–present), a platform aimed at teaching children game design principles, which supports a community of over 250,000 active designers, most of whom are between the ages of seven and fourteen. Over the past several years, a sizeable number of high-profile child game developers have moreover been featured on tech blogs and in the news media. One twelve-year-old app developer, Thomas Suarez, even gave a TED Talk that, as of February 2019, had been viewed nearly nine million times. Game-making activities also appear in a wide range of lesson plans, after-school clubs, library programs, and other educational contexts where game design is mobilized as an entry point for learning computer coding, procedural thinking, effective communication, and a wide range of other curricula. An extreme example is the Quest to Learn school, a public middle and high school launched in 2009 by the Institute of Play and the New York City Department of Education, in which every piece of curriculum follows game design principles.

The emergence of child game makers coincides with broader trends found in mainstream culture, such as the rise of indie (or independent) game development and the spread of the "maker movement." As with children's game making, the growth in popularity and participation in indie game development is strongly linked to the concurrent introduction of more accessible, more affordable, and more user-friendly game engines and design tools over the past decade.[7] Similarly, many of the products and programs aimed at supporting children's game making echo aspects of the maker movement's DIY ethos and emphasis on hands-on technical creation and intervention. Indeed, in some cases, the game-making tools are overtly positioned – within corporate communications and marketing materials – as part of the maker movement, particularly in its widespread mobilization within and outside of schools as a conduit for STEM-based learning.[8]

A notable example of this trend is Scratch. Created by researchers at MIT's Lifelong Kindergarten Group and aimed at children aged eight to sixteen, Scratch is at once a media creation platform, a social networking forum, and a programming language. It aims to teach children and teens computational thinking and other skills associated with coding, and to offer them experience with collaborative design more generally. The site design draws heavily on constructionism, specifically as the theory appears in the works of Papert, an early proponent of using games and play to teach children how to code. As Resnick and his colleagues explain, Scratch aims to meet three criteria proposed by Papert as crucial for making coding accessible to children: "Papert argued that programming languages should have a 'low floor' (easy to get started) and a 'high ceiling' (opportunities to create increasingly complex projects over time). In addition, languages need 'wide walls' (supporting many different types of projects so people with many different interests and learning styles can all become engaged)."[9] The platform is a success on many levels. In 2016 alone, nearly two hundred million people used Scratch to make their own games, animations, and interactive stories. As Resnick relayed in a recent interview, Scratch is now the "19th most popular coding language in the world – and the only one with a core userbase of 8- to 16-year-old kids."[10] Accordingly, there is a significant body of academic research on Scratch, much of it supporting the creators' claims that the platform is useful for teaching children to code. Resnick and his associates have produced numerous studies focused on assessing (or demonstrating) the effectiveness of using Scratch to support children's development of

"21st century skills," including multimodal literacies and computational thinking.[11] Other studies examine the use of Scratch's social networking features for peer-to-peer learning and reciprocal apprenticeship.[12] Still others affirm its potential to serve as a stepping stone into more advanced, textual, and professional coding languages.[13]

Children's game making should not be seen solely as a conduit to computer programming, however. DIY game making is a subset of a greater cross-media trend in which children are assuming the roles of producers, writers, artists, and creators with increased frequency. For instance, as Nicoll and Nansen observe, children are prominently involved in the creation of toy unboxing videos, a YouTube phenomenon that is enormously popular among audiences of all ages.[14] In their study of one hundred randomly selected toy unboxing videos, thirty-four either featured a child or a "disembodied child" (filmed in the first person, so that only the child's hands and voice were discernible) in the role of "unboxer." In addition to making their own games, or collaborating with others on a local level, some children share their creations by publishing them online or submitting them to a digital distribution platform (e.g., Steam or the Apple App Store). Still others broadcast themselves playing existing game titles, using Twitch or other screen capture software to produce "Let's Play" videos. While at first glance these examples may seem far removed from game design, the practices have much in common beyond consisting of forms of media production. In each case, children are engaging in the co-creation, shaping, and negotiation of shared experiences – actively participating in the new public fora of connected culture.

From games to unboxing videos and everything in between, children's growing involvement in digital media production is an exciting development with enormous potential for the advancement of children's cultural rights online. In addition to providing important outlets for children's own self-expression, agency, civic engagement, and creative autonomy, increased access to media made *by* other children stands to disrupt several of the dominant patterns and power relations that have long characterized children's shared popular culture (or what Cook calls "children's commercial culture"). As in other areas of Web 2.0, the rise of child-made DIY productions would shift power away from the systematic privileging of advertising, brand management, and risk aversion that currently permeates so much of the children's digital landscape. It would also challenge the idealized and deeply ideological visions of childhood that are generally found in adult-made cultural texts and technologies. Indeed, there is something important that happens when anyone – children or adults – shares personal creations. The act of sharing is beneficial not only for learning or for exercising cultural rights, but also for the meaning-making that is associated with the experience itself. As Papert argues, "Construction that takes place 'in the head' often happens especially felicitously when it is supported by construction of a more public sort 'in the world' – a sand castle or a cake, a LEGO house or a corporation, a computer program, a poem, or a theory of the universe. Part of what I mean by 'in the world' is that the product can be shown, discussed, examined, probed, and admired."[15]

Overall, the literature indicates that more children engaging in media production, sharing, critique, and discussion translates into a richer and more diverse culture for everyone. Yet although tools and platforms for making games are increasingly available, they are far from universally accessible. Programs like Scratch, which contain supports –formal and informal – to accommodate the needs of new (not to mention young) users are unusual. After all, Scratch was created by university researchers with expertise in children's learning and technology use. It is a great ambassador of the children's learn-to-code movement, but it is also an exceptional case. The enthusiasm among educators and scholars for children learning to code through game playing and making may be widespread, but children are being taught using a variety of tools, approaches, and programs – not all of which are of the same standard as Scratch. The available resources contain different levels of support, are of uneven quality, and respond in varying degrees to children's particular needs and interests. In many instances, questions about quality, access, and equity remain unaddressed.

Critiques and concerns are slowly emerging regarding how game-maker tools and programs are designed and whom they are targeted to; what level and type of skills, supports, and pre-existing knowledge novice users are assumed (and in many instances required) to already have; as well as how norms, stereotypes, and discourses associated with maker and hacker subcultures might carry over to children's programs. For instance, Blikstein and Worsley argue that maker culture often promotes a sink-or-swim approach: minimal facilitation is meant to encourage tinkering, making mistakes, self-driven exploration, and autonomous discovery. This approach, however, can be problematic for novices, especially those belonging to groups that have historically been excluded from technical professions and activities including girls and women, and Black, Indigenous, and people of colour. If novices are not suitably oriented and acclimatized to a new tool or set of activities, Blikstein and Worsley note, they can feel "lost and frustrated" and become more susceptible to "stereotype threat," wherein "individuals can perform below their ability level when they suspect that they belong to a group that historically does not do well at a particular activity."[16]

There is a certain amount of elitism hidden within the "minimal facilitation" approach, as it configures even the novice user as a subject position reserved to those who feel and identify themselves as *authorized* to mess around with unfamiliar technologies. This is a privileged subject position – and one that not everyone has immediate access to. Design also plays a crucial role in delimiting the accessibility of specific tools, platforms, and programs. Design features can exclude users in a wide range of ways – from implicit assumptions about their pre-existing skills and knowledge to the inclusion of overt barriers to entry (intentional or otherwise). Lastly, the costs associated with media production tools (e.g., initial purchase, subscription fees) and with the equipment required to run them (e.g., a computer with internet connection, a webcam, or a smartphone) limit access in important ways. Within Canada, this is particularly the case for children living in rural or remote areas, and those from lower socio-economic backgrounds (which in turn includes a disproportionate number of children from Indigenous, Black, and racialized communities). Even where free tools or public access points may be available (for instance, at school or at the library), limits on how or for how long these technologies can be used can often prohibit involved activities such as designing a game or making a video.

Within this context, the advent of UGC games is an especially compelling development. As tools for game making, most UGC game titles are markedly "easy access," in that they can be used by novices "without previously required skills."[17] Most UGC games feature a "what you see is what you get" (WYSIWYG) interface, allowing users to make selections from a finite number of options, using familiar or intuitive inputs such as "point and click" or "drag and drop," instead of asking them to write or edit actual software code. The games themselves also tend to be marketed to a more inclusive audience, in terms of targeted demographics (all ages and genders) and how the ideal user is configured. Moreover, UGC games function largely as self-contained software programs designed for immediate, out-of-the-box use. Using them rarely requires any additional hardware or infrastructural supports, beyond a device to run it on (e.g., a gaming console, tablet computer) and occasional internet access. While certainly not free, the starting costs associated with UGC game titles are relatively low. Moreover, although the pre-existing skills required to use a UGC game are decidedly less technically sophisticated than those of traditional game-making programs, many researchers suggest that creating in a UGC game can have benefits for children's learning similar to engaging in more traditional game design.[18] Much of the recent scholarship in this area focuses on *Minecraft* as a key site of informal learning and skill development. For instance, Niemeyer and Gerber propose that playing and making in *Minecraft* fosters participatory learning.[19] Other scholars focus on the creative dimensions of *Minecraft*, arguing that the game's unique combination of "limitless" tools and building materials, emergent design, and social aspects functions as a catalyst for invention.[20]

In some ways, UGC games provide an inclusive, affordable, and accessible entry point into game making, especially for children who don't have access to more sophisticated tools and skills, or who don't see themselves as coders and makers, or who simply aren't interested in designing at a higher level. Instead, they can use UGC games to explore aspects of game creation, see their own and other children's ideas expressed as game features, and disrupt some of the trends that dominate the adult-made children's digital playground. In other ways, however, the experiences and activities afforded by UGC games are incongruent with key aspects of the DIY ethos, specifically its emphasis on hands-on interaction, original creation, and technical intervention. For one, many UGC games enable only superficial levels of creative and technical engagement, with a limited range of possible outcomes and few opportunities to move up to more advanced actions. This is typical of easy-access technologies, Logler explains, as "making technologies easy for beginners often results in hiding, abstracting or eliminating more advanced capabilities and complex processes."[21]

To use Papert's framework, while many UGC games may indeed have low floors, they also tend to have low ceilings and narrow walls. It is easy for users to get started, but there is not much room to them to grow, diverge, or innovate. Another key point of disconnect between DIY and UGC game making is that titles in the latter category are frequently focused on affording and promoting transmedia intertextuality. Many UGC games revolve around customizing and remixing characters, scenarios, or actions drawn from existing games or media brands. While this emphasis on transmedia intertextuality is consistent with broader trends found across children's culture (digital and analogue), it stands in stark contrast with the handmade, homemade aesthetic associated with the DIY movement, as well as the importance that is placed on original works within much of the literature in this area.

At least part of this disconnect can be explained by the genre's equally strong associations with long-held cultures of practice that centre on transmedia, remix, and fandom. As mentioned, engaging with media brands and transmedia play are common activities for children. They surface within many of the spaces and activities of childhood, at school and at home, and are recurring themes in children's art, stories, songs, and make-believe play. Notably, similar practices are also found across teen and adult gaming cultures and in their associated fan communities. From cosplay and crafting to fanfiction and modding, many players appropriate game characters, storylines, contents, or program codes in original and "derivative" creations. The game industry has a long and convoluted history in its relationship with transmedia and UGC – which is embraced at times, and at other times shut down or threatened with lawsuits.

Today, UGC has become a formal part of numerous game titles and systems. For the past two decades, there has been a growing trend towards providing players with increasingly sophisticated tools for customizing their gameplay experience. Initially, these tools were focused on game aesthetics (e.g., intricate avatar personalization menus) and narrative (e.g., through the provision of branching storylines). However, some game titles now include tools for customizing aspects of the game mechanics, including creating new level maps, altering action outcomes, or modifying in-game physics. Normally, these custom creations exist outside of and in addition to the principal game world. While UGC games clearly emerge out of this broader trend, they are also unique in that the entire game is centred on user-created or customized content. Creating content *is* the main mode of play.

Several of the best-selling games in this category are either targeted specifically to children or are child-friendly in their design, language, and player management strategies. One of the first blockbuster UGC game titles was Media Molecule's *LittleBigPlanet*, a platform game maker rated "E for Everyone" and advertised as a quasi-educational creative children's game. The look and feel of the game is dominated by a yarn-and-cardboard aesthetic, and many of the level-design tools are styled after materials and supplies used by children for arts and crafts activities (e.g., scissors, glue, stickers, paints and paint brushes). In addition to an extensive toolset and high degree of creative flexibility, the game features a long series of story-mode levels and tutorials, narrated by British actor Stephen Fry (in his trademark style), and aimed at introducing a beginner player to the game's creation system and to the broader remix ethos. While the game appeals to many teens and adults, it is heavily coded as a children's game – in its themes, imagery, didacticism, and vocabulary, as well as in its embedded safety mechanisms and rules of play (e.g., rules for what constitutes appropriate content).

Another prominent example, *Minecraft* (Mojang/Microsoft) is a sandbox game focused on the collection and use of resources and on building. Although reportedly inspired by the creator's own childhood memories of playing Lego, the game itself was not originally designed for children, and it was initially devoid of any of the types of features and policies commonly found in a children's connected play space, such as safety mechanisms and law-abiding privacy policies. As the game became popular among child players, it was repositioned as a children's title. Today it carries an E10+ rating and is widely used in classrooms and after-school programs aimed at elementary and middle school–aged children. Yet another example in this genre – and arguably the most popular at the time of writing – is *Roblox*, a *Minecraft*-esque platform for designing and editing game levels and assets, with the unique attribute of enabling users to buy and sell their creations to each other for real-world money.[22]

The UGC game genre emerged at the convergence of three trends – the game maker/STEM movement, the decades-long spread of UGC tools in digital games, and the prominence of remix and transmedia intertextuality across children's culture. The genre's amalgamation of these trends is enabled by a shared emphasis on everyday amateur creation, while underlying tensions are sublimated by design, glossed over by promotional discourses, or both. Similar combinations of trends and tactics are found across children's media and technologies, where education, play, and industry trends frequently merge in innovative and appealing ways. Indeed, many of the UGC games discussed in this chapter reproduce patterns found throughout children's commercial culture. Primary among them is the mobilization of transmedia and other branded content for promotional ends. Popular media characters do not merely surface in children's own creations and remixes, but are sold and controlled as downloadable add-on commodities. In a new iteration of the velvet-rope strategy described in chapter 3, branded content is reconfigured as exclusive content, available only to those who are willing and able to purchase access to it.

Notably, in the case of UGC games such as *LittleBigPlanet* or *Minecraft*, players are asked to purchase content *in order to* remix it into new or derivative works. In a sense, they are purchasing permission to use the copyrighted works – even in instances where such permissions are not necessarily required by law. Meanwhile, unsanctioned fan creations are discouraged through heavy-handed copyright rules, which include the threat of deletion of levels and player-made content containing copyright-infringing imagery or sounds. Ironically, as early entrants in this category, *LittleBigPlanet* and *Minecraft* initially aligned themselves with the "free culture" ethos of the remix movement. In fact, many of *LittleBigPlanet*'s early promotional materials showcased player-made homages of well-known game titles and media properties produced using the game's flexible game-creation platform. As these games evolved and grew in popularity, however, the emphasis on remix was subsumed by a prioritization of paid-for content and corporate copyright interests.[23]

As previously discussed, the role of transmedia intertextuality in the children's digital landscape is deep-rooted and complex. Children love interacting with their favourite media characters and story-worlds. They regularly incorporate media characters and plots into their play, creative activities, stories, songs, peer interactions, and other everyday life scenarios. Research in the areas of children's culture, education, and literacy highlights the diverse ways transmedia engagement can be meaningful to children. While there are certainly scholars who critique the expanding presence of media characters and other commercial elements in children's lives, others maintain that there are important benefits for children's learning, socialization, identity formation, and well-being. In any case, transmedia intertextuality is so prevalent within Western cultures (and beyond) that it is almost impossible to avoid. It is unsurprising that it has assumed a comparably strong presence within digital contexts as well.

However, the digitization and online transmission of children's engagement with transmedia intertextuality introduces new issues and considerations into the fray. For one, it raises unprecedented questions about children's relationship with copyright and fair use/fair dealing. Moreover it problematizes dominant contemporary assumptions about children's supposedly innate digital literacy. For instance, most children may have no trouble figuring out how to turn on an iPad, but far fewer have a firm grasp of legal concepts such as copyright or liability, let alone their implications for their rights and experiences. As children's play and creative practices migrate onto connected platforms and digital spaces, the significant power imbalance between media companies and young media users is increasingly exposed. While UGC games hold a lot of potential for inclusivity, creativity, and the collaborative construction of new "secret spaces" of childhood, they also contain a problematic tendency to reframe children's creativity as a paid-for experience, and they reimagine remixing and artistic expression as commercial practices. Many UGC game titles thus afford a sort of playing *at* making – a preliminary, corporately controlled set of creative practices that reconfigure game making as a new form of consumer subjectivity.

Children's Literacy, Agency, and Cultural Rights

The most urgent issue to emerge out of the legal and commercial relationships taking shape within UGC games and other forums for DIY creation is how children's authorship and ownership – over their play, utterances, and creative works – are addressed by the corporate owners of these platforms. Today, the task of determining the scope and nature of children's roles and responsibilities as content creators is left largely to corporate entities. In most cases, this work is further delegated to the site's accompanying TOS contract or EULA – policies to which all players must agree before entering the digital playground. Most TOS contracts and EULAs consist of notoriously long documents, written largely by lawyers (or adapted from lawyer-written boilerplate). These contracts are written using sophisticated technical language, often considered cryptic by those outside the legal professions and derogatorily referred to as "legalese." Many of the terms delineated in these documents extend beyond the text, informing design and player management strategies. There, they manifest as design features and are policed as (seemingly) incontestable rules of the game.

In addition to making sweeping claims that disproportionately benefit the games' owners, TOS contracts tend to offer a highly limited vision of children's authorship. Although the current trend is to acknowledge users as the lawful proprietors of any UGC that is posted or uploaded, this is done largely to legitimize the concurrent claim that lawful ownership of the content is automatically transferred to the game company upon submission, as well as to limit corporate liability in cases involving copyright infringement. Most TOS contracts fail to address children's potential rights as the creators and owners of content and other data, including children's moral rights, such as the right of attribution. Very few explain fair use/fair dealing exceptions or implement these exceptions in their policing of (potential) copyright infringement in player-made remixes, homages, or other non-monetized forms of transmedia intertextuality. The contents of the legal contracts found in children's UGC games and other digital playgrounds – what they include and exclude – merit closer consideration. Notably, when it comes to ownership and copyright issues, many of the TOS contracts found in UGC games and other DIY media platforms targeted to children reproduce norms first established in the late 1990s. The continued proliferation of this outdated model across the children's digital playscape contributes to the systematic suppression of children's cultural rights and to the enclosure of children's culture.

Before delving into problematic contractual terms, however, it is worth questioning the very practice of including a TOS or EULA when the intended userbase consists of children. Even if children *did* read them (and there is much to suggest that very few children do), it is unlikely that many children would fully understand what they were agreeing to, let alone comprehend the broader implications of the agreement or be able to identify omissions and oversights regarding how their own rights were delineated. Furthermore, it is doubtful that children can truly consent to the terms they are asked (or often assumed) to agree to in any contract – a problem that has led many jurisdictions to enact laws either delimiting contracts with children or preventing children from entering into contractual relationships with corporations in the first place. Of course, many children are savvy about connected technologies, and many children have high levels of situated knowledge about the artefacts they engage with and practices they engage in. Literacy and experience levels also vary greatly from one child to the next, particularly when age and socio-economic background are taken into consideration. Nonetheless, the academic literature strongly supports the idea that many children are lacking in literacy in the legal and economic dimensions of life on-line. Indeed, this particular literacy deficit is shared by many teens and adults as well. The gaps in children's knowledge are furthermore not always immediately apparent. Many children might know the words or hold a basic understanding of a general concept, without having deeper knowledge of the processes and interests involved.

For instance, in a recent study of young *Minecraft* players, Willet found that while all the children "were able to identify numerous revenue-generating mechanisms," there was a marked "variation in relation to in-depth understanding of revenue-generation processes and owner-ship of gaming companies."[24] Those with the deepest knowledge of *Minecraft*'s business processes were more likely to enjoy "social resources (including siblings, parents and other family members) [that] informed children about monetary aspects of online gaming industries, and also shaped their dispositions, including critical awareness and evaluation of consumer industries more generally." Socio-economic background and individual investment in the game (and in the "gamer" identity) were also identified as contributing factors to the children's varying media literacy skills. These findings are reminiscent of those uncovered in a previous study by Shade et al., who found although many children knew about "cookies," they could not accurately explain what they did or how they worked. Similar conclusions emerge from research conducted by Kafai, who discovered that even although most of the children and teens in her study were familiar with the term "computer virus," a large major-ity had "little understanding" of what a computer virus *actually* was or of how it worked.[25]

In 2016, I conducted my own study of children's thoughts on content ownership and copyright in UGC games.[26] Over the course of three "game-jam" focus groups with seven participants each (twenty-one in total), my team and I asked child game makers aged six to twelve a se-ries of questions about who owns UGC game titles, who owns UGC (i.e., player-made) game content, how copyright works, and how much control corporations have over players' creations. The children's understanding of content ownership varied greatly – not only across age groups, as was expected, but across experience levels as well. For instance, some of the children with the largest gaps in their knowledge of intellectual property ownership were those who had some form of formal training in game design, through learn-to-code summer camps or after-school programs centred on game making. In fact, increased age and experience seemed to be correlated with a narrower understanding of these processes, one that was more in line with corporate definitions of copyright and standard Web 2.0 appropriations of UGC. Our youngest participants expressed a relatively fluid understanding about the ownership of player-made and in-game content, viewing it all as a shared resource or as a sort of commons, while also viewing the content they made as their own. Conversely, many of the older participants reported that another entity – the company that owned the UGC game title, other players, or the server host – had some claim and incontestable power over their creations. As one nine-year-old respondent described it, "I own my build, but Mojang technically owns Minecraft." As such, the company could come to her house and take away her build by taking back her copy of their game.

We know very little about how, when, and where children learn about idea ownership, copyright, and related concepts. Cultural discourses are certainly an important source, as are the other elements that make up an individual child's *habitus* – including household socio-economic status, which technologies are present (and accessible) at school and at home, as well as the types of leisure activities engaged in by and with parents.[27] However, it is increasingly important to consider the role of corporate discourses and formal pedagogy within these processes. There are a range of actors already engaged in teaching children about legal issues, including educators and child advocacy groups, as well as copyright holders such as game developers, media companies, and advertisers. In some instances, these different groups might even collaborate on the creation of materials and lesson plans. For instance, the US-based Internet Keep Safe Coalition (iKeepSafe), a major player in children's online privacy regulation, works closely with industry giants such as Google to provide (among other things) educational resources to schools. Such initiatives are widespread. They also vary significantly in the depth and quality of the materials and messages produced.

At school, many children learn about copyright as part of a media or digital literacy curriculum. Some teachers use curriculum packages, such as those produced by iKeepSafe, or by MediaSmarts (a Canadian non-profit focused on media literacy and youth advocacy), while others rely on their own or their school board's resources. However, previous studies of the contents of digital literacy materials indicate a tendency to place heavy emphasis on the prevention of copyright infringement and piracy. Meanwhile, the students' own potential rights and responsibilities as creators, remixers, and users of copyrighted materials are regularly minimized or omitted. Gillespie argues that materials that prioritize corporate copyrights often downplay user rights such as fair use/fair dealing exceptions.[28] There is a tendency within digital literacy programs, particularly those aimed at children, to position children as potential copyright infringers, rather than as content creators and potential copyright holders. When media literacy programs *do* take fair use/fair dealing exceptions into account, as Moore and Landis observe, "much of the focus has, understandably, been on teaching teachers about their rights to use copyrighted material [made by others] and to encourage their students to do the same." Less attention is given to children's roles as potential "owners" or creators of their own copyrighted materials.

While concepts such as intellectual property, author rights, and user rights can be challenging, the systematic omission of children's potential rights as users and creators is problematic, as well as unwarranted. Moore and Landis's research demonstrates that even kindergartners are quite capable of grasping the underlying principles of authorship, attribution, and fair use/fair dealing. These researchers advocate for a more comprehensive approach to teaching copyright at every grade level, one that encourages children "to confidently and thoughtfully claim their rights as both creators and users of copyrighted material."[29] In the meantime, however, children are instead asked to agree to ambiguous terms and conditions that disproportionately advantage corporate copyright holders and data brokers, with little to no protections or supports to ensure that their own rights as content creators and users are upheld.

For younger children, filling some of these literacy gaps is not merely a matter of having access to more nuanced and comprehensive digital literacy materials. A whole series of developmental milestones and capacities is required to understand many of the abstract, and at times contestable, ideas that drive legal and economic processes. Take, for example, the concept of transfer of ownership, which is not only a key tenet of modern intellectual property law, but one that fuels much of the online data economy. It is also a term found in many of the TOS contracts found in children's UGC games and other digital playgrounds. Yet facets of this singular concept can be challenging for young children to comprehend. As Berti and her colleagues describe it, understandings of ownership generally evolve as part of children's economic socialization. Initially, children might believe that the person who made the object is the person who owns it. It is only once they become aware of the roles involved in manufacturing and production (e.g., boss, worker, seller) that children can differentiate between ownership and labour.[30] Even then, the ownership of certain goods is easier to identify than others. For instance, children will often be able to identify ownership of a personal clothing item (i.e., that it belongs to the person wearing it) before they are able to pinpoint who owns the family car or the desks at school.

Cram similarly suggests that it is not until children reach a certain level of maturity and experience that they are able to accurately identify ownership of many different goods. Moreover, Cram and her colleagues argue that while children grasp the rights of use and control quite easily, the right of transfer is much more difficult.[31] They note that this challenge is partly due the fact that most children experience ownership as something that is partial, tenuous, and mutable. Typically, children's possessions, including their clothing, books, and toys, are given to them "by adults who, for most practical purposes, retain the right of transfer. This makes it difficult for young children to connect the rights of use and control with the right of transfer."[32] Indeed, most children do not fully understand the right of transfer until they are older. It is therefore unreasonable to ask a child to transfer ownership to a corporate entity "forever and throughout the universe" – to use the type of language found in many child-targeted TOS contracts.

Yet just because some concepts may be excessively challenging for younger children to comprehend does not mean that all legal and economic concepts are beyond their grasp. It has long been assumed, for instance, that because the ownership of things is such a challenging and evolving concept for many children, the ownership of ideas must be doubly so. Traditional child development models posit that the ability to understand the concept of idea ownership does not emerge until well into the later stages of children's cognitive development. The dominant assumption, within the literature and across popular culture, is that younger children are fundamentally unable to grasp related concepts such as intellectual property and plagiarism. As Olson and Shaw point out, however, very little research has directly engaged with this assumption or explored "what young children understand about their own and other people's *ideas*."[33] Their work disrupts the traditional models and assumptions by showing that children can develop nuanced understandings of abstract, idea-related concepts and can even form opinions and beliefs about their associated practices. In a recent study of how children view the concept of plagiarism, for example, Olson and Shaw found that children as young as six made "negative moral evaluations about those who plagiarize as compared to those who produce unique work."[34] Although it is unclear *how* children develop a sense of idea ownership, Shaw, Li, and Olson suggest that sociocultural contexts likely play a role, such as the high "value placed on ideas ... in Western cultures that place a lot of value on individuality and uniqueness."[35]

The terms and parameters of ownership and other legal dimensions of children's online content creation are established largely by companies and their legal teams, and to a lesser extent by federal and provincial/state regulations. The primary mechanisms that most companies use to set these terms consist of TOS and TOU contracts, complex documents that are ubiquitous across the children's digital landscape, even though few children actually read them, and despite that fact that contracts made with minors for non-essentials are generally considered voidable in Canada and the United States (in that minors can usually seek to void a contract they have entered into, especially if it does not benefit them).[36] Some companies try to get around this by naming the parent as the agreeing party, setting up agreements that often fail to fully account for the laws limiting parental authority to enter into a contract on their child's behalf, and which few parents ever read anyway.[37] Yet, despite their many shortcomings and questionable enforceability, TOS contracts nonetheless guide major decisions about how players and player-made content are managed (e.g., what is censored or removed, how accounts are suspended). They also serve to legitimize – or at least corroborate – the current industry practice of claiming sweeping intellectual property ownership of players' creations, as well as of their data. While often ignored by child players, their parents, and their teachers, TOS contracts play a monumental role in shaping digital play and supporting the underlying data economies upon which many digital playgrounds are built.

Terms of Service, Terms of Play

Within mainstream game studies literature, numerous works examine how TOS and EULA contracts are used by game and/or platform owners to limit their responsibility to players and to establish their authority over players' in-game communications, activities, and creations. As mentioned above, these documents are included in more or less every program, app, game, virtual world, and website. They seek to set the economic and legal terms of the relationship between users and operators/owners – from delimiting the operator's liability and establishing jurisdiction to making sweeping intellectual property ownership claims over players' in-game utterances and UGC. Many also contain terms that are more reflective of cultural norms and expectations, such as rules against "griefing" or bullying other players. The research in this area demonstrates that analysing the contents and specifics of TOS contracts can provide insight into how games, and their players, are governed.

In the case of children's games, where the mere inclusion of a TOS contract is problematic, the need to scrutinize these documents and to consider their implications is even greater. First, as Lastowka argues, many countries grant minors special status within contract law that could make TOS contracts voidable if ever challenged in court. In Canada, this was most recently confirmed by the British Columbia Supreme Court, when Justice Peter Willcock ruled that, under the Infants Act of BC, a parent cannot sign away a child's right to sue for negligence.[38] This decision established that parents are not able to legally renounce their child's right (or future right) to litigate – a clause that is nonetheless commonly included in permission slips and liability waivers. Second, TOS contracts commonly contain complex language, terminology, and concepts, making any claim that children can give or have given informed consent problematic. Further, the contracts themselves are often presented in ways that facilitate clicking "agree" without reading their entire contents.[39] It is unlikely that TOS contracts would withstand a challenge in a court of law, should one ever arise. However, in the absence of such a challenge, they currently function as though they were legitimate and enforceable. There is therefore a need to better understand their largely hidden function within the children's digital play landscape – and the ideas, relationships, and rules they introduce into children's digital play.

Who Owns Children's Content in Digital Playgrounds?

Over the past eighteen years, I have conducted six separate studies analysing the contents of TOS contracts contained in games, websites, and apps designed for, or targeted primarily to, elementary school–aged children.[40] The first study was completed in 2005[41] and the most recent was completed in 2018.[42] All six studies used a coding protocol based on Russo's checklist of "fifteen significant points" to look for when analysing EULAs.[43] As Russo reports, these documents tend to follow a rigid format, reproducing the same (or a similar) set of terms initially established by the PC software industry in the late 1990s. Notably, although Russo's model is nearly twenty years old, it remains just as relevant and applicable today as it was when it was published in 2001. Although many of the technologies and practices that make up the children's digital landscape have evolved over the years, the industry's approach to legal and regulatory issues has changed surprisingly little since the early 2000s. TOS contracts are largely used to claim intellectual property rights over players' contributions and data. In turn, this content is used to fuel data economies, supply sites with content, generate added value, contribute to brand identity, and engage users in viral marketing. Players' contributions and data, therefore, have enormous value. Indeed, many games and connected playgrounds are based on business models that hinge on the legitimacy of the UGC and data ownership claims made in the accompanying TOS or EULA. For instance, games that sell user data rely on the belief that they are legally permitted to do so.

A comparative analysis of TOS contracts collected between 2007 and 2012 shows just how similar, and unchanged, these documents tend to be (table 6.1).[44] All sixteen of the TOS documents reviewed contained the same "fifteen significant points" identified by Russo as standard in EULAs aimed at managing market-based relationships between informed, consenting adults. This itself is problematic, as many of the stipulations included on Russo's list may not actually be applicable to children. Some of the contracts attempted to bypass the question of age appropriateness by naming the child's parent or guardian as the agreeing party. Others contained a vague stipulation that if the user was under the age of eighteen, *implied agreement* to the terms automatically extended to the user's parent or guardian. None of the games reviewed contained evidence that any effort was made to ensure that an adult had read or consented to the terms. Instead, many of the contracts required children to assume responsibility for securing their own parental consent.

For example, as the TOS for tween-targeted MMOG *Dizzywood* (2007–10) outlined,

> By uploading or otherwise submitting any Posted Content to us and/or the Site, you (and your parents, if you're under age 18) automatically grant (or warrant that the owner of such rights has expressly granted) to Dizzywood, a perpetual, royalty-free, irrevocable, nonexclusive right and license to use, reproduce, modify, adapt, publish, translate, create derivative works from, and distribute such materials or incorporate such Posted Content into any form, medium, or technology (now known or hereafter developed or devised) throughout the world. In addition, you warrant that all "moral rights" and other similar rights recognized throughout the world in that Posted Content has been waived.[45]

The confusion about whether children or their parents are the ones consenting to these contracts is troubling. While parents are often held responsible for their children's actions online, parents and children are still distinct legal persons. Moreover, this distinction is extremely important: not all parents act in their child's best interests, and children often do things against their parents' wishes. A recent ruling in favour of parents whose children spent large sums on in-app purchases, unbeknownst to them until they saw the charges on their credit card statements, demonstrates that the courts will not unilaterally hold parents liable for their children's actions. Just as parents cannot legally bind their children

Table 6.1. Children's Connected Games TOS Contracts Analysed

Name	Corporate owner	Game genre	Date of TOS retrieval
BarbieGirls	Mattel	MMOG	9 August 2008
Build-A-Bearville	Build-A-Bear Workshop	Play-based virtual world	15 November 2007
Club Penguin	Walt Disney Company	MMOG	27 November 2008 9 February 2009
Pixie Hollow	Walt Disney Company	MMOG	24 October 2008
Dizzywood	Rocket Paper Scissors	MMOG	23 June 2008
Free Realms	Sony Online Entertainment	MMOG	11 February 2010
Fusion Fall	Cartoon Network	MMOG	15 January 2009
GalaXseeds	Corus Entertainment	MMOG	24 May 2009 27 September 2012
Lego Universe	The Lego Group	MMOG	5 January 2011
LittleBigPlanet	Sony Computer Entertainment	UGC game	11 November 2010 26 September 2012
Magi-Nation	Cookie Jar	MMOG	8 October 2009
MoshiMonsters	Mind Candy	Game-themed virtual world	16 May 2008
Nicktropolis	Nickelodeon/Viacom	MMOG	9 August 2010
Roblox	Roblox Corporation	UGC game	15 June 2011
Stardoll	Stardoll	MMOG	23 May 2007 27 September 2012
Toontown	Walt Disney Company	MMOG	8 October 2009

Source: Adapted from Grimes (2013).

to unfair contractual agreements, children cannot bind their parent to a contract merely by playing a game or using a service.

Overall, the TOS contracts I have reviewed focused on restricting players' rights and interactions, as well as limiting corporate accountability and liability. When analysed together, the TOS contracts suggest a culture that privileges corporate interests. The scope and nature of the terms delineated in these documents maintain the traditional, imbalanced power relations between children and the children's industries, and extend these power relations into new areas of children's play and creative practice. Notably, some of the most problematic terms were found in the portions pertaining to intellectual property. All sixteen of the TOS contracts listed in table 6.1 claimed either full or partial copyright over players' submissions, including UGC creations. This was even true in contracts that overtly acknowledged that children were the authors and original owners of their content. For instance, the TOS for the paper doll and fashion design–themed virtual world *Stardoll* (2005–present) specified, "You own the rights to the material which you have created yourself on Stardoll's websites, but in this agreement you give Stardoll the right, without special compensation, to publish the material for an unlimited time throughout the world and irrespective of the medium used."[46]

The insistence that players waive their moral rights and other author rights is a common clause in TOS contracts. This is apparent in the above excerpt from the *Dizzywood* TOS, which requires the player to waive "all 'moral rights' and other similar rights." Another example is found in the TOS for *Pixie Hollow*, a Disney Fairies–themed MMOG, which not only claimed worldwide, perpetual licence to use, reproduce, and modify users' submissions in all formats and channels "now known or hereafter devised," but asserted that they could do so without adhering to standard attribution practices, "all without further notice to you, with or without attribution, and without the requirement of any permission from or payment to you or to any other person or entity (the 'Submissions License')."[47]

The TOS contracts unilaterally paired the requirement that children (and/or their parents) waive all rights and privileges normally bestowed to creators of content with the assertion that the children nonetheless remained responsible for ensuring that said content respected the rights of *other* copyright holders. For example, the EULA for *LittleBigPlanet* included the following term at the end of its lengthy (two single-spaced page) section on UGC: "You hereby ... Warrant and represent that A) you created your User Generated Content; B) You have all necessary rights to your User Generated Content to fulfill your obligations under this Agreement; C) your User Generated Content does not infringe on the intellectual property or other rights of any third party and is not obscene, defamatory, offensive or an advertisement of solicitation of business."[48] This last excerpt illustrates a trend found in many of the TOS contracts reviewed, but it is one that becomes particularly problematic within the context of a UGC game such as *LittleBigPlanet*. Here, posting others' copyrighted materials is forbidden in the EULA, but it is concurrently encouraged in the game's promotional materials and in-game store – a contradiction that is explored in greater detail below. Moreover, a blanket ban on posting content that contains others' copyrighted materials omits the possibility that the use of such material may fall under fair use/fair dealing exceptions, as with parodies or satires.

As explored above, because TOS contracts are so rarely read and understood, it is unlikely that children or parents ever gave verifiable, informed consent to the terms and conditions outlined in these contracts. Moreover, the scope and extent of the claims made within these contracts are sweeping and clearly not to the benefit of the children involved. As mentioned, this industry practice has thus far attracted very little academic attention or public concern. However, until recently, there were relatively few opportunities for children to directly shape the contents of their games, media, or virtual environments, particularly in the realm of children's digital games and play, where opportunities to contribute "user submissions" were often limited to participating in in-game chat conversations. While some games invited children to submit fan art and news items, their submissions were commonly curated, and the topics were largely determined, by adults. For instance, little more than half of the sites included in my early study of children's online games allowed participants to contribute creative submissions such as game reviews, poetry contest entries, or fan art. Even fewer allocated space within the sites for players to create webpages and user polls or contribute other features to the website's design. Similar trends appeared in my subsequent analysis of children's virtual worlds, where user contributions were limited mostly to avatar customization and decorating personal spaces with virtual items acquired through gameplay or purchase (as opposed to items or decorative elements created by the players themselves). Children did engage in more visible forms of fandom and meta-participation during this period, but such activities tended to occur outside of the official game environment.

Of course, the conversations that children engage in while playing games together frequently involve creative activities, as they share ideas, engage in make-believe play, negotiate rules, and tell each other stories. For most users, however, these forms of creative engagement are seemingly ephemeral. In text or voice chat, for example, the engagement occurs in real time and disappears as it unfolds (or soon after). Although most commercial multiuser forums keep records of players' conversations, which become categorized as data and used in business transactions, for the players and the public such user contributions appear transient and immaterial. It is notable that during this same period, a new sector emerged within the children's digital play space, which centred on the collection, analysis, and sale of children's data; this of course included children's online chat and other immaterial submissions (e.g., content, information, or selections uploaded to a connected digital system). Perhaps because the types of UGC that children were submitting predominantly in those early years were less clearly distinguishable as creative, it was more difficult to see their contributions as worthy of intellectual property rights. In any case, historically, very little consideration was given to children's potential authorship or intellectual property rights during the decade or so in which the terms described here silently became the industry standard.

New Creative Opportunities, Same Old Terms

Examining the TOS contracts contained within UGC games – games that provide players with the tools to make and share their own creative content – provides compelling evidence of just how problematic the enduring use of the standard EULA format has become. For this phase of my research, conducted between 2011 and 2016, I focused on fifty-five digital game titles identified as containing a significant number or meaningful depth of features for players to make and share game levels, mods, maps, or other playable content. The analysis included several genres, from UGC games such as *LittleBigPlanet 2* and *Super Mario Maker*, to games with build-in level editors such as *Torchlight II* (2012–present) and *The Elder Scrolls V: Skyrim* (2011–present), as well as several of the more playful WYSIWYG game-making platforms such as *Scratch* and *Roblox*. Not all the games examined in this study were targeted to children, and one of the research questions was whether the games' target demographics influenced the games' treatment of player creativity and creative freedoms, intellectual property ownership, and UGC submissions. Therefore, only fifteen of the TOS contracts (listed in table 6.2) reviewed were for games that carried an E or E10+ ESRB rating, or were otherwise indicated as for children (e.g., described as such in promotional texts and privacy policies).

While the contents and structures of the fifteen documents examined in this study were not identical, the majority contained most or all of Russo's fifteen points. Several of the TOS contracts acknowledged that users were the owners of their submissions and were therefore responsible for the contents (e.g., if the submission constituted copyright infringement, the users were responsible). At the same time, many of the agreements required players to transfer or waive significant aspects of their ownership rights (a key exception here was *Minecraft*, discussed in the next section). For instance, the Disney Interactive EULA that accompanied the Steam download version of *Disney Infinity 2.0: Marvel Superheroes* (2014) stipulated,

> We do not claim ownership to your User Generated Content; however, you grant us a non-exclusive, sublicensable, irrevocable and royalty-free worldwide license under all copyrights, trademarks, patents, trade secrets, privacy and publicity rights and other intellectual property rights to use, reproduce, transmit, print, publish, publicly display, exhibit, distribute, redistribute, copy, index, comment on, modify, adapt, translate, create derivative works

Table 6.2. TOS Contracts in Children's UGC Games, Game Design Platforms, and Games Containing UGC Tools, 2011–2016

Name	Corporate owner	Game genre
Angry Birds	Rovio	Game app containing UGC tools
Create	EA	UGC game
Disney Infinity 2.0: Marvel Superheroes	Disney	Toys-to-life game containing UGC tools
Kerbal Space Program	Squad/Private Division	Game containing UGC tools
LittleBigPlanet 2	Media Molecule	UGC game
Minecraft	Mojang/Microsoft	UGC game
Roblox	Roblox	UGC game
Scratch	MIT	DIY game/animation design platform
Scribblenauts Unmasked	WB Interactive	UGC game/game containing UGC tools
SimCity	EA	UGC game
Sound Shapes	Queasy Games/Sony	Game containing UGC tools
Spore	EA	UGC game
Stardoll	Stardoll	DIY avatar/game design platform
Super Mario Maker	Nintendo	UGC game
Train Simulator	Railsimulator.com	UGC game

based upon, publicly perform, make available and otherwise exploit such User Generated Content, in whole or in part, in all media formats and channels now known or hereafter devised (including in connection with the Disney Services and on third-party sites and platforms such as Facebook, YouTube and Twitter), in any number of copies and without limit as to time, manner and frequency of use, without further notice to you, with or without attribution, and without the requirement of permission from or payment to you or any other person or entity.

The terms and language used here are typical of child-targeted TOS contracts. The claims of unlimited, irrevocable licensing rights, in any form or format "now known or hereafter devised," with or without attribution to the content creator, are found across children's websites, digital games, and other software. This paragraph could easily have been drawn from any number of the TOS and EULAs I have examined over the past eighteen years. Despite their pervasiveness and apparent obscurity, I am consistently surprised by how little the terms and contents of most TOS contracts have changed since the early 2000s. During this period, monumental shifts have taken place in how and where children access digital tools – from the widespread adoption of mobile and touch devices by children of increasingly younger ages, to the massive expansion in the volume and forms of digital creation and communication that children engage in. Indeed, across the digital landscape, traditional, top-down relationships between media industries and audiences are being replaced by a more dynamic (albeit rarely tension-free) exchange of participatory culture. Yet somehow these participatory, user-driven Web 2.0 spaces and practices are still largely underwritten by contractual agreements designed for traditional, unidirectional producer-consumer transactions. What *has* changed is that in the current climate, where users produce much of the content and value upon which the data economy flows, these outdated agreements represent an increasingly grotesque imbalance of power, as corporate copyright owners are disproportionately and unfairly advantaged, while users see their cultural and other rights systematically undermined.

Recent works by Zuboff and Pasquale provide useful insight into why users' intellectual property is still framed in these seemingly outdated terms.[49] Although the things users do online have shifted, the underlying workings of the information or data economy have not changed so much as they have expanded over the past two decades. This is also true of children's digital games. A key function of many popular titles has been – and still is – to collect data from young users. These spaces are troves of children's personal information, and they provide unfettered access to children's thoughts, preferences, and behaviours. All of this information can be (and indeed is) used for a range of purposes, from influencing children's purchasing habits to creating predictive algorithms. From *Neopets* and *Habbo Hotel* to *Facebook* and *Minecraft*, users are configured as a resource that fuels business-to-business exchange, which in turn generates a sizeable portion of the profits made by companies online. Along with the enormous immaterial value that UGC can produce for a brand (similar to the value produced by the "brand ambassadors" and "premium members" found in the children's virtual worlds discussed in chapter 3) and for the user community, UGC also contributes to this larger, very material exchange as a form of user data to be packaged and sold. Here, intellectual property is envisioned as a corporate asset to be secured, extended, and controlled. Within this dynamic, player contributions are acknowledged primarily as a form of intellectual property so that they can then be claimed, mined, and exploited by the site's corporate owner.

Over a decade ago, Lastowka argued that, given children's limited commercial power, "it would seem very difficult for a virtual world owner to bind a child to the terms of an online contract, since minors generally lack the capacity to enter into legal contracts."[50] This sentiment has been echoed more recently by other legal scholars, including Wayne, who explains, "Most contracts entered into by a person that is underage (referred to as 'minors' or 'infants') are voidable at the minor's option."[51] To this day, however, the legality and legitimacy of TOS contracts and EULAs made with children have not been addressed by a court of law, at least not directly. While TOS contracts found in mainstream games (i.e., those targeted primarily to adults) were debated at length in a series of high-profile, mostly US-based court cases that essentially confirmed their legitimacy, the conclusions reached in those cases are unlikely to apply to minors. For one, the players involved consisted of consenting adults deemed to have received "adequate" notice of the terms they were agreeing to before engaging in practices that overtly defied the EULA. In at least one instance, *Davidson & Associates v Internet Gateway*, the defendants consisted of computer programmers with specialized, insider knowledge of the legal frameworks typically used by the game and software industries. In that case, the players' familiarity with EULAs was a key factor in the court's decision to reject their claim that the agreement was "unconscionable." It is unlikely that these same conclusions would apply if the rule-breakers consisted of children.

The above argument finds some support in the conclusions reached following a 2013 FTC investigation into unauthorized in-app purchases made by minors, which resulted in high-profile settlements with Apple and Google. The FTC action was launched in response to complaints filed by parents who had been billed for apps and for in-app purchases made by their children without their consent. Here "unauthorized" charges were deemed to include accidental purchases (such as the ones described in chapter 2), as well as purchases made by minors without the authorization of the parent/account holder. Aspects of the settlements the companies reached with the FTC highlight the legal limitations of the widespread assumption that parents automatically consent to and are responsible for the online actions of their minor children. As part of its settlement, for instance, Apple agreed to refund millions of dollars to affected parents. It was also required to change its billing practices to better ensure parental consent was secured before app and in-app purchases were processed (e.g., by enabling the account holder to require a password every fifteen minutes or with every purchase). Court decisions on some of the class-action lawsuits associated with the FTC's investigation are also useful when considering the legality of TOS contracts involving children. For instance, in his 2014 denial of Amazon's motion to dismiss the FTC's suit against it, Judge John C. Coughenour refused to consider the company's "terms and conditions," stating, "This Court has previously held that neither legal terms nor similar customer terms of use were 'beyond reasonable controversy.'"[52] The court noted that it was not inclined to extend the "apparent authority" that account-holder parents had allegedly bestowed onto child users under Amazon's terms and conditions, in part because the contents of the TOS agreements were not deemed applicable, and in part because of what the judge described as a lack of "more persuasive legal authority."

On the one hand, such developments are promising, as they suggest that there is opportunity and legal justification for questioning – and possibly challenging – the industry standards that have emerged regarding TOS contracts, children's agency, and parental consent within digital environments. On the other hand, the issue of minors' contracts in the digital realm remains for the most part an obscure subplot within the larger, much more visible story about adults' online rights and relationships. When children's rights do appear, it is in a narrative that is focused on the recurring conflicts that arise between adults – parents, governments, companies – as they fight for authority and control over children's lives online. Meanwhile, the absence of a focused public debate about TOS contracts and the relationships these contracts seek to establish with children has enabled industry standards to emerge unquestioned and largely unhindered. Over the past two decades, these standards of practice have evolved, spread, and taken root, withstanding new trends and resisting change. In the process, the contracts have come to exert an overlooked but significant amount of influence over how children's digital spaces are designed, managed, and monetized. The terms contained in these agreements do more than establish liability or licensing rights. They lay out a particular world view: a political position and *positioning* on the role and responsibility of children, their parents, the company, and the government, within the quasi-public sphere of a commercially owned virtual space. This is a *positioning* as well as a position because the contracts enact these politics onto the players, presenting the contracts' terms as a status quo that is embedded at the level of design and enforced through the constant threat of exclusion via censorship, account suspension, or even legal action.

Notably, TOS contracts represent one of the only places where children's relationship to intellectual property and other authorship rights are addressed and delineated. They thereby set the terms of what little public discourse *is* accorded to these issues – or at least *shape* these terms in meaningful ways. For instance, the specific approach to copyright found in many children's TOS contracts is consistent with the messages promoted in many child-targeted digital literacy materials. In some cases, TOS contracts are explicitly deferred to as the source of authority in determining who owns children's UGC creations and other content.[53] Children and their parents are surrounded by a singular interpretation of what children's relationship to copyright is. This interpretation is corporately constructed and undeniably biased towards the interests of commercial entities concerned with maintaining and securing the rights over as much content as possible, including user creations, personal information, and behavioural data. The content is valuable on many levels: it may be used in the short term for developing new features or targeting advertisements, or it may be packaged and sold as "big data" now or in the future. Very few alternative visions of what children's relationship to their online content is or could be are available. The question thus becomes whether this narrow vision of online creativity in turn constrains children's sense of themselves as persons who belong and contribute to a shared culture. How does the (re)positioning of cultural participation as a corporately owned commodity (re)shape children's experience, autonomy, and identity as digital creators and citizens?

User Rights in Minecraft

While this book is concerned primarily with revealing the overarching patterns and underlying politics of the children's digital landscape, it is worth considering some of the exceptions as well, particularly when a key exception happens to be one of the most popular digital games of all time. As mentioned above, there is now an impressive amount of academic literature on the blockbuster sandbox/UGC game *Minecraft* – and for good reason. The game is (or has been) used in schools, libraries, and after-school programs for a wide range of applications. It is available on virtually every gaming device and system, and it has spawned its own transmedia (and product licensing) empire. The game has surfaced multiple times in my own research, first as a primary example of UGC games and children's game making, then as a locus of hyperbolic public optimism about its educational benefits, and most recently as an influential source of children's knowledge and experiences of creativity and copyright within commercially owned digital spaces. Over the past several years, *Minecraft* has also been an outlier in my ongoing analysis of TOS contracts and privacy policies, breaking from the norms found throughout the children's and digital games industries, and carving a distinct trajectory in how it approaches UGC, copyright, and user rights.

After an extended period of open testing, a full version of *Minecraft* was officially released in late 2011. A year later, it was the sixth-best-selling game of all time. By 2018, it had sold over 154 million copies worldwide across all platforms, and it became the second-best-selling game of all time – bested only by *Tetris*.[54] Today, it remains one of the most popular games in the world, with over ninety-one million active monthly players. While not designed specifically for children, market research, news coverage, and academic literature all show that it is extremely popular among children. The game is the focus of innumerable grassroots curricula and after-school programs aimed at elementary school–aged children, and an official *Minecraft: Education Edition* containing tools to help teachers incorporate the game into their classes was launched in 2016. *Minecraft*'s creators have furthermore teamed up with teachers in the United States and Finland to run an online network for educators (which also provides technical and peer support for users of the *Education Edition*), called *MinecraftEdu*. The game is heralded as a key conduit for teaching computing skills and STEM skills, and is reportedly used in social studies–, art-, and humanities-based lesson plans as well. *Minecraft*'s flexibility and simplicity make it amenable to creativity and appropriation, and it has been used by millions to make a vast assortment of creations and to participate in an array of cultural practices. It is the subject of countless YouTube channels, fan sites, artworks, and handmade crafts. It has been used to build detailed replicas of Hogwarts, Winterfell, and the USS *Enterprise*. It is a place where people of all ages engage in role-playing games, have heartfelt conversations, and compete in ruthless battles. Its applications are seemingly endless.

The first step in playing and creating in *Minecraft* is to generate a "world" or instance of the game. Worlds can be generated (i.e., built and saved) on the player's device, where they exist as single-player or "local multiplayer" games (also known as a "couch co-op," meaning that all players are in the same room together). Worlds can also be generated and made playable for others online, but the system for this is largely decentralized and mostly unsupervised. Most recently, *Minecraft* has introduced the option of purchasing a game realm, in which a player essentially rents server space directly from Mojang/Microsoft rather than going through a third party. Otherwise, online worlds are hosted on player-run (i.e., owned or rented and operated) servers. In either case, an inordinate amount of responsibility is delegated to the players themselves for moderation, player management, and policing unacceptable or illegal activities. Online *Minecraft* worlds usually contain some form of player-to-player communication tool (e.g., text-based chat, VoIP), unless these features have been turned off. Player interactions are therefore also monitored by other players, albeit to wildly varying degrees. Despite this conflux of unusual regulatory (or non-regulatory) circumstances, since its introduction *Minecraft* has been consistently and almost uniformly celebrated within popular and academic contexts.

Unlike most other examples and areas of the children's digital land-scape, *Minecraft*'s individual server system, lack of oversight, and absence of top-down moderation services are rarely discussed in terms of risk and safety. Instead, they are more likely to be positioned as opportunities for educators, libraries, or families to build and control their own game worlds. A similar rhetoric appears in the promotional descriptions for *Minecraft*'s Realms service: "The internet can be a wild place – but with Realms, only people you invite can join your world, making it the safest way to play with friends!"[55] Indeed, in her textual analysis of US and UK popular media coverage of *Minecraft* from November 2010 to April 2013, Willett found that on the topic of *Minecraft* and safety, the dominant discourse was that the game presented an appealing, "family friendly" alternative to the blood and violence of mainstream videogames.[56] Other reviewers claimed that *Minecraft*'s emphasis on interaction and exploration provides an antidote to the types of risks linked to "sedentary media" consumption.[57] During the period reviewed in Willett's study, me-dia coverage of the game was overwhelmingly positive. She concludes, "The indie component and the creative learning aspects of [*Minecraft*] seem to trump any concerns about risks, even high-profile risks such as 'stranger danger.' The emphasis is almost entirely on the high quality of *Minecraft*, with parents being encouraged to understand their children's activities on the site."[58] Given that children's culture has long been and remains a locus of critique, concern, and contradiction, the special status accorded to Minecraft by the popular press is difficult to comprehend.

Similarly, although there is a substantial body of academic literature on *Minecraft*, very little scholarship has addressed the game's unconventional approach to children's privacy, copyright, commercialization, and other legal and regulatory issues. The game was originally based in Sweden but was sold to the US-based Microsoft in 2014. In the United States and Canada, *Minecraft* carries an ESRB rating of E10+, along with a disclaimer that it contains "online features that may expose players to unrated user-generated content."[59] While it was not originally designed for chil-dren, *Minecraft* is widely known to be popular among children, and it has official relationships with elementary schools and cross-sector initiatives aimed at children and teens. Its merchandising strategies also indicate that children are a core target demographic of the *Minecraft* transmedia supersystem. It is clearly subject to the same rules, laws, and social ex-pectations accorded to other digital playgrounds frequented by young children in these countries, and yet it has not been held to the same stand-ards. Within the academic literature, there is a surprising lack of critical analysis or discussion of the political economy of *Minecraft*, its relation-ship to Microsoft, or its privileged position within so many educational and cultural institutions. Concurrently, until relatively recently, the game and its owners also avoided addressing many of these issues. For many years, player age was not even mentioned in the game's TOS agreement or scant privacy policy. In the early 2010s, when I first started researching *Minecraft* and its users, both documents were unusually terse and hard to locate. For a time, they could be found only by searching the game's official website and were not included in the computer, mobile, handheld, and console downloads of the game itself. Since COPPA requirements include the prominent display of a privacy notice or policy containing clear information about how children's information might be used, as well as information about parental rights vis-à-vis their child's information, during this period *Minecraft* was not COPPA compliant.

In 2016, however, Mojang significantly altered its approach to the myriad legal implications and relationships associated with *Minecraft* and its players (i.e., the types of issues normally covered by a standard TOS contract and COPPA-compliant privacy policy). The policies themselves are still difficult to locate for the majority of players who purchase the game somewhere other than on the company's own website (for instance, through the Microsoft Xbox Marketplace or Sony PlayStation Store). By contrast, when purchasing a copy from Mojang's Minecraft.net, the policies are posted prominently and incorporated into the new account registration process. But it is the contents of the policies themselves that are unique and noteworthy. This is particularly true of their TOS contract or EULA, which has seemingly been reimagined as serving the double function of contractual agreement and comprehensive policy statement. The agreement spans four distinct documents that the user must open individually and scroll down to read. They are written almost entirely in friendly, informal language, in a stark departure from the legalese that dominates most of the other TOS contracts I have examined. They do not mention user age but do suggest that the agreement applies to children, stating, "If you are young and you are having trouble understanding these terms and conditions, please ask a responsible adult such as your parent or guardian."

The terms themselves also contain numerous significant departures from the status quo. First, and most notable, is the company's approach to copyright as it relates to players' UGC and meta-participation. Unlike most of the TOS contracts analysed as part of my UGC games study, the agreement contains an explicit approval of players using and sharing their own UGC, and it even encourages them to do so: "We are very relaxed about things you create for yourself. Pretty much anything goes there – so go for it, have fun, and just don't distribute anything we've made. We are also quite relaxed about other non-commercial things so feel free to create and share videos, screen shots, independently created mods (that don't use any of our Assets), fan art, machinima, etc."

The agreement also addresses commercial uses of player-made content, although they warn, "We are less relaxed about commercial things." Players who wish to make money from their *Minecraft*-based or *Minecraft*-related creations are pointed to a separate document (the Commercial Usage Guidelines), which contains limits on how much money any one player is allowed to earn in a single year from selling original works inspired by *Minecraft* (US$5,000), as well as a cap on the number of items that can be manufactured from a single design (twenty). In general terms, the agreement explains, "We love the idea of people doing cool things with our games and sharing those things with the community. That's something we totally support and encourage. So please feel free to do so but please also make sure you don't go too far." Many of the limitations placed on players' commercial and non-commercial uses of their UGC are concerned with preventing pseudo-counterfeiting activities (i.e., activities that could result in the UGC being confused with official *Minecraft* content or merchandise). The agreement also contains an "essential requirement" that any shared content must "*NOT* be unlawful, deceptive, obscene, harmful or disparaging." Throughout the TOS agreement, and particularly in the Commercial Usage Guidelines section, acceptable or unproblematic UGC is described as player-made (as opposed to commercially made) and original (as opposed to derivative), with many of the examples centred on activities that Consalvo would identify as forms of meta-participation.

For example, many of the descriptions and examples of UGC found in the agreement could be interpreted as references to Let's Play videos. In a section dedicated to outlining player rights regarding screenshots and video footage, the agreement states,

> You may create, use and distribute videos of you playing or using our game for any lawful reason provided that you don't make any money from them. However, you may make money using your videos of our game by, for instance, through ad revenue, as long as you also add your own unique content to the video, such as audio commentary. The amount you add must also be enough to make it fair and worthwhile for someone to pay for it or for you to make money from it. For example you couldn't just include your logo, web address or indent [*sic*] but you could add an audio commentary or your own music if you are creating a music video.

The policy also contains a section on handcrafted creations, allowing users to make and even sell (limited) crafts and other things that they have made that feature a *unique design* inspired by *Minecraft* (defined as "something that adds enough personal creativity to make the work distinctive and original"). It also includes sections on mods and books, both of which are deemed acceptable as long as certain "essential" rules are followed. It is notable that each of these listed activities consists of a form of meta-participation that is already well-established within gaming culture (and well documented within game studies), where they are deeply associated with games-based fandoms and grassroots maker movements. Within that context, these activities are the territory of everyday users, rather than corporations.

Second, the agreement is among a mere handful of such documents I have seen that overtly address fair use/fair dealing copyright exceptions. This acknowledgment surfaces in the section pertaining to commercial uses of UGC and states, "You may also make money using videos and screen-shots if it is covered by so called 'fair dealing' or 'fair use' exceptions to copyright, such as where it is for criticism and review, reporting current affairs etc." Although the document does not provide any additional information or clarification about these exceptions and where they may apply, the mere mention of fair use/fair dealing is significant. Few sources include these terms in their copyright policies, resulting in a digital landscape where fair use/fair dealing is largely obscured. Acknowledging these and other user rights is an important step towards confirming them.

A third important feature of the new *Minecraft* TOS agreement is the repeated distinction it makes between individual players, on the one hand, and corporations and other entities, on the other hand. Most, if not all, of the commercial and non-commercial use rights contained in the agreement are accorded solely to players. The TOS states, "We also want to make it clear that these Guidelines are for the community of Minecraft players and fans. They do not authorize commercial companies, corporate brands, advertising agencies, non-profits, or governments to use or exploit Minecraft for promoting products or services unrelated to Minecraft."[60] It is this part of the new policy that received the most media attention when it was first introduced in 2016. Industry news sources described the policy change as a move intended to curtail advertising in *Minecraft*, specifically for "unrelated" third-party products. The new policy would prevent companies and advertisers from bypassing *Minecraft*'s business-to-business services, which generate a substantial amount of revenue for the game company. Now, instead of launching immersive advertising campaigns under the guise of a branded or sponsored server, companies could purchase ad space only in traditional forms such as pop-up banners or video ads. The image of the innocent child was heavily mobilized within the corporate communications and press interviews that followed the policy change. On the developer blog, a spokesperson for Mojang highlighted the company's desire to exert more control over what and how products were marketed to minors: "We want to empower our community to make money from their creativity, but we're not happy when the selling of an unrelated product becomes the purpose of a Minecraft mod or server. That doesn't feel right, or more importantly, fun. The new rules are an attempt to stop these things from happening."[61]

The picture painted by Mojang and the news media during this period is slightly misleading, however. Some articles even made it sound as if the game was removing promotional content altogether. For example, Grubb's article on *Venture Beat* carried the headline "Microsoft Bans Corporations from Using Minecraft as a Marketing Tool." Yet the game continues to offer select businesses the option of purchasing immersive advertising and other integrated promotional content through licensing deals that result in paid-for DLC or "add-ons" such as skins, story packs, maps, and levels featuring popular transmedia properties. At the time of writing, for instance, the Sony PlayStation Store contained 206 different *Minecraft* DLC products available for purchase, sixty-eight (33 per cent) of which featured third-party properties. For example, players could buy a *Minecraft: Steven Universe* pack containing avatar skins, building block textures, locations, and original music from the popular Cartoon Network television series and transmedia property *Steven Universe* (2013–20).[62] The presence and promotion of licensed content packs contrasts with the tone and terms contained in the TOS, which work to configure the game as a welcoming site for fandom and player creativity. On the one hand, the stipulation that only players acting of their own volition are allowed to "build products or movie environments that you are a fan of into a Minecraft mod/map/server," combined with the assertion that companies and other entities are forbidden from doing so for any sort of promotional means, can indeed be interpreted as a move aimed at fostering participatory culture while restricting the game's colonization by commercial interests. On the other hand, now that corporations are legally prevented from building their own promotional worlds, dealing with Mojang/Microsoft directly (through a business-to-business transaction) becomes the only viable way of entering an exceptionally popular digital environment. With this policy shift, Mojang/Microsoft cemented its authority and control over the promotional content appearing in its game space, enabling the company to better align third-party content with *Minecraft*'s own brand identity and player population, while also securing a lucrative revenue stream in the process.

It is important that a game with the popularity and influence of *Minecraft* has adopted such a player-centric approach in the way it addresses fair use/fair dealing, remix, and other forms of meta-participation. Although it is too soon to know what impact, if any, *Minecraft*'s approach will have on broader industry standards of practice, it already provides a viable alternative model for how UGC can be not only accommodated but also supported by the commercial entities that enable and oftentimes profit from such activities. The agreement's explicit acknowledgment of a wide range of players' cultural rights sets an example that can be evoked in policy discussions and public debates about the role and function of player creativity and agency across Web 2.0-style contexts. In many ways, *Minecraft*'s agreement stands in opposition to the widespread trends and assumptions that have dominated many corporations' approach to player contributions. As such, it provides an opening for rethinking trends and assumptions, and for finding a way forward that is more consistent with how people use digital tools, why they use them, and what they expect from the corporate entities that supply them.

Yet it is also important to remember that *Minecraft* and its corporate owners do also reproduce other problematic patterns found across the children's digital playground. Here the lack of critical engagement with the game and its many uses becomes troubling. The political-economic underpinnings of *Minecraft* – its business model, how it makes money, what it does with players' personal information and other data – are largely the same as the ones found within more overtly commercial game titles. Just as too few people questioned the game's lack of privacy policy or detailed TOS agreement in its first few years of existence, the dearth of attention given to *Minecraft*'s unique brand of immersive advertising, and its subsequent evocation of children's affective bonds and labour, enables these patterns to continue unfettered. There is a tendency to let games such as *Minecraft* – games that contain some high-quality, ethical design features or policy approaches – off the hook for their commercial practices. Willett came to a similar conclusion in her review of the game's early media coverage, which mostly downplayed the commercial and profit-making dimensions of *Minecraft*, while emphasizing its "indie" and "labour of love" origins. She found that the game, its owners, and its original creator (Persson) were predominantly discussed in terms of their perceived commitment to players, their belief in making a unique and high-quality play experience, and their contrast to the business practices of the mainstream global games industry. This narrative, she argues, is "part of the discursive construction which designates *Minecraft* as a safe, high-quality game for children and young teens with no risk of commercial exploitation."[63] In systematically ignoring and sublimating the commercial dimensions of the game, we not only normalize the commercial presence, but also passively accept the unfair and potentially exploitative dynamics that they introduce to children's lives.

Fandom and Fair Use as Consumer Practice

As a game that is centred on making and customizing, *Minecraft*'s inclusion of licensed third-party content necessitates a delicate balancing act. The cross-promotional *Minecraft* DLC that is available for purchase in the Sony PlayStation Store (and elsewhere) represents a series of thematically consistent partnerships, described in the store as "mash-ups," with popular transmedia brands owned by large media conglomerates such as Disney, and Triple-A game companies such as EA. The packs themselves are designed for players to appropriate and engage with core aspects of a third-party transmedia property, while playing and building in a *Minecraft* world. The packs contain tools and materials for creating remixed content. Some players might use them in ways that stay true to the property's canon, using the texture blocks and skins to reproduce the official story and locations (at least, to the extent that they are able to do so). Others will use them in new ways and contexts, utilizing them for satire, juxtaposing them with their own ideas or with other properties, appropriating and subverting them in all kinds of unanticipated ways. Many players will share their creations with others, and together they will create communities of practice embedded in player-driven readings, interpretations, and meta-participation.[64] Throughout much of this process, the brand's copyright owners have little control over what players will do with their DLC.

This state of affairs contrasts significantly with the extensive systems of control and censorship that were found in commercial children's virtual worlds in the mid- to late 2000s. As discussed in chapter 3, games such as *BarbieGirls* were highly limited in the action opportunities they afforded to players. Some even censored in-game chat to prevent anything remotely negative from being uttered within the game world (e.g., as found in the predetermined safe chat systems). In those games, straying from the official, brand-consistent script was difficult, and the rules were enforced at multiple levels. Today, however, transmedia-based communities of practice and fandoms are very common, as well as frequently sought after by transmedia property owners, even though fan communities often feature transgressive readings and subversive reimaginings of the original text. Some of these "transformational fan" practices, as

Woo describes them, have resulted in tensions or even conflicts with the transmedia property's original creators (or its copyright holders).[65] Overall, however, the media industry seems to have learned that attempts to exert too much control over fans can often fail or even result in backlash. Nonetheless, even though the approach may have changed, the underlying goals are much the same. The companies who have partnered with *Minecraft* to produce licensed DLC packs are doing so to extend their brand, to cross-promote their texts and products, and to foster what Woo refers to as the "affirmational fan" – the sort of fan who engages in the type of meta-participation and other fan activities that align "with the interests of media companies and tends to be encouraged by them."[66] Facilitating this by providing players with corporately approved content and tools to use in their (branded) remix creations, which the players must moreover pay for, is first and foremost a branding strategy. These are some of the competing interests that Mojang must try to balance as it strives to sustain a game world where players' and businesses' interests are met.

The fact that the branded content packs can be accessed only if purchased using real-world money is itself significant. While there is a clear marketing or cross-promotional function to the branded DLC, these packs are never described as a form of advertising within the *Minecraft* store, its TOS agreement, or its corporate communications. This is consistent with the type of rhetoric that surrounded similar cross-promotional features found in *Club Penguin* and *Nicktropolis*, wherein integrated forms of marketing and brand expansion were consistently presented as something other than an ad. Indeed, *Club Penguin* was often described as "ad free." Yet the DLC products promoting third-party transmedia brands are not self-referential tie-ins, and there is a wide range of *Minecraft* original DLC available for purchase as well. In this respect, promotional DLC is the most recent evolution of the "immersive advertising" strategy first introduced by *Neopets* in the early 2000s. The key difference between *Minecraft* and these earlier examples is that here the players pay to interact with this new form of promotional content. Notably, *Minecraft* is not the first or only UGC game to sell third-party licensed content to its players in the form of DLC. The *LittleBigPlanet* games also contain for-purchase, third-party licensed DLC. For example, the Adventure Time Level Creator Kit includes character costumes, materials, ready-made objects, stickers, and a Land of Ooo background image, all recognizable elements from the popular transmedia brand *Adventure Time* (2010–18).[67] Within UGC games, where transmedia engagement, meta-participation, and remix are not only popular among players but often encouraged in the game's own promotional materials, this commodification of source materials has serious implications.

As mentioned above, while both *Minecraft* and *LittleBigPlanet* emphasize the creation of original content in their promotional and corporate communications, as well as in the games themselves (e.g., in tutorials), players are also encouraged to create fan levels and remixes. At first glance, this appears to include making DIY homages to characters, objects, or locations drawn from transmedia properties. And indeed, both games contain examples of impressive and detailed fan levels, made entirely by players using only the tools and templates available in the basic versions of the games. However, there is also a subtle privileging of fan creations that utilize licensed DLC, as the DLC is promoted as something that will grant unique entry into a particular fandom. For instance, the description for the *Adventure Time* DLC states, "Create your very own funny and fantastical adventures in the mysterious Land of Ooo with this Adventure Time Level Creator Kit." The licensed DLC contains assets (objects, textures) and other contents that cannot be reproduced using the game's built-in tools and materials. Purchasing DLC gives the player access to exclusive content and features, which they can then incorporate into their own creations and make them "exclusive" as well. This constructs a "hierarchy of access," wherein players who pay for DLC are given special privileges and advantages that set them, and their creations, apart from the general player community.[68] In *Minecraft*, where the TOS agreement grants players explicit permission to make things inspired by existing media while acknowledging that they may do so under fair use/fair dealing exceptions, the hierarchy of access functions as a velvet rope. Players see advertisements for the DLC, or they encounter its exclusive by-products firsthand while visiting someone else's world, which may in turn entice them to purchase DLC themselves.

In *LittleBigPlanet*, however, where any and all forms of copyright infringement are formally prohibited in the EULA, a much more problematic dynamic unfolds. At issue is the inherent contradiction of first inviting players to engage in fan homage and remix, and then telling them that they can do so only with the explicit permission of the copyright holder. No mention is made of fair use/fair dealing exceptions, such as those for works of parody and for sufficiently transformative derivative works. Instead, purchasing an officially licensed DLC pack is presented as the easiest (and possibly only) way for players to engage in authorized forms of fandom. By purchasing a DLC pack, the EULA-required permission from the copyright holder is implicitly secured, and the fan level can be published without fear of removal. Conversely, player-made DIY remixes and fan creations are formally restricted, and they can be flagged for copyright infringement and removed at any time. Public outcry about players' levels being completely deleted in the early years of *Minecraft* eventually led to the implementation of a review process, where the player's level was instead taken offline after being flagged, and the player was given the opportunity to revise and resubmit it. The policing of copyright within the *LittleBigPlanet* network was never thorough – throughout the period of my research, the game remained populated by unsanctioned fan tributes featuring a wide range of transmedia properties. Nonetheless, it was widely understood by the press and within the player community that user-made *LittleBigPlanet* games were reviewed for copyright infringement, and that the threat of removal or a cease-and-desist letter was real.[69]

Unfortunately there is no literature or data on the frequency or volume of child-made content and UGC games that have been flagged or otherwise embroiled in copyright disputes. This would certainly be a compelling area to explore, and it would fill a critical gap in our understanding of children's evolving relationship to copyright and culture in the digital environment. Just as important, however, are the mundane encounters that children have with corporate copyright definitions and approaches as they hear about player-levels being removed and read product descriptions that promote the idea of remixing as a paid-for experience. Such encounters are not only much more common than legal disputes, but they are likely to have a much broader impact on children's understanding and behaviour. The strict interpretations of copyright and fan engagement that are advanced in *LittleBigPlanet* and most other UGC games carry a discursive power, through which player-driven forms of participatory culture are criminalized, and remix is reimagined as a commercial transaction. Through this problematic commodification of remix and fandom, cultural participation itself is reduced to just another form of consumer subjectivity. Absent from this configuration are the many ways participatory culture provides a forum for children to master, challenge, and reshape the worlds they live in. As seen in the literature, children often express an understanding of copyright that closely mirrors the vision presented by corporate copyright holders and the mainstream media industries. It is perhaps no wonder, since children are utterly immersed in this vision: it appears in digital literacy curricula, it circulates throughout the popular media, and – as seen in this chapter – it is embedded in the very tools and spaces where children play and create.

Conclusion

The spread of increasingly accessible tools and platforms for making and sharing media and other content brings with it myriad opportunities for children to have a more direct impact in shaping our shared culture. It also introduces challenges, questions, and concerns, many of which have not yet been adequately addressed by public discussions of children's role in and relationship with digital technologies. The dominant policy, popular discourses, and academic commentary in this area all focus on the educational value and impact of these technologies; issues relating to children's rights with respect to, access to, and inclusion in the political economy of the digital DIY landscape are either under-examined or omitted altogether. So much more needs to be included in this discussion, and there are more worthy goals than just using the technologies to provide children with "twenty-first-century skills": better frameworks for involving a greater and more diverse number of children in digital media production; more comprehensive and nuanced media/digital literacy programs for children of all ages, including very young children who are already starting to access – and be accessed by – connected technologies and their associated business practices; deeper consideration of the potential role of DIY and maker movements for expanding children's access, skills, and agency vis-à-vis the information society and its underlying data economy; and some acknowledgment of the importance of rule breaking for children's learning and development, and the need to ensure that there is space and support for them to engage in, and recuperate from, risky activities as well.

Equally important is the continued exploration of the potential of many of the less technical, less specialized, and less sophisticated forms of cultural participation, including those made possible by UGC tools and other Web 2.0 consumer technologies. Although these technologies may not foster the same depths of learning and agency as the coding and maker programs described above, they have other attributes that should not be discounted, including broad accessibility, established popularity, and clear alignment with children's cultural traditions and everyday practices. Player-made *LittleBigPlanet* levels and "Let's Play *Minecraft*" videos on YouTube have a lot in common with the types of creative reappropriations that children's scholars have consistently identified as a crucial means through which children retain interpretive and transformative power in their interactions with the adults and corporations that produce most of our cultural texts and artefacts.[70] The widespread emergence of these practices across genres and formats also has relevance to questions about children's rights in the online environment, in that they represent an area where children have already assumed prominent roles as cultural producers.

Undermining this potential, however, is the problematic technical regime that has emerged around children's digital playgrounds, including UGC game-making platforms. The term "technical regime" is used by critical theorists of technology to describe how professional norms and customs arise within particular technical disciplines and how they establish "standard ways of looking at problems and solutions."[71] In the context of children's digital playgrounds and copyright, the technical regime affords a corporately biased approach to children's newfound roles as content producers, one that maintains power relations and overlooks children's best interests. Within most digital playgrounds, children's rights are diminished and corporate rights are amplified. While it is not yet clear what this inequality means for children's legal standing or their potential intellectual property claims, it has a persistent impact on children's lived experience within these spaces. The impact is pedagogical to some extent, but it likely extends into other areas. When children are perceived as having no rights or authority over their fan creations, the copyright holder can always just take their creations away. Children's everyday practices are thereby shaped by the threat itself, to varying degrees and mostly in ways that are implicit and hard to recognize. As Feenberg points out, the limits of technological systems often become apparent to its users only when something goes wrong. It is likely that most children engaged in UGC game making and other forms of meta-participation will never have their content removed for copyright infringement, or will never receive a cease-and-desist notice. Only one of the children in my study of child game makers had experienced this first-hand, although several others were uncertain about whether any of their creations had ever been removed. This does not mean that children are unaffected by the threat itself, however, or that the tensions between children and corporate copyright holders cannot reveal themselves in other ways.

An illustration of this occurred in late 2017, when Sony announced that Disney would be leaving *LittleBigPlanet*; this meant that Disney-licensed DLC would no longer be available for purchase in the Sony PlayStation Store.[72] The end of a license agreement between two corporate entities had an immediate and tangible impact on the game's players. Not only did Disney-licensed DLC make up a substantial proportion of the total inventory of add-on content that players could access through the store, but the company itself is the largest and most prominent owner of children's transmedia properties – and perhaps of transmedia properties in general. In addition to its own impressive roster, Disney is the parent company of Pixar, Marvel, and Lucasfilm (among others). Losing Disney meant losing several transmedia properties with tight linkages to children's culture, including *Frozen*, *Toy Story*, *The Incredibles*, and *Pirates of the Caribbean* (in addition to the Marvel-licensed DLC the company had removed in late 2015).[73] At the time, there was substantial protest on player-run blogs and community forums, and there was sizeable media coverage as well. Because players who had already purchased the DLC were told they would be able to keep it indefinitely, even after Disney had left, the key message relayed in Sony PlayStation's communications about the move was "buy now, before it's too late." Despite the public outcry, the DLC was indeed removed. *LittleBigPlanet* players are no longer able to purchase Disney content, nor can they copy or receive any from players who had purchased it before it was removed from the market. Moreover, because of *LittleBigPlanet's* strict stance on fan creations and copyright infringement, homemade versions are forbidden and subject to removal.

Then as now, public attention was focused on one small aspect of the event, while very little consideration was given to the systematic imbalances that had produced this absurd situation in the first place. Here we see a big media company under the uncontested impression that it is authorized to announce to children and other players that they are no longer allowed to pay for the "permission" to legally make games featuring a character that is plastered all over their bedroom walls, T-shirts, and backpacks – a character they read books about before bedtime, who perhaps provided the entertainment at their birthday party last month. Unless they were already owners of the DLC before the end date, in-game access to this character is no longer possible. Instead of pondering the ethics or even legality of this situation, the story became a promotional opportunity for Sony PlayStation and a lesson on the limits of consumer sovereignty.

The issues surrounding children's creativity and cultural rights online echo and overlap with other points of tension in the children's online landscape, including privacy, censorship, safety, and commercialization. For example, problems with informed consent and parental consent surround TOS contracts and privacy policies, as evidenced by ongoing research on children's experiences online, including studies by Livingstone in the EU and Steeves in Canada. The work in this area – or in interrelated areas – demonstrates that the current standards for informing parents and children about their rights and responsibilities in the digital realm, and for obtaining their consent to the corporate appropriation of children's personal information and content that unfolds daily via digital platforms, have long been inadequate. From the current discussion, it is clear that TOS contracts often include terms that attempt to pre-emptively resolve regulatory grey zones that have not yet been subject to legal debate, let alone decision. Other contracts, meanwhile, work to expand corporately advantageous power relations into new areas of children's lives. As young users continue to create and share their ideas, information, and content online, the need for a formal acknowledgment and delineation of their roles as cultural producers, authors, and consumers has become critical. As children's involvement in cultural production and media has been identified as a key entry point for the advancement of all children's rights, it is crucial that their emerging status as cultural producers be properly addressed, protected, and fostered within regulatory frameworks, as well as within industry standards of practice.

7
The Politics of Children's Digital Play

The idealization of children's play is hard to avoid. For most of us, the sight or thought of children playing is a deeply affective experience – nostalgic, emotional, and symbolic for a wide range of reasons, both personal and cultural. In play, we see possibility and opportunity. We see joy and meaning. We see ourselves and what we aspire to be. We see our babies discovering the world around them, and we picture the leaders, athletes, and innovators we hope they will someday become. Play is also mundane and uneventful. It is convenient and contrite. It can be contentious, and it is at times utterly unsatisfying. It passes the time and keeps little hands occupied while the grownups are making dinner. Children's play is all of this and more. And because it is so expansive, paradoxical, and ambiguous, children's play becomes a locus onto which our deeper, unresolved questions about childhood, selfhood, and society can find a focus and a means of expression. In many ways, therefore, children's play functions primarily as a venue, an idea, or a metaphor. In the process, configurations of the child come to supplant and at times supersede the motivations and practices of actual children. The idealization of children's play is well documented within the literature, but a clean break from the powerful rhetorics that shape our academic and social understandings of play is not easily attained. Instead, the ideas and assumptions that are promulgated within dominant discourses about children's play inform many of our decisions about the types of play that children can (or at least should) engage in, as well as when, where, and with whom.

Our tendency to idealize children's play can make it difficult to perceive idealization as having its own set of politics and biases – but of course it does. Taking a position on what constitutes appropriate or ideal play necessarily involves an act of demarcation, through which the non-ideal or inappropriate is othered and excluded. The literature shows that in contemporary – and specifically in Western – contexts these boundaries are consistently out of touch with the lived experiences of most children. First, such idealizations of play often omit or even vilify forms of play that are prevalent among children. This includes a range of activities that most children engage in at least some of the time, including transgression and cheating, rough and mean behaviour, and vulgar and explicit themes. Moreover, idealizations of children's play are often contingent upon a hegemonic vision of the child that assumes and privileges a very narrow segment of the overall population. The child in this vision is most often a white, heterosexual, cisgender boy from a middle-class family, although today other, slightly more inclusive permutations are also increasingly common (e.g., white middle-class boys *and* girls). Forms of play that are closely aligned with this configuration of the child are subsequently most likely to be identified as examples of ideal play. Concurrently, play practices that are associated primarily with children who are not part of this configuration are more likely to be labelled inappropriate.

Within an increasingly technologized childhood, the act of demarcation involved in the perpetuation of such ideals and their associated configurations is not only discursive but also structural. Demarcation emerges in technological decisions and user management strategies, as well as in regulatory policies, laws, and industry standards. It becomes concretized as features of an artefact's design, which in turn enacts a set of affordances and places parameters on how that artefact can be used. Technological artefacts for children thus reflect and reproduce the same underlying ideological values that inform our broader social understandings of play and childhood. But this is only part of the story of the social construction of children's digital playgrounds. Myriad other influences, priorities, assumptions, needs, limitations (e.g., financial, material, etc.), and interests contribute to the technical code, or broader socio-political climate, out of which such artefacts emerge. For instance, new manifestations of the fears that drove many of the public controversies about videogame violence in the 1990s (as explored chapter 1) surface regularly, as do articulations of the hope that play technologies will serve as a conduit for children's learning and for closing the lingering digital divide. Added to this are plenty of contemporary debates and concerns that the makers (and to some extent, users) of digital playgrounds must respond to. Moreover, commercial initiatives, which make up the majority of the examples discussed in this book, are driven by market imperatives and the ideological values of advanced capitalism. As iterative technological forms that depend on player participation in order to function, digital playgrounds are also informed and shaped by their users (i.e., children), both real and imagined. In many cases, parents and educators have central roles as well.

Indeed, an entire matrix of actors, ideologies, and objectives feed into the way these spaces are designed and ultimately performed.

Many relevant social groups are implicated in the social construction of children's digital playgrounds. There are also dominant, industry-wide, and industry-driven patterns to why these spaces are typically made and how they tend to operate. These patterns are obscured by rhetoric that evokes ideological values that often have little to do with the artefact's design and daily operations. They include children's hopes for friendship and their desire to explore fantastical new worlds, as well as parents' concerns about their children's safety and their wish to secure constructive and appropriate technological interactions for their children. The mobilization of these ideals within promotional materials, rule books, and tutorials detracts attention from the games' underlying business motivations and mechanisms. Within many popular digital playgrounds, commercial features are integrated into the gameplay and the narrative. Commercial priorities are advanced through design affordances, reward systems, and strategies that enrol the players in advancing brand identity or viral marketing campaigns. Relatedly, players' actions, interactions, and creations within these spaces are often subject to multiple forms of control and surveillance. These range from embedded censorship (e.g., in the form of safety mechanisms), to opaquely strict moderation practices, to corporately biased copyright policies. Some games are presented as sites for children's autonomy and DIY creativity but operate primarily as storefronts for branded DLC. Other games are promoted as children's spaces, yet they are designed in ways that not only privilege adult interests but severely limit opportunities for children to contribute their own ideas and priorities. Within many children's digital playgrounds, there is a systematic disconnect between discourse and practice.

In this final chapter, I provide a synthesis of key themes and arguments made throughout the book about how digital playgrounds tend to be designed, how they are run, as well as how kids are typically addressed by and within them. Out of this analysis, I revisit the four key problem areas that warrant urgent public attention and debate: privacy, censorship, ownership, and commercialization. Each of these areas has a long history – emerging over a period of nearly two decades, they have gradually established hidden yet hegemonic sets of norms and standards of practice within an environment that is largely perceived as ever changing and user driven. The concretization of these four problematic tendencies raises broader questions about children's cultural rights online, some of which will be discussed below. The chapter ends with a call to action and proposes an alternative way of thinking about children's digital playgrounds as public spheres from which a diversity of spaces and practices can be carved, but which must foremost be actualized as places where children's rights are supported and children's digital citizenship is acknowledged.

Where We Are, and How We Got Here

While the news coverage of children's digital play technologies and trends may seem incessant, it also remains, for the most part, as conflicted as it was in the 1980s and 1990s. Every week a new controversy: critics bemoaning teenage boys' addiction to *Fortnite*, or a new study claiming that iPad use causes children to develop ADHD. Such stories are counterbalanced by regular bursts of techno-utopianism: a review of an amazing new app that will magically teach three-year-olds to read, or an article maintaining that *Pokémon Go* has reduced childhood obesity. Policy developments are also unfolding with unprecedented frequency, and they often add to the ambivalence that surrounds children's relationship to the online world. In the past few years alone, the American Academy of Pediatrics and the World Health Organization have released starkly incongruous recommendations about screen time limits for children. In 2019, the FTC imposed a record-breaking US$5.7 million fine on social media app TikTok for collecting personal information from users under the age of thirteen without parental consent (breaking COPPA rules), while Facebook was fined US$5 billion for its systematic privacy violations. Meanwhile, legislation containing expanded protections for children's privacy (the General Data Protection Regulation, or GDPR) was launched across the EU, with implications felt around the world. As always, media depictions and associated public discourses on these developments are most often murky and polarized.

It remains extremely difficult for parents, caregivers, and educators to navigate the conflicting information they receive about children's use of digital technologies. Parents report increasing anxiety as they struggle to keep up with the technological and cultural changes unfolding in their children's lives (and in their own), and they describe a lack of support and resources for parenting questions about digital technologies.[1] Children and young people have similar concerns, especially about the political-economic implications of the online world and the companies who control their favourite sites and apps. Recall that a recent survey conducted in the United States discovered that although more than two thirds (69 per cent) of teens agreed that it was "extremely important" for sites to ask permission before selling or sharing their personal information, just over a third (36 per cent) thought that social networking sites and apps did a "good job of explaining what they do with users' data."[2]

Research on the experiences of Canadian youth supports the idea that young people are increasingly distrustful of the business interests that shape much of the online environment. A series of focus groups conducted by Steeves in 2014 found that most youth aged eleven to seventeen did not read TOS contracts and only half had ever had the contents of a TOS explained to them. Nonetheless, most agreed that reading a TOS would not help them to understand the business processes at work within websites and connected platforms, "because corporations purposely hid what they were doing with their information."[3]

It's easy to blame the current state of affairs on the newness of digital technologies and their applications. High-profile scandals, such as the revelation that data analysis firm Cambridge Analytica used user data purchased from Facebook to sway public opinion during the 2016 US election, serve as important catalysts for raising public awareness about the business side of connected platforms and their possible negative consequences if left unchecked. In turn, this can fuel new social movements, policies, and research initiatives aimed at changing specific practices. Today, there is renewed interest in articulating stronger privacy rights for people vis-à-vis digital technologies and their associated processes, especially in relation to the impacts of biased algorithms and the always-on surveillance enabled by devices associated with the internet of things. The Office of the Privacy Commissioner of Canada (OPC) recently announced that it was taking Facebook to Federal Court for its numerous breaches of Canadian privacy laws, and for the company's subsequent refusal to implement the OPC's recommended changes for bringing it to PIPEDA compliance. Books about the dark side of big data economies appear with increasing frequency on non-fiction bestseller lists, contributing to the deepening public engagement with questions of privacy and data politics. Meanwhile, universities across Canada and the United States are launching new institutes and programs of study focused on ethics in computing with the aim of establishing themselves as leaders in "socially responsible technology."[4]

For the most part, these developments are framed as responsive interventions into an emerging problem – working to ensure that technological advances unfold in ways that benefit and enhance our daily lives, while minimizing potential risks. There is thus a sort of collective amnesia found within much of the current discussion of big data economies and online privacy. The tendency to frame these issues as new – unanticipated and as yet unexamined – works to perpetuate a dehistoricization of the problems and their proposed solutions.[5] For while their current incarnations may be unprecedented, many of the systems, norms, and political-economic underpinnings of the data exchange that are at the centre of public attention have actually been in place for several years. The cultivation, collection, and sale of people's data is a well-established business model in the online realm. In this respect, *Neopets* is merely one among several early examples of how and where contemporary data market models first took shape. It is by looking at this history, and by revisiting the controversies that unfolded previously around these very same issues, that we can begin to not only better understand but also more effectively address the problematic structures of digital technology.

The dual tendency of ignoring the past while highlighting polarizing (i.e., newsworthy) aspects of an issue is common within public discourses about children's play and technology. Children also served as the focus of high-profile controversies about privacy rights and commercial practices in the mid-1990s, fuelling lengthy debates and even leading to the enactment of early legislation (e.g., COPPA) aimed at curbing data collection from users under the age of thirteen. For the most part, however, discussions about children's digital experience have been caught in a pendulum swing between moral panics and techno-utopianism. As discussed in chapter 1, the stakes are raised considerably in the process, as using or not using a device today is regularly presented as having an irrevocable effect on children's future development and success. When it comes to children and technology, the emphasis is almost always on long-term, overarching outcomes. This draws notice away from the situated, everyday experience of the children and away from the details – what Arisaka calls "the stuff" – of technology.[6] Paying attention to the actual stuff requires taking a closer look at a game's design and contents, mapping out the different ways a popular app generates income, and trying to figure out what happens to UGC creations once they are posted. Children's scholars emphasize the profound importance of examining the "contexts of play" if we are to move beyond traditional tendencies of idealization and develop a balanced, nuanced, and child-centric understanding of childhood. Within the connected digital environment, these contexts are significantly expanded to include a range of new actors, new relationships, hidden agendas, and political dimensions. Attending to emerging concerns about children's privacy or many of the other issues associated with connected technologies means delving deeper into the quotidian aspects of the spaces and artefacts where children's digital play – as a situated, socio-technical practice – unfolds.

For one, many of the commercial processes found within the children's digital landscape occur at the level of the mundane. Within children's games and other digital play spaces, commercial features are frequently made part of the background, the "taken for granted" and ordinary facets of the play world. In some cases, they are part of the fun (e.g., *GalaXseeds*'s Hive'n'Seek game), while in others, they become a perk or advantage (e.g., *Club Penguin*'s velvet rope membership model). Most of the interactions and data that are gathered from and about the players can also be characterized as mundane. This is, after all, the goal of most market research: to discover intimate details about common habits, popular aspirations, and shared preoccupations with the aim of inserting a brand, product, or idea into the everyday lives of a particular demographic group (e.g., *Habbo Hotel*'s Habble service). Indeed, some of the most manipulative commercial strategies to emerge within the children's digital landscape over the past two decades have been those that seek to tap into children's interactions with peers and with beloved media characters. These include attempts to mobilize children's affective bonds, mine their conversations, and enlist them in viral marketing and branding campaigns. Throughout their brief history, children's connected play technologies and spaces have consistently and predominantly functioned as promotional venues. Many have also served as data farms, where designers and moderators cultivate the types of interactions and solicit the type of inputs deemed most useful for future content development, market research, and sale on the data market. The strategies first developed in *Neopets* can still be found today. They appear in *Minecraft*'s third-party licensed DLC Build Kits, for instance, and in *Smurf Village*'s incorporation of pay-to-progress game mechanics.

Commercial digital playgrounds typically support multiple concurrent business activities, from making direct sales in the form of DLC (e.g., *Minecraft*, *LittleBigPlanet*) or tie-in toys (e.g., *Disney Infinity*), to fostering transmedia engagement and building brand loyalty among players. Often commercial priorities are further promoted at various levels of the game's design and operations. These commercial priorities are implemented in safety features, unveiled as plot developments, and written into TOS agreements and privacy policies. Through repetition, their message is not merely amplified but normalized. When comparing the commercial features of children's digital games across time, format, and genre, several patterns emerge. The resultant hegemonic norm advances a vision of digital play as a consumer activity, and it invites the child player to assume a highly idealized and heavily commercialized set of subject positions. Together, the affordances, rhetorics, and configurations that dominate the children's digital playground merge to form a sort of rule system through which a preferred mode of play is articulated and encouraged.

Many of the commercial priorities reflected in popular digital games, apps, and other playgrounds are found across children's commercial culture, where they appear in the multitude of texts and artefacts associated with popular media brands or supersystems. At least some of these similarities trace back to shared ownership. The companies that have long dominated traditional children's industries (media and toys) seem to be especially adept at expanding into new cultural and technological forms as they emerge. Disney is a prime example. A significant number of the titles discussed in this book were either created or purchased by Disney, and it is unsurprising that these titles exhibit a common approach to copyright and immersive advertising. Disney's consistent and widespread implementation of its own response to unresolved questions (e.g., children's intellectual property ownership) in turn informs broader industry practices. Disney's approach helps establish the technical regime out of which other games and artefacts are subsequently developed. It is true that Disney is but one voice in a diverse chorus of interests, ideals, and politics, all of which contribute to the social shaping of the children's digital landscape. But it is also an extremely powerful one.

The power imbalance that transpires within this realm is widespread and substantial. Although it is only by looking at specific artefacts that we can effectively identify and contextualize how the politics of children's digital playgrounds manifest, it is also clear that the implications extend far beyond the borders of any one game or app. Rules are much harder to bend and disobey when they appear to be ubiquitous, manifesting across a vast assortment of game titles, resurfacing with every new technological form. Such rules are also less likely to be viewed as open to negotiation, let alone challenge. At a micro level, this becomes apparent when rules are enforced at multiple levels of a game – from design affordances and player management strategies to narrative and visual elements. In virtual worlds such as *BarbieGirls*, for instance, official rules about appropriate behaviour surfaced in storylines, in the TOS agreement, and in the types of utterances made available to players through the game's safe chat system. While some of the rules can be bent and are broken (in some cases, with great frequency), others function as though they were physical properties of the game world itself. Still others become stand-ins for laws and other social realities, as biased interpretations are so consistently and authoritatively presented across the digital landscape that they take on the appearance of objective fact. This is especially the case when responsibility for enforcing a rule is delegated to the technology's design, and power is resituated in an allegedly neutral technological system. Throughout this exchange, the interpretive dimensions of the rule – its articulation, its ideological assumptions, its purpose – are obscured. As design and policy decisions become normalized and concretized through repetition, their sociocultural origins are soon forgotten. Children will indeed continue to test and challenge the systems of social order that seek to define and contain them in the digital landscape. They will engage in acts of symbolic interaction, some of which may result in transgression of that social order, or assimilation to the order, or both. The question becomes, How is the social order articulated within children's digital spaces? What interests, norms, and agendas are represented, and what is excluded in the process?

Such questions become critical where the rules of play conflict with established systems of social order, such as laws and government regulations. The conflation of children's privacy and safety is a key example of such conflict, one that gains increased significance in the current climate of mounting public concern about the use and abuse of people's data. Within many digital playgrounds, children's privacy rights are sublimated – reframed in terms of safety that serve primarily, if not solely, as promotional and rhetorical devices. Meanwhile, minimal details are provided to children or their parents about the corporations' responsibilities in collecting, storing, and sharing children's data. Similar tensions are found in the way that children's authorship and ownership of their online contributions are routinely superseded by corporate copyright claims – even though core aspects of children's rights as creators have yet to be addressed by intellectual property law. The presentation of these issues as resolved, by including proclamations to that effect in a TOS agreement, is a radical interpretation of children's authorial status. More troubling still is the industry's apparent disregard for existing laws (e.g., legal limitations on minors' contracts) and precedent-setting court cases, which together suggest a high likelihood that TOS agreements made with minors are voidable and unenforceable. If left unchallenged, the reinterpretations of children's rights currently advanced in TOS agreements could eventually weaken or even dismantle existing protections, as new cultural norms are established through industry standards of practice and widespread social acceptance. The disconnect between rules and legislation is not merely a lapse in policy compliance, but a deeply political repositioning of children's rights in the service of corporate interests. In time, this repositioning could reshape actual legislation pertaining to key facets of children's cultural participation.

Other interests, agendas, politics, and ideals also contribute to the social shaping of children's connected play spaces. They surface in different places and at various points during children's interactions with digital playgrounds, their players, their corporate owners, and the other actors involved (e.g., parents, regulators, advertisers, service providers, data harvesters and analysts). Children themselves are a primary *relevant social group* (to use the STS term) within this dynamic, and their preferences and habits are often chief factors in determining the artefacts' designs and discourses. The children's industries spend a great deal of time and money finding out what types of games children find most fun, which characters they love – and what products they are likely to want to buy. A great many of the interests and agendas that contribute to the social shaping of children's digital technologies support children's access and encourage children's participation in the digital environment. Many others, however, centre on notions of risk, protection, and safety, and instead seek to contain and direct children towards specific experiences and away from others. There are obvious tensions between the interests at play, but risk avoidance is often a top priority.

As a result, many children's digital playgrounds are designed and de-scribed in ways that emphasize safety while minimizing perceived risks – including potential threats to children's innocence and well-being, as well as liability and reputational risks to corporate owners and adver-tisers. Often safety manifests as programmed design limitations and systematic restrictions on children's freedom of expression. While such mechanisms are described largely as child-friendly or in children's best interests, in any other context they would almost certainly be classified as censorship. Ensuring children's safety is exceptionally important for most parents and caregivers, even though there is little consensus on what that is or what it entails. Trepidation about the risks associated with digital technologies often informs parents' decision making about digi-tal technologies, from what devices or apps are purchased (and at what age) to what limits or conditions are placed on children's use of them. In the process, other aspects of children's online experience, including many of their cultural rights, can start to seem superfluous, or at least secondary. The lack of debate about the impact of automated and sys-tematic censorship on children's freedom of expression in the digital environment is a key example of how some rights become expendable when children's "best interests" are framed in terms of external threats and traditional ideas about what constitutes "appropriate" play. Another example is found in the contradictions and concessions that have emerged around children's privacy, from how privacy is defined to the type of data that is protected at the regulatory level.

Cultural norms and expectations regarding children's privacy are in flux, as new surveillance technologies are integrated into children's every-day lives, and as parenting styles continue to trend towards increased su-pervision and involvement. As a result, there are fewer opportunities for children to construct the types of secret spaces that once characterized childhood. Instead, children are offered adult-made children's spaces, many of which contain a heavy commercial presence, and all of which embody an idealized vision of what children and children's play should be. At the same time, through their designs and player management strategies, the spaces themselves afford an ambiguous fusion of freedoms and constraints. Here, children are invited to imagine, explore, and create with peers in an environment made just for them. Meanwhile, their words and actions within these spaces are restricted. Their creations and interactions are seized as intellectual property and then commodified as sellable data. These spaces contribute to a growing social confusion about children's privacy – its value and limits, and its greatest sources of infringement. The blurring of privacy and safety found within commercial discourses, for instance, redefines privacy infringement as what other users might do. This rhetorical strategy disassociates children's privacy from the corporate surveillance and data collection that fuel a great proportion of online businesses. At a certain level, it lets the companies involved in the data economy off the hook, allowing them to operate with very little transparency or accountability about the information they collect from children or how they use it. Yet children's digital culture unfolds in a state of constant corporate surveillance, through which operators, lawyers, moderators, data analysts, algorithms, and advertisers have established an always-on conduit into children's peer groups and imaginations. This not only challenges traditional notions of privacy but also redefines privacy as something that does not extend to commercial entities and market relations.

Corporate-friendly (re)interpretations of complex ethical and legal issues are also shaping children's authorship rights, particularly as they relate to who owns the creations, contributions, and remixes that children make and share online. The spread of accessible, easy-to-use tools, forums, and systems for DIY and UGC media introduces exciting opportunities for children to have a more direct role in and impact on our shared culture. Children often assume these new roles as producers in spaces and platforms that are owned and controlled by corporate entities. These businesses frequently seek to absorb children's creations as part of their own intellectual property claims, and they look to embed children's creative practice in real money exchange (e.g., by making fan homages and remixes a paid-for experience through licensed DLC). Just as much of the data harvesting that permeates the children's digital landscape was established over decades and across genres, current norms around intellectual property and user contributions stem from longstanding industry trends. Two decades ago, it was standard practice within connected games and virtual worlds to include TOS agreements that made sweeping copyright claims over "any and all" user creations, forever and throughout the universe. While today most TOS agreements acknowledge users as the owners of their own contributions – and therefore liable for their contents – the terms still include claims that the users grant the corporate owners the rights to use these contributions for "any and all" purposes, forever and throughout the universe. Even more notable is the way that access to branded content is now positioned as a special privilege. While user-made creations featuring branded media (e.g., characters, locations) often function as a form of grassroots promotion or viral marketing, children are nonetheless told they need permission to engage in remixes and fan homages, including for the creation of works that would likely fall under fair use/fair dealing exceptions. Increasingly, this permission is tied to a financial transaction, as users are invited to purchase the licensed assets required to make "legal" paratexts. Meanwhile, users are told that their own DIY versions qualify as copyright infringement. While such interpretations are partial and biased, they are also pervasive – found not only within commercial discourses but also in digital literacy curriculum, popular media, and public debates.

The (Four) Problems with Digital Playgrounds

Years of research on the topic has shown that the connected digital landscape is filled with great opportunities for children and that it generates many positive experiences. There are myriad options available for children to play, learn, create, and interact online, and many of the companies involved in building and maintaining such spaces do a fine job of keeping up to date with cultural trends. The children's digital play ecosystem contains lively multiplayer games and quiet creative platforms, forums for connecting with other children, and tools for playing dress-up with beloved media characters. While there are clearly many problems with the current state of children's digital culture, it nonetheless holds significant value, meaning, and potential. These many benefits are what makes it so important that we make a concerted effort to address and eventually resolve the problems inherent in digital playgrounds, even though these problems are complex and often linked to broader trends found across the information society.

Children's play is always political, and it follows that as new trends and technologies enter the realm of play, they too will become associated with the tensions, idealizations, hopes, and fears historically linked to children's leisure. Children's play is also ambiguous, which means that discussions about children's games and playthings are situated within a conflicting amalgam of controversies and rhetorics; a general lack of consensus on the issues surrounding children's play can make it seem as if they are at best debatable and at worst irresolvable. However, although the ideological dimensions of children's digital play are clearly conse-quential, the importance of the play itself should not detract from the need to think more critically about the technologies – the actual artefacts and the designs, relationships, and processes that they contain. It is be-cause children's play is ambiguous and contentious that we must work even harder to understand the practices and relationships involved. This knowledge must then be applied to proactively support children's rights and well-being within digital contexts – especially because these contexts are increasingly ubiquitous, but also increasingly emergent and unfixed. For now, at least, the digital playground is still very much a site of struggle.

For many years, governments in Canada and the United States largely resisted passing new digital policy. A hands-off approach to the commu-nication and information industries – and their associated technologies and business practices – became mainstream just as many of the trends described in this book were solidifying. In Canada, under the leadership of Harper's Conservatives from 2006 to 2015, the federal government not only rejected public calls to regulate then-emerging internet ser-vices and wireless infrastructures, they also ignored recommendations introduced by several of its own task forces and studies that suggested revising the country's privacy and telecom policies. In the United States, the interests and ethos of a largely neo-liberal tech industry aligned well with the country's first "social media president," and with the Obama administration's emphasis on economic recovery in the wake of the Great Recession.[7] Today, however, a marked shift is unfolding: around the world, new rules, federal regulations, and transnational policies are emerging on a range of digital issues. In democratic countries, many of these shifts are associated with a greater involvement of public interest and consumer groups in policymaking, as with the GDPR in the EU, and in the recent affirmation of net neutrality rules in Canada.[8] The perspectives and interests of users-as-people are increasingly included in the discussion. Meanwhile, policymakers and other stakeholders are paying more attention to the hidden facets and structures of life online, especially as awareness of biased algorithms, manipulation through fake news, and surveillance capitalism deepens.

The time has come for intervention – and above all change – in the standards, practices, and structures that dominate the digital environ-ment. In the current climate, there is an opportunity for change that avoids reproducing the same tendencies that plagued previous attempts to regulate children's online experience. Rather than simply mobiliz-ing an abstract image of "the child" as a rhetorical tool for advancing adult-driven political or economic agendas, there is an opportunity for action that is child-centric and includes children themselves in reshaping the digital realm to better support children's rights, cultures, and communities of practice. Whether this change involves policy discussions, design interventions, or transforming industry norms, any action for and with children can and should unfold alongside the broader efforts to democratize the digital landscape that are currently underway. Indeed, there are a handful of notable initiatives to draw on in this regard. At the time of writing, for instance, the UN is set to release a new General Comment on children's rights in relation to the digital environment, aimed at updating and expanding the Convention on the Rights of the Child to address the global spread of digital technologies in children's lives and the related new opportunities and challenges. This development is significant, as assertions of children's rights can provide a starting point for other actions to support children's participation within specific contexts, areas, and artefacts. As Livingstone and Third argue, "Before identifying practical pathways one must imagine desired goals and then build sufficient consensus by discursive means to pursue them collectively."[9]

When thinking about children's digital playgrounds from a children's rights perspective, several issues not addressed in this book rise to the forefront. They include access and persisting digital divides, questions about how to ensure fair representation and prevent discrimination, and the many challenges associated with defining children's best interests and ensuring that these interests are respected. Relatedly, disparities in forms of literacy and situated knowledge required to master digital technologies are widespread and deep-rooted. It can indeed seem as if there are innumerable hurdles to overcome before all children are able to equally access, use, and enjoy digital tools and environments. Yet, as this book has attempted to show, children's relationship with any technology is also much more complex than the media coverage and public controversies would have us believe. The tendency within popular discourse to simplify and polarize means that access alone can too often become the focus, while the details of how, whom, when, and what children are accessing is pushed to the margins. It certainly doesn't help that so much of the academic literature – particularly what gets cited most frequently in the press and in policy debates – exhibits similar tendencies towards essentialism and technological determinism. Although a diverse and inclusive internet is essential, access alone will not produce an equitable, empowering digital environment where children's rights can flourish. In many online spaces and platforms, there is also much work to be done in design, business practices, and player management strategies, as well as data and content policies.

As established in previous chapters, there are four key areas relating to the "stuff" of children's digital playgrounds that warrant further attention and action. These four areas are the normalization of corporate surveillance and its erosion of children's privacy and the secret spaces of childhood; the regular censorship of children's speech that unfolds online, often in the name of safety; the question of children's authorship and ownership of their own ideas and creations, and how their creative rights conflict with corporate copyright; and the predominance of commercial content, relationships, and control in child-populated areas of the digital environment. Each of these issues emerges as the culmination of multiple historical and cultural factors, including several years of overlooked industry practices, incomplete or ineffectual policy responses, as well as the everyday choices of children and parents, and their strategies for managing the contradictions and promises of life online. These four areas are starting points to address how the actors engaged in the social construction of children's digital playgrounds – designers and regulators, children and parents – can make these spaces more supportive of children and their rights.

Privacy, Secrets, and Selfhood

For many years, studies showed that public awareness of the surveillance unfolding in digital environments was partial at best. Children reported gaps in their knowledge about privacy policies and what happened to their online data.[10] The relationship between children's data and children's privacy was often obscured within popular and promotional discourses. Within commercial spaces, privacy was often defined as keeping personally identifiable information safe from unwelcome strangers and bullies. However, recent research indicates that children and parents are increasingly concerned about children's online privacy in relation to business activities and the potential, hidden uses of children's data.[11] Following a series of high-profile scandals surrounding the "data economy" and its associated business practices, there are mounting questions about how children's privacy can be protected when so many of their activities and relationships are already embedded in big data flows.[12] Research conducted since the late 1990s traces the continued proliferation of corporate surveillance and data collection throughout the children's digital landscape. From websites and videogames to virtual assistants and the "internet of toys," businesses have used each new digital trend to gather information from children.[13] Children's participation in digital playgrounds is often turned into a "natural resource" for in-house business activities and for third-party sale on the data markets. The full implications of ubiquitous "dataveillance" and the ways that children's information is ultimately used and abused by corporations, governments, and other adult-run entities are not yet known.[14] What is clear, however, is that fundamental experiences of childhood are becoming transformed in the process. Accordingly, there is now a growing call for increased regulation and protection of children's privacy vis-à-vis connected digital technologies.

In Canada, the United States, and elsewhere, privacy laws regulate to widely varying degrees what and how personal information can be gathered from children. The fact that children's privacy is already on the regulatory radar means that there are already some important protections and supports in place, some of which are amenable to further expansion. Yet some of these protections have their own challenges, especially when interpretations of children's privacy laws result in arbitrary age restrictions that limit children's access to online tools and experiences, or when the implementation of safety features infringe on children's freedom of expression. For instance, many multiplayer games and social media forums have opted to ban children under the age of thirteen in order to avoid the costs and trouble associated with ensuring COPPA compliance, moderating children's content, and reducing corporate liability. Moreover, in spite of privacy protections, a significant number of the websites, games, and applications that do target (or otherwise include) younger users collect vast amounts of data from them for advertising, sale, and other undisclosed purposes. Some of these practices contravene or bend regulatory requirements, while others are perfectly legal – exploits of regulatory grey areas or activities that are simply not covered by legislation. Overall, the policies lack the authority and enforceability required to provide effective regulation in this area. An expansion of these policies may not be sufficient to resolve their limitations.

Covert business activities based on the collection, sale, and manipulation of children's personal and behavioural data are the largest and most pervasive threat to children's privacy online. This has been the case since the late 1990s. Although the specific methods and sites of data collection have changed, the market for children's data has not only persisted, but flourished. The rhetorical link between privacy and safety has served multiple functions within this process, from obscuring the original function of privacy policies to downplaying the commercial implications of in-game moderation. The link is effective because it connects with deeper trends and concerns common among contemporary Western families, where constant supervision and parental involvement are increasingly viewed as not only desirable, but mandatory. The notion of secret spaces of childhood plays a paradoxical role within this dynamic. It provides a nostalgic justification for the inclusion of safety mechanisms, such as limited chat options and action opportunities, which are promoted as restricting entry to the playground so that only (good) children are allowed. At the same time, the perceived safety of a digital playground is contingent on the promise of constant surveillance, carried out by (adult) moderators or (adult-made) filters and algorithms. While contradictory, both aspects are informed by the diminishing value that our culture accords to secret spaces of childhood, along with vaguely defined societal fears about what happens within these spaces. Delegating responsibility to corporations for ensuring children's safety or for providing virtual secret spaces is equally problematic. Whether the surveillance is enacted by human moderators or by algorithms, it eliminates important opportunities for children to engage in the types of boundary-making and boundary-breaking that are so crucial to their cultural experience and selfhood. Moreover, both approaches routinely result in the datafication of children's private thoughts, secret acts, and interactions, as they are recorded, tracked, collated, analysed, and stored for "any and all uses, forever, and throughout the universe."

What would children's online privacy look like if privacy was configured as one important part of a framework of rights and responsibilities that children carry with them across space and time? In Canada and elsewhere, there is a clear and immediate need to address the widespread encroachment of children's privacy rights in the digital environment. To do so, we will first need to articulate a holistic, nuanced definition of what children's privacy is and what it entails, not only as an analytic category but also as a set of experiences that extend beyond personally identifiable information or data. Out of this revised definition, we need to devise more effective strategies for protecting and fostering privacy in ways that also respect children's other rights, as well as the cultural practices that form a core part of children's identities. Notably, a better balance must be achieved in supporting children's privacy and freedom of expression. Including children themselves in this process is critical for ensuring that any new policies or regulations reflect the rich diversity of children's cultures, the ever-changing nature of their needs and capacities, and a fuller range of their rights as digital citizens.

Censorship and Freedom of Expression

Participating in digital culture means interacting with others, creating and remixing content, and commenting and posting in public forums. Not only are these activities central to the online experience, but they also have significant implications for the companies who make and operate connected spaces and platforms, as well as for the regulatory infrastructures. While some of these implications, such as privacy, are the focus of growing public attention, debate, and regulatory response, others remain unaddressed. A primary example is the profound challenge involved in moderating children's online contributions, and the tensions between the expectation that child-specific spaces will censor inappropriate or dangerous content and the need to protect children's right to freedom of expression. While many businesses have come up with their own responses to this challenge, they have done so largely without input from policymakers, consistent access to relevant academic research, or public input. It is often only when a site or service fails to prevent harm that the issue receives public attention, often tinged with media panic about the dangers of allowing children on the internet. What these stories fail to consider is that every day, companies around the globe are managing children's content and interactions online. These businesses have taken on the significant task of curating children's communications and creations, and they are deciding what type of content will be published, what will be censored, and why. We know almost nothing about how such decisions are made, what they are based on, or how they are implemented. Apart from those relatively rare instances when one of these systems misfires or malfunctions, their inner workings and ideological underpinnings are almost completely obscured.

Although some developers have independently devised innovative, child-centric solutions to the challenges of children's privacy, safety, and freedom of expression, such examples are neither well documented nor widely shared.[15] Other developers, such as those at *Minecraft*, have elected not to engage in moderation and instead leave it up to the players to determine their own rules and delineate their own spaces. Many developers include children in the moderation, through features that allow users to flag or report offensive (or inappropriate, or copyright infringing) content. In general, however, the strategy tends to be that developers avoid controversy and minimize risk by implementing sweeping restrictions on what children can say and do within the confines of child-specific digital environments. These restrictions are enforced in a range of ways – by moderators, for instance, but also through the inclusion of programmed design barriers and filtering algorithms. Such restrictions result in the omission or removal of many children's contributions, and the systematic censorship of a wide range of words, themes, and ideas. Conversely, moderation that is effective, context aware, fair, and age appropriate requires trained professionals who can look over all content and comments. This requires a significant amount of time and financial investment. Even then, there is always a risk that dangerous people, activities, or themes will slip through. Added to this are the additional complications introduced by regulatory requirements, such as those associated with COPPA, which prohibits the public display of children's real names or other personally identifiable information unless parental consent is secured. Overall, the tasks of moderating, screening, and censoring a children's digital playground can be a thankless, expensive, and monumental responsibility. The lack of guidance and support available to the people engaged in these tasks is troubling, and it is likely a contributing factor in the existence of this particular problem area.

Resolving the tensions that emerge between the need for some censorship within spaces designed for and used by children and children's right to freedom of speech and right to information will be challenging. When it comes to media, content, and spaces for children, certain forms of restriction are not only acceptable and anticipated, but indeed desirable. This remains the case even though there is significant debate about the details – what themes or images should be excluded, at what ages or maturity levels, and by what justification. We know that content-based age restrictions, such as those applied to films or videogames, are often problematic, essentialist, and easily bypassed. Nonetheless, there is an established and widespread need for age-appropriate options – texts, artefacts, and experiences that children can enjoy and connect with without being exposed to ideas or imagery that they are simply not ready for. However, children themselves are often the originators of such ideas, and they frequently engage in dark, aggressive, or subversive activities that defy normative classifications of what is appropriate for children. Moreover, it is not always possible to know the age or identity of the users themselves, especially in open multiplayer spaces, where the presence of older children and adults is likely (and is not necessarily dangerous or disruptive). Children's freedom of expression comes with an assortment of risks, and finding a way to address these risks while respecting children's rights is a formidable undertaking.

However, we already have models to draw on, including some from the world of teens and adults. Online service providers are generally reluctant to impose restrictions on adults' freedom of expression, as adults' claim to this right is not only universally recognized but legally protected. When bans on certain forms of expression, such as hate speech, are implemented, it is usually the result of informed and legally grounded decision-making. While the actual restrictions and their justifications will be different when children are involved, the decision processes that lead to these restrictions can nonetheless follow a similar trajectory. Every ban of a word or theme from a children's digital playground should be comparably justifiable within a child-specific context. Each of these decisions must be weighed against the very real costs associated with diminishing children's freedom of expression. Restrictions on children's speech and creative output in the digital environment must therefore never be arbitrary or imposed simply because it is easier or more cost effective to do so. Thinking back to some of the examples discussed in chapter 5, it is paramount that censorship is never enacted as a way of advancing commercial activities.

Respecting children as participants and digital citizens means giving flexible and concerted space for children's voices – spaces that reflect children's diverse needs, interests, abilities, and challenges. Moderation and other curation policies must therefore be grounded in research and theory, inclusive of different perspectives and identities, and in touch with the realities of childhood development, emerging literacies, and cultural practices. There is a growing need for governments to make clear statements on children's rights in the digital environment, and there is a specific need for a direct affirmation of children's right to freedom of expression – a right that carries over to both digital and commercial contexts. Legislators need to be proactive in addressing regulatory grey areas, and they must provide the same level of support for children's rights as they do for adults' rights. Concurrently, regulations and guidelines must not be so complex or ambiguous that businesses look for loopholes or require professional assistance to meet them. Resources must be developed to encourage businesses that operate children's digital playgrounds to support and enhance child rights; at the same time, these resources must address social expectations and manage the risks associated with life online.

Ownership, Authorship, and Copyright

Children bring their creative practices, activities, and outputs into the digital world. Many are engaged in digital media making, remixing, and sharing their own DIY and UGC works with others online. A great number of opportunities and benefits are associated with children's increased participation in shaping the contents of our shared culture, and the shift has generally been met with enthusiasm. However, children's increased participation also raises myriad new questions about what exactly their rights and responsibilities are as authors, artists, producers, and distributors of digital content. In both Canada and the United States, these roles are not well delineated within current laws and policies when minors are involved. Simultaneously, widespread assumptions about children's limited ability to understand complex legal concepts such as intellectual property have led to a tendency within media and digital literacy materials to oversimplify or even exclude legal topics from curricula aimed at younger children.[16] When children are taught about copyright, the emphasis is most often placed on delineating corporate copyrights.[17] Meanwhile user rights, such as fair use/fair dealing, are either downplayed or omitted altogether. As a result, many digital literacy materials position children as copyright *infringers*, rather than as content creators or potential copyright *holders*. Yet recent research indicates that contrary to traditional models and assumptions about children's capacity for understanding legal concepts, many children do develop an early awareness, and at least a burgeoning understanding, of these concepts. Even children aged four to six have nuanced opinions about the ownership of ideas and what makes a work original.[18] Scholars in this area advocate for a more comprehensive approach to teaching copyright at every grade level, one that encourages children "to confidently and thoughtfully claim their rights as both creators and users of copyrighted material."[19]

Children, as well as their parents and educators, must be better informed about the legal terms and relationships they enter when they bring their creative practices into the online realm. They must be given the opportunity to make informed decisions, and must be provided with better supports for developing a sense of ownership and authorship over their creations. However, many of the legal questions that children are encountering as they engage in digital content production do not yet have clear answers. Increased digital literacy alone is unlikely to provide a remedy to the widespread inequities and unfair terms contained in so many TOS contracts and advanced by common business practices. Meanwhile, corporations are quietly determining the terms and conditions of children's online participation, including children's authorship and ownership rights, as well as their access to fair use/fair dealing and their rights to claim access to material that is part of the public domain. While these processes are unfolding largely under the radar, or more accurately *in the fine print*, the resulting norms and standards could have important and lasting repercussions for children's rights and their emerging status as cultural producers. Although the terms contained in a typical TOS contract are contentious and unenforceable, their presence has received little critical attention or challenge. Beyond simply asking children to start reading the fine print, addressing the problem of ownership in children's digital playgrounds requires a significant shift within public and policy priorities for children online. We need to acknowledge children's roles as content producers who are already engaged in ambiguous and largely disadvantageous legal and economic relationships.

There is an urgent need for children's emerging status and rights as cultural producers to be properly addressed, protected, and fostered within public and policy discourses. The relationships children enter into with commercial entities and legal processes need to be reviewed, clarified, and most likely regulated. Above all, there is a need for a better informed, democratically crafted articulation of children's rights and responsibilities as cultural producers, authors, and consumers. Increased participation in media and cultural production has been identified as an entry point for the advancement of all children's rights.[20] However, full participation requires a certain amount of agency, autonomy, and ownership – the very things that are being diminished by longstanding industry trends aimed at expanding corporate copyright, as well as at appropriating and commodifying users' creations.

Commercial Content and Control

The prevalence of media supersystems, branded characters, and licensed properties within children's commercial culture is well documented, as is the tendency for children to draw meaning from and build affinity spaces based upon them. In addition to the intimate relationships that individual children form with beloved media characters and tie-in toys, groups of children often create shared stories and experiences based on media brands, regardless of firsthand experience or exposure. The research indicates that children have their own ways of generating and managing references to consumer culture, which are then mobilized to secure entry into the conversations of and play with their peers. A child who does not play *Minecraft* or watch *Paw Patrol* might nonetheless memorize the material types and character names in order to fit into the larger community.[21] In this way, elements of commercial culture are often part of the childhood zeitgeist. Consumption, particularly access to specific consumer goods and the regulation of access, often plays a key role in children's cultural practices and boundary-setting. For example, store-bought candies had a central role in children's delineation of the special child-only spaces and practices observed by James; several feminist scholars, meanwhile, have argued that even highly gendered technologies, such as baby dolls, can serve as key sites for children's negotiation and subversion of hegemonic gender ideals.[22] At the same time, the creative and social practices associated with transmedia intertextuality – what Jenkins and others refer to as participatory culture – are increasingly acknowledged as crucial entry points for learning, literacy, and skill development. While licensed toys and media supersystems are the subjects of ongoing debate within both popular and academic discourses, their centrality within contemporary childhood is undeniable.

However, many transmedia properties also incorporate invasive business practices within their digital games, apps, and website tie-ins. From enlisting children as brand ambassadors and charging them with promoting licensed content and exclusive features to other children, to enclosing and commodifying fandom through branded, for-purchase creation kits in UGC games, the commercial activities that pervade the children's digital landscape reveal that property owners are cultivating unprecedented levels of intimacy with their young fan base. Meanwhile, vast quantities of data are harvested, analysed, packaged, and sold as children's words, behaviours, and creations are mined and mobilized for new product ideas, cunning advertising strategies, and social profiling. Many of these behind-the-scenes tactics seem far removed from children's own strategies, meanings, and uses of commercial culture. But they are indeed deeply intertwined. The problem is not (necessarily) that when children play online they are playing mostly in branded spaces, employing tie-in toys, and engaging with transmedia intertextuality. Rather, the problem is the hidden and embedded cascade of commercial processes unfolding beyond the purview of parents, policymakers, and the children themselves. These processes are designed to manipulate children at a personal, emotional level. They often confuse and obscure legal and economic boundaries, including laws and policies aimed at protecting children from commercial exploitation. Together, the embedded nature of commercial practices results in an environment based on inequality and longing.

The children's digital landscape is increasingly underwritten by business practices and design standards that are driven by unbridled, or at least minimally regulated, forms of commercialization. These practices are moreover implicated in all of the other problem areas identified above, and throughout this book. A technical regime that advances such forms and levels of commercialization fosters – and in many ways, depends upon – concurrent systems of corporate surveillance, censorship, and copyright control. Commercialization and privacy infringement are deeply linked within these processes, for instance, and are set to become even more entangled in future. The spread of smart devices, the prevalence of DLC, lootboxes, and pay-to-progress mechanics across media, genres, and age groups, and the lack of public attention to how these processes are designed to work in concert all suggest that current trends are likely to continue unless radical change or action is taken.[23] Ironically, the commercialization of children's digital culture, and its associated business activities, may also be an area where meaningful intervention and policy development are least likely to occur. Recent studies showing the prevalence of in-game ads in children's apps, for instance, have received little media coverage or public debate.[24] While there is a need for direct regulatory intervention in this area, there is also much work to be done in laying the groundwork, providing the evidence, and initiating public discussion of what, why, and how commercial processes in children's digital playgrounds undermine children's rights and well-being.

The Digital Playground as Public Sphere

In 1906, the Playground Association was founded in the United States. The organization was dedicated to the advancement of "rational recreation," and its early activities were focused on convincing municipalities to build dedicated playgrounds and community parks. These spaces were envisioned as a means of keeping working-class children and youth off the streets and out of trouble, and providing them with opportunities for personal improvement. By 1915, Cross notes, "430 American municipalities had park programs and thousands more followed."[25] The playground movement was not limited to the United States; during the same period, similar trends unfolded in Canada, the United Kingdom, and around the world. The movement was deeply ideological, driven by puritanical concerns about the activities of unsupervised working-class youth, especially boys, and by racism and xenophobia. After all, the movement aimed to homogenize a growing, diverse population and imbue its members with the values and priorities of the white dominant culture by engaging youth and new immigrants in "respectable," "modern" leisure practices. Although the politics and agendas have shifted significantly in the past century, certain aspects of the playground movement's original ethos are still felt today. They appear in the controversies and configurations that surround contemporary playgrounds, from the ongoing debates about risk and safety to decisions about locations and access – as well as in broader social tensions about what constitutes "appropriate" or "good" children's play. But the playground movement's most profound and long-lasting impact was on our cultural understanding of what playgrounds are and the function they serve within our society. From the very beginning, playgrounds were configured as a public service.[26] To this day they remain largely public spaces, regulated and maintained for public use, and unique in their prioritization of children's needs, sizes, and play habits.[27]

The idea of the playground as a public space surfaces within many of the digital iterations explored in this book as well. Virtual worlds such as *Club Penguin* and connected UGC games such as *Minecraft* are promoted as digital places where children can interact with others, socialize and play, collaborate and chat. Many of these games are designed and configured as places for children to build communities, engage in popular assemblies, and form cultures of practice. The implicit promise, and the apparent hope of many of the more optimistic scholars in this area, is that digital playgrounds foster a sort of virtual public sphere, where children from diverse locations and backgrounds can come together around shared interests, and where children engage in the important meaning-making activities that unfold when they play together. In theory, this would include opportunities to engage in and negotiate the adult-controlled social order, create peer cultures and secret spaces, exercise agency and make decisions, as well as uncover, break, follow, and reinterpret the rules of play. While very few of the game titles examined in this book fulfil that promise entirely, many nonetheless retain that potential. Although currently limited by tendencies towards restrictive designs, stringent rule systems, and the privileging of business interests, the potential for the digital playground to function as a child's version of the public sphere is evidenced by its frequent realization in different games over the past twenty years. Moreover, the children who enter digital playgrounds seem to experience them largely as public spaces. It is often only when things go wrong that the incongruity (e.g., political, structural) between digital and real-life playgrounds is revealed.

What would a digital playground need to look like to function effectively and consistently as a children's public sphere? Perhaps it would need to look much like the playground around the corner from your house. At the playground mentioned in the introduction to this book, as in community playgrounds across the country, a loose circle of parents monitor the children as they play. Some parents, especially the ones accompanying toddlers and preschoolers, are active players, providing their child with close supervision, companionship, and a helping hand. Most parents, however, stand along the periphery of the playground, watching, but also carrying water bottles and snacks, checking their phones, and chatting with each other. The parents intervene in the activities that unfold on the playground to widely varying degrees. Despite the media outcry over helicopter parenting, some of them are in fact very hands off and wait before reacting to a skinned knee or minor scuffle, providing the children with opportunities to work it out themselves. Meanwhile, the children engage in individual pursuits or find ways to play together, negotiate turns on the swing and slide, and carve out moments and spaces out of the sight and earshot of the adults. It is a balancing act – supervised place and secret space, adult-made social order and child-made interpretive reproduction, constraint and freedom, all in constant flux. It is an ongoing negotiation made up of contextualized responses, with performative dimensions, peer pressure, and surprises added in for good measure. At the same time, and as in digital playgrounds, commercial culture, transmedia intertextuality, corporate sponsorships, and even third-party surveillance systems are integral parts of this space. The children wear clothes that feature media characters and they re-enact scenarios from the latest Disney movie, parents shop on Amazon using their smartphones, and signs advertising an app made by the builders of the playground structures are on prominent display. The key difference is that here, companies are not pre-eminent and all powerful. In this place, parents and children are people with rights, first and foremost. These rights are upheld and protected by the state and its mechanisms, as well as by the community itself.

Having spent an enormous amount of time exploring children's digital playgrounds, it is not difficult for me to imagine one where children are treated as people, and where space is afforded for the balancing act that unfolds in so many other areas of children's lives. Some of the games I researched came very close to achieving this, at least on the surface. Yet, given the patterns that have shaped so much of the children's commercial digital landscape, and given how deeply the hidden politics and processes examined in this book extend, it seems unlikely that such an alternative trajectory will take hold any time soon – at least not without major cultural shifts, interventions, or both. Leaving children and their parents on their own to deal with the imbalance of power that pervades a digital environment in which children's rights are ill-defined and rarely respected is an untenable response. There is an urgent need for support and guidance among almost all the actors involved in the social construction of children's digital technologies – from the developers building the games and the legal teams drafting the TOS contracts, to the children playing and making in digital spaces and the parents struggling to make the right choices (or at least avoid the wrong ones). A clear and formal articulation of children's rights and interests, through statements and new policy development, is an important first step. In this regard, the UN's upcoming General Comment on children's rights in relation to the digital environment is especially timely. As we take these first steps towards building a better digital landscape for children, it is important to remember that children's relationship to technology and play is permeated with conflicting politics and ideologies. It is also changeable. Any efforts made today must therefore be sustainable, built from the ground up to include mechanisms and procedures that will ensure that the policies and supports for children's rights introduced today are subsequently reviewed and maintained. Our response to current trends and problems must be revisited as new technologies and practices are introduced, and policies must be reconsidered as new cultural norms and social expectations emerge. Childhood is ambiguous, and regulating its parameters will always be controversial and complex. But as anyone who knows one will tell you, children are well worth the effort.

Notes

Introduction

1 Brian Sutton-Smith, *The Ambiguity of Play* (Cambridge, MA: Harvard University Press, 1997), 8.

2 A high-profile example is an adventure playground in North Wales called "The Land." As of July 2016, The Land has been the subject of a short-form documentary and a cover story in the *Atlantic*. See Hanna Rosin, "The Over-protected Kid," *Atlantic*, April 2014, https://www.theatlantic.com /magazine/archive/2014/04/hey-parents-leave-those-kids-alone/358631/; Erin Davis, *The Land* (Newburgh, NY: New Day Films, 2015). For an analysis of adventure playgrounds in Canada, see Marianne B. Staempfli, "Reintro-ducing Adventure into Children's Outdoor Play Environments," *Environ-ment and Behavior* 41, no. 2 (2009): 268–80.

3 See, for example, Alison Mott, Kim Rolfe, Rosie James, Rupert Evans, Alison Kemp, Frank Dunstan, Kenneth Kemp, and Jo Sibert, "Safety of Surfaces and Equipment for Children in Playgrounds," *Lancet* 349 (1997): 1874–6.

4 For a discussion of the recent trend of reducing – and in some cases, eliminating – recess in American elementary schools, see Anthony D. Pellegrini, *Recess: Its Role in Education* (New Jersey: Lawrence Erlbaum, 2005); for a discussion of reduced resources, equipment, and support for recess play in Canadian elementary schools, see Lauren McNamara, "What's Getting in the Way of Play? An Analysis of the Contextual Factors That Hinder Recess in Elementary Schools," *Canadian Journal of Action Research* 14, no. 2 (2013): 3–21.

5 Daphna Bassok, Scott Latham, and Anna Rorem, "Is Kindergarten the New First Grade?" *AERA Open* 1, no. 4 (January–March 2016): 1–31.

6 David Manno, "How Dramatic Shifts in Perceptions of Parenting Have Exposed Families, Free-Range or Otherwise, to State Intervention: A Com-mon Law Tort Approach to Redefining Child Neglect," *American University Law Review* 65, no. 3 (2016): 675.

7 Research has shown that this is the case in multiple states in the United States, and that the correlation exists for both minority and low socio-economic neighbourhoods; see Latetia V. Moore, Ana V. Diez Roux, Kelly R. Evenson, Aileen P. McGinn, and Shannon J. Brines, "Availability of Recreational Resources in Minority and Low Socioeconomic Status Areas," *American Journal of Preventative Medicine* 34, no. 1 (2008): 16–22.

8 See, for example Daniel Goldowitz, Jean-Paul Collet, and Keiko Shikako-Thomas, "Children with Disabilities Need Better Access to Sport," Conversation, 8 August 8, 2018, http://theconversation.com/children-with-disabilities-need-better-access-to-sport-99493.

9 For a discussion of the early results of this landmark longitudinal study, see Iona Opie and Peter Opie, *The Lore and Language of Schoolchildren* (Oxford: Clarendon, 1961).

10 In "Mother May I?" every time the player assigned to be the "mother" looks away, the other players inch forward to undermine her authority and collectively conceal the transgression. For an analysis of the game and its implications, see Helen B. Schwartzman, *Transformations: The Anthropology of Children's Play* (New York: Plenum, 1978).

11 Schwartzman, *Transformations*, 124.

12 Lydia Plowman, Christine Stephen, and Joanna McPake, *Growing Up with Technology: Young Children Learning in a Digital World* (London: Routledge, 2010).

13 Neil Narine and Sara M. Grimes, "The Turbulent Rise of the Child Gamer: Public Fears and Corporate Promises in Cinematic and Promotional Depictions of Children's Digital Play," *Communication, Culture and Critique* 2, no. 3 (2009): 319–38; Matteo Bittanti, "The Technoludic Film: Images of Video Games in Movies (1973–2001)" (MA thesis, San Jose State University, 2001); Sherry Turkle "'Spinning' Technology: What We Are Not Thinking About When We Are Thinking About Computers," in *Technological Visions: The Hopes and Fears that Shape New Technologies*, ed. Marita Sturken, Douglas Thomas, and Sandra J. Ball-Rokeach, 19–33 (Philadelphia: Temple University Press, 2004).

14 Pål Aarsand and Karin Aronsson, "Gaming and Territorial Negotiations in Family Life," *Childhood* 16, no. 4 (2009): 514.

15 The term "actors" is used here to describe entities involved in the determination and use of a technical system or network through their associations, interests, and actions, in keeping with how the term is used in STS, specifically in actor-network theory (ANT). See Bruno Latour, *Science in Action: How to Follow Scientists and Engineers through Society* (Cambridge, MA: Harvard University Press, 1987).

16 Andrew Feenberg, *Alternative Modernity: The Technical Turn in Philosophy and Social Theory* (Berkeley: University of California Press, 1995); Andrew

Feenberg, *Questioning Technology* (London: Routledge, 1999); Sara M. Grimes and Andrew Feenberg, "Rationalizing Play: A Critical Theory of Digital Gaming," *Information Society* 25, no. 2 (2009): 105–18.

17 In *Alternative Modernity*, Feenberg calls this the "technical code," described as "those features of technologies that reflect the hegemonic values and beliefs that prevail in the design process," which form a "background of un-examined cultural assumptions literally designed into the technology itself" (4, 87). This notion is explored further in subsequent chapters of this book.

18 See, for example, the description of children playing with overly prescriptive "smart" toys, in Lydia Plowman, "Hey, Hey, Hey! It's Time to Play: Children's Interactions with Smart Toys," in *Toys, Games, and Media*, ed. Jeffrey Goldstein, David Buckingham, and Gilles Brougère, 207–23 (Mahwah, NJ, L. Erlbaum Associates, 2004). Comparable findings in children's negotiations of media themes in their make-believe play are found in Karen E. Wohlwend, "Damsels in Discourse: Girls Consuming and Producing Gendered Identity Texts through Disney Princess Play," *Reading Research Quarterly* 44, no. 1 (2009): 57–83.

19 The importance of noting small, ephemeral acts of user agency in digital games and the meaning such actions hold for players was first argued by Cindy Poremba, "Patches of Peace: Tiny Signs of Agency in Digital Games" (paper presented at Level Up: Digital Games Research Conference, University of Utrecht, The Netherlands, November 2003).

20 Sara M. Grimes and Leslie Regan Shade, "Neopian Economics of Play: Children's Cyberpets and Online Communities as Immersive Advertising in Neopets.com," *International Journal of Media & Cultural Politics* 1, no. 2 (2005): 181–98; Grace Chung and Sara M. Grimes, "Data Mining the Kids: Surveillance and Market Research Strategies in Children's Online Games," *Canadian Journal of Communication* 30, no. 4 (2005): 527–48; Sara M. Grimes, "Online Multiplayer Gaming: A Virtual Space for Intellectual Property Debates?," *New Media & Society* 8, no. 6 (2006): 969–90; Grimes, "Researching the Researchers: Market Researchers, Child Subjects and the Problem of 'Informed' Consent," *International Journal of Internet Research Ethics* 1, no. 1 (2008): 66–91; Grimes, "Kids' Ad Play: Regulating Children's Advergames in the Converging Media Context," *International Journal of Communications Law and Policy* 8, no. 12 (2008): 162–78; Grimes, "Saturday Morning Cartoons Go MMOG," *Media International Australia* 126, no. 1 (2008): 120–31; Narine and Grimes, "Turbulent Rise."

21 Deborah A. Fields and Yasmin B. Kafai, "Knowing and Throwing Mudballs, Hearts, Pies, and Flowers: A Connective Ethnography of Gaming Practices," *Games and Culture* 5, no. 1 (2010): 88–115; Jackie Marsh, "Young Children's Play in Online Virtual Worlds," *Journal of Early Childhood Research* 8, no. 1 (2010): 23–39; David Gauntlett and Lizzie

Jackson, "Virtual Worlds, Users and Producers: Case Study: *Adventure Rock*" (paper presented at Children in Virtual Worlds Conference, University of Westminster, London, May 2008); Victoria Carrington and Katherine Hodgetts, "Literacy-Lite in *BarbieGirls*™," *British Journal of Sociology of Education* 31, no. 6 (2010), 671–82; Nic Crowe and Simon Bradford, "'Hanging Out in *Runescape*': Identity, Work and Leisure in the Virtual Playground," *Children's Geographies* 4, no. 3 (2006): 331–46.

22 Not all children in this broad age group played with the same frequency. For instance, children aged eight to eleven were more likely to play digital games and for longer periods of time than older children and teens, while nearly half of children six and under owned a videogame console. In 2006, industry analyst NPD Funworld reported that 45 per cent of "heavy gamers" and nearly one-third of "avid console gamers" were between the ages of six and seventeen; see Victoria J. Rideout, Ulla G. Foehr, and Donald F. Roberts, *Generation M: Media in the Lives of 8- to 18-Year-Olds* (Washington, DC: Kaiser Family Foundation, 2005); Victoria J. Rideout, Elizabeth A. Vandewater, and Ellen A. Wartella, *Zero to Six: Electronic Media in the Lives of Infants, Toddlers and Preschoolers* (Washington, DC: Kaiser Family Foundation, 2003).

23 Amanda Lenhart, Joseph Kahne, Ellen Middaugh, Alexandra Rankin Macgill, Chris Evans, and Jessica Vitak, *Teens, Video Games, and Civics* (Washington, DC: Pew Internet and American Life Project, 2008).

24 Amanda Lenhart, Aaron Smith, Monica Anderson, Maeve Duggan, and Andrew Perrin, *Teens, Technology, and Friendships* (Washington, DC: Pew Internet and American Life Project, 2015).

25 Hilda K. Kabali, Matilde M. Irigoyen, Rosemary Nunez-Davis, Jennifer G. Budacki, Sweta H. Mohanty, Kristin P. Leister, and Robert L. Bonner Jr., "Exposure and Use of Mobile Media Devices by Young Children," *Pediatrics* 136, no. 6 (October 2015): 1044–50.

26 Joan Ganz Cooney Centre, "Digital Games and Family Life: Understanding When, Where, and How Kids Play Video Games," news release, 13 September 2016.

27 "Four out of five US households own a device used to play video games," according to a 2015 report from the Entertainment Software Association; see *Essential Facts about the Computer and Video Game Industry* (Entertainment Software Association, April 2015).

28 Valerie Steeves, *Young Canadians in a Wired World – Phase II* (Ottawa: Media Awareness Network, 2005); Robyn Greenspan, "Kids Are Media Users Too," ClickZ, 9 October 2003; Rideout, Foehr, and Roberts, *Generation M*.

29 Nic Mitham, "Virtual Worlds and MMOs: Universe and Radar Charts" (paper presented at Digital Kids Expo, Los Angeles, April 2012), http://www.slideshare.net/nicmitham/digital-kids-expo-kzero-presentation.

30 Feenberg, *Questioning Technology*; Judy Wajcman, *TechnoFeminism*
    (Cambridge: Polity, 2004); Tyler J. Veak, ed., *Democratizing Technology:*
    Andrew Feenberg's Critical Theory of Technology (Albany: SUNY Press, 2006);
    Graeme Kirkpatrick, *Critical Technology: A Social Theory of Personal Computing*
    (London: Ashgate, 2004).

31 Madeleine Akrich, "The De-Scription of Technical Objects," in
    Shaping Technology/Building Society, ed. Wiebe E. Bijker and John Law,
    205–24 (Cambridge, MA: MIT Press, 1992); Madeleine Akrich, "User
    Representations: Practices, Methods and Sociology," in *Managing Technology*
    in Society: The Approach of Constructive Technology Assessment, ed. Arie Rip,
    Thomas J. Misa, and Johan Schot (London: Pinter, 1995), 167–84; Nelly
    Oudshoorn, Els Rommes, and Marcelle Stienstra, "Configuring the
    User as Everybody: Gender and Design Cultures in Information and
    Communication Technologies," *Science, Technology, & Human Values* 29,
    no. 1 (2004): 30–63; Ellen C.J. van Oost, "Materialized Gender: How
    Shavers Configure the Users' Femininity and Masculinity," in *How Users*
    Matter: The Co-Construction of Users and Technology, ed. Nelly Oudshoorn and
    Trevor Pinch, 193–208 (Cambridge, MA: MIT Press, 2005); Steve Woolgar,
    "The Turn to Technology in Social Studies of Science," *Science, Technology, &*
    Human Values 16, no. 1 (1991): 20–50.

32 Vincent Mosco, *The Political Economy of Communication: Rethinking and Renewal*
    (London; Thousand Oaks, CA: SAGE, 1996); Vincent Mosco, *The Digital Sub-*
    lime: Myth, Power, and Cyberspace (Cambridge, MA: MIT Press, 2004).

33 Henry Jenkins, "'Complete Freedom of Movement': Video Games
    as Gendered Play Spaces," in *From Barbie to Mortal Kombat: Gender*
    and Computer Games, ed. Justine Cassell and Henry Jenkins, 262–97
    (Cambridge, MA: MIT Press, 1998); Claudia Mitchell and Jacqueline
    Reid-Walsh, *Researching Children's Popular Culture: The Cultural Spaces of*
    Childhood (London: Routledge, 2002); Daniel Thomas Cook, *The Commod-*
    ification of Childhood: The Children's Clothing Industry and the Rise of the Child
    Consumer (Durham, NC: Duke University Press, 2004).

34 Allison James, Chris Jenks, and Alan Prout, *Theorizing Childhood* (Cambridge:
    Polity, 1998).

35 Seymour Papert, *The Children's Machine: Rethinking School in the Age of*
    the Computer (New York: Basic Books, 1993), 142; Kaveri Subrahman-
    yam, Robert E. Kraut, Patricia M. Greenfield, and Elisheva F. Gross,
    "The Impact of Home Computer Use on Children's Activities and
    Development," *Future Child* 10, no. 2 (2000): 123–44; James Paul Gee,
    Good Video Games + Good Learning: Collected Essays on Video Games, Learning
    and Literacy (New York: Peter Lang, 2007); Mizuko Ito, Heather Horst,
    Matteo Bittanti, and danah boyd, eds., *Hanging Out, Messing Around, Geek-*
    ing Out: Living and Learning with New Media (Cambridge, MA: MIT Press,

2010); Plowman, Stephen, and McPake, *Growing Up*; Yasmin B. Kafai and Deborah A. Fields, *Connected Play: Tweens in a Virtual World* (Cambridge, MA: MIT Press, 2013); John Coleman, Chris Davies, and Sonia Livingstone eds., *Digital Technologies in the Lives of Young People* (London: Routledge, 2014); Sonia Livingstone and Julian Sefton-Green, *The Class: Living and Learning in the Digital Age* (New York: NYU Press, 2016).

36 Nelly Oudshoorn and Trevor Pinch, eds., *How Users Matter: The Co-Construction of Users and Technology* (Cambridge, MA: MIT Press, 2005), 1.

37 Mizuko Ito, *Engineering Play: A Cultural History of Children's Software* (Cambridge, MA: MIT Press, 2009)

38 Jesper Juul, *Half-Real: Video Games between Real Rules and Fictional Worlds* (Cambridge, MA: MIT Press, 2005); Ian Bogost, *Persuasive Games: The Expressive Power of Videogames* (Cambridge, MA: MIT Press, 2007); Drew Davidson, ed., *Well Played 1.0: Video Games, Value and Meaning* (Pittsburgh: ETC, 2009);

39 Some foundational examples can be found in Justine Cassell and Henry Jenkins, eds., *From Barbie to Mortal Kombat: Gender and Computer Games* (Cambridge, MA: MIT Press, 1998); as well as Yasmin B. Kafai, Carrie Heeter, Jill Denner, and Jennifer Y. Sun, eds., *Beyond Barbie and Mortal Kombat: New Perspectives on Gender and Gaming* (Cambridge, MA: MIT Press, 2008).

40 Doris Bergen, "Preschool Children's Play with 'Talking' and 'Nontalking' Rescue Heroes: Effects of Technology-Enhanced Figures on the Types and Themes of Play," in *Toys, Games, and Media*, ed. Jeffrey Goldstein, David Buckingham, and Giles Brougère, 295–306 (Mahwah, NJ: Lawrence Erlbaum, 2004); Plowman, "'Hey, Hey, Hey!'"; Allison Druin, ed., *The Design of Children's Technology* (San Francisco: Morgan Kauffman, 1999); Alissa N. Antle, "Designing Tangibles for Children: What Designers Need to Know" (paper presented at the Conference on Human Factors in Computing Systems, San Jose, CA, February 2007); Mark Allen, "Tangible Interfaces in Smart Toys," *Toys, Games, and Media*, ed. Jeffrey Goldstein, David Buckingham, and Gilles Brougère, 179–94 (Mahwah, NJ: Lawrence Erlbaum, 2004).

41 Plowman, "Hey, Hey, Hey!," 99.

42 For instance, all of the following address aspects of materiality and design in their discussion of gendered toys: Heather Hendershot, "Dolls: Odour, Disgust, Femininity and Toy Design," in *The Gendered Object*, ed. Pat Kirkham, 90–102 (Manchester: Manchester University Press, 1996); Judy Attfield, "Barbie and Action Man: Adult Toys for Girls and Boys, 1959–93," in *The Gendered Object*, ed. Pat Kirkham (Manchester: Manchester University Press, 1996), 80–9; Ellen Seiter, *Sold Separately: Children and Parents in Consumer Culture* (New Brunswick, NJ: Rutgers University Press

1993); Merris Griffiths, "Blue Worlds and Pink Worlds: A Portrait of Intimate Polarity," in *Small Screens*, ed. David Buckingham, 159–84 (Leicester, UK: Leicester University Press, 2002); Matthew P. McAllister, "'Girls with a Passion for Fashion': The Bratz Brand as Integrated Spectacular Consumption," *Journal of Children and Media* 1, no. 3 (2007): 244–58.

43 Miriam Forman-Brunell, *Made to Play House: Dolls and the Commercialization of American Girlhood, 1830–1930* (New Haven, CT: Yale University Press, 1993).

44 Stephen Kline, *Out of the Garden: Toys and Children's Culture in the Age of TV Marketing* (Toronto: Garamond, 1993); Marlys Pearson and Paul R. Mullins, "Domesticating Barbie: An Archaeology of Barbie Material Culture and Domestic Ideology," *International Journal of Historical Archaeology* 3, no. 4 (1999): 225–59.

45 David Buckingham and Julian Sefton-Green, "'Gotta Catch 'em All': Structure, Agency and Pedagogy in Children's Media Culture," *Media, Culture & Society* 25, no. 3 (2003): 379–400.

46 Aarsand and Aronsson, "Territorial Negotiations"; Seth Giddings, "'I'm the One Who Makes the Lego Racers Go': Studying Virtual and Actual Play," in *Growing Up Online: Young People and Digital Technologies*, ed. Sandra Weber and Shanly Dixon, 35–48 (New York: Palgrave Macmillan, 2007); Mary Celeste Kearney, "Pink Technology: Mediamaking Gear for Girls," *Camera Obscura* 25, no. 2 (2010): 1–39.

47 Ian Bogost, *Unit Operations: An Approach to Videogame Criticism* (Cambridge, MA: MIT Press, 2006).

48 T.L. Taylor, "Beyond Management: Considering Participatory Design and Governance in Player Culture," special issue, *First Monday* 7 (2006), https://firstmonday.org/ojs/index.php/fm/article/view/1611.

49 Allison Druin, Ben Bederson, Angela Boltman, Adrian Miura, Debby Knotts-Callahan, and Mark Platt, "Children as Our Technology Design Partners," in *The Design of Children's Technology*, ed. Allison Druin (San Francisco: Morgan Kaufmann Publishers, 1999), 52.

50 Druin, *Design*; Plowman, Stephen, and McPake, *Growing Up*; J. Alison Bryant, Anna Akerman, and Jordana Drell, "Diminutive Subjects, Design Strategy, and Driving Sales: Preschoolers and the Nintendo DS," *Game Studies: An International Journal of Computer Game Research* 10, no. 1 (2010), http://gamestudies.org/1001/articles/bryant_akerman_drell.

51 Oudshoorn, Rommes, and Stienstra, "Configuring the User."

52 Trevor Pinch and Weibe E. Bijker, "The Social Construction of Fact and Artefacts: Or How the Sociology of Science and the Sociology of Technology Might Benefit Each Other," in *The Social Construction of Technological Systems: New Directions in the Sociology and History of Technology*, ed. Wiebe E. Bijker and Trevor Pinch, 17–50 (Cambridge, MA: MIT Press, 1987).

53 Kline, *Garden*; Cook, *Commodification*.

54 Langdon Winner, *The Whale and the Reactor: A Search for Limits in an Age of High Technology* (Chicago: University of Chicago Press, 1986).

55 Stuart S. Blume, "The Rhetoric and Counter-Rhetoric of a 'Bionic' Technology," *Science, Technology, & Human Values* 22, no.1 (1997): 31–56; Blume, "Land of Hope and Glory: Exploring Cochlear Implantation in the Netherlands," *Science, Technology, & Human Values* 25, no. 2 (2000): 139–66; Jörg Niewöhner, Martin Döring, Michalis Kontopodis, Jeannette Madarász, and Christoph Heintze, "Cardiovascular Disease and Obesity Prevention in Germany: An Investigation into a Heterogenous Engineering Project," *Science, Technology, & Human Values* 36, no. 5 (2011): 723–51.

56 Ruud Hendricks, "Egg Timers, Human Values, and the Care of Autistic Youths," *Science, Technology, & Human Values* 23, no. 4 (1998): 399–424; H.M. Collins, "Socialness and the Undersocialized Conception of Society," *Science, Technology, & Human Values* 23, no. 4 (1998): 494–516.

57 Rayna Rapp, "Chasing Science: Children's Brains, Scientific Inquiries, and Family Labors," *Science, Technology, & Human Values* 36, no. 5 (2011): 662–84.

58 Robert J. Weber, Stacey Dixon, and Antolin M. Llorente, "Studying Invention: The Hand Tool as a Model System," *Science, Technology, & Human Values* 18, no. 4 (1993): 480–505.

59 For example, see Alfred Moore and Jack Stilgoe, "Experts and Anecdotes: The Role of 'Anecdotal Evidence' in Public Scientific Controversies," *Science, Technology, & Human Values* 34, no. 5 (2009): 654–77; and William A. Stahl, "Venerating the Black Box: Magic in Media Discourse on Technology," *Science, Technology, & Human Values* 20, no. 2 (1995): 234–58.

60 Kavita Philip, Lilly Irani, and Paul Dourish, "Postcolonial Computing: A Tactical Survey," *Science, Technology, & Human Values* 37, no. 1 (2012): 3–29.

61 Anne-Jorunn Berg and Merete Lie, "Feminism and Constructivism: Do Artefacts Have Gender?," *Science, Technology, & Human Values* 20, no. 3 (1995): 345.

62 Judy Wajcman, *Feminism Confronts Technology* (University Park, PA: Penn State University, 1991), 62.

63 For example, see James, Jenks, and Prout, *Theorizing Childhood*.

64 Sara Margrét Ólafsdóttir, Susan Danby, Jóhanna Einarsdóttir, and Maryanne Theobald, "'You Need to Own Cats to Be a Part of the Play': Icelandic Preschool Children Challenge Adult-Initiated Rules in Play," *European Early Childhood Education Research Journal* 25, no. 6 (2017): 826; see also William Corsaro, "Collective Action and Agency in Young Children's Peer Cultures," in *Studies in Modern Childhood: Society, Agency, Culture*, ed. Jens Qvortrup, 231–47 (New York: Palgrave Macmillan, 2005).

65 Jackie Marsh, *Childhood, Culture and Creativity: A Literature Review* (Newcastle upon Tyne, UK: Creativity, Culture and Education, 2010), 10.

66 Johannes Fromme, "Computer Games as a Part of Children's Culture," *Game Studies: An International Journal of Computer Game Research* 3, no. 1 (2003), http://www.gamestudies.org/0301/fromme/.

1. The Importance of Digital Play

1 See, for example, Maria Cipollone, Catherine C. Schifter, and Rick A. Moffat, "Minecraft as a Creative Tool: A Case Study," *International Journal of Game-Based Learning* 4, no. 2 (2014): 1–14; and Josef Nguyen, "Minecraft and the Building Blocks of Creative Individuality," *Configurations* 24, no. 4 (2016): 471–500.

2 Nicholas Kardaras, *Glow Kids: How Screen Addiction Is Hijacking Our Kids – And How to Break the Trance* (New York: St. Martin's, 2016).

3 Nicholas Kardaras, "It's 'Digital Heroin': How Screens Turn Kids into Psychotic Junkies," *New York Post*, 27 August 2016.

4 Brian Sutton-Smith, *Toys as Culture* (New York: Gardner, 1986), 123.

5 The quote "Play is the work of children" is in fact associated with several influential childhood experts, from Maria Montessori and Jean Piaget, to Dr. (Benjamin) Spock and Mister (Fred) Rogers.

6 In the wake of the 2012 Sandy Hook Elementary School massacre in Newtown, Connecticut (in which a young man killed twenty children, six staff members, his mother, and himself), National Rifle Association CEO Wayne LaPierre reportedly pointed to "vicious, violent videogames with names like *Bulletstorm, Grand Theft Auto, Mortal Kombat,* and *Splatterhouse*" as an underlying cause of the man's murderous rampage; see Ian Bogost, "Rage against the Machines," *Baffler* 24 (2014), https://thebaffler.com/salvos/rage-against-the-machines.

7 Gary S. Cross, *A Social History of Leisure since 1600* (State College, PA: Venture, 1990), 117.

8 Brian Sutton-Smith, *The Ambiguity of Play* (Cambridge, MA: Harvard University Press, 1997).

9 Sutton-Smith, *Ambiguity*, 8.

10 See Jaak Panksepp, "Rough and Tumble Play: A Fundamental Brain Process," in *Parent-Child Play: Descriptions and Implications*, ed. Kevin MacDonald (New York: State University of New York Press, 1993), 25, 26. Despite the "nondefinitive state of the evidence," many play theorists remain committed to the idea that play serves some adaptive function. As Sutton-Smith argues, "The rhetorics of play express the way play is placed in context within broader value systems, which are assumed by the theorists of play rather than studied directly by them" (Sutton-Smith *Ambiguity*, 8).

11 See, for example, Narine and Grimes, "Turbulent Rise."

12 World Health Organization, "Addictive Behaviours: Gaming Disorder," 14 September 2018, https://www.who.int/features/qa/gaming-disorder/en/.

13 WHO, "Gaming Disorder."

14 In a response to the WHO's initial proposal to pathologize gaming addiction, a group of twenty-six game scholars from around the world argued, "Concerns about problematic gaming behaviors deserve our full attention. Some gamers do experience serious problems as a consequence of the time spent playing video games. However, we claim that it is far from clear that these problems can or should be attributed to a new disorder, and the empirical basis for such a proposal suffers from several fundamental issues." The group also highlighted the formalization of a game-specific addiction disorder would have sweeping negative impacts on the lives of the millions of young players who engage with digital games in a normal, healthy way. See Espen Aarseth, Anthony M. Bean, Huub Boonen, Michelle Colder Carras, Mark Coulson, Dimitri Das, Jory Deleuze et al., "Scholars' Open Debate Paper on the World Health Organization IDC-11 Gaming Disorder Proposal," *Journal of Behavioral Addictions* 6, no. 3 (2017): 268.

15 Norma O. Pecora, *The Business of Children's Entertainment* (New York: Guilford, 1998).

16 Victoria J. Rideout, Elizabeth A. Vandewater, and Ellen A. Wartella, *Zero to Six: Electronic Media in the Lives of Infants, Toddlers and Preschoolers* (Washington, DC: Kaiser Family Foundation, 2003), 4.

17 Maya Götz, Dafna Lemish, Amy Aidman, and Heysung Moon, *Media and the Make-Believe Worlds of Children: When Harry Potter Meets Pokémon in Disneyland* (Mahwah, NJ: Lawrence Erlbaum, 2005); Vivian Gussin Paley, *A Child's Work: The Importance of Fantasy Play* (Chicago: University of Chicago Press, 2004); Stephen Kline, *Out of the Garden: Toys and Children's Culture in the Age of TV Marketing* (Toronto: Garamond, 1993); Jerome L. Singer, *The Child's World of Make-Believe: Experimental Studies of Imaginative Play* (New York: Academic, 1973).

18 Kline, *Garden*; Susan Linn, *Consuming Kids: The Hostile Takeover of Childhood* (New York: New Press, 2004).

19 Seiter, *Sold Separately*; Sutton-Smith, *Culture*; Susan Willis, *A Primer for Daily Life* (New York: Routledge, 1991).

20 For a discussion of ongoing debates and controversies on the gendering of childhood and children's toys, see Cordelia Fine, *Delusions of Gender: How Our Minds, Society, and Neurosexism Create Difference* (New York: W.W. Norton, 2010); for an overview of trends and concerns relating to the central role played by guns in toys and media targeted to boys, see Lyn

Mikel Brown, Sharon Lamb, and Mark Tappan, *Packaging Boyhood: Saving Our Sons from Superheroes, Slackers, and Other Media Stereotypes* (New York: St. Martin's, 2009).

21 Marsha Kinder, *Playing with Power in Movies, Television, and Video Games: From Muppet Babies to Teenage Mutant Ninja Turtles* (Berkeley: University of California Press, 1991).

22 Götz et al., *Media and the Make-Believe Worlds of Children*; Paley, *Child's Work*; Kline, *Out of the Garden*; Singer, *Child's World*.

23 Beryl Langer, "The Business of Branded Enchantment: Ambivalence and Disjuncture in the Global Children's Culture Industry," *Journal of Consumer Culture* 4, no. 2 (2004): 251–77; Eileen R. Meehan, "'Holy Commodity Fetish, Batman!' The Political Economy of a Commercial Intertext," in *The Many Lives of Batman: Critical Approaches to a Superhero and His Media*, ed. Roberta E. Pearson and William Uricchio, 47–65 (New York: Routledge, 1991); Buckingham and Sefton-Green, "'Gotta Catch 'em All.'"

24 As argued, for instance, by Kline, *Out of the Garden*; and Linn, *Consuming Kids*.

25 Kinder, *Playing with Power*.

26 Giddings, "'I'm the One.'"

27 Kline, *Out of the Garden*; Linn, *Consuming Kids*.

28 Patricia M. Greenfield, Emily Yut, Mabel Chung, Deborah Land, Holly Kreider, Maurice Pantoja, and Kris Horsley, "The Program-Length Commercial: A Study of the Effects of Television/Toy Tie-Ins on Imaginative Play," *Psychology and Marketing* 7, no. 4 (1990): 237–55.

29 Kline, *Out of the Garden*; Stephen Kline and Kristin Stewart, *The Role of Communication in Supporting Pro-Social 'Play Scripts' in Young Boys' Imaginative Play with Action Hero Toys: A Pilot Study of Rescue Heroes* (Vancouver: Simon Fraser University Press, 1999).

30 Kline, *Out of the Garden*, 327.

31 Götz et al., *Media and the Make-Believe Worlds of Children*; Vivian Gussin Paley, *Boys & Girls: Superheroes in the Doll Corner* (Chicago: University of Chicago Press, 1984); Paley, *Child's Work*; Seiter, *Sold Separately*; Willis, *Primer for Daily Life*.

32 Sutton-Smith, *Toys as Culture*.

33 Merris Griffiths and David Machin, "Television and Playground Games as Part of Children's Symbolic Culture," *Social Semiotics* 13, no. 2 (2003): 147–60; Helen B. Schwartzman, *Transformations: The Anthropology of Children's Play* (New York: Plenum, 1978); Sutton-Smith, *Toys as Culture*.

34 Seiter, *Sold Separately*, 190–1.

35 Willis, *Primer for Daily Life*, 31.

36 Giddings, "'I'm the One'"; see also Deborah A. Fields and Yasmin B. Kafai, "'Stealing from Grandma' or Generating Cultural Knowledge?

Contestations and Effects of Cheats in a Teen Virtual World," *Games and Culture* 5, no. 1 (2010): 64–87; David Gauntlett and Lizzie Jackson, "Virtual Worlds, Users and Producers: Case Study: *Adventure Rock*" (paper presented at the Children in Virtual Worlds Conference, University of Westminster, London, May 2008).

37 Giddings, "'I'm the One,'" 41.

38 Henry Jenkins, "Why Heather Can Write: Media Literacy and the Harry Potter Wars," in *Convergence Culture: Where Old and New Media Collide*, ed. Henry Jenkins, 175–216 (New York: New York University Press, 2008); Götz et al., *Media and the Make-Believe Worlds of Children*.

39 Jackie Marsh and Chris Richards, "Play, Media and Children's Playground Cultures," in *Children, Media and Playground Cultures*, ed. Rebekah Willett, Chris Richards, Jackie Marsh, Andrew Burn, and Julia C. Bishop, 1–20 (London: Palgrave Macmillan, 2013); Rebekah Willett, "Superheroes, Naughty Mums and Witches: Pretend Family Play among 7- to 10-Year-Olds," in Willett et al. *Children, Media and Playground Cultures*, 145–69.

40 Bill Jeffrey, "The Supreme Court of Canada's Appraisal of the 1980 Ban on Advertising to Children in Québec: Implications for 'Misleading' Advertising Elsewhere," *Loyola of Los Angeles Law Review* 39, no. 1 (2006): 249.

41 MMOGs are viewed as promoting a unique, innovative form of cultural participation through their emphasis on multiplayer communication, collaborative authorship, and open-ended gameplay environments. Researchers in digital game studies have uncovered instances of meaningful cultural reappropriation among teen and adult MMOG players, including the establishment of unsanctioned, player-driven virtual economies, the co-authoring of complex storylines, and the widespread circulation of player-modified game code.

42 Some key examples include Kafai and Fields, *Connected Play*; Alicia Blum-Ross, Kristiina Kumpulainen, and Jackie Marsh, *Enhancing Digital Literacy and Creativity: Makerspaces in the Early Years* (New York: Routledge, 2019); as well as Livingstone and Sefton-Green, *Class*.

43 For a succinct, critical reflection on this aspect of digital game history and its problematic representation, see Greame Kirkpatrick, *The Formation of Gaming Culture: UK Gaming Magazines, 1981–1995* (Basingstoke: Palgrave Macmillan, 2015).

44 Gary Cross, *The Cute and the Cool: Wondrous Innocence and Modern American Children's Culture* (New York: Oxford University Press, 2004), 176.

45 Cross, *Cute and the Cool*, 176.

46 Entertainment Software Association, *2019 Essential Facts about the Computer and Video Game Industry* (Washington, DC: Entertainment Software Association, 2019).

47 The terms "lightning rod of controversy" and "controversial lightning rod" appear in numerous publications. For an in-depth analysis of the

phenomenon, see Dmitri Williams, "The Video Game Lightning Rod: Constructions of a New Media Technology, 1970–2000," *Information, Communication and Society* 6, no. 4 (2003): 523–50; Bob Rehak, "Genre Profile: First-Person Shooting Games," *The Video Game Explosion: A History from PONG to and Beyond*, ed. Mark P. Wolf, 187–93 (Westport, CT: Greenwood, 2008), 187–93.

48 Williams, "Video Game Lightning Rod," 524.

49 Brian McKernan, "The Morality of Play: Video Game Coverage in *The New York Times* from 1980 to 2010," *Games and Culture* 8, no. 5 (2013): 325.

50 Christopher J. Ferguson, "Violent Video Games, Mass Shootings, and the Supreme Court: Lessons for the Legal Community in the Wake of Recent Free Speech Cases and Mass Shootings," *New Criminal Law Review* 17, no. 4 (2014), 553–86.

51 The bills sought to make compliance to ESRB age guidelines mandatory and enforceable, much in the way that movie theatres in many parts of the United States were once required to abide by the film industry's MPAA ratings.

52 Williams, "Video Game Lightning Rod," 544.

53 Williams, "Video Game Lightning Rod," 543.

54 Sharon Dunwoody and Patrice A. Kohl, "Using Weight-of-Experts Messaging to Communicate Accurately about Contested Science," *Science Communication* 39, no. 3 (2017): 338–57.

55 Alison Harvey, *Gender, Age and Digital Games in the Domestic Context* (London: Routledge, 2015), 70.

56 Stephen Kline, "Media Effects: Redux or Reductive?," *Particip@tions* 1, no. 1 (2003), https://www.participations.org/volume%201/issue%201/1_01_kline_reply.htm.

57 Craig A. Anderson and Karen E. Dill, "Video Games and Aggressive Thoughts, Feelings, and Behavior in the Laboratory and in Life," *Journal of Personality and Social Psychology* 78, no. 4 (2000): 772–90.

58 Andrea Millwood Hargrave and Sonia Livingstone, *Harm and Offence in Media Content: A Review of the Evidence* (Bristol: Intellect, 2006).

59 While beyond the purview of this discussion, Canada's widespread adoption of a US-based ratings system (the contents of which are determined through undisclosed methods by a board composed solely of Americans) bears additional consideration, particularly as our two countries have historically diverged on identifying what content and themes are appropriate for children.

60 Originally developed by the industry-led Interactive Software Federation of Europe, the PEGI system came into effect in 2003 and is currently overseen and administered by several boards and committees, each of which comprises cross-sector experts and representatives from a range of participating countries.

61 Raphael Cohen-Almagor, "Ethical Considerations in Media Coverage of Hate Speech in Canada," *Review of Constitutional Studies* 6, no. 1 (2001): 79–100. See also Canadian Charter of Rights and Freedoms, Part I of the Constitution Act, 1982, being Schedule B to the Canada Act 1982 (UK), 1982, c 11, s 91(24); R v Keegstra [1990] 3 SCR 697; Canadian Human Rights Commission et al. v Taylor et al. [1990], 75 DLR (4th) 577 (SCC); R v Butler [1992] 1 SC 452.

62 See, for instance, Jacob Gershman, "Do Theaters Have to Enforce Movie Ratings?" *Law Blog, Wall Street Journal,* 25 October 2013, http://blogs.wsj .com/law/2013/10/25/do-theaters-have-to-enforce-movie-ratings/.

63 Valerie Walkerdine, "Playing the Game: Young Girls Performing Femininity in Video Game Play," *Feminist Media Studies* 6, no. 4 (2006): 525.

64 Narine and Grimes, "Turbulent Rise."

65 Adrienne Shaw, "Do You Identify as a Gamer? Gender, Race, Sexuality, and Gamer Identity," *New Media & Society* 14, no. 1 (2012): 29.

66 Shira Chess, "A 36-24-36 Cerebrum: Productivity, Gender, and Video Game Advertising," *Critical Studies in Media Communication* 28, no. 3 (2011): 230–52.

67 Gareth R. Schott and Kirsty R. Horrell, "Girl Gamers and Their Relationship with the Gaming Culture," *Convergence* 6, no. 4 (2000): 36–53.

68 Tracy Fullerton, Janine Fron, Celia Pearce, and Jacki Morie, "Getting Girls into the Game: Towards a 'Virtuous Cycle,'" in *Beyond Barbie and Mortal Kombat: New Perspectives on Gender and Gaming,* ed. Yasmin B. Kafai, Carrie Heeter, Jill Denner, and Jennifer Y. Sun, 161–76 (Cambridge, MA: MIT Press, 2008).

69 Janine Fron, Tracy Fullerton, Jacquelyn Ford Morie, and Celia Pearce, "The Hegemony of Play" (paper presented at the Situated Play: Digital Games Research Association International Conference, University of Tokyo, Tokyo, 24–8 September 2007), 1.

70 Brenda Laurel, *Utopian Entrepreneur* (Cambridge, MA: MIT Press, 2001), 4.

71 Fine, *Delusions of Gender.*

72 Patricia M. Greenfield and Kaveri Subrahmanyam, "Computer Games for Girls: What Makes Them Play?," in *From Barbie to Mortal Kombat: Gender and Computer Games,* ed. Justine Cassell and Henry Jenkins, 46–71 (Cambridge, MA: MIT Press, 1998).

73 Greenfield and Subrahmanyam, "Computer Games."

74 Heather Gilmour, "What Girls Want: The Intersections of Leisure and Power in Female Computer Game Play," in *Kids' Media Culture,* ed. Marsha Kinder (Durham, NC: Duke University Press, 1999), 263.

75 Shaw, "Do You Identify as a Gamer?"

76 Anna Vitores and Adriana Gil-Juárez, "The Trouble with 'Women in Computing': A Critical Examination of the Deployment of Research on the Gender Gap in Computer Science," *Journal of Gender Studies* 25, no. 6 (2016): 668.

77 Valerie Walkerdine, *Children, Gender, Video Games: Towards a Relational Approach to Multimedia* (New York: Palgrave Macmillan, 2007).

78 Jennifer Jenson and Suzanne de Castell, "Girls@Play," *Feminist Media Studies* 11, no. 2 (2011): 171.

79 Jenson and de Castell, "Girls@Play," 175.

80 Forman-Brunell, *Made to Play House.*

81 For instance, Walkerdine found that when parents purchased digital games for their daughters, they were more likely to enforce an educational-content criterion.

82 Sharon Lamb, *The Secret Lives of Girls: What Good Girls Really Do – Sex Play, Aggression, and Their Guilt* (Toronto: Free Press, 2001).

83 Walkerdine, *Children, Gender, Video Games*, 111.

84 Cassell and Jenkins, *From Barbie*, 24.

85 Helen W. Kennedy, "Illegitimate, Monstrous and Out There: Female *Quake* Players and Inappropriate Pleasures," in *Feminism in Popular Culture*, ed. Joanne Hollows and Rachel Moseley, 183–201 (Oxford: Berg Publishers, 2006); T.L. Taylor, "Multiple Pleasures: Women and Online Gaming," *Convergence: The International Journal of Research into New Media Technologies* 9, no. 1 (2003): 21–46.

86 Kishonna L. Gray, *Intersectional Tech: Black Users in Digital Gaming* (Baton Rouge: Louisiana State University Press, 2020); Bonnie Ruberg, *Video Games Have Always Been Queer* (New York: New York University Press, 2019); Nicholas Taylor and Gerald Voorhees, eds., *Masculinities in Play* (Cham, Switzerland: Palgrave Macmillan, 2018); Harvey, *Gender, Domestic Context.* As in other fields, including children's studies, game studies increasingly draws on intersectionality theory, a praxis-based approach established by Black feminist scholars and activists aimed at understanding the complex and historically overlooked experiences and social justice actions of Black women, while challenging and de-centring the "hegemonic whiteness in the naming and legitimating of particular kinds of politics, policy-making and knowledge production" (Konstantoni and Emejulu, 2017, 8). See Kristina Konstantoni and Akwugo Emejulu, "When Intersectionality Met Childhood Studies: The Dilemmas of a Travelling Concept," *Children's Geographies* 15, no. 1 (2017): 6–22; Kimberle Crenshaw, "Demarginalizing the Intersection of Race and Sex: A Black Feminist Critique of Antidiscrimination Doctrine, Feminist Theory and Antiracist Politics," *University of Chicago Legal Forum* 1 (1989): 139–67; Patricia Hill Collins, *Black Feminist Thought: Knowledge, Consciousness and the Politics of Empowerment* (New York: Routledge, 2000.)

87 Shira Chess, Nathaniel J. Evans, and Joyya JaDawn Baines, "What Does a Gamer Look Like? Video Games, Advertising and Diversity," *Television & New Media* 18, no. 1 (2017): 37–57.

88 Johanna Weststar, Marie-Josée Legault, Chandell Gosse, and Vicki O'Meara, *Diversity in the Game Industry*, International Game Developers Association, 12 June 2016.

89 Marc Graser, "Videogame Biz: Women Still Very Much in the Minority," *Variety Online*, 1 October 2013, https://variety.com/2013/digital/features /womengamers1200683299-1200683299/.

90 Joanne Cohoon and William Aspray, "A Critical Review of the Research on Women's Participation in Postsecondary Computing Education," in *Women and Information Technology*, ed. Joanne Cohoon and William Aspray (Cambridge, MA: MIT Press, 2006), ix.

91 Caroline Clarke Hayes, "Computer Science: The Incredible Shrinking Woman," in *Gender Codes: Why Women Are Leaving Computing*, ed. Thomas J. Misa (Hoboken, NJ: IEEE-CS Press/Wiley, 2010), 27.

92 Sian Tomkinson and Tauel Harper, "The Position of Women in Video Game Culture: Perez and Day's Twitter Incident," *Continuum: Journal of Media & Cultural Studies* 29, no. 4 (2015): 617–34.

93 For example, in the wake of the Sandy Hooks massacre, Senator Dianne Feinstein and others called for the industry to tighten its self-regulation, describing violent video games as "a kind of simulator to practice on." See Charlie Spiering, "Sen. Dianne Feinstein: Violent Video Games Act as Death Simulators," *Washington Examiner*, 13 April 2013.

94 Vikki B., "Sony Santa Monica Supports Girl Scouts Game Design Badge," IGN, 23 September 2016, http://ca.ign.com/articles/2016/09/23/sony -santa-monica-supports-girl-scouts-game-design-badge.

95 Mizuko Ito, "Education v. Entertainment: A Cultural History of Children's Software," in *Ecology of Games*, ed. Katie Salen (Cambridge, MA: MIT Press, 2008), 90.

96 Fields and Kafai, *Connected Play*; Jackie Marsh, "Purposes for Literacy in Children's Use of the Online Virtual World Club Penguin," *Journal of Research in Reading* 37, no. 2 (2014): 179–95; Rebecca W. Black and Stephanie M. Reich, "Affordances and Constraints of Scaffolded Learning in a Virtual World for Young Children," *International Journal of Game-Based Learning* 1, no. 2 (2011): 52–64; Carrington and Hodgetts, "Literacy-Lite in *BarbieGirls*™."

97 Ian Hutchby and Jo Moran-Ellis, "Introduction: Relating Children, Technology and Culture," in *Children, Technology and Culture: The Impacts of Technologies in Children's Everyday Lives*, ed. Ian Hutchby and Jo Moran-Ellis (London: Routledge, 2000), 3.

98 A number of scholars have examined the economic (e.g., Dyer-Witheford and de Peuter, 2009), legal (e.g., Lastowka and Hunter, 2004), commercial (e.g., Brookey and Booth, 2006), and structural dimensions (Bogost, 2007)

of traditional, or teen- and adult-oriented MMOGs: see Nick Dyer-Witheford and Greig de Peuter, *Games of Empire: Global Capitalism and Video Games* (Minneapolis, MN: University of Minnesota Press, 2009); Greg F. Lastowka and Dan Hunter, "The Laws of the Virtual Worlds," *California Law Review* 92, no. 1 (2004): 3–73; Robert Alan Brookey and Paul Booth, "Restricted Play: Synergy and the Limits of Interactivity in the *Lord of the Rings: The Return of the King* Video Game," *Games and Culture* 1, no. 3 (2006): 214–30; and Bogost, *Persuasive Games*. While research on children's digital media tends to focus on users, a growing number of studies examine the political-economic dimensions of child-specific digital games and trends. Examples include Jaron Harambam, Stef Aupers, and Dick Houtman, "Game Over? Negotiating Modern Capitalism in Virtual Game Worlds," *European Journal of Cultural Studies* 14, no. 3 (2011): 299–319; Vili Lehdonvirta, Terhi-Anna Wilska, and Mikael Johnson, "Virtual Consumerism: Case Habbo Hotel," *Information, Communication & Society* 12, no. 7 (2009): 1059–79; and Sara M. Grimes, "Playing by the Market Rules: Promotional Priorities and Commercialization in Children's Virtual Worlds," *Journal of Consumer Culture* 15, no. 1 (2015): 110–34.

99 Juho Hamari and Vili Lehdonvirta, "Game Design as Marketing: How Game Mechanics Create Demand for Virtual Goods," *International Journal of Business Science and Applied Management* 5, no. 1 (2010): 27.

100 For interface design and game engine coding structures, see Katie Salen and Eric Zimmerman, *Rules of Play: Game Design Fundamentals* (Cambridge, MA: MIT Press, 2004); for the relationship between narrative and game rules, see Espen J. Aarseth, "Genre Trouble: Narrativism and the Art of Simulation," in *First Person: New Media as Story, Performance, and Game*, ed. Noah Wardrip-Fruin and Pat Harrigan, 45–69 (Cambridge, MA: MIT Press, 2004); Gonzalo Frasca, "Ludology Meets Narratology: Similitude and Differences between (Video) Games and Narrative," Ludology, http://www.ludology.org/articles/ludology.htm; Jesper Juul, *Half-Real: Video Games between Real Rules and Fictional Worlds* (Cambridge, MA: MIT Press, 2005); for questions about human-computer interaction, see Pippin Barr, James Noble, and Robert Biddle, "Video Game Values: Human-Computer Interaction and Games," *Interacting with Computers* 19, no. 2 (2007): 180–95; Michael Mateas and Andrew Stern, "Interaction and Narrative," in *The Game Design Reader: A Rules of Play Anthology*, ed. Katie Salen and Eric Zimmerman, 642–69 (Cambridge, MA: MIT Press, 2006). It is worth mentioning that within the broader games studies literature (where digital games are most often approached as a cultural form or practice), design is often listed as one among many factors contributing to the social construction of digital gameplay – even though the design

features themselves are not commonly included in the ensuring analysis. Nonetheless, design is frequently described within the literature as an important facet of the relationship between play (players) and games, as well as between structure and agency.

101 Salen and Zimmerman, *Rules of Play*, 34.

102 Cassell and Jenkens, *From Barbie*; Sheri Graner Ray, *Gender Inclusive Game Design: Expanding the Market* (Hingham, MA: Charles River Media, 2004); Kafai et al., *Beyond Barbie*; Brenda Laurel, *Utopian Entrepreneur* (Cambridge, MA: MIT Press, 2001).

103 Forman-Brunell, *Made to Play*; Jacqueline Reid-Walsh and Claudia Mitchell, "'Just a Doll?' 'Liberating' Accounts of Barbie-Play," *Review of Education, Pedagogy, and Cultural Studies* 22, no. 2 (2000): 175–90; Seiter, *Sold Separately*.

104 Miriam Forman-Brunell and Julie Eaton, "The Graceful and Gritty Princess: Managing Notions of Girlhood from the New Nation to the New Millennium," *American Journal of Play* 1, no. 3 (2009): 340.

105 Sutton-Smith, *Toys as Culture*, 26.

106 Sutton-Smith, *Toys as Culture*, 251.

107 Sutton-Smith, *Ambiguity*, 47.

108 Mikhail M. Bakhtin, *Rabelais and His World* (Bloomington: Indiana University Press, 1984), 43.

109 Allison James, "Confections, Concoctions and Conceptions," *Journal of the Anthropological Society of Oxford* 10, no. 2 (1979), 83–95; Seiter, *Sold Separately*; Hendershot, "Dolls."

110 Hendershot, "Dolls," 98.

111 Peter Stallybrass and Allon White, *The Politics and Poetics of Transgression* (London: Methuen, 1986), 43.

112 Schwartzman, *Transformations*.

113 Sutton-Smith, *Ambiguity*, 41.

114 Towards the end of his life and following several decades of ground-breaking research and theorizing on the topic of play, Sutton-Smith concluded that, contrary to his own earlier definitions, play was neither just fun nor simply "pleasurable for its own sake." Rather, "Play's positive pleasure typically transfers to our feelings about the rest of our everyday existence and makes it possible to live more fully in the world, no matter how boring or painful or even dangerous ordinary reality might seem. It appears to me that in this way play genetically refreshes or fructifies our other, more general, being." Thus, play is inherently worthwhile, but its benefits also permeate other aspects of our lives, our selves. Brian Sutton-Smith, "Play Theory: A Personal Journey and New Thoughts," in *The Handbook for the Study of Play*, ed. James E. Johnson, Scott G. Eberle, Thomas S. Henricks, and David Kuschner (New York: Rowman & Littlefield, 2015), 249.

115 Sutton-Smith, *Ambiguity*.
116 Mizuko Ito, "Education vs. Entertainment: A Cultural History of Children's Software," in *The Ecology of Games: Connecting Youth, Games, and Learning*, ed. Katie Salen, 89–116 (Cambridge, MA: MIT Press, 2008).

2. Small Worlds and Walled Gardens

1 Greenspan, "Kids Are Media."
2 Max Heineman and Grace Kim, "Kids Account for One out of Five Internet Surfers in the U.S.: More Than 27 Million American Kids Connect Online According to Nielson//Netratings," news release, Nielsen//Netratings, 21 October 2003.
3 Amanda Lenhart, Aaron Smith, Monica Anderson, Maeve Duggan, and Andrew Perrin, "Teens, Technology and Friendships: Video Games, Social Media and Mobile Phones Play an Integral Role in How Teens Meet and Interact with Friends," Pew Research Center, August 2015, http://www.pewinternet.org/2015/08/06/teens-technology-and-friendships/.
4 For studies showing that children are playing longer, see Rideout, Foehr, and Roberts, *Generation M*; for the console ownership of young children, see Rideout, Vandewater, and Wartella, *Zero to Six*.
5 NPD Group, "Amount of Time Kids Spend Playing Video Games Is on the Rise," news release, 16 October 2017, http://www.npd.com/press/releases/press_071016a.html.
6 NPD Group, "Avid Omni Gamers Close to Surpassing Free & Mobile Gamers as the Largest Gamer Segment in the U.S.," news release, 12 September 2016, https://www.npd.com/wps/portal/npd/us/news/press-releases/2016/the-npd-group-reports-on-gamer-segmentation/.
7 Joan Ganz Cooney Center, "Digital Games."
8 Joan Ganz Cooney Center, "Digital Games."
9 Reliable statistics on Canadian children's media use and participation rates are not as prevalent as those pertaining to US children, but supporting evidence that digital gaming is equally popular among children in Canada can be found in the Entertainment Software Association of Canada's yearly Essential Facts reports, including a 2018 iteration, which found that 71 per cent of Canadian parents "play video games with their children at least once a week." See Entertainment Software Association of Canada, "Essential Facts about the Canadian Video Game Industry: 2018," report, 29 October 2018, http://theesa.ca/wp-content/uploads/2018/10/ESAC18_BookletEN.pdf. Additional support is found in Steeves, *Young Canadians II*.
10 Nielsen//Netratings, "Nearly 20 Percent of the Active Online Population Are Kids and Teens, Creating Opportunities for Marketers," news release, 13 August 2002; and Greenspan, "Kids Are Media."

11 ESA, "2019 Essential Facts," 10.

12 As Henry Jenkins describes it, "Many sites depend on self-disclosure to police whether the participants are children or adults. Yet, many young people seem willing to lie to access those communities." See Henry Jenkins, *Confronting the Challenges of Participatory Culture: Media Education for the 21st Century* (Cambridge, MA: MIT Press, 2009), 25. See also Valerie Steeves, "It's Not Child's Play: The Online Invasion of Children's Privacy," *University of Ottawa Law & Technology Journal* 3, no. 1 (2006): 169–88; Joseph Turow, *Privacy Policies on Children's Websites: Do They Play by the Rules?* (Philadelphia: Annenberg Public Policy Center of the University of Pennsylvania, 2001); Leslie Regan Shade, Nikki Porter, and Wendy Sanchez, "'You Can See Anything on the Internet, You Can Do Anything on the Internet!: Young Canadians Talk about the Internet," *Canadian Journal of Communication* 30, no. 4 (2005): 503–26; Sonia Livingstone, "Internet Literacy: Young People's Negotiation of New Online Opportunities," in *Digital Youth, Innovation, and the Unexpected*, ed. Tara McPherson, 101–22 (Cambridge, MA: MIT Press, 2008).

13 T.L. Taylor, "Does WoW Change Everything? How a PvP Server, Multinational Player Base, and Surveillance Mod Scene Caused Me Pause," *Games and Culture* 1, no. 4 (2006): 318–37.

14 Nick Yee, "Maps of Digital Desires: Exploring the Topography of Gender and Play in Online Games," in *Beyond Barbie and Mortal Kombat: New Perspectives on Gender and Gaming*, ed. Yasmin B. Kafai, Carrie Heeter, Jill Denner, and Jennifer Y. Sun, 83–96 (Cambridge, MA: MIT Press, 2008).

15 David Kleeman, "Study: How Fortnite Is Doing Right by Kids," KidScreen, 11 May 2018, https://kidscreen.com/2018/05/11/study-how-fortnite-is-doing-right-by-kids/; William D'Angelo, "Fortnite Tops 350 Million Registered Players – Sales," VGChartz, 6 May 2020, https://www.vgchartz.com/article/443407/fortnite-tops-350-million-registered-players/.

16 For a detailed discussion of the impact of the dot com boom on the emergence and eventual regulation of the early children's internet industry, see Kathryn C. Montgomery, *Generation Digital: Politics, Commerce, and Childhood in the Age of the Internet* (Cambridge, MA: MIT Press, 2007).

17 "Flash games" is generally used as a catch-all term to describe browser-based, two-dimensional games that appear in a regular web browser or in a pop-up window. These games normally have fairly basic structures and graphics, particularly when contrasted with the standards of other online games that began to appear during this same period, not to mention those found in console and computer-based games.

18 Grimes, "Saturday Morning Cartoons."

19 Nielsen/Netratings, "Nearly 20 Percent"; Greenspan, "Kids Are Media Users."

20 See, for example, Jack Loechner, "Where Kids Go for Games and Toys Online," MediaPost Research Brief, 23 December 2005.

21 Norma Pecora, "Nickelodeon Grows Up: The Economic Evolution of a Network," in *Nickelodeon Nation: The History, Politics, and Economics of America's Only TV Channel for Kids* ed. Heather Hendershot (New York: New York University Press, 2004), 38.

22 Smith and Just provide a useful, inclusive definition of advergames as those "whose main purpose is to boost sales of a product or service, whether through increased brand recognition, increased liking or other methods"; see Jonas Heide Smith and Sine Nørholm Just, "Playful Persuasion: The Rhetorical Potential of Advergames," *Nordicom Review* 30 (2009): 54. Here, the term "advergame" is understood as a flexible category that includes games that share the characteristic of having been designed first and foremost as promotional devices. This broader definition thus opens up the discussion to include more ambiguous applications, such as licensed games or games that feature multiple and distinct advertising strategies. A major influence in thinking about advergames as a diverse and evolving genre is Jane Chen and Matthew Ringel's early research report on advergames and the future of interactive advertising. Cited throughout both the academic and practice-oriented literature, their research outlines three different types or ways products and brands can be integrated into digital games. The first type, associative advergaming, attempts to drive "brand awareness by associating the product with the lifestyle or activity featured in the game" (3). The second, illustrative advergaming, consists of games that "prominently feature the product itself in game play" (4). The third, demonstrative advergaming, invites the player to interact with and "experience the product within the virtual confines of the gaming space ... boost[ing] messaging effectiveness by presenting the product in its natural context" (4); see Jane Chen and Matthew Ringel, "Fast Forward 2001" (Los Angeles: KPE, 2001); see also David Radd, "The Secrets of Advergaming," *BusinessWeek*, 23 May 2007.

23 Jennifer Culp, Robert A. Bell, and Diana Cassady, "Characteristics of Food Industry Web Sites and Advergames Targeting Children," *Journal of Nutrition Education and Behavior* 42, no. 3 (2010): 197–201, cited in Katarina Panic, Verolien Cauberghe, and Patrick De Pelsmacker, "Comparing TV Ads and Advergames Targeting Children: The Impact of Persuasion Knowledge on Behavioral Responses," *Journal of Advertising* 42, no. 2–3 (2013): 264–73.

24 Between 2004 and 2005, I conducted a content analysis of seventeen of the most popular online games among children and youth. In selecting my case studies, I drew on published rankings of the most highly rated and heavily frequented websites among children and youth, based on

polls conducted by market analyst firms Nielsen/Netratings and Hitwise in 2003. The study aimed to record and analyse the contents and emerging standards of practice found within the terms of service (TOS) or terms of use (TOU) agreements contained within popular children's gaming sites. Data were also gathered on the scope and content of the sites themselves, through extensive "play throughs" of the games, and a comprehensive survey of the sites' pages, texts, images, and other features. The results of this study have been published elsewhere; see Sara M. Grimes, "Terms of Service, Terms of Play in Children's Online Gaming," in *The Players' Realm: Studies on the Culture of Video Games and Gaming*, ed. J. Patrick Williams and Jonas Heide Smith, 33–55 (Jefferson, NC: McFarland, 2007).

25 In 2002, I contributed to a large-scale research project investigating ICT use among Canadian children and young people in the home, led by Leslie Regan Shade (then at the University of Ottawa). I was asked to find examples of popular children's websites and do a preliminary study of the then-current trends in kids' online gaming. While watching cartoons one Saturday morning, I saw an ad for Post Honey Nut Cheerios cereal that ended with a link to a website called *Neopets*. Over the course of the next year, Shade and I collected data on the site and conducted interviews with some of its young users. I expanded upon this study of *Neopets* in two subsequent research projects, and by the end of 2005, I had tracked the site and its evolution from independently run virtual community to poster child for the commercialization of children's digital play. With *Neopets'* emphasis on social interaction and its integrated, persistent game environment, it was also a precursor to the children's virtual worlds and MMOGs that would soon populate the digital landscape.

26 In a 2014 article that appeared on Kidscreen detailing the launch of a then-new *Neopets* digital comic by the site's current owners, JumpStart, the following statistics were provided: "According to JumpStart, Neopets currently has 71 million registered users who have created more than 279 million Neopets. Visitors to the site each spend an average of two hours per month on the virtual world, which also has 67 million monthly game plays." While these numbers likely include a fair number of inactive registered users (e.g., my own account still exists, even though I once let several years pass between logins), the monthly game plays number – if accurate – is impressive; see Daniela Fisher, "JumpStart, Madefire Bring Neopets to Interactive Comics," *Kidscreen*, 11 November 2014.

27 Rob Shaw, "Viacom Buys Neopets: Media Giant's $160-Million (U.S.) Deal Allows Access to Millions of Children," *Globe and Mail*, 21 June 2005.

28 Lisa M. Bowman, "Who Let the NeoPets Out?" C/Net, 26 February 2002.

29 The information relayed here about Neopets Inc.'s business activities in the early 2000s, including some of its unsuccessful initiatives, was drawn

from the company's "NeoPets Press Kit (2003–2004)," which I obtained
from the corporate website in 2004.

30 Mathew Ingram, "Club Penguin Got Bought – Is Webkinz Next?" *Globe and
Mail,* 2 August 2007.

31 It was widely publicized at the time that Disney had valued the purchase
of *Club Penguin* at US$700 million. However, they paid only half of that
amount up front, with a commitment to pay the remainder in two instal-
ments based on undisclosed profit goals. As the site failed to meet both
targets, the other US$350 million was never paid to the site's original own-
ers; see Brooks Barnes, "Club Penguin Misses Goals, Giving Disney a Half-
Price Deal," *New York Times,* 12 May 2010, http://www.nytimes.com/2010
/05/13/business/media/13penguin.html.

32 Karyn M. Peterson, "A Season for Sales," Playthings, January 2008, 19.

33 eMarketer, "Virtual Worlds Are Trendiest Spot Online for Kids and Teens,"
news release, 24 September 2007.

34 Virtual Worlds Management, "Updated: Virtual Worlds Management
Report: 100+ Youth-Oriented Worlds Live or Developing," *Virtual
Worlds News,* 11 April 2008; and Virtual Worlds Management, "Report:
200+ Youth-Oriented Worlds Live or Developing," *Virtual Worlds News,*
26 January 2009.

35 Virtual Worlds Management, "Report: 200+."

36 Jackie Marsh and Anne Burke, *Children's Virtual Play Worlds: Culture, Learn-
ing and Participation* (New York: Peter Lang, 2013); Mia Consalvo, *Cheating:
Gaining Advantage in Videogames* (Cambridge, MA: MIT Press, 2007);
Kaveri Subrahmanyam, "Developmental Implications of Children's Virtual
Worlds," *Washington & Lee Law* Review 66, no. 1065 (2009): 1065–83.

37 Shortly after the lists were published, I conducted a content analysis of
the titles listed in the first Virtual Worlds Management report, which were
described as "100+ youth-oriented [virtual] worlds live or developing."
I reviewed the original list by cross-referencing it with contemporaneous
news stories, trade press coverage, and corporate press releases, removing ten duplicate entries and adding three missing items. I subsequently
conducted a content analysis of 106 individual titles, the vast majority of
which were drawn directly from the list provided in the report. I applied
a standardized coding protocol to produce inventories of each world's
contents and associated publicity materials, privacy policies, and TOU
contracts. For an in-depth discussion of this content analysis, see Sara M.
Grimes, "Penguins, Hype and MMOGs for Kids: A Critical Re-Examination
of the 2008 'Boom' in Children's Virtual Worlds Development," *Games and
Culture* 13, no. 6 (2018): 624–64.

38 Nick Gibson, "Child's Play: Why the Tide Is Turning toward Making Games
for Kids," *Develop Magazine,* 30 June 2008, 18.

39 NPD Group, "Amount."

40 The commonly used criterion – that the virtual world environment con-
    sist of a three-dimensional space – was not applied in this study, as this
    requirement was deemed to be more a consequence of the forms and
    contents of the specific T-rated titles that have dominated the literature,
    rather than an essential property of virtual worlds.

41 Examples include *Be-Bratz* and *BarbieWorld,* both of which were described
    as MMOGs by Greene, as well as *Nicktropolis,* which was described as
    an MMOG by Zenke. See Maggie Greene, "Fascinating yet Horrifying:
    The Barbie and Bratz MMOs," *Kotaku,* 12 August 2007; and Michael
    Zenke, "How Stuffed Animals and Penguins Clobber World of Warcraft,"
    GameSetWatch, 3 April 2007.

42 Jeremiah Spence, "Virtual Worlds Research: Consumer Behaviour in
    Virtual Worlds," *Journal of Virtual Worlds Research* 1, no. 2 (2008): 1–45.

43 Virtual Worlds Management, "Report: 200+ Youth-Oriented Worlds Live or
    Developing," *Virtual Worlds News,* 26 January 2009.

44 *Club Penguin Blog,* "Important Announcement Regarding Club Penguin on
    Desktop and Mobile Devices," 30 January 2017.

45 Dubit Limited, "More Than Half of Children Own a Toy Based on a Virtual
    World Like Moshi Monsters and Club Penguin," news release, 1 December
    2011, http://www.sourcewire.com/releases/rel_display.php?relid=68822.

46 Wendy Smolen, "Making It to the Top: Tweens Rule the Virtual World
    Space," Kidscreen, 5 December 2012.

47 The majority of my preliminary research into children's virtual worlds
    was conducted as part of my doctoral dissertation: Sara M. Grimes, "The
    Digital Child at Play: How Technological, Political and Commercial Rule
    Systems Shape Children's Play in Virtual Worlds" (PhD diss., Simon Fraser
    University, 2010).

48 Gibson, "Child's Play."

49 Statista, "Value of the Global Game Market from 2007 to 2016, by Region
    (in billion U.S. Dollars)," June 2012.

50 In my research on game-themed virtual worlds and MMOGs, I have used
    five criteria for determining whether a game fits this category: (1) the
    virtual world must contain features and activities that unfold in a real-time,
    persistent environment; (2) multiple players are present and visually repre-
    sented within a shared GUI "space"; (3) multiple players are able to interact
    with one another and the environment simultaneously; (4) play activities
    are available and undertaken by users; and (5) the organizing themes and
    narrative of the virtual world operate as components of a "game."

51 Sal Humphreys, "Ruling the Virtual World," *European Journal of Cultural
    Studies* 11, no. 2 (2008): 149–71; Greg F. Lastowka and Dan Hunter, "The

Laws of the Virtual Worlds," *California Law Review* 92, no. 1 (2004): 3–73; Edward Castronova, *Synthetic Worlds: The Business and Culture of Online Games* (Chicago: University of Chicago Press, 2005); Julian R. Kücklich, "Virtual Worlds and Their Discontents: Precarious Sovereignty, Governmentality, and the Ideology of Play," *Games and Culture* 4, no. 4 (2009): 340–52; Nic Crowe and Simon Bradford, "'Hanging Out in *Runescape*': Identity, Work and Leisure in the Virtual Playground," *Children's Geographies* 4, no. 3 (2006): 331–46.

52 Since 2011, I have conducted four studies focused specifically on unpacking the "UGC games" phenomenon, analysing the games' designs and contents, and understanding the role of UGC and DIY game-making within children's culture: the User-Generated Content Games project (2011–12), the DigiKidz: Children's Cultural Media Making project (2012–15), the Playing at Making project (2013–16), and the Children's Making Game Study (2014–16).

53 CBC News, "Most Families with Kids Have a Gaming Console," 11 April 2013, http://www.cbc.ca/news/technology/most-families-with-kids-have -a-gaming-console-1.1325831; Statista, "Daily Personal Device Usage among Children in Canada as of August 2014," https://www.statista.com /statistics/494706/canada-personal-device-usage-children/.

54 Amanda Lenhart, Aaron Smith, Monica Anderson, Maeve Duggan, and Andrew Perrin, "Teens, Technology and Friendships: Video Games, Social Media and Mobile Phones Play an Integral Role in How Teens Meet and Interact with Friends," Pew Research Center, August 2015. http://www .pewinternet.org/2015/08/06/teens-technology-and-friendships/.

55 Entertainment Software Association, "2016 Essential Facts," report, 28 April 2016.

56 ESA, "2016 Essential Facts."

57 Between 1999 and 2018, the ESRB ratings system included a separate category for games suitable for children aged three years and older, labelled "EC for Early Childhood." The EC rating was given to games deemed to contain no material inappropriate for young children. It was abruptly discontinued in 2018.

58 This stipulation appears in the service's privacy policy, under Children's Privacy, which starts with the following statement (in all caps): "IF YOU ARE UNDER 13 YEARS OF AGE, THEN PLEASE DO NOT USE OR ACCESS THE TWITCH SERVICES AT ANY TIME OR IN ANY MANNER." https://www.twitch.tv/p/legal/privacy-notice/.

59 For instance, in the 2007 book *Persuasive Games*, Bogost claims that licensed properties represent only approximately 20 per cent of all console game sales; see Bogost, *Persuasive Games*.

60 Eddie Makuch, "Lego Star Wars Franchise Sells 30 Million," GameSpot, 13 February 2012, http://www.gamespot.com/articles/lego-star-wars -franchise-sells-30-million/1100-6350252/.

61 Craig Elvy, "Pokémon Is Now the Highest Grossing Media Franchise," ScreenRant, 28 August 2018, https://screenrant.com/pokemon-highest -grossing-media-franchise/.

62 For example, see Aaron Katersky, "Online Gaming Is Becoming Predator's Playground," ABC News Online, 5 April 2012, http://abcnews.go.com/US /online-gaming-predators-playground/story?id=16081873.

63 Entertainment Software Association of Canada, "2010 Essential Facts," report, 29 October 2010.

64 Victoria Rideout, "Zero to Eight: Children's Media Use in America, 2013," Common Sense Media, 28 October 2013, https://www.commonsensemedia .org/research/zero-to-eight-childrens-media-use-in-america-2013.

65 Statista, "Daily Personal Device Usage."

66 Hilda K. Kabali, Matilde M. Irigoyen, Rosemary Nunez-Davis, Jennifer G. Budacki, Sweta H. Mohanty, Kristin P. Leister, and Robert L. Bonner Jr., "Exposure and Use of Mobile Media Devices by Young Children," *Pediatrics* 136, no. 6 (2015): 1044–50, https://doi.org/10.1542/peds.2015-2151.

67 NPD Group, "Kids Are Gaming on Mobile Devices Almost as Much as They Are on Consoles and Computers," news release, 10 September 2013, https:// www.npd.com/wps/portal/npd/us/news/press-releases/kids-are-gaming-on -mobile-devices-almost-as-much-as-they-are-on-consoles-and-computers/.

68 Alysia Judge, "Kids' Mobile Games Worth Nearly 8% of Global Market," PocketGamer, 20 August 2015, http://www.pocketgamer.biz/news/61804 /kids-mobile-games-8-global-market-children-spending/.

69 Scott Traylor, "Is the Children's App Market Overripe? Developers Discuss," Kidscreen, 1 June 2016, http://kidscreen.com/2016/06/01/is-the -childrens-app-market-overripe-developers-discuss/.

70 Ito, *Engineering Play*.

71 Sarah Vaala, Anna Ly, and Michael H. Levine, *Getting a Read on the App Stores: A Market Scan and Analysis of Children's Literacy Apps* (New York: Joan Ganz Cooney Center at Sesame Workshop, 2015).

72 Dean Takahashi, "Pokémon Go Generated Revenues of $950 Million in 2016," VentureBeat, 17 January 2017, http://venturebeat.com/2017/01 /17/pokemon-go-generated-revenues-of-950-million-in-2016/.

73 Wendy Goldman Getzler, "Infinity's End: Disney Closes Console Games Business," Kidscreen, 11 May 2016, http://kidscreen.com/2016/05/11 /infinitys-end-disney-closes-console-games-business/.

74 Willie Clark, "Nintendo's Amiibo Succeed and Fail at the Same Time," VentureBeat, 16 December 2015, http://venturebeat.com/2015/12/16 /nintendos-amiibo-succeed-and-fail-at-the-same-time/.

75 See, for instance, the discussion of stuffed animals as "transitional objects," in D.W. Winnicott, *Playing and Reality* (London: Tavistock Publications, 1971); or Erikson's description of toys as symbols of power and identity, in Erik Erikson, *Toys and Reasons: Stages in the Ritualization of Experience* (New York: W.W. Norton, 1977).

76 Cecilia Kang, "FTC to Review Apple iPhone In-App Purchases," *Washington Post*, 22 February 2011.

77 Chris Pereira, "Free-to-Play Game Controversy Sparks FTC Investigation," 1Up.com, 23 February 2011.

78 Joshua Gardner, "Apple Loses $100 Million Class Action Suit to Parents of Kids Who Went on Unauthorized App Spending Sprees," *Daily Mail*, 16 June 2013, http://www.dailymail.co.uk/news/article-2349003/Apple -loses-100MILLION-class-action-suit-parents-kids-went-unauthorized-app -spending-sprees.html.

3. Commercializing Play(grounds)

1 Pecora, *Business of Children's Entertainment*; Jyotsna Kapur, "Out of Control: Television and the Transformation of Childhood in Late Capitalism," in *Kids' Media Culture*, ed. Marsha Kinder, 122–36. (Durham, NC: Duke University Press, 1999); Rideout et al., *Zero to Six*; Kinder, *Playing with Power*; Linn, *Consuming Kids*; Juliet B. Schor, *Born to Buy: The Commercialized Child and the New Consumer Culture* (New York: Scribner, 2004); Agnes Nairn, "Commercialization of Childhood? The Ethics of Research with Primary School Children," *International Journal of Market Research* 48, no. 2 (2006): 113–14.

2 Kinder, *Playing with Power*.

3 Kinder, *Playing with Power*, 85.

4 Kinder, *Playing with Power*, 67.

5 Jack Zipes, *Happily Ever After: Fairy Tales, Children, and the Culture Industry* (New York: Routledge, 1997), 96.

6 Zipes, *Happily Ever After*, 99.

7 Dan Fleming, *Powerplay: Toys as Popular Culture* (Manchester: Manchester University Press, 1996), 95.

8 Fleming, *Powerplay*, 56.

9 Fleming, *Powerplay*, 128.

10 Fleming, *Powerplay*, 164.

11 Fleming, *Powerplay*, 162.

12 Dan Fleming, "Managing Monsters: Videogames and the 'Mediatization' of the Toy," in *The International Handbook of Children, Media and Culture*, ed. Kirsten Drotner and Sonia Livingstone (Thousand Oaks, CA: SAGE, 2008), 67.

13 Wolfgang Fritz Haug, *Critique of Commodity Aesthetics: Appearance, Sexuality, and Advertising in Capitalist Society*, trans. Robert Bock (Cambridge: Polity Press, 1986), 16.

14 Willis, *Primer for Daily Life*.

15 van Oost, "Materialized Gender," 194.

16 Adrienne Shaw, "Encoding and Decoding Affordances: Stuart Hall and Interactive Media Technologies," *Media, Culture & Society* 39, no. 4 (2017): 592–602.

17 Shaw, "Encoding and Decoding," 8.

18 Shaw, "Encoding and Decoding," 9.

19 Pearson and Mullins, "Domesticating Barbie."

20 Buckingham and Sefton-Green, "'Gotta Catch 'em All,'" 394; see also Daniel Thomas Cook, "Exchange Value as Pedagogy in Children's Leisure: Moral Panics in Children's Culture at Century's End," *Leisure Sciences* 23, no. 1–2 (2010): 81–98; Marina Bianchi, "Collecting as a Paradigm of Consumption," *Journal of Cultural Economics* 21, no. 4 (1997): 275–89.

21 Hendershot, "Dolls"; Forman-Brunell, *Made to Play House*; Attfield, "Barbie and Action Man"; Seiter, *Sold Separately*; McAllister, "Passion for Fashion."

22 Bergen, "Preschool Children's Play," 205, 203.

23 A short summary of this work can be found in Lydia Plowman and Rosemary Luckin, "Interactivity, Interface and Smart Toys," *IEEE Computer* 37, no. 2 (2004): 98–100. For an in-depth analysis of the findings, see Plowman, "Hey, Hey, Hey!"

24 Plowman, "Hey, Hey, Hey!," 213.

25 Plowman, "Hey, Hey, Hey!," 216.

26 Plowman, "Hey, Hey, Hey!," 220.

27 For an in-depth discussion of how these elements first became prominent, as well as a critical analysis of the impact this has had on game design and culture, see Christopher A. Paul, *The Toxic Meritocracy of Video Games: Why Gaming Culture Is the Worst* (Minneapolis, MN: University of Minnesota Press, 2018).

28 Kinder, *Playing with Power*, 41.

29 Kinder, *Playing with Power*, 6.

30 Bogost, *Persuasive Games*, 195.

31 From 2011 to 2013, I conducted an in-depth analysis of the *LittleBigPlanet* titles, along with several other user-generated content (UGC) games, as part of a broader study called Adaptive Games and Inclusive Play. The findings from the LittleBigPlanet analysis can be found in Sara M. Grimes, "Little Big Scene: Making and Playing Culture in Media Molecule's *LittleBigPlanet*," *Cultural Studies* 29, no. 3 (2015): 379–400.

32 Bogost, *Persuasive Games*, 223.

33 Jennifer Pybus, "Affect and Subjectivity: A Case Study of Neopets.com," *Politics and Culture* 2 (2009), https://politicsandculture.org/2009/10/02/jennifer-pybus-affect-and-subjectivity-a-case-study-of-neopets-com/.

34 Edward Castronova, "The Right to Play," *New York Law School Law Review* 49, no. 1 (2004–5): 185–210.

35 Dallas W. Smythe, *Dependency Road: Communications, Capitalism, Consciousness and Canada* (Norwood, NJ: Ablex, 1981).

36 Grimes and Shade, "Neopian Economics"; Montgomery, *Generation Digital*; Nairn, "Commercialization of Childhood?"; Steeves, "Not Child's Play"; Valerie Steeves and Cheryl Webster, "Closing the Barn Door: The Effect of Parental Supervision on Canadian Children's Online Privacy," *Bulletin of Science, Technology & Society* 28, no. 1 (2008): 4–19.

37 van Oost, "Materialized Gender"; Feenberg, *Questioning Technology*; Winner, *The Whale*; Akrich, "De-Scription."

4. From Rules of Play to Censorship

1 This remains the case, despite the growing popularity of participatory design involving children within academic settings, a movement pioneered by Allison Druin, and more recently advanced in the works of Rilla Khaled. Druin, *Design*; Rilla Khaled and Asimina Vasalou, "Bridging Serious Games and Participatory Design," *International Journal of Child-Computer Interaction* 2 (2014): 93–100.

2 Johan Huizinga, *Homo Ludens: A Study of the Play-Element in Culture* (1950; Boston: Beacon Press, 1955), 10.

3 Roger Caillois, *Man, Play, and Games*, trans. Meyer Barash (1958; Chicago: University of Illinois Press, 2001), 29.

4 Bernard Herbert Suits, *The Grasshopper: Games, Life and Utopia* (Toronto: University of Toronto Press, 1978), 34.

5 Richard Gruneau, *Class, Sports, and Social Development* (Chicago: Human Kinetics, 1999), 27.

6 Schwartzman, *Transformations*.

7 Salen and Zimmerman, *Rules of Play*, 121.

8 Grimes and Feenberg, "Rationalizing Play," 105.

9 Salen and Zimmerman, *Rules of Play*, 159.

10 John H. Holland, *Emergence: From Chaos to Order* (Reading, MA: Helix, 1998); cited in Salen and Zimmerman, *Rules of Play*, 160.

11 Salen and Zimmerman, *Rules of Play*, 160.

12 Michael Mateas and Andrew Stern, "Interaction and Narrative," in *The Game Design Reader: A Rules of Play Anthology*, ed. Katie Salen and Eric Zimmerman (Cambridge, MA: MIT Press, 2006), 653.

13 J.L. Austin, *How to Do Things with Words* (Cambridge, MA: Harvard University Press, 1962). As Hall describes it, "Statements such as 'I now pronounce you husband and wife' ... are performative, not constative, because it is by the utterance of the words that the act is performed." See Kira Hall, "Performativity," *Journal of Linguistic Anthropology* 9, no. 1–2 (2000): 184.

14 A key exception here is *Whyville*; see Kafai and Fields, *Connected Play*.

15 Matthew Weise, "The Future of Sandbox Gaming," *Confessions of an Aca /Fan* (blog), 9 December 2007, http://henryjenkins.org/2007/12/gambit .html.

16 Elizabeth King, "Possibility Spaces: Using the Sims 2 as a Sandbox to Explore Possible Selves with At-Risk Teenage Males," *International Journal of Game-Based Learning* 1, no. 2 (2011), 34–51.

17 Meredith A. Bak, "Building Blocks of the Imagination: Children, Creativity, and the Limits of Disney Infinity," *Velvet Light Trap* 78 (2016): 58.

18 *Disney Infinity* was one of the titles analysed as part of my contribution to the DigiKidz study (2012–15).

19 Feenberg, *Questioning Technology.*

20 van Oost, "Materialized Gender"; Akrich, "De-Scription"; Akrich, "User Representations."

21 These dimensions of technology design and use can be addressed using a broad interpretation of Feenberg's notion of the technical code, which refers to "those features of technologies that reflect the hegemonic values and beliefs that prevail in the design process," which form a "background of unexamined cultural assumptions literally designed into technology itself" (*Alternative Modernity*, 4, 87).

22 Judy Wajcman, *Feminism Confronts Technology* (University Park, PA: Penn State University, 1991); see also Ruth Schwartz Cowan, "The Consumption Junction: A Proposal for Research Strategies in the Sociology of Technology," in *The Social Construction of Technological Systems: New Directions in the Sociology and History of Technology*, ed. Wiebe E. Bijker, Thomas P. Hughes, and Trevor Pinch, 261–80 (Cambridge, MA: MIT Press, 2001); Berg and Lie, "Feminism and Constructivism."

23 Adrian Chen, "The Laborers Who Keep Dick Pics and Beheadings Out of Your Facebook Feed," *Wired Online*, 23 October 2014.

24 As Roberts, one of the few scholars who has paid concerted attention to the work and culture of online moderators, describes it,

> The sign of a good CCM worker is invisibility – a worker who leaves no trace. This makes it seem as though content just magically appears on a site, rather than there being some sort of curation process and a set of logics by which content is determined to be appropriate or inappropriate. When the content contains racist, homophobic, or sexist aspects, this

invisibility is particularly problematic. It can appear that such content just naturally exists, and should exist, in the digital ecosystem, rather than it often being the result of a decision-making process that has weighed the merits of making it available against the results of removing it, or a system that simply has not been able to deal with it yet.

Sarah T. Roberts, "Commercial Content Moderation: Digital Laborers' Dirty Work," in *The Intersectional Internet: Race, Sex, Class and Culture Online*, ed. Safiya Umoja Noble and Brendesha M. Tynes (New York: Peter Lang, 2016), 148, 149.

25 Jean Piaget, *The Moral Judgment of the Child* (New York: Free Press, 1965).

26 For a thorough critical assessment of Piaget's study and overall approach, see Schwartzman, *Transformations*, 51–3.

27 Piaget, *Moral Judgment*, 28.

28 See, for example, Marjorie Harness Goodwin, "The Serious Side of Jump Rope: Conversational Practices and Social Organization in the Frame of Play," *Journal of American Folklore* 98, no. 389 (1985): 315–30; Cathrin Martin and Ann-Carita Evaldsson, "Affordances for Participation: Children's Appropriation of Rules in a Reggio Emilia School," *Mind, Culture, and Activity* 19 (2012): 51–74; Amanda Bateman, "Huts and Heartache: The Affordance of Playground Huts for Legal Debate in Early Childhood Social Organization," *Journal of Pragmatics* 43, no. 2 (2011): 3111–21; Amanda Bateman and Cary W. Butler, "The Lore and Law of the Playground," *International Journal of Play* 3, no. 3 (2014): 235–50; Magnus Karlsson, Eva Hjörne, and Ann-Carita Evaldsson, "Preschool Girls as Rule Breakers: Negotiating Moral Orders of Justice and Fairness," *Childhood* 24, no. 3 (2017): 396–415.

29 Karlsson et al., "Preschool Girls," 397.

30 For example, Alcock uses sociocultural play theory in her own work on children's meaning-making through unsanctioned mealtime play and rule breaking, and reviews works by other play scholars with similar theoretical frameworks. See Sophie Alcock, "Playing with Rules around Routines: Children Making Mealtimes Meaningful and Enjoyable," *Early Years* 27, no. 3 (2007): 281–93.

31 Karlsson et al., "Preschool Girls," 397.

32 Martin and Evaldsson, "Affordances," 53.

33 Charlotte Cobb-Moore, Susan Danby, and Ann Farrell, "Young Children as Rule Makers," *Journal of Pragmatics* 41, no. 8 (2009): 1477–92.

34 Alcock, "Playing with Rules," 282.

35 Ólafsdóttir et al., "'You Need to Own Cats'"; see also Bateman, "Huts and Heartache."

36 Cobb-Moore, Danby, and Farrell, "Rule Makers," 1478.

37 Karlsson et al., "Preschool Girls," 397.

38 Sutton-Smith, *Ambiguity*; Forman-Brunell, *Made to Play House*; James, "Confections," 74; Lamb, *Secret Lives of Girls*; Schwartzman, *Transformations*.

39 Ólafsdóttir et al., "'You Need to Own Cats,'" 825.

40 William A. Corsaro, *The Sociology of Childhood*, 2nd ed. (Bloomington: Indiana University Press, 2005), 18.

41 Heather Hendershot, "Dolls," 98.

42 Forman-Brunell, *Made to Play House*, 30.

43 Forman-Brunell and Eaton, "Graceful and Gritty," 340.

44 James, "Confections," 83.

45 Examples include Seth Giddings, *Game Worlds: Virtual Media and Children's Everyday Play* (London: Bloomsbury, 2014); Kafai and Fields, *Connected Play*; and Marsh and Burke, *Children's Virtual Play Worlds*.

46 Since the 1990s, the Lego company has expanded operations from its traditional building block sets to include an array of cross-media partnerships and digital media ventures, including a hugely successful series of videogames based upon the Star Wars movies (*Lego Star Wars*). See Giddings, "'I'm the One.'"

47 Yasmin B. Kafai and Deborah A. Fields, "Cheating in Virtual Worlds: Transgressive Designs for Learning," *On the Horizon* 17, no. 1 (2009): 15.

48 During my three-year study of children's MMOGs and virtual worlds, I conducted regular and ongoing observations of the public actions and interactions of the player populations (in aggregate) of two games. The two titles selected for this phase of the study were especially popular among children at the time: Disney's *Club Penguin* and Mattel's *BarbieGirls*. The primary objective of these observations was to better understand how players negotiated the rule systems contained within child-specific virtual worlds. Emphasis was placed on identifying instances where interactions between players and rules were in some way revealed or made manifest. I was interested in identifying moments where players and rules came into overt, observable conflict. I was also looking for instances where play appeared to accord with multiple rule systems, such as design affordances, storylines, and promotional priorities.

49 Most of these interactions were observed in October 2018, leading up to Halloween which is traditionally celebrated on 31 October.

50 Kristen Schilt, "Queens of the Damned: Women and Girls' Participation in Two Gothic Subcultures," in *Goth: Undead Subculture*, ed. Lauren M.E. Goodlad and Michael Bibby (Durham, NC: Duke University Press, 2007), 69.

51 Victoria Carrington, "'I'm in a Bad Mood. Let's Go Shopping': Interactive Dolls, Consumer Culture and a 'Glocalized' Model of Literacy," *Journal of Early Childhood Literacy* 3, no. 1 (2003): 83–98; McAllister, "Girls with a Passion for Fashion"; Claudia Mitchell and Jacqueline Reid-Walsh, *Researching Children's Popular Culture: The Cultural Spaces of Childhood* (London: Routledge; 2002).

52 Pearson and Mullins, "Domesticating Barbie," 229.

53 All six of these "movies" drew from an existing animated web series called *My Scene*, which was used to promote a "Barbie: *My Scene*" doll line. During this same period, Barbie dolls were often sold packaged with a DVD containing a number of episodes from this same web series. The *My Scene* sub-brand was Mattel's response to the popularity of MGA's Bratz line, which similarly revolved around a group of friends, rather than a single titular character.

54 This quote was drawn from the "Parents" page of BarbieGirls.com in 2008.

55 Carrington, "'I'm in a Bad Mood,'" 92.

56 Schwartzman, *Transformations*, 115.

57 Brian Sutton-Smith, "A Structural Grammar of Games and Sports," *International Review of Sport Sociology* 11, no. 2 (1976): 128.

58 Siegfried Kracauer, *The Mass Ornament: Weimar Essays*, trans. Thomas Y. Levin (Cambridge, MA: Harvard University Press: 1995).

59 Feenberg, *Questioning Technology*, 113.

60 Salen and Zimmerman, *Rules of Play*, 160.

61 Grimes and Feenberg, "Rationalizing Play."

62 Giddings, *Game Worlds;* Giddings, "I'm the One"; Kafai and Fields, *Connected Play;* and Marsh and Burke, *Children's Virtual Play World.*

5. Safety First, Privacy Later

1 Kapur, "Out of Control"; Kathryn Montgomery, "Digital Kids: The New On-Line Children's Consumer Culture," in *The Handbook of Children and the Media*, ed. Dorothy G. Singer and Jerome L. Singer, 635–48 (Thousand Oaks, CA: SAGE, 2000); Linn, *Consuming Kids;* Ellen Seiter, *The Internet Playground: Children's Access, Entertainment, and Mis-Education* (New York: Peter Lang, 2005); Douglas Rushkoff, *Screenagers: Lessons in Chaos from Digital Kids* (Cresskill, NJ: Hampton, 2006); Nairn, "Commercialisation of Childhood?"

2 Steeves, "Not Child's Play"; Turow, *Privacy Policies.*

3 Kate Raynes-Goldie, "Aliases, Creeping, and Wall Cleaning: Understanding Privacy in the Age of Facebook," *First Monday* 15, no. 1 (2010): 4.

4 The introduction of the General Data Protection Regulation (GDRP) in 2018 marked the first time a Europe-wide regulation specifically addressed the privacy of children, through the inclusion of specific requirements for the collection, use, and disclosure of children's data. As Livingstone describes, the reasons for these protections is set out in the GDPR's recital 38:

> Children merit specific protection with regard to their personal data, as they may be less aware of the risks, consequences and safeguards concerned and their rights in relation to the processing of personal data. Such

specific protection should, in particular, apply to the use of personal data of children for the purposes of marketing or creating personality or user profiles and the collection of personal data with regard to children when using services offered directly to a child. The consent of the holder of parental responsibility should not be necessary in the context of preventive or counselling services offered directly to a child.

Livingstone also points out, however, that a "recital" only provides guidance on how to implement the GDPR, without the "legal force of an article." It also leaves a lot up to interpretation. See Sonia Livingstone, "What Will the General Data Protection Regulation (GDPR) Mean for Children's Privacy and Rights?," *Parenting for a Digital Future* (blog), 25 May 2018, https://blogs.lse.ac.uk/parenting4digitalfuture/2018/05/25/what-will-the -gdpr-mean-for-childrens-privacy-and-rights/; and Milda Macenaite, "From Universal towards Child-Specific Protection of the Right to Privacy Online: Dilemmas in the EU General Data Protection Regulation," *New Media & Society* 19, no. 5 (2017): 765–79.

5 Montgomery, *Generation Digital*, 67–9.
6 Steeves, "Not Child's Play," 175.
7 Chung and Grimes, "Data Mining."
8 Lisa Lazard, Rose Capdevila, Charlotte Dann, Abigail Locke, and Sandra Roper, "Sharenting: Pride, Affect and the Day-to-Day Politics of Digital Mothering," *Social and Personality Psychology Compass* 13, no. 4 (2019): 1–10; Merike Lipu and Andra Siibak, "'Take It Down!': Estonian Parents' and Pre-Teens' Opinions and Experiences with Sharenting," *Media International Australia* 170, no. 1 (2019): 57–67; Carol Moser, Tianying Chen, and Sarita Schoenebeck, "Parents' and Children's Preferences about Parents Sharing about Children on Social Media" (paper presented at CHI 2017, Denver, CO, 6–11 May 2017); Alicia Blum-Ross and Sonia Livingstone, "'Sharenting,' Parent Blogging, and the Boundaries of the Digital Self," *Popular Communication* 15, no. 2 (2017): 110–25.
9 Sonia Livingstone, Kjartan Ólafsson, and Elisabeth Staksrud, *Social Networking, Age and Privacy* (London: EU Kids Online, 2011), http://eprints.lse .ac.uk/35849/.
10 Valerie Steeves, *Young Canadians in a Wired World, Phase III: Life Online* (Ottawa: MediaSmarts, 2014).
11 Kantar, "Share of Children Using Selected Social Media in Norway 2019, by Platform," Statista, 17 September 2019, https://www.statista.com /statistics/1051525/share-of-children-using-selected-social-media-in-norway -by-platform/. Notably, although the specific platforms children use may have changed over the years, new entrants like TikTok and Snapchat espouse a similar approach, restricting use of their (primary) service by

children under the age of thirteen years. The popular video-sharing platform TikTok announced a child-specific version of the app after being fined $5.7 million by the FTC for its widespread mishandling of children's personal information. The children's version would allow younger users to create videos but not share them. Marie Loreto, "TikTok Announces Child Friendly Version of App after Being Fined Nearly $6 Million," Fresh Toast, 2 March 2019, https://thefreshtoast.com/culture/tiktok-announces-child -friendly-version-of-app-after-being-fined-nearly-6-million/.

12 Federal Trade Commission, "The Future of the COPPA Rule: An FTC Workshop," FTC Website: Events Calendar, 7 October 2019, https://www .ftc.gov/news-events/events-calendar/future-coppa-rule-ftc-workshop. See also Lesley Fair, "New Block on the Kids? FTC Announces COPPA Review and Workshop," *Federal Trade Commission Business Blog*, 17 July 2019, https://www.ftc.gov/news-events/blogs/business-blog/2019/07/new -block-kids-ftc-announces-coppa-review-workshop.

13 Sarah Perez, "The FTC Looks to Change Children's Privacy Law Following Complaints about YouTube," TechCrunch, 18 July 2019, https:// techcrunch.com/2019/07/18/the-ftc-looks-to-change-childrens-privacy -law-following-complaints-about-youtube/. Notably, the age requirements outlined in YouTube's Terms of Service were updated six months later to reflect "the specific age requirements for your country ... and included a notice that, if you are a minor in your country, you must always have your parent or guardian's permission before using the Service." This description is somewhat misleading, however, at least in regard to the Canadian version, which now says, "You must be at least 13 years old to use the Service. However, children of all ages may use YouTube Kids (where available) if enabled by a parent or legal guardian." The new wording does not address the widespread presence of children under 13 on the platform or how parental consent might remove this restriction. See Google LLC, "Terms of Service," Terms, 10 December 2019, https://www.youtube.com /t/terms.

14 Regulation (EU) 2016/679 (General Data Protection Regulation) in the current version of the OJ L 119, 04.05.2016; cor. OJ L 127, 23.5.2018, applicable as of 25 May 2018.

15 danah boyd, Eszter Hargittai, Jason Schultz, and John Palfrey, "Why Parents Help Their Children Lie to Facebook about Age: Unintended Consequences of the 'Children's Online Privacy Protection Act,'" *First Monday* 16, no. 11 (2011), https://firstmonday.org/ojs/index.php/fm /article/view/3850/3075.

16 Parents are not the only ones who share children's personal information online – a wide range of other adults do so as well, often with few restrictions or regulatory interventions. For instance, an increasing number of

schools, child care centres, and recreational organizations use social networking forums and connected apps to communicate with attendees and parents, and they sometimes share their posts with the community-at-large. Photos of children and information about their everyday lives are circulated among family members and relatives, between parents and caregivers, and shared with friends and various others. Through such exchanges, family ties are fostered, relationships are sustained, and the child's personal network is built and maintained. In the process, however, an enormous amount of information about children is circulated publicly on the internet and is added to information flows more generally. Although these practices are rarely included in discussions or studies of children's internet use, they represent a key means through which children's lives unfold online.

17　C.S. Mott Children's Hospital, "Parents on Social Media: Likes and Dislikes of Sharenting," *Mott Poll Report* 23, no. 2 (16 March 2015): 1–2.

18　Stacey B. Steinberg, "Sharenting: Children's Privacy in the Age of Social Media," *Emory Law Journal* 66 (2017): 856.

19　Steinberg, "Sharenting," 862.

20　Sonia Livingstone, "Mediating the Public/Private Boundary at Home: Children's Use of the Internet for Privacy and Participation," *Journal of Media Practice*, 6, no. 1 (2005): 41–51; Steeves and Webster, "Closing the Barn Door"; Turow, *Privacy Policies*.

21　The general lack of information literacy among users of connected technologies supports the idea that there is a growing need for transparency, accountability, and oversight across the digital industries, as was advanced in a large-scale canvassing of technology experts (scholars, practitioners, and policymakers) conducted in 2017 by the Pew Research Centre and Elon University. Respondents argued that "those who create and evolve algorithms are not held accountable to society and argued there should be some method by which they are. They also argued there is great need for education in algorithm literacy, and that those who design algorithms should be trained in ethics and required to design code that considers societal impacts as it creates efficiencies." Lee Rainie and Janna Anderson, *Code-Dependent: Pros and Cons of the Algorithm Age* (Washington: Pew Research Center, 2017).

22　Steinberg, "Sharenting," 877.

23　Alexis Hiniker, Sarita Y. Schoenebeck, and Julie A. Kientz, "Not at the Dinner Table: Parents' and Children's Perspectives on Family Technology Rules" (paper presented at the Conference Proceedings of 19th ACM Conference on Computer-Supported Cooperative Work and Social Computing, San Francisco, 27 February–2 March 2016).

24　Hiniker et al., "Dinner Table," 1385.

25　Hiniker et al., "Dinner Table."

26 Steinberg, "Sharenting," 881.
27 In a COPPA "compliance plan for businesses" published in 2018, the FTC clarified that "connected toys or other Internet of Things devices" were covered by the Rule under the current definition of "Website or online service." See Federal Trade Commission, "Children's Online Privacy Protection Rule: A Six-Step Compliance Plan for Your Business," June 2017, https://www.ftc.gov/tips-advice/business-center/guidance/childrens-online-privacy-protection-rule-six-step-compliance.
28 Kapur, "Out of Control"; Montgomery, "Digital Kids"; Steeves, "Not Child's Play."
29 Chung and Grimes, "Data Mining."
30 Federal Trade Commission, "Children's Online Privacy Protection Rule," Federal Register 78, no. 12, 17 January 2013, s. 1302, p. 8.
31 J. Walker Smith and Ann Clurman, *Rocking the Ages: The Yankelovich Report on Generational Marketing* (New York: HarperCollins Publishers, 1997); Anne Sutherland and Beth Thompson, *Kidfluence: Why Kids Today Mean Business* (Toronto: McGraw-Hill Ryerson, 2001); Montgomery, *Generation Digital.*
32 The Final Rule, published in 2013, states, "A persistent identifier that can be used to recognize a user over time and across different Web sites or online services, where such persistent identifier is used for functions other than or in addition to support for the internal operations of the Web site or online service." According to the FTC, persistent identifiers includes a range of data forms, from cookies and IP addresses, to device serial numbers.
33 Karen Louise Smith and Leslie Regan Shade, "Children's Digital Playgrounds as Data Assemblages: Problematics of Privacy, Personalization, and Promotional Culture," *Big Data & Society* 5, no. 2 (2018): 1–12.
34 Grimes and Fields, "Children's Media Making," 112–22.
35 Turow, *Privacy Policies.*
36 There is also evidence that there are often deep discrepancies between what is outlined in a privacy policy and how users' data are in fact collected and handled. Recent research comparing privacy policies and privacy practices in large samples of mobile apps, conducted by Zimmeck et al., suggests "the occurrence of potential privacy requirement inconsistencies on a large scale." Similar trends were uncovered in Reyes et al.'s analysis of 5,855 of the most popular free child-specific apps available on the Google Play Store between 2016 to 2018. While more than half of the apps analysed contained links to privacy policies, the majority used third-party SDKs in direct violation of COPPA requirements. This was even the case of apps that had been approved under COPPA's Safe Harbor program, a designation ostensibly reserved for "privacy practices that go above and beyond COPPA's minimum requirements." See Sebastian Zimmeck, Ziqi Wang, Lieyong Zou, Roger Iyengar, Bin Liu, Florian Schaub,

Shomir Wilson, Norman Sadeh, Steven M. Bellovin, and Joel Reidenberg, "Automated Analysis of Privacy Requirements for Mobile Apps" (paper presented at Proceedings of NDSS Symposium, San Diego, 26 February–1 March 2017); and Irwin Reyes, Primal Wijesekera, Joel Reardon, Amit Elazari Bar On, Abbas Razaghpanah, Narseo Vallina-Rodriguez, and Serge Egelman, "'Won't Somebody Think of the Children?': Examining COPPA Compliance at Scale," *Proceedings on Privacy Enhancing Technologies* 3 (2018): 63–83.

37 Sulake, "Habbo Hotel Privacy Pledge" (2006).

38 Firma Studios, "*GalaXseeds* Privacy Policy" (2008).

39 Steeves, *Young Canadians, Phase III*, 22.

40 Leslie Regan Shade, "Surveilling the Girl via the Third and Networked Screen," in *Mediated Girlhoods: New Explorations of Girls' Media Cultures*, ed. Mary Celeste Kearney (New York: Peter Lang, 2008), 264.

41 As Vittrup et al. describe it, "Several studies have shown discrepancies between parents' and children's reports of the children's media use (e.g., Kaiser Family Foundation, 2003; Lenhart, 2005; Vittrup, 2009; Wang et al., 2005)." In their own study of parents and young children, they found that "less than 50 percent of parents could accurately identify their children's level of proficiency with various technologies" (48); see Brigitte Vittrup, Sharla Snider, Katherine K. Rose, and Jacqueline Rippy, "Parental Perceptions of the Role of Media and Technology in Their Young Children's Lives," *Journal of Early Childhood Research* 14, no. 1 (2016): 43–54.

42 Significantly, Disney's *The Mickey Mouse Club* (which ran on ABC from 1955 to 1959) is often credited with being one of the first programs to fully merge content and advertising, as the show essentially functioned as "one big advertisement for Walt Disney's theme park"; see Lynn Spigel, "Seducing the Innocent: Childhood and Television in Postwar America," in *The Children's Culture Reader*, ed. Henry Jenkins (New York: New York University Press, 1998), 127.

43 As discussed in Grimes, "Kids' Ad Play"; see also Report and Order and Further Notice of Proposed Rule Making In the Matter of Children's Television Obligations of Digital Television Broadcasters ("2004 Order"), MB Docket No. 00-167, FCC 04-221, 23 November 2004; Second Order on Reconsideration and Second Report and Order ("Second Order"), MM Docket No. 00-167, FCC 06-143, 29 September 2006.

44 Wendy Goldman Getzler, "Virtually Gone? Think Again," Kidscreen, 6 April 2017, http://kidscreen.com/2017/04/06/virtually-gone-think-again/.

45 Sonia Livingstone, "Making the Internet a Safer (and Better) Place for Children," Media Policy Project Blog, 5 December 2017, https://blogs.lse .ac.uk/mediapolicyproject/2017/12/05/making-the-internet-a-safer-and -better-place-for-children/.

46 Ofcom, *Children and Parents: Media Use and Attitudes Report*, 29 November
    2017, https://www.ofcom.org.uk/__data/assets/pdf_file/0020/108182
    /children-parents-media-use-attitudes-2017.pdf.

47 Rob Marvin, "76 Percent of Parents Concerned for Children's Online
    Safety," *PC Magazine*, 13 August 2018, https://www.pcmag.com/news
    /363054/76-percent-of-parents-concerned-for-childrens-online-safety.

48 Alexandra Whyte, "Common Sense Finds Social Media Privacy Matters to
    Teens," Kidscreen, 11 June 2018, http://kidscreen.com/2018/06/11
    /common-sense-finds-social-media-privacy-matters-to-teens/.

49 Charlene Simmons, "Protecting Children While Silencing Them: The
    Children's Online Privacy Protection Act and Children's Free Speech
    Right," *Communication Law and Policy* 12, no. 2 (2007): 139; moreover,
    Simmons highlights that other legal critics have raised the point that "pro-
    tecting children's privacy for safety reasons is not inherently compelling
    for First Amendment purposes" (137).

50 Some of the games contained multiple chat levels or options, ranging
    from less to more restrictive, depending on the user's age. For instance,
    Club Penguin also offered a membership level that included a less restric-
    tive chat system, as well as a "child safe'" membership level in which chat
    was limited to pre-formulated sentences selected from a drop-down menu.

51 For example, see Annabelle Timsit, "Alexa Is Very Confused by Little
    Kids," Quartz, 12 August 2018, https://qz.com/1352272/when-alexa-and
    -other-smart-speakers-misunderstand-little-kids/.

52 James, "Confections," 83.

53 Irwin Altman, "Privacy Regulation: Culturally Universal or Culturally
    Specific?" *Journal of Social Issues* 33, no. 3 (1977): 66–84.

54 Julie E. Cohen, "The Inverse Relationship between Secrecy and Privacy,"
    Social Research 77, no. 3 (2010): 889.

55 Salen and Zimmerman, *Rules of Play*, 280.

56 Sonia Livingstone, "Internet Literacy: Young People's Negotiation of New
    Online Opportunities," in *Digital Youth, Innovation, and the Unexpected*, ed.
    Tara McPherson, 101–22 (Cambridge, MA: MIT Press, 2008); Shade et
    al., "You Can See Anything on the Internet"; Steeves, "Not Child's Play";
    Turow, *Privacy Policies*.

57 Victoria J. Rideout, Ulla G. Foehr, and Donald F. Roberts, *Generation M:
    Media in the Lives of 8- to 18-Year-Olds* (Washington, DC: Kaiser Family Foun-
    dation, 2005); Cheryl K. Olson, Lawrence A. Kutner, Dorothy E. Warner,
    Jason B. Almerigi, Lee Baer, Armand M. Nicholi II, and Eugene V. Beresin,
    "Factors Correlated with Violent Video Game Use by Adolescent Boys
    and Girls," *Journal of Adolescent Health* 41, no. 1 (2007): 77–83; Patti M.
    Valkenburg, *Children's Responses to the Screen: A Media Psychological Approach*
    (Mahwah, NJ: Lawrence Erlbaum Associates, 2004); Joanne Cantor, "'I'll

Never Have a Clown in My House': Why Movie Horror Lives On," *Poetics Today* 25, no. 2 (2004): 283–304.

58 Peter Nikken and Jeroen Jansz, "Playing Restricted Videogames," *Journal of Children & Media* 1, no. 3 (2007): 227–43; Brad J. Bushman and Angela D. Stack, "Forbidden Fruit versus Tainted Fruit: Effects of Warning Labels on Attraction to Television Violence," *Journal of Experimental Psychology: Applied* 2, no. 3 (1996): 207–26.

59 Nikken and Janz, "Playing Restricted Videogames," 238.

60 David Buckingham, "Selling Childhood?," *Journal of Children and Media* 1, no. 1 (2007): 20.

61 See, for instance, danah boyd et al., "Why Parents Help Their Children Lie."

62 Sara M. Grimes, "Kids and Moms Harassed in Xbox Live," Gamine Expedition, 12 August 2007, http://gamineexpedition.blogspot.com/2007/08/kids-and-mom-harrassed-in-xbox-live.html.

63 Many of these characteristics are described in the Bakhtinian scholarship on children's play conducted by Sutton-Smith; see Sutton-Smith, *Ambiguity*; Schwartzman, *Transformations*; Lamb, *Secret Lives*; Giddings, "'I'm the One."

64 Fields and Kafai, "Stealing from Grandma"; Livingstone, "Internet Literacy."

65 Taylor, "Does WoW Change Everything," 324.

66 Burcu S. Bakioglu, "Spectacular Interventions of Second Life: Goon Culture, Griefing, and Disruption in Virtual Spaces," *Journal of Virtual Worlds Research* 1, no. 3 (2009); Consalvo, *Cheating*.

67 Gregory T. Donovan and Cindy Katz, "Cookie Monsters: Seeing Young People's Hacking as Creative Practice," *Children, Youth and Environments* 19, no. 1 (2009): 198.

68 Theresa Tanenbaum, "How I Learned to Stop Worrying and Love the Gamer: Reframing Subversive Play in Story-Based Games," *Proceedings of the 2013 DiGRA International Conference: DeFragging Game Studies*, http://www.digra.org/digital-library/publications/how-i-learned-to-stop-worrying-and-love-the-gamer-reframing-subversive-play-in-story-based-games/.

69 Sonia Livingstone and Peter K. Smith, "Annual Research Review: Harms Experienced by Child Users of Online and Mobile Technologies: The Nature, Prevalence and Management of Sexual and Aggressive Risks in the Digital Age," *Journal of Child Psychology and Psychiatry* 55, no. 6 (2014): 647.

70 Rosin, "Overprotected Kid," n.p.

71 David J. Ball, "Policy Issues and Risk-Benefit Trade-Offs of Safer Surfacing for Children's Playgrounds," *Accident Analysis and Prevention* 36, no. 4 (2004): 661–70.

72 For a thorough overview of the literature promoting risky play, see Heather A. Coe, "Embracing Risk in the Canadian Woodlands: Four Children's Risky Play and Risk-Taking Experiences in a Canadian Forest Kindergarten," *Journal of Early Childhood Research* 15, no. 4 (2017): 374–88.

73 Ellen Beate Hansen Sandseter, "Children's Expressions of Exhilaration and Fear in Risky Play," *Contemporary Issues in Early Childhood* 10, no. 2 (2009): 103.

74 Brian W. Sturm, "Imaginary 'Geographies' of Childhood: School Library Media Centers as Secret Spaces," *Knowledge Quest* 36, no. 4 (2008): 46–9.

75 Dorothy G. Singer and Jerome L. Singer, *The House of Make-Believe: Children's Play and the Developing Imagination* (Cambridge, MA: Harvard University Press, 1990), 43.

76 Smith and Shade, "Children's Digital Playground," 1.

6. Playing as Making and Creating

1 Aldo Tolino, "Beyond Play: Analyzing Player-Generated Creations," Gamasutra, 14 May 2009, http://www.gamasutra.com/view/feature/4008 /beyond_play_analyzing_.php.

2 See Consalvo, *Cheating;* Tolino, "Beyond Play."

3 Consalvo, *Cheating,* 9.

4 Fields and Kafai, "Stealing from Grandma," 74.

5 Fields and Kafai, "Stealing from Grandma," 80.

6 As Consalvo writes, cheating emerges when top-down forces associated with the gaming industry clash and compete with bottom-up resistance and actions of the players.

7 Chris J. Young, "Game Changers: Everyday Gamemakers and the Development of the Video Game Industry" (PhD diss., University of Toronto, 2018), http://hdl.handle.net/1807/89734.

8 Paulo Blikstein and Marcelo Worsley, "Children Are Not Hackers: Building a Culture of Powerful Ideas, Deep Learning, and Equity in the Maker Movement," in *Makeology: Makerspaces as Learning Environments,* ed. Kylie Peppler, Erica Halverson, and Yasmin B. Kafai, 64–79 (New York: Routledge, 2016).

9 Mitchel Resnick, John Maloney, Andrés Monroy-Hernández, Natalie Rusk, Evelyn Eastmond, Karen Brennan, Amon Millner, Eric Rosenbaum, Jay Silver, Brian Silverman, and Yasmin Kafai, "Scratch: Programming for All," *Communications of the ACM* 52, no. 11 (2009): 63.

10 David Walter, "Scratch That," *Princeton Alumni Weekly,* 25 October 2017, https://paw.princeton.edu/article/scratch.

11 Resnick et al., "Scratch."

12 Karen Brennan, Amanda Valverde, Joe Prempeh, Ricarose Roque, and Michelle Chung, "More Than Code: The Significance of Social Interactions in Young People's Development as Interactive Media Creators," in *Proceedings of ED-MEDIA 2011 – World Conference on Educational Multimedia, Hypermedia & Telecommunications,* ed. T. Bastiaens & M. Ebner,

2147–56 (Lisbon, Portugal: Association for the Advancement of Computing in Education, 2011).

13 Michal Armoni, Orni Meerbaum-Salant, and Mordechai Ben-Ari, "From Scratch to 'Real' Programming," *ACM Transactions on Computing Education* 14, no. 4 (2015): 1–15.

14 Benjamin Nicoll and Bjorn Nansen, "Mimetic Production in YouTube Toy Unboxing Videos," *Social Media + Society* 4, no. 3 (2018): 1–12.

15 Papert, *The Children's Machine*, 142.

16 Blikstein and Worsley, "Children Are Not Hackers," 71.

17 Nick Logler, "Arduino and Access: Value Tensions in the Maker Movement," *Ethics and Information Technology* (2018), https://doi.org/10.1007/s10676 -018-9479-z.

18 Jennifer Jenson and Milena Droumeva, "Revisiting the Media Generation: Youth Media Use and Computational Literacy Instruction," *E-Learning and Digital Media* 14, no. 4 (2017): 212–25; Yasmin B. Kafai and Quinn Burke, *Connecting Gaming: What Making Video Games Can Teach Us about Learning and Literacy* (Cambridge, MA: MIT Press, 2016).

19 Dodie J. Niemeyer and Hannah R. Gerber, "Maker Culture and Minecraft: Implications for the Future of Learning," *Educational Media International* 52, no. 3 (2015): 216–26.

20 Nguyen, "*Minecraft* and the Building Blocks"; Cipollone et al., "*Minecraft* as a Creative Tool."

21 Logler, "Arduino and Access," 2.

22 In this context, the term "assets" refers to the objects, props, costumes, and other aesthetic components that make up the game world.

23 For a more detailed description of this shift, see Grimes, "Little Big Scene."

24 Rebekah Willett, "'*Microsoft* Bought *Minecraft* … Who Knows What's Going to Happen?!': A Sociocultural Analysis of 8–9-Year-Olds' Understanding of Commercial Online Gaming Industries," *Learning, Media and Technology* 43, no. 1 (2016): 101–16.

25 Yasmin B. Kafai, "Understanding Virtual Epidemics: Children's Folk Conceptions of a Computer Virus," *Journal of Science Education Technology* 17, no. 6 (2008): 523–9.

26 Sara M. Grimes and Vinca Merriman, "'Technically They're Your Creations, But …': Children Making, Playing, and Negotiating UGC Games," in *The Routledge Companion to Digital Media and Children*, ed. Lelia Green, Donell Holloway, Kylie Stevenson, Tama Leaver, and Leslie Haddon, 275–84 (London: Routledge, 2020).

27 "Habitus" is a term coined by Bourdieu to describe the matrix of conditions, contexts, and behaviours that converge to shape our expectations and world views; see Pierre Bourdieu, *Sociology in Question*, trans. Richard Nice (London: Sage, 1993).

28 Tarleton Gillespie, "Characterizing Copyright in the Classroom: The Cultural Work of Anti-Piracy Campaigns," *Communication, Culture, & Critique* 2, no. 3 (2009): 274–318.

29 David Cooper Moore and John Landis, "'I Got It from Google': Re-contextualizing Authorship to Strengthen Fair Use Reasoning in the Elementary Grades," in *The Routledge Companion to Media Education, Copyright, and Fair Use*, ed. Renee Hobbs (London: Routledge, 2018), 272.

30 Anna Emilia Berti, Anns Silvia Bombi, and Adriana Lis, "The Child's Conceptions about Means of Productions and Their Owner," *European Journal of Social Psychology* 12, no. 3 (1982): 221–39.

31 Fiona Cram, Sik Hung Ng, and Nileena Jhaveri, "Young People's Understanding of Private and Public Ownership," in *Economic Socialization: The Economic Beliefs and Behaviours of Young People*, ed. Peter Lunt and Adrian Furnham, 110–29 (Cheltenham, UK: Edward Elgar, 1996).

32 Cram et al., "Young People's Understanding," 114.

33 Kristina R. Olson and Alex Shaw, "'No Fair, Copycat!': What Children's Response to Plagiarism Tells Us about Their Understanding of Ideas," *Developmental Science* 14, no. 2 (2011): 431.

34 Olson and Shaw, "No Fair," 438.

35 Alex Shaw, Vivian Li, and Kristina R. Olson, "Children Apply Principles of Physical Ownership to Ideas," *Cognitive Science: A Multidisciplinary Journal* 36, no. 8 (2012): 1383–1403.

36 As Waddams explains,

> The protection of weaker parties is an essential part of any civilized law of contracts. It was argued in the chapter on unconscionability that freedom of contract cannot be an absolute value but that other values such as fairness, equity, and the avoidance of unjust enrichment, must weighed [*sic*] in the balance. For these reasons the law of contracts has always given special protection to minors. On the other hand, some protection is needed for a party dealing with a minor, and entire freedom to avoid contracts might in the long term rebound to the detriment of minors, for few would advance credit even for necessaries to one whose promise to pay was not binding. The complexity of the present law springs from these conflicting objectives.

See Stephen M. Waddams, *The Law of Contracts* (Toronto: Canada Law Book, 2005), 471; see also Sara M. Grimes, "Persistent and Emerging Questions about the Use of End-User Licence Agreements in Children's Online Games and Virtual Worlds," *UBC Law Review* 46, no. 3 (2013): 681–738.

37 Jonathan A. Obar and Anne Oeldorf-Hirsch, "The Biggest Lie on the Internet: Ignoring the Privacy Policies and Terms of Service Policies of Social Networking Services" (paper presented at TPRC 44: The 44th Research Conference on Communication, Information and Internet

Policy, George Mason University, Arlington, VA, 24 August 2016),
http://dx.doi.org/10.2139/ssrn.2757465; see also Christian Sandvig,
"The Internet at Play: Child Users of Public Internet Connections,"
Journal of Computer-Mediated Communication 11, no. 4 (2006): 932–56;
Turow, *Privacy Policies*; Yannis Bakos, Florencia Marotta-Wurgler and David R. Trossen, "Does Anyone Read the Fine Print? Consumer Attention
to Standard-Form Contracts," *Journal of Legal Studies* 43, no. 1 (2014):
1–35.

38 See Wong v Lok's Martial Arts Centre Inc., [2009] BCSC 1385.

39 Steeves, "Not Child's Play"; Grimes, "Terms of Service."

40 Chung and Grimes, "Data Mining"; Grimes, "Terms of Service"; Grimes,
"Persistent and Emerging Questions"; Sara M. Grimes, "Digital Play
Structures: Examining the Terms of Use (and Play) Found in Children's
Commercial Virtual Worlds," in *Children's Virtual Play Worlds: Culture,
Learning and Participation*, ed. Anne Burke and Jackie Marsh, 151–72 (New
York: Peter Lang, 2013); Grimes, "Child-Generated Content: Children's
Authorship and Interpretive Practices in Digital Gaming Cultures," in
Dynamic Fair Dealing: Creating Canadian Culture Online, ed. Rosemary J.
Coombe and Darrin Wershler, 336–45 (Toronto: University of Toronto
Press, 2014); Sara M. Grimes and Deborah A. Fields, "Children's Media
Making, but Not Sharing: The Potential and Limitations of Child-Specific
DIY Media Websites," *Media International Australia* 154 (2015): 112–22.

41 The findings of this study have been published previously, in Grimes,
"Terms of Service."

42 This study began as part of the Playing at Making project, and focused specifically on TOS contracts found in digital games containing a significant
UGC or DIY component, including thirteen UGC games, thirty-four games
featuring extensive UGC tools, and eight DIY game-making platforms.

43 Jack Russo, "How to Read 'Terms of Use' Agreements" (paper presented
at the Computer Systems Laboratory Colloquium, Stanford University,
Palo Alto, CA, 11 April 2001).

44 In 2012, I revisited sixteen of the TOS contracts I had originally collected
in two previous studies of the legal relationships underlying children's
MMOGs (2007–10) and UGC games (2010–11) in order to compare their
contents and track any changes that may have unfolded across time and
genre. See Grimes, "Digital Play Structures."

45 *Dizzywood*, "Terms of Use," 2008.

46 *Stardoll*, "Terms of Use," 2012.

47 *Disney Fairies*, "Terms of Use," 2008.

48 *LittleBigPlanet*, "Online User Agreement," 2012.

49 Shoshana Zuboff, *The Age of Surveillance Capitalism: The Fight for a Human
Future at the New Frontier of Power* (New York: PublicAffairs, 2019); Frank

Pasquale, *The Black Box Society: The Secret Algorithms That Control Money and Information* (Cambridge, MA: Harvard University Press, 2014).

50 Greg Lastowka, *Virtual Justice: The New Laws of Online Worlds* (New Haven, CT: Yale University Press, 2010), 66.

51 Wayne R. Barnes, "Arrested Development: Rethinking the Contract Age of Majority for the Twenty-First Century Adolescent," *Maryland Law Review* 76, no. 2 (2017): 405–48.

52 Federal Trade Commission v Amazon.com Inc. USDC: Western district of Washington at Seattle, case no. C14-1038-JCC, Order Denying Defendant Amazon's Motion to Dismiss, https://wlflegalpulse.files.wordpress.com /2015/05/248945035-14-ftc-v-amazon-order-denying-defendant-s-motion -to-dismiss.pdf.

53 For instance, the Office of the Privacy Commissioner of Canada, which provides media literacy resources produced by child advocacy group MediaSmarts for use by Canadian teachers, includes the following defini-tion of a TOS in its online information lesson plan for students in Grades 6 to 8: "Terms of Use (also called Terms of Service) are a more general explanation of the conditions under which you use a website, app or service. These include what kind of behaviour is acceptable and unaccept-able, *who owns the content you create or share,* how you can close your account, what you can do if you think the policy has been violated, and many other rules"; see MediaSmarts "Getting the Toothpaste Back into the Tube: A Lesson on Online Information," 2018, https://priv.gc.ca/en/about-the -opc/what-we-do/awareness-campaigns-and-events/privacy-education-for -kids/educational-resources-for-teachers/lesson-plans-for-the-classroom /lesson_02/?wbdisable=true.

54 Ben Gilbert, "Minecraft Is Still One of the Biggest Games in the World, with over 91 Million People Playing Monthly," *Business Insider: Deutschland,* 10 January 2018, https://www.businessinsider.de/minecraft-has-74-million -monthly-players-2018-1?r=US&IR=T.

55 Minecraft.net, "Minecraft Realms: Your Own World, Always Online," accessed 23 April 2019, https://www.minecraft.net/en-us/realms/.

56 Rebekah J. Willett, "The Discursive Construction of 'Good Parenting' and Digital Media – The Case for Children's Virtual World Games," *Media, Culture & Society* 37, no. 7 (2015): 1060–75.

57 Willett, "Discursive Construction," 1067.

58 Willett, "Discursive Construction," 1071–2.

59 ESRB.org, accessed 11 November 2013, http://www.esrb.org/ratings /synopsis.jsp?Certificate=32799&Title=Minecraft%3A%20Xbox%20360 %20Edition.

60 See "Minecraft Commercial Usage Guidelines," updated 22 June 2017; it is unclear how this term interacts with the above-mentioned

acknowledgment of fair use/fair dealing, since companies also have access to that particular exception.

61 The original post was no longer online at the time of writing, but this portion was cited in a news article written shortly after the policy change occurred; see Jeff Grubb, "Microsoft Bans Corporation from Using Minecraft as a Marketing Tool," *Venture Beat*, 31 May 2016, https://venturebeat.com/2016/05/31/microsoft-bans-corporations-from-using-minecraft-as-a-marketing-tool/.

62 PlayStation Store, "Minecraft: Steven Universe (Mojang)," https://store.playstation.com/en-ca/product/UP4433-CUSA00744_00-KMP0000000000015?smcid=pdc%3Aca-en%3Aweb-pdc-games-minecraft-ps4%3Awaystobuy-buy-download%3Anull%3A.

63 Willett "Discursive Construction," 1068.

64 In addition to creating remixes and fan homages using licensed DLC, the players of UGC games also create a sizeable amount of "original" content, characters, game levels, and mods. These freely available mods provide a seemingly endless array of "homemade alternatives" to the implicitly promotional games that are often made with licensed DLC. Indeed, Robinson and Simon argue that this type of UGC creation not only makes up most player-made content available in Little Big Planet, but can be understood as a "form of resistance" that helps "break the ideological stranglehold held by studio franchises by allowing players to communicate and interact with one another." See William Robinson and Bart Simon, "*Little Big Planet*: La Créativité Numérique à L'œuvre," *Tracés* 28 (2015): 99–118.

65 Benjamin Woo, *Getting a Life: The Social Worlds of Geek Culture* (Montreal and Kingston: McGill-Queen's University Press, 2018), 196.

66 Woo, *Getting a Life*, 196.

67 Adventure Time (Cartoon Network, 2010–18).

68 Sara M. Grimes and Deborah A. Fields, *Kids Online: A New Research Agenda for Understanding Social Networking Forums* (New York: Joan Ganz Cooney Center at Sesame Workshop, 2012).

69 See, for instance, Frank Caron, "LittleBigPlanet IP Infringing Levels Being Silently Deleted," Ars Technica, 10 November 2008, https://arstechnica.com/gaming/2008/11/littlebigplanet-ip-infringing-levels-being-silently-deleted/.

70 Willis, *Primer for Daily Life*; Götz et al., *Media and the Make-Believe*; Henry Jenkins, *Convergence Culture: Where Old and New Media Collide* (New York: New York University Press, 2008),

71 See Feenberg, *Questioning Technology*, 87; "technical regimes" are also described as "technological frames" or "paradigms"; see Pinch and Bijker, "Social Construction."

72 Sony Computer Entertainment Europe, "Last Chance to Buy the Disney
DLC Packs!" *PlayStation: LittleBigPlanet* (blog), 14 December 2017, https://
littlebigplanet.playstation.com/news/last-chance-buy-disney-dlc-packs.

73 Owen S. Good, "LittleBigPlanet's Marvel DLC to Be Pulled from PlayStation
Store," *Polygon*, 26 December 2015, https://www.polygon.com/2015/12/26
/10667768/littlebigplanets-marvel-dlc-to-be-pulled-from-playstation-store.

7. The Politics of Children's Digital Play

1 Sonia Livingstone and Alicia Blum-Ross, *Parenting for a Digital Future: How
Hopes and Fears about Technology Shape Children's Lives* (New York: Oxford
University Press, 2020).

2 Common Sense Media, "Common Sense and SurveyMonkey Poll Finds
'Privacy Matters' for Parents and Teens on Social Media," 11 June 2018,
https://www.commonsensemedia.org/about-us/news/press-releases
/common-sense-and-surveymonkey-poll-finds-privacy-matters-for-parents.

3 Steeves, *Young Canadians, Phase III*, 22.

4 *U of T News*, "The New Schwartz Reisman Innovation Centre Will
Turbocharge the Next Wave of Canadian Innovation, Advancing How
AI, Biomedicine and Other Disruptive Technologies Can Enrich Lives,"
March 25, 2019, https://www.utoronto.ca/news/landmark-100-million-gift
-university-toronto-gerald-schwartz-and-heather-reisman-will-power.

5 A good illustration of this tendency can be found in both the coverage
and contents of Cathy O'Neil's best-selling book on "the dark side of big
data," *Weapons of Math Destruction: How Big Data Increases Inequality and
Threatens Democracy* (New York: Crown, 2016). In an article appearing in
the *New York Times*, O'Neil made the controversial claim that there was
little to no academic research exploring the workings and social implications of digital technologies. For instance, she wrote, "But academics
have been asleep at the wheel.... We need academia to step up to fill in
the gaps in our collective understanding about the new role of technology
in shaping our lives." This stance ignores the large volumes of academic
literature and ongoing research on the very issues she claims are ignored
by academia, including an entire area of study, Science and Technology
Studies, as well as numerous affiliated departments and fields, from
Philosophy of Technology to Communication; see Cathy O'Neil, "The
Ivory Tower Can't Keep Ignoring Tech," *New York Times*, 14 November
2017, https://www.nytimes.com/2017/11/14/opinion/academia-tech
-algorithms.html. For a summary of some of the backlash from academics
and others, see Andy Thomason, "Are Academics 'Asleep at the Wheel'?
Op-ed on Tech's Influence Draws Scholars' Ire," *Chronicle of Higher*

Education, 14 November 2017, https://www.chronicle.com/article/Are
-Academics-Asleep-at-the/241769.

6 Yoko Arisaka, "Women Carrying Water: At the Crossroads of Critical
   Theory and Technology," in *New Critical Theory: Essays on Liberation*, ed.
   Jeffrey W. Paris and William S. Wilkerson, 155–74 (Lanham, MD: Rowman
   and Littlefield, 2001).

7 Elizabeth Losh, "Channelling Obama: YouTube, Flickr, and the Social
   Media President," *Comparative American Studies* 10, no. 2–3 (2012): 255.

8 Michael Geist, "The Policy Battle over Information and Digital Policy
   Regulation: A Canadian Perspective," *Theoretical Inquiries in Law* 17, no. 2
   (2016): 417.

9 Sonia Livingstone and Amanda Third, "Children and Young People's
   Rights in the Digital Age: An Emerging Agenda," *New Media & Society* 19,
   no. 5 (2017): 659.

10 Steeves, *Young Canadians, Phase III*.

11 Common Sense Media, "Privacy Matters."

12 Zuboff, *Age of Surveillance Capitalism*.

13 Giovanna Mascheroni and Donell Holloway, *The Internet of Toys: Practices,
    Affordances and the Political Economy of Children's Smart Play* (London:
    Palgrave Macmillan, 2019).

14 Deborah Lupton and Ben Williamson, "The Datafied Child: The Dataveil-
    lance of Children and Implications for Their Rights," *New Media & Society*
    19, no. 5 (2017): 780.

15 Grimes and Fields, *Kids Online*.

16 Moore and Landis, "'I Got It from Google,'" 258.

17 Gillespie, "Characterizing Copyright," 274.

18 Olson and Shaw, "No Fair," 431; Shaw et al., "Children Apply Principles,"
    1383.

19 Moore and Landis, "'I Got It from Google,'" 272.

20 Livingstone and Third, "Young People's Rights."

21 Rebekah Willett, "Online Gaming Practices of Preteens: Independent En-
    tertainment Time and Transmedia Game Play," *Children & Society* 30, no.
    6 (2016): 467–77; Allison J. Pugh, *Longing and Belonging: Parents, Children,
    and Consumer Culture* (Berkeley: University of California Press, 2009).

22 James, "Confections"; Heather Hendershot, *Saturday Morning Censors: Tel-
    evision Regulation before the V-Chip* (London: Duke University Press, 1998);
    Forman-Brunell, *Made to Play House*.

23 The spread of loot boxes as a core game mechanic is now the focus of
    a growing body of academic literature, as it represents an important
    shift in how games are monetized, as well as how players progress in
    games and are rewarded for in-game achievements. The emergence of
    loot boxes in games has also been a source of controversy, within the

gaming community and the broader public, leading to a new round of regulatory inquiries and motions to pass new laws to limit their presence and impact – particularly in games played by children. Scholars such as Mark R. Johnson and Tom Brock highlight that, in certain cases, there are deep similarities between lootbox systems and casino games, at the level of the design and in how they are configured, a process they describe as the "gamblification" of digital games. It should be noted that while there are clear linkages between gambling and addiction, Johnson and Brock seek to distance their own research from the gaming addiction debate, emphasizing that the notion of gaming addiction is heavily contested, and that gamblification has much wider impacts involving a range of groups, including players, as well as developers and policymakers. Mark R. Johnson and Tom Brock, "Loot Boxes: Video Game Gambling, Paying to Win, and the Question of Game Design" (paper, *Semaphore Critical Gaming Series*, Faculty of Information, University of Toronto, Toronto, 2018).

24 Reyes et al., "'Won't Somebody Think of the Children?'"
25 Gary S. Cross, *A Social History of Leisure since 1600* (State College, PA: Venture Publishing, 1990), 117.
26 As Cross describes it, the Playground Association played a key role in advancing the idea that "alternatives to the street and degrading commercial leisure must be provided by the government in safe, regulated fun"; see Cross, *Social History*, 117.
27 There are important exceptions to this trend, which are often embedded in the same systematic racism and xenophobia found in the early playground movement. Tamir Rice, a twelve-year-old Black boy, was playing in and near a playground when he was murdered by two white on-duty police officers in Cleveland, Ohio. See Nathaniel Bryan, "Remembering Tamir Rice and Other Black Boy Victims: Imagining *Black PlayCrit Literacies* Inside and Outside Urban Literacy Education," *Urban Education* (January 2020), https://doi.org/10.1177/0042085920902250.

Bibliography

Akrich, Madeleine. "The De-Scription of Technical Objects." In *Shaping Technology/ Building Society*, edited by Wiebe E. Bijker and John Law, 205–24. Cambridge, MA: MIT Press, 1992.

Bergen, Doris. "Preschool Children's Play with 'Talking' and 'Nontalking' Rescue Heroes: Effects of Technology-Enhanced Figures on the Types and Themes of Play." In *Toys, Games, and Media*, edited by Jeffrey Goldstein, David Buckingham, and Gilles Brougère, 295–306. Mahwah, NJ: L. Erlbaum Associates, 2004.

Bovill, Moira, and Sonia Livingstone. "Bedroom Culture and the Privatization of Media Use." In *Children and Their Changing Media Environment: A European Comparative Study*, edited by Sonia Livingstone and M. Bovill. London: Lawrence Erlbaum Associates, 2001.

Buckingham, David, and Rebekah Willett, eds. *Digital Generations: Children, Young People and New Media*. Mahwah, NJ: Lawrence Erlbaum, 2006.

Castronova, Edward. *Synthetic Worlds: The Business and Culture of Online Games*. Chicago: University of Chicago Press, 2005.

Chung, Grace, and Sara M. Grimes. "Data Mining the Kids: Surveillance and Market Research Strategies in Children's Online Games." *Canadian Journal of Communication* 30, no. 4 (2005): 527–48.

Cobb-Moore, Charlotte, Susan Danby, and Ann Farrell. "Young Children as Rule Makers." *Journal of Pragmatics* 31 (2009): 1477–92.

Consalvo, Mia. *Cheating: Gaining Advantage in Videogames*. Cambridge, MA: MIT Press, 2007.

Corsaro, William A. *The Sociology of Childhood*. 2nd ed. Bloomington: Indiana University Press, 2005.

Druin, Allison, ed. *The Design of Children's Technology*. San Francisco: Morgan Kauffman, 1999.

Feenberg, Andrew. *Alternative Modernity: The Technical Turn in Philosophy and Social Theory*. Berkeley: University of California Press, 1995.

– *Questioning Technology*. London: Routledge, 1999.

Fields, Deborah A., and Yasmin B. Kafai. "Knowing and Throwing Mudballs, Hearts, Pies, and Flowers: A Connective Ethnography of Gaming Practices." *Games and Culture* 5, no. 1 (2010): 88–115.

– "'Stealing from Grandma' or Generating Cultural Knowledge? Contestations and Effects of Cheats in a Teen Virtual World." *Games and Culture* 5, no. 1 (2010): 64–87.

Fleming, Dan. *Powerplay: Toys as Popular Culture*. Manchester: Manchester University Press, 1996.

Forman-Brunell, Miriam. *Made to Play House: Dolls and the Commercialization of American Girlhood, 1830–1930*. New Haven, CT: Yale University Press, 1993.

Forman-Brunell, Miriam, and Julie Eaton. "The Graceful and Gritty Princess: Managing Notions of Girlhood from the New Nation to the New Millennium." *American Journal of Play* 1, no. 3 (2009): 338–64.

Giddings, Seth. *Game Worlds: Virtual Media and Children's Everyday Play*. London: Bloomsbury, 2014.

– "'I'm the One Who Makes the Lego Racers Go': Studying Virtual and Actual Play." In *Growing up Online: Young People and Digital Technologies*, edited by Sandra Weber and Shanly Dixon, 35–48. New York: Palgrave Macmillan, 2007.

Götz, Maya, Dafna Lemish, Amy Aidman, and Heysung Moon. *Media and the Make-Believe Worlds of Children: When Harry Potter Meets Pokémon in Disneyland*. Mahwah, NJ: Lawrence Erlbaum, 2005.

Grimes, Sara M. "Kids' Ad Play: Regulating Children's Advergames in the Converging Media Context." *International Journal of Communications Law and Policy* 8, no. 12 (2008): 162–78.

– "Online Multiplayer Gaming: A Virtual Space for Intellectual Property Debates?" *New Media & Society* 8, no. 6 (2006): 969–90.

– "Penguins, Hype and MMOGs for Kids: A Critical Re-examination of the 2008 'Boom' in Children's Virtual Worlds Development." *Games and Culture* 13, no. 6 (2018): 624–44.

– "Researching the Researchers: Market Researchers, Child Subjects and the Problem of 'Informed' Consent." *International Journal of Internet Research Ethics* 1, no. 1 (2008): 66–91.

– "Saturday Morning Cartoons Go MMOG." *Media International Australia* 126, no. 1 (2008): 120–31.

Grimes, Sara M., and Andrew Feenberg. "Rationalizing Play: A Critical Theory of Digital Gaming." *Information Society* 25, no. 2 (2009): 105–18.

Grimes, Sara M., and Deborah A. Fields. "Children's Media Making, but Not Sharing: The Potential and Limitations of Child-Specific DIY Media Websites," *Media International Australia* 154 (2015): 112–22.

Grimes, Sara M., and Leslie Regan Shade. "Neopian Economics of Play: Children's Cyberpets and Online Communities as Immersive Advertising in Neopets.Com." *International Journal of Media and Cultural Politics* 1, no. 2 (2005): 181–98.

Hamari, Juho, and Vili Lehdonvirta. "Game Design as Marketing: How Game Mechanics Create Demand for Virtual Goods." *International Journal of Business Science and Applied Management* 5, no. 1 (2010): 14–29.

Harvey, Alison. *Gender, Age and Digital Games in the Domestic Context.* London: Routledge, 2015.

Hendershot, Heather. "Dolls: Odour, Disgust, Femininity and Toy Design." In *The Gendered Object*, edited by Pat Kirkham, 90–102. Manchester: Manchester University Press, 1996.

Hutchby, Ian, and Jo Moran-Ellis, eds. *Children, Technology and Culture: The Impacts of Technologies in Children's Everyday Lives.* The Future of Childhood Series. London: Routledge, 2000.

Ito, Mizuko. *Engineering Play: A Cultural History of Children's Software.* Cambridge, MA: MIT Press, 2009.

James, Allison. "Confections, Concoctions and Conceptions," *Journal of the Anthropological Society of Oxford* 10, no. 2 (1979): 83–95.

James, Allison, Chris Jenks, and Alan Prout. *Theorizing Childhood.* Cambridge: Polity, 1998.

Jenkins, Henry. *Confronting the Challenges of Participatory Culture: Media Education for the 21st Century.* Cambridge: MIT Press, 2009.

Kafai, Yasmin B., and Deborah A. Fields. *Connected Play: Tweens in a Virtual World.* Cambridge, MA: MIT Press, 2013.

Kapur, Jyotsna. "Out of Control: Television and the Transformation of Childhood in Late Capitalism." In *Kids' Media Culture*, edited by Marsha Kinder, 122–36. Durham, NC: Duke University Press, 1999.

Kinder, Marsha. *Playing with Power in Movies, Television, and Video Games: From Muppet Babies to Teenage Mutant Ninja Turtles.* Berkeley: University of California Press, 1991.

Lastowka, Greg. *Virtual Justice: The New Laws of Online Worlds.* New Haven, CT: Yale University Press, 2010.

Livingstone, Sonia. "Mediating the Public/Private Boundary at Home: Children's Use of the Internet for Privacy and Participation." *Journal of Media Practice* 6, no. 1 (2005): 41–51.

Livingstone, Sonia, and Alicia Blum-Ross. *Parenting for a Digital Future: How Hopes and Fears about Technology Shape Children's Lives.* New York: Oxford University Press, 2020.

Livingstone, Sonia, and Amanda Third. "Children and Young People's Rights in the Digital Age: An Emerging Agenda." *New Media & Society* 19, no. 5 (2017): 657–70.

Marsh, Jackie. "Young Children's Play in Online Virtual Worlds." *Journal of Early Childhood Research* 8, no. 1 (2010): 23–39.

Marsh, Jackie, and Anne Burke. *Children's Virtual Play Worlds: Culture, Learning and Participation.* New York: Peter Lang, 2013.

Mascheroni, Giovanna, and Donell Holloway. *The Internet of Toys: Practices, Affordances and the Political Economy of Children's Smart Play.* London: Palgrave Macmillan, 2019.

McPherson, Tara, ed. *Digital Youth, Innovation, and the Unexpected.* John D. and Catherine T. Macarthur Foundation Series on Digital Media and Learning. Cambridge, MA: MIT Press, 2007.

Montgomery, Kathryn C. *Generation Digital: Politics, Commerce, and Childhood in the Age of the Internet.* Cambridge, MA: MIT Press, 2007.

Olson, Kristina R., and Alex Shaw. "'No Fair, Copycat!': What Children's Response to Plagiarism Tells Us about Their Understanding of Ideas." *Developmental Science* 14, no. 2 (2011): 431–9.

Oudshoorn, Nelly, Els Rommes, and Marcelle Stienstra. "Configuring the User as Everybody: Gender and Design Cultures in Information and Communication Technologies." *Science, Technology, & Human Values* 29, no. 1 (2004): 30–63.

Paley, Vivian Gussin. *A Child's Work: The Importance of Fantasy Play.* Chicago: University of Chicago Press, 2004.

Pearce, Celia, and Artemesia. *Communities of Play: Emergent Cultures in Multiplayer Games and Virtual Worlds.* Cambridge, MA: MIT Press, 2009.

Pearson, Marlys, and Paul R. Mullins. "Domesticating Barbie: An Archaeology of Barbie Material Culture and Domestic Ideology." *International Journal of Historical Archaeology* 3, no. 4 (1999): 225–59.

Pecora, Norma O. *The Business of Children's Entertainment.* New York: Guilford, 1998.

Plowman, Lydia. "'Hey, Hey, Hey! It's Time to Play': Children's Interactions with Smart Toys." In *Toys, Games, and Media,* edited by Jeffrey Goldstein, David Buckingham, and Gilles Brougère, 207–23. Mahwah, NJ: Lawrence Erlbaum, 2004.

Plowman, Lydia, Christine Stephen, and Joanna McPake, *Growing Up with Technology: Young Children Learning in a Digital World.* London: Routledge, 2010.

Reid-Walsh, Jacqueline, and Claudia Mitchell. "'Just a Doll?' 'Liberating' Accounts of Barbie-Play." *Review of Education, Pedagogy, and Cultural Studies* 22, no. 2 (2000): 175–90.

Schwartzman, Helen B. *Transformations: The Anthropology of Children's Play.* New York: Plenum, 1978.

Seiter, Ellen. *The Internet Playground: Children's Access, Entertainment, and Mis-Education.* New York: Peter Lang, 2005.

– *Sold Separately: Children and Parents in Consumer Culture.* New Brunswick, NJ: Rutgers University Press, 1993.

Stallybrass, Peter, and Allon White. *The Politics and Poetics of Transgression.* London: Methuen, 1986.

Steeves, Valerie. "It's Not Child's Play: The Online Invasion of Children's Privacy." *University of Ottawa Law & Technology Journal* 3, no. 1 (2006): 169–80.

Steeves, Valerie, and Cheryl Webster. "Closing the Barn Door: The Effect of Parental Supervision on Canadian Children's Online Privacy." *Bulletin of Science, Technology & Society* 28, no. 1 (2008): 4–19.

Sutton-Smith, Brian. *The Ambiguity of Play.* Cambridge, MA: Harvard University Press, 1997.

– *Toys as Culture.* New York: Gardner, 1986.

Tapscott, Don. *Growing Up Digital: The Rise of the Net Generation.* New York: McGraw-Hill, 1997.

Taylor, T.L. "Does WoW Change Everything? How a PvP Server, Multinational Player Base, and Surveillance Mod Scene Caused Me Pause." *Games and Culture* 1, no. 4 (2006): 318–37.

Turow, Joseph. *Privacy Policies on Children's Websites: Do They Play by the Rules?* Philadelphia: Annenberg Public Policy Centre of the University of Pennsylvania, 2001.

van Oost, Ellen C.J. "Materialized Gender: How Shavers Configure the Users' Femininity and Masculinity." In *How Users Matter: The Co-Construction of Users and Technology,* edited by Nelly Oudshoorn and Trevor Pinch, 193–208. Cambridge, MA: MIT Press, 2005.

Wajcman, Judy. *TechnoFeminism.* Cambridge: Polity, 2004.

Walkerdine, Valerie. *Children, Gender, Video Games: Towards a Relational Approach to Multimedia.* New York: Palgrave Macmillan, 2007.

Wasko, Janet. "The Commodification of Youth Culture." In *The International Handbook of Children, Media and Culture,* edited by Kirsten Drotner and Sonia Livingstone, 460–74. Los Angeles: Sage, 2008.

Weber, Sandra, and Shanly Dixon, eds. *Growing Up Online: Young People and Digital Technologies.* New York: Palgrave Macmillan, 2007.

Willett, Rebekah. "'Microsoft Bought Minecraft ... Who Knows What's Going to Happen?!': A Sociocultural Analysis of 8–9-Year-Olds' Understanding of Commercial Online Gaming Industries." *Learning, Media and Technology* 43, no. 1 (2016): 101–16.

Willett, Rebekah, Chris Richards, Jackie Marsh, Andrew Burn, and Julia C. Bishop, eds. *Children, Media and Playground Cultures.* London: Palgrave Macmillan, 2013.

Willis, Susan. *A Primer for Daily Life.* New York: Routledge, 1991.

Wohlwend, Karen E. "Damsels in Discourse: Girls Consuming and Producing Gendered Identity Texts through Disney Princess Play." *Reading Research Quarterly* 44, no. 1 (2009): 57–83.

Zipes, Jack. *Happily Ever After: Fairy Tales, Children, and the Culture Industry.* New York: Routledge, 1997.

Index